THE LETTERED MOUNTAIN

THE LETTERED MOUNTAIN

A Peruvian Village's Way with Writing

FRANK SALOMON AND

MERCEDES NIÑO-MURCIA

DUKE UNIVERSITY PRESS

DURHAM AND LONDON 2011

Printed in the United States of America on acid-free paper ∞

Designed by Heather Hensley

Typeset in Warnock Pro by Keystone Typesetting, Inc.

Library of Congress Cataloging-in-Publication Data appear on
the last printed page of this book.

TO OUR PARENTS

George Salomon and Mathilde Loewen Salomon

Marco Antonio Niño Gómez y Soledad Murcia Ballén

The romance of the precise is not the elision
Of the tired romance of imprecision.

It is the never ever-changing same,
An appearance of Again, the diva dame.

❖ ❖ ❖

WALLACE STEVENS

CONTENTS

ILLUSTRATIONS

FIGURES

(all photographs by the authors, unless otherwise noted within the figure captions)

MAP

TABLES

PREFACE

One makes an ethnography by weaving research experiences together with threads of friendship. We are deeply indebted to many Tupicochans who shared their knowledge with us. For some fifteen years they have enriched our research with their kindness, generosity, and wit. Don Alberto Vilcayauri and his daughter Elba Vilcayauri literally kept us going with their help in lodging and feeding. By sharing their family tradition of community-bonded learning—even walking us to the doors of those who care for the local document legacy—they helped us bring papers to life in conversation. Don León Modesto Rojas Alberco, Tupicocha's homegrown paleographer, has proven a true colleague in working with both documents and oral traditions. Aurelio Ramos Antiporta, a young Tupicochan full of curiosity and enterprise, guided us in learning about his ancient-rooted *ayllu* (the kinship corporation of Cacarima) through its archive. In Huarochirí (the provincial capital), Abelardo Santisteban Tello afforded memorable insight into the long trajectory of his region's Andean mythology. Celso Alberco, Lidia Ramos, Rómulo Velapatiño Navarro, and Doris Alberco gave invaluable access to their documentary heirlooms. We regret that the sacristan of San Damián, Roberto Sacramento, did not live to see the fruits of our lively conversations in print. Two mayors—Roy Vilcayauri and his successor, Armando Rojas Capistrano—enabled us to study municipal papers. The officers of Tupicocha's ten ayllus rotate yearly, so our debts to them and the people they represent have multiplied beyond counting, but we are indebted to all of them. We feel humbled by their gift: every single ayllu allowed us to study the papers and *khipus* that form its consecrated legacy.

Likewise we are deeply grateful to the friends and colleagues who helped us find our way to scholarly happiness in Lima. The Scurrah-Mayer family and the Vich-Zavala family gave our research the kitchen-table treatment, helping us see specifically Peruvian uses of theories and data, and they were also incalculably generous with practical help. Among linguistic colleagues, Susana De los Heros, Bonnie Urciuoli, and Jorge Pérez Silva enriched our sense of Peruvian language and writing. Emilio Chambi, of Puno, contributed fieldwork insight into the life of scripts in the countryside. Many of the far-flung historians, anthropologists, and literary humanists who enliven current debate about the media world of "the people called Indians" have proven valuable interlocutors. Among them are Kathryn Burns, John Charles, Tom Cummins, Marco Curátola, Alan Durston, Sabine Hyland, Catherine Julien, Patricia Oliart, Tristan Platt, José Luís de la Puente, Rocío Quispe-Agnoli, Joanne Rappaport, Karen Spalding, Gary Urton, and Germaine Warkentin. We thank them all.

The research reported here began as far back as 1994, and it has grown thanks to many agencies: the Instituto de Estudios Peruanos in Lima, the John Simon Guggenheim Memorial Foundation, the National Science Foundation under grant 144-FW88, and the School of American Research (now School for Advanced Research) under its National Endowment for the Humanities Resident Fellowship. But above all, we owe everything to the Comunidad Campesina San Andrés de Tupicocha together with its ten component ayllus.

At Madison, the University of Wisconsin's Institute for Research in the Humanities provided writing time, a big desk, a nonringing phone, and a seminar of like-minded people. For these boons we warmly thank David Sorkin, Susan Stanford Friedman, and Loretta Freiling.

The University of Iowa aided us through its Arts and Humanities Initiative and its International Programs by supporting travel and transcriptions. The project's "cyber-godmothers," Mindy Tuttle and Virginia Drake —our technical mentors on Iowa's Information Technology Services team—gave of their expertise with Iowan good cheer, never counting the hours. Also at Iowa, Daniel Balderston and Brian Gollnick furnished many a valuable lead and heard us out with critical sympathy. We warmly appreciate our research assistants Tony Chapa, Elizabeth Palumbo, Esther Hill, Jennifer Heacock-Renaud, and Will Marquardt for good talk as well as good work.

And what can we be more thankful for than for each other?

INTRODUCTION

Peru and the Ethnography of Writing

Almost half a millennium has passed since Spanish invaders began building an empire of letters over the lands of the Inka state. As much as Spanish law strove to keep writing harnessed as the specialized language of command for legal and religious conquistador elites, the people called *yndios* quickly became actors in the transatlantic web of alphabetic writing. This study tells the neglected story of how they made the alphabet their own, and goes on to analyze rural Andean writing practices of our times.

The fact of Andean literacy, which so many have contrived to overlook, centrally affects whom we take Andean Americans to be. Historically, peoples who spoke Quechua and Aymara (like other Native South Americans) have long been described as eternal outsiders to the world of letters. Indeed some authors have stereotyped them as "oral" cultures, and assigned to them a role as tragic Rousseauian resisters against alphabetic regimentation. But this is mistaken. The more one reads in the lesser-known archives of the countryside, the more one realizes that much of what we know as Andean culture has grown in and through literacy. If this damages the appeal of the Andean as a "non-Western" culture, so much the better. It brings us toward a more realistic encounter with the peoples of highland South America, in all their cultural distinctiveness, as actors within the creation of modernity.

READING BEHIND ADOBE WALLS

Today, campesino households in high-altitude villages cherish their goatskin-wrapped packets of titles and lawsuits (see figure 1) as vital endowments. They and their ancestors have for centuries known legal writing as a battlefield for livelihood. Historical accounts of Peruvians and other Andean peoples abound in cases of bloodshed over bad paperwork.

But were campesinos themselves writers, or only clients of writers? Did they evolve distinctive ways of writing? What role has script played in their self-government? What role in self-representation, expressive lore, and the sharing of historic memory? Does script have a role in the practices classed as Andean, such as devotion to deified mountains? In short, are Andean local societies in any deep and comprehensive sense literate societies?

Peasants everywhere are routinely treated as marginal members of the world of letters. They are not widely considered even as consumers of the written word, much less as producers. Discussions of rural inequality routinely treat high levels of "illiteracy" almost as if they inhered in the peasant condition.

This is an outsider's view, and an illusory one. Ethnography and sociolinguistics provide a very different image. In this book we explore how one peasant village has made the alphabet its own and developed an internal graphic community. Formerly speaking an Aymara-related ethnic tongue as well as Quechua, it is today a monolingually Spanish-speaking community. The fact that its people are native speakers of Spanish hugely invigorates their participation in writing; this would have been quite a different book had it concentrated on one of the decreasing number of Peruvian villages where Spanish is only known as a lingua franca.

But the village we studied is at the same time strikingly Andean in its social organization, mythology, and expressive culture. We are concerned here with the distinctive characteristics of writing that arise in the vernacular-literate process of living out this culture. They include original developments of codification and norms, rules of performativity, lexical change, diglossia between spoken and written language, framing of writing within Andean ritual scenarios, and a characteristic folk theory of writing. Changes over time in these facets of vernacular literacy reflect the face-to-face dynamics of a small community as much as they do interaction with greater powers. To read behind adobe walls, in the archives

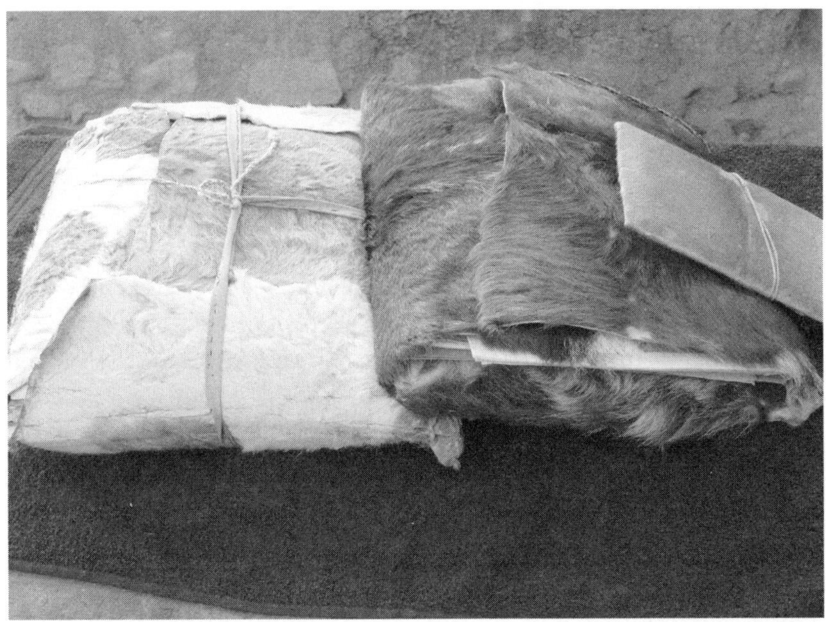

1. Campesino households protect their titles and other papers in goatskin packets. (Photos by the authors unless otherwise indicated.)

of an Andean village, is to encounter different processes from the ones registered in studies of metropolitan systems. They have implications for the way we imagine writing as a discourse of power.

This study is the work of an ethnographer and a sociolinguist of literacy who have shared fieldwork in one small Peruvian village: Tupicocha (province of Huarochirí, department of Lima). It proposes that exploring the outermost and least-studied reaches of the worldwide alphabetic order will expand and vary our notions of literacy. For the internal writings of this village, the main corpus of this study, attest to an old and largely self-generated conquest of the alphabet. It preceded and still stands apart from the work of state schools, which continue to project the ideology of "alphabetization" in indifference to the heritage of rural writings. Local writings are amazingly profuse and detailed. If many of them also seem crabbed, obscure, formulaic, or formally defective to the metropolitan eye, that only means we have not understood how they are made or what they are good for: a system in which the accumulation of writing is felt to create that virtual thing, "community." Writing is felt to give community a body and a physical presence immune to the flaws and dangers of daily interaction.

More formally Tupicocha, like any sphere of information exchange, can also be characterized as a *graphic network* or *graphic community*, by analogy to speech community. Like the idea of speech community, the concept of graphic community can be scaled up or down to adjust to the scope of a code's application. Scripts as well as tongues vary from broad lingua franca usage to the highly specific vernacular whose peculiarities mark local or other group boundaries. The oral counterpart of village literate practice is a form of the dialect called Andean Spanish by Rodolfo Cerrón-Palomino (2003) and Ana María Escobar (1990). But, as we will show, rural writing is very far from being a transcript of the spoken vernacular. Most village writing is register specific, requiring a mode of discourse derived from legal genres even when the content is Andean-ritual or folk-legal rather than official. Document writing is omnipresent in daily life, more so than in metropolitan life, yet it marks an exaggerated contrast with everyday speech. We consider this dichotomy a form of diglossia between writable and conversational Andean Spanish. Indeed villagers see writing as a separate semiotic sphere. It can be rendered into speech, but its social force is independent of speech, and this is its virtue.

That is how villagers see it. As observers, however, we are concerned with how Tupicochans produce text out of talking events, no less than with internal properties of their texts. From the sociolinguist's viewpoint, the oral and the written products of the village do address each other and do change each other. Despite themselves, village writers produce writing influenced by varying oral sociolinguistic contexts, and we are attentive to the ways in which written lexicon and format respond to them. The corpus illustrates how vernacular literacy in Tupicocha has continually been remodeled according to the practices of the institutions whose social life it has recorded. It is in the whole field of discourse, not in writing alone, that the written text—its meanings and functions—are co-constructed. Shared meanings of terms and forms are continually negotiated and renegotiated (Mannheim and Tedlock 1995:3). Innovations in community accordingly leave traces in ways of writing as well as in overt written content.

Attentive to this interaction, we complement the reading of Tupicochan writings from the past with observation of "writing events" (Heath 1982:93)—which are also talking events—and with ethnographic study of the forces that shape content. We are concerned with literacy as a social practice, a play of meaningful signs emerging in social interaction and dialogical exchanges (Roberts and Street 1997:168).

ORIGINS OF MODERN ANDEAN GRAPHIC CULTURE

Indigenous Andean engagement with the Roman alphabet has for the most part a hidden history. We do not know who was the first native of Inka lands to take up the quill. The army of Francisco Pizarro invaded Peru in 1532; already in 1535, when Spaniards were still ransacking the sacred Inka capital of Cuzco, Fray Vicente Valverde was appointed its bishop and founded a school for Andean lords. Only five years later crown policy mandated (but did not actually create) schools for "Indian" nobles in all major provincial towns (Andrien 2001:116). Informal literacy may have spread early among the translators who helped produce catechisms, or among the Inka nobles who had become enmeshed by marriage with the Pizarran invaders within a decade of the invasion. By 1560 an influential dictionary and grammar of "general" Quechua was in print (Santo Tomás 1951 [1560], 1995 [1560]). In 1570 Peru's first Jesuit mission was set up in Huarochirí, the main scene of this book, and it promoted elite literacy for native nobles. In 1576 King Philip II gave the Jesuits general responsibility for teaching Andean elites, and in 1578 he provided funding for the venture.

Jesuit efforts to rework Quechua as a missionary tongue for the Christianization of Andean peoples (Wood 1986:15–29) were, among other things, a practical solution for catechizing peoples whose non-Inka ethnic languages were so diverse as to defy the church's linguistic resources. Huarochiranos were a case in point, being speakers of an ethnic language related to Aymara (Adelaar 1994).The viceroyal university, San Marcos, installed Quechua as a required course for future clergy, while rivals in the cathedral chapter established another Quechua professorate (Durston 2007a:55).

As a part of its campaign to create a standardized process of conversion, the Archbishopric's highest councils published bilingual and trilingual (Spanish, Quechua, and Aymara) sermonaries, catechisms, and devotional songs. Demand for Quechua training of the clergy fueled some superb lexicography, from 1583 through the 1610s (most importantly, González Holguín 1952 [1608]; 1984 [1612]). Prescriptive and doctrinal in intent, it nonetheless compiled a great descriptive store of information about Quechua lexicon and rhetoric. Clergymen put great effort into choosing Quechua glosses for Christian terms, and also deciding which should not be translated lest pagan semantic traces foster heresy. Literacy in "pastoral Quechua" (as Alan Durston calls it in his commanding monograph; 2007a) did produce some splendid works, such as the devotional poetry of Juan Pérez Bocanegra (1631) and Luis Jerónimo de Oré (1992 [1598]). But it was meant to be, and remained, a channel of indoctrination —almost an Orwellian Newspeak. It may never even have been a spoken language in the sense that any speech community freely produced it. Rather, pastoral Quechua seems to have been a "high" sociolect reserved for specifically Catholic roles and contexts. (A sociolect means a variety of a given language used in one part of society, such as a class, ethnic group, age group, or religious community.) Writers of Tupían and Arawakan languages on the Jesuit mission frontier in what is now Paraguay and eastern Bolivia found contrasting sociolinguistic niches; see Clara López Beltrán (2005).

Church documents and books form the overwhelming majority of colonial Quechua writings. Written Quechua did, nonetheless, develop a presence in the "civil" literate orbit. During the first century of Spanish rule, some local "Indian" nobles learned to write Quechua the way clerics did, and at times used it in their political correspondence (Itier 1991). During the first colonial century, Spanish courts recognized papers brought forward by bilingual *escribanos de naturales* ('scribes for natives'; Burns 2007n62). Although no whole protocol book of such a writer has yet come to light, Burns's *Into the Archive* (2010) identifies one such scribe and studies newly unearthed work from his office. Durston's compilation of twelve known cases of "mundane" Quechua for private or administrative-legal purposes (2008; see also Durston 2003) indicates Quechua adaptation of scribal conventions. At least one series, from near Cuzco (1605–8), seems to be notarial. The *cabildos* ('village councils') established as part of the Toledan "reduction" government were supposed to keep alphabetic records as well as *khipus* (knotted-cord records, the pre-Hispanic medium), the former concerning testaments and criminal proceedings (Burns 2004). By 1616 Lima's famous Indian school in El Cercado had opened. (El Cercado was a reserved district wherein the colonial City of the Kings tried to corral its native and African labor pool.) Similar institutions existed in other cities (Cárdenas Ayaipoma 1977; Olachea Labayen 1958). Toward 1615 the bicultural chronicler Felipe

Guaman Poma de Ayala drew a *regidor* ('village councilman') holding both a book and a khipu, and a "scribe of the [village] council" (1980 [1615]:759) in indigenous headgear working with paper only (see figures 2–3).

Nonetheless Peru, unlike Mesoamerica with its immense accumulations of native-language papers, never saw indigenous languages stably inserted into the civil part of the alphabetic graphic community (Restall 1997, 1999; Sousa and Terraciano 2003; Terraciano and Restall 1992). One reason Quechua literacy did not become massive or habitual among native Peruvians may be that the clergy decided not to promote the "general language" or lingua franca variety of Quechua, which was already known among many ethnic groups before the 1532 Spanish invasion. Instead they published and promoted a southern dialect which they considered nobler because they associated it with the Inka royal city of Cuzco. Supposedly faithful to the high diction of nobles, and therefore more worthy of sacred usage, it became the dialectal base of church Quechua.

Rather, Spanish became the general language for writing long before the Huarochiranos made it their spoken vernacular. In the civil sphere, by the early seventeenth century the imperial state, increasingly saturating the countryside, exerted its power chiefly through translators and non-indigenous rural scribes who wrote Spanish only. In 1596 the Council of the Indies asked the king to forbid official paperwork in Andean tongues. Although no broad decree to this effect followed, state officials became ever less receptive to Quechua (Mannheim 1992:90). By the late sixteenth century officials perceived the onslaught of "Indian" lawsuits as a problem which bilingual administration might only increase. As the governmental fortunes of Quechua declined, the insertion of Spanish-language writing into Andean society deepened apace. Spanish literacy was not universal or demotic in colonial times (1532–1825 for Peru), but it was omnipresent and immensely productive. Archives on both sides of the Atlantic are crammed with the papers Andean rural people tendered via the testimony-translation-transcription chain (see Lienhard 1992:153–307 for a sampling).

Some *curacas* (a hispano-Quechua term for Andean nobles, derived from *kuraka*) were avid readers of Spanish, and writers as well, to a degree that disturbed Spanish onlookers. Monique Alaperrine-Bouyer (2002:155–57) cites a 1588 memorandum by a Cuzco cleric, Bartolomé Alvarez, which complains against one kuraka who bought a *monterroso*,

2. Toward 1615, Felipe Guaman Poma de Ayala drew a village councilman holding both a book and a khipu (1980 [1615]: 746).

3. Guaman Poma also drew a "scribe of the [village] council" (1980 [1615]: 759) working with paper only.

or specialized lawbook for scribes. In the 1620s one kuraka's estate included a collection of drama, history, law, and theology that would have looked handsome in the home of a Castilian notable (Hampe Martínez 1989). Alcira Dueñas's *Indians and Mestizos in the "Lettered City"* (2010) brings to light important writings by seven kurakas who, during the seventeenth and eighteenth centuries, addressed their claims to upper levels of the Spanish empire. They were not men of the Hispanicized Inka elite that adorned Cuzco, but politically and sometimes intellectually ambitious champions of eroding ethnic aristocracies over most of the former Inka state: from Lambayeque in Peru's far north to Chuquisaca (now Sucre) in the south of Bolivia. Their papers show that command of prestigious genres such as memoranda to the king was not rare among native elites. Such men may have played a role in the diffusion of literacy through rural Quechua-speaking society.

Meanwhile, literally every one of the plebeian "people called Indians" (Anonymous: 1991:41) underwent, with death-and-taxes regularity, the experience of having his or her tributary status written into state inspections and ledgers (Salomon and Guevara Gil 1994). It was the endless contestation of routine plebeian complaints, noble's requests for revisits or succession rulings, and endemic litigation over lands and tributes which would form rural Peruvians' ideas of genre and prose style. By the later seventeenth century and throughout the eighteenth, some kurakas and Andean commoners close to the scribal establishment could emulate the ponderous legalistic prose that spoke to power. Baltazar Jaime Martínez Compañón, an archbishop on Peru's north coast and the author of a remarkable illustrated book on the region's biota and cultures, designed a general system of schooling for Andean pupils in the middle eighteenth century (Ramírez 2008). Official schooling as such, however, penetrated only the aristocratic level of society. Pablo Macera (cited in Klaren 2000:105) estimates the number of pupils in formal primary schools toward the end of the eighteenth century at only 5,000 for "yndios" and others. The actual diffusion of writing to plebeian society took place outside schoolhouse walls.

The intervention of public rural schooling, with its ideology of universal literacy, thus marks a relatively recent impact on a very old literate order. In most places rural education was only implemented from the 1920s on. (It had been legislated but not funded fifty years earlier: Fell 1990; Mac-Lean y Estenós 1944; Macera 1990). Higher-lying and more remote villages first received public schooling as late as the 1960s, when the first presidency of Fernando Belaúnde Terry promoted "alphabetization" as an economic development strategy. Rural Andean villages were and to some degree still are perceived in cities as a linguistically and racially stigmatized margin of the transatlantic community of the Roman alphabet. Yet as the independent Republic of Peru took shape after 1825, villagers had already thoroughly internalized the graphic order despite having no schools of their own.

These growing edges of literacy, sponsored by church and by state, were not expanding into a graphic void. For when Spaniards brought the alphabet, they brought it to a society which already had its own advanced resources for recording information. The ancient medium of the khipu, or knot-cord record, was thriving and continued to thrive during at least the first colonial century. The relation between Andean traditions of the legible and "writing proper" was therefore not one of simple replacement, but one of durable coexistence. The widespread view of writing as a cognitive revolution, a cultural thunderbolt piercing previously "oral" societies, reflects the ideology of educators and not the historic evidence.

How decisive, then, was alphabetic interaction? Taking into account the interface between khipu and paper, should we think of script production as taking place in a distinctive indigenous domain affected by distinctive Andean ideas and practices of literacy? Were Andean literacy practices articulated with nonalphabetic inscriptive techniques in a distinctive hybrid semiosis? Is there any prospect of understanding the intertextual relation between deeply different literacies, as Serge Gruzinski (1993) has accomplished in Mexico?

In sum, to understand the roots of Andean graphic practice we need to imagine Andean literacy in two ways. On one hand, the importation of the alphabet, a code molded to sonic units of language, created an alternative to the khipu code molded on the categorical units of action (Salomon 2004a). Although colonial authority made use of khipus, Spaniards never learned the corded graphic order enough to prescribe its details. It was a process largely internal to the "republic of Indians" which shaped the graphic pluralism reflected in late khipu use (Salomon 2007). Some scholars think the colonial development of khipus included elite attempts to retool cords as a syllabary, that is, as a writing on phonographic principles (Hyland 2003:136).

On the other hand, the growth of Andean graphic habits also connected the Andean peoples quite early with a global textual community. The image of so-called "yndios" as illiterate latecomers to the bookish world is an oversimplification. As soon as Spain and the papacy sought to reduce them to a regulated peasantry, it also unintentionally made them privy to the scripts and protocols of regulation. In their own way, colonial native nobles knew very well what Michel Foucault meant when he spoke of documents "producing or objectifying the subjects that use them" (Read 2006:158). Although "yndios" responded from positions of disadvantage, often through mediators, they did respond in kind. Amerindian peoples thus joined the empire of letters, and some learned to write almost as early as mass literacy was emerging in Europe itself.

It is by no means obvious why these processes remain almost invisible in the historiography of literacy. The habit of describing rural Andean people as "natives," a term which unreflectively invokes nonliteracy, has blinded us to the fact that the institutions we think of as Andean were built through active engagement in literate media.

NEW LITERACY STUDIES AND THEIR SEQUELS IN AND BEYOND THE AMERICAS

The case study we will present fits into a wide literature of cross-cultural approaches, which can be overviewed from the general to the particular. First, it benefits from works on theories and practices of literacy as such, including anthropological classics (Basso 1974; Goody 1986; Heath 1983; Street 1984) and sociolinguistic work on theories of context and language socialization (Gee 1986, 2000; Gumperz 1982; Schieffelin and Ochs 1986). Among ethnographies, Brinkley Messick's *The Calligraphic State* (1993), a historical study of oral and written practices within highland Yemeni Shari'a polities, provides a uniquely full and deep analysis of writing as "discursive formation" along Foucauldian lines. Many of the most influential ethnographies of writing contemplate an "oral/literate continuum" (Biber 1988; Chafe and Tannen 1987; Finnegan 1988), an idea also entertained here. We also take some note of wider debates in grammatology and semiology (Connerton 1989; N. Goodman 1976; Harris 1995; Lafont et al. 1984; Sampson 1985).

A related branch of comparative and theoretical discussion concerns the nature of documents as cultural forms (Foucault 1989:129). As for the definition of documentation, we follow Buckland (1997:215) in adopting

Suzanne Briet's precise but capacious four-part definition: a document is a material object, intended to be used as evidence, processed so as to serve this purpose, and recognized as serving it. We sympathize with Annelise Riles's call for ethnographers to get beyond Foucauldian harping on the hegemony of document technology, which "tends itself to become fairly hegemonic," and ask "how else documents may be 'good to think with' as for scholars as much as for their subjects" (2006:13).

Second, this Peruvian case enters into an already large field of empirical studies about the "effects of literacy." This literature began as debate around sweeping assertions by Jack Goody and Ian Watt (1962). It continued with a barrage of "New Literacy Studies" (or NLS; Besnier 1988, Roberts and Street 1997) rebutting Goody and Watt on ethnological grounds. In anthropology and sociolinguistics, the "NLS debate" began with what is called the "great divide" controversy (Goody and Watt 1962; Olson 1994; Ong 1982). Extending "Toronto school" theses rooted in Greco-Roman studies toward non-Western cases, Goody and Watt argued that the perceived "great divide"between the cognitive modes of simple and complex societies or primitive and modern ones arises, at bottom, from the difference between handling information as speech (intersubjective, transient) and as script (objectlike, durable). By giving discourse a physical presence independent of the conversations that produce it, writing radically alters its possibilities. While in oral interaction meaning can largely be derived from context, writing is decoded out of context and needs therefore to be more explicit. Transformed to an object out of context, discourse becomes susceptible to distancing and critique in a way that conversation rarely fosters. Writing is therefore associated with logic and critical cognitive habits. These include the fundamentals of historicist and analytical mentalities.

"New Literacy Studies" (NLS) arose in the 1980s as an interdisplinary challenge to this "great divide" argument. (Goody himself, as his valuable comparativist researches advanced, had by then adopted more nuanced positions.) New Literary Studies writers approach literacy as a symbolic system rooted in social practices (Barton and Hamilton 1998; Gee 1986, 2000; Heath 1982; Scollon and Scollon 1981; Street 1984, 1993; among others). The NLS theoretical framework does not affirm any "effect of literacy" as such, but instead postulates that the effects of literacy inhere in the nature of the social relations articulated through it. In a crucial moment Sylvia Scribner and Michael Cole (1981) studied the triply literate Vai-speaking population of Liberia and concluded that neither literacy in English (acquired in school), nor in Vai (an indigenous system of syllabic writing), nor in Arabic (associated with the reading of the Koran) demonstrated a direct relation with abstract cognitive performance. Rather, each graphic practice heightened the kind of cognition its social context demanded, such as memorization for Quranic learners of Arabic or lyric prosody for Hanunoo (Phillippine) learners of an Indic syllabary (Frake 1983:371). Scholars of NLS see literacy as inherently socially situated, and necessarily plural even within a single graphic code insofar as the practices it articulates are multiple.

New Literary Studies monographs have strongly influenced methodology for studying writing (e.g., Barton and Hamilton 1998; Baynham 1995). Several edited volumes provided worldwide samplings of vernacular literacy research (Barton, Hamilton, and Ivanič 2000; Boyarin 1993; Dubin and Kuhlman 1992; Hamilton, Barton, and Ivanič 2000; Street 1993). Perspectives of NLS proved important not only because they distanced ethnography from the suppositions of the "great divide," but also because they gave an empirical idea of the range of diversity in lettered practice.

Having moved the term *literacy* to its plural, a recent current in NLS now attempts to find empirical regularities that might reunite literacy studies on a new common ground. James Collins and Richard Blot (2003) point out that the NLS paradigm has fostered a relativist vision within which the study of "writing" as a unitary topic tends to dissolve. As an alternative they propose looking for consistent tendencies within the diversity of literacy events. Like Claude Lévi-Strauss in the famous "writing lesson" chapter of *Tristes Tropiques* (1992 [1955]:294–304), they find such an avenue in the sociological and power-freighted aspects of writing rather than in purported cognitive implications. Their discussion takes up currents from an earlier, mostly French, round of theorizing on texts, education, discourse, and power (Bourdieu 1991; Derrida 1972; Foucault 1989). Sociolinguistics too has evolved a nomothetic common ground. But we sympathize with Messick's judgment that despite "family resemblances found in other places and times, a discursive history . . . must always be resolutely specific" (1993:254).

Moving from the vast field of general literacy studies to a domain of closer comparability, the Peruvian case might be considered in a third body of cases: those belonging to imperial "edges" where indigenous-language communities come under the literate hegemony of royal or colonial languages, and graphic practice therefore acquires a context of unequal pluralism. This includes Mesoamerica (Kowalewski and Saindon 1992; Restall 1999; Van Acker 1995; Vaughan 1990), the Philippines (Rafael 1988), Africa (Bledsoe and Robey 1993; Blommaert 2004; Janzen 1985; MacGaffey 1986; Maxwell 1983; Prinsloo and Breier 1996; Twaddle 1974), Amazonia (Aikman 1999; Gow 1990; Perrin 1986; Vidal 1992), the West Indies (Roberts 1997), Oceania (Besnier 1995; Bloch 1993; Gewertz and Errington 1991), Asia (Ahearn 2001), the Guarani-speaking lowlands (Meliá 1998), and the Andes themselves (Adelaar 1997; Dedenbach 1997; Itier 1995; Jouve Martín 2005; Mannheim 1991; Rappaport 1994). A subset of this literature concerns the reception, or sometimes the nonrecognition, of Amerindian forms of inscription by those who introduced the alphabet. Germaine Warkentin's influential essay (1999) on Algonkian "hieroglyphs" and wampum, like Elizabeth Boone's introduction to *Writing without Words* (1998:3–26), argues that such problems are concrete instances of basic dissensus on what writing is. Richard Rubinger (2007) provides a deep study about the plebeian appropriation of Japanese script from the sixteenth century onward. It too is a study of "edges," but in this case of social classes marginal to elite literacy, rather than outlying lands.

Jan Blommaert's *Grassroots Literacy: Writing, Identity and Voice in Central Africa* (2008) stands out as a particularly close counterpart to our work. Through study of vernacular texts from the Democratic Republic of the Congo, Blommaert measures the gulf separating "homemade" arts of writing from elite norms and demonstrates how the former are discounted. Other researches in rural Africa also reveal the riches of provincial writing that result when, as Philippe Lavigne-Delville puts it (2002), "farmers use 'pieces of paper' to defend resources in Francophone Africa." Ever more "reservoirs" of vernacular literacy are coming to light in many countries at the periphery of the older "republic of letters."

Contemporary studies about literacy in Latin America emphasize the swarming variety of literacies and demonstrate that these practices are likewise situated in vernacular social webs, not just in literate institutions. Studies about the endogenous spread and teaching of writing tend to contrast European "fetishism of writing" (in Lienhard's words) with plebeian appropriations of it as a means of self-defense (Rappaport 1994). Brooke Larson remarks of Bolivia after 1860 that "as some peasant leaders entered the Hispanic world of 'print capitalism,' they or their scribes mastered literacy in order to make their collective views known to Creole politicians" (2004:53–54). However, this contrast no longer satisfies as a full description. Ethnographic approaches demonstrate that writing also has a long history as an internal structure of nonelite societies. Students of locally placed literacy include Judy Kalman (1999), who analyzed the writing practices of a group of scribes practicing their trade in a public plaza in Mexico City, and later those of a group of women in the neighborhood of Mixquic at the edge of the city (Kalman 2005). Some of these studies have ethnohistoric depth. Among the most surprising studies is Clara López Beltrán's and Akira Saito's fascinating ethnographic volume (2005) on Mojos, in eastern lowland Bolivia. It concentrates on vernacular innovations evolving from sacred literacy after the Jesuit missions were expelled in 1767. Jorge Pavez's compilation *Cartas mapuche* (2008) illuminates how Chilean and Argentinian indigenous groups put secretaries and even newspapers to work diffusing the political correspondence of their still-unconquered war leaders in the mid- to late nineteenth century.

While Latin America comes late to the NLS arena, it has a distinguished record in humanistic studies of literacy. Probably no single work has affected humanists' understanding of New World literacy more than Angel Rama's remarkable *La ciudad letrada* (1984; translated as *The Lettered City* 1996). In reviewing the English translation, Eric Metcalf (1997) distills Rama's emphasis on writing in Latin America as a profession which stamped its products with a peculiar diction:

> Inextricably woven into the urban system [of the viceroyalties] was a culture of writing that would administer the city and extend its influence over the rural areas beyond its walls. The interpretation and implementation of a steady flow of imperial and ecclesiastic directives required a vast lettered elite Rama described as the "letrados." This class of educated men documented legal decisions, drafted governmental edicts, maintained church records and authored the literature of Latin America for three hundred years. The letrados were tightly condensed within the confines of the city. A diverse bureaucratic corps, they mingled exclusively among their peers and served their urban institutions in an increasingly successful effort to duplicate the hierarchical divisions of power in the uncivilized territories. Irrespective of their particular offices, these minor functionaries were linked by a common skill: literacy.

From their ranks would arise the intellectuals, the poets and the writers of Latin America, as well as a characteristic Baroque style drawn from their Spanish superiors. Trained and practiced in the art of writing, the letrados employed a formal speech divorced from the rural vulgarities of the subservient illiterate.

The scribal register of language was more than just "divorced from the rural vulgarities." It was propagated, according to Rama, as an earthly vehicle of divine authority. Human order was felt to emanate seamlessly down from transcribed divine utterance (in scripture) to the detailed conduct of everyday life through the mediation of royal and other authoritative writ. In the ideology of the lettered city, writing did not simply reflect social order ex post facto; order was *created* in the act of writing. Script was taken to be the originating, determining form of human discourse, and speech its defective by-product. This premise—in polar contrast to the speech-centered Quranic ethos Messick studied—still holds firm in much of rural Latin America, including Tupicocha.

Our stance toward Rama might be characterized as loyal opposition. His persuasive view of the colonial "lettered city" provides a compelling image of the world of scribal letters. Yet it lacks a full insertion into the America it sets out to explain. The scribal and notarial power structure he describes did not grow in a vacuum. The societies it enmeshed in the most populous parts of America, Mexico, and the Andes, had already possessed complex webs of graphic practices. Whatever else the effects of literacy may have been in the viceroyalties of Peru and New Spain, they were surely interaction effects. As Serge Gruzinski argued in *La conquête de l'imaginaire* (published in English as *The Conquest of Mexico* [1993]), these interactions were not just content-neutral changes of medium. By concurrently using Mexican glyphs and alphabetic writing, Mexicans internalized such entities of the European imaginary as saints, kings, and revelations. It was in the process of revising Mexican writing so as to contain these cultural entities that Mexican thinking became imbued with Iberian categories. In this way Mexicans became capable of acting as Americans within Christendom: became "yndios." The process of absorbing icons from Spain went along with the incorporation of alphabetic writing, and with it, of a throroughly changed mentality concerning the relation between visual and verbal knowledge. The analogous changes in the Andes are harder to trace because Andean graphic media were even more dissimilar from alphabetic media than Mesoamerican ones were (Cummins 1998). But we will treat the nature of interaction between khipus and alphabetic representation in Tupicocha as far as the state of khipu studies allows.

A fourth literature—namely, reports on writing and reading among contemporary Andean people—is springing up copiously around local NGOs. With the help of NGOs, Rainer Hostnig, Ciro Palomino Dongo, and Jean-Jacques Decoster (2007) have published a vast corpus of primary sources from village archives in Apurímac Department. Projects for bilingual education are especially prolific (e.g., Cotacachi 1994; Godenzzi 1992; Jung and López 1988; Zúñiga 1990). A Bolivian monograph by Denise Arnold and Juan de Dios Yapita (2000), like Gruzinski's, argues that the infiltration of literacy into a local graphic order alters the fundamentals of culture. The work of Nancy Hornberger (2000), an ethnographer-educator and Andean specialist, constitutes the main bridge between school studies and inquiries into out-of-school literacy such as Sarah Lund's (1997). Peruvian inquiries into the "ethnography of schooling" concentrate on the diffusion of alphabetic writing in rural regions and in indigenous communities (Ames 2002; Ansión 1989; Montero 1990).

An interesting Andean vein of discussion concerns the dark side of literacy. To Walter Mignolo (1995:29–124), throughout the New World literacy is inseparable from "the colonization of languages" and the suffocation of native knowledge. Some peasant voices also speak of the high cost of letters. A radiant "myth of progress" centered on schooling (Degregori 1986, 1991) promises modern enrichment, but has as its obverse the blackly grotesque "school myth" about cannibal demons who beguile with an offer of learning (Ortiz Rescaniere 1973:143–49). In a fascinating study of letters written between highland villagers and their peers who have emigrated to jungle frontier zones, Lund (1997) observes that letters arrive in the home community carrying greater significance than what is overtly written, because letters may carry an invisible freight of magic. Peter Wogan's Ecuadorian ethnography *Magical Writing in Salasaca* (2004) reports on a belief that one can kill people by writing their names in a book—a suggestion of Rama's idea as seen in the mirror of local conflict. We view negativity about writing as a corollary of involvement with it, rather than resistance to it.

Studies from the Peruvian Amazon demonstrate enormous divergences in perceptions of literacy. Sheyla Aikman (1999, 2004) and Peter

Gow (1990, 1991) both studied communities which became acquainted with the alphabet within living memory. Amazonian communities studied by Aikman perceive bilingual literacy acquisition as an innovation, but Gow reports that the Piro say they "already had writing" when teachers arrived because shamanic traditionalists view letters as part of the same class of legible signs as the patterns manifested in *yona* (hallucination-inspired painted patterns). The notion that Amerindian peoples "already" had writing has been documented from a number of societies (Hugh-Jones 1989:65–68; Perrin 1986; Platt 1992:143), which too raises questions about the cultural basis of lettered authority in Amerindia.

A final focus of Peruvian discussion, closely relevant to the present study, concerns degrees of endogenous versus outside-imposed literacy. In the fullest ethnography of literacy in the Andean highlands to date, *(Des)encuentros con la escritura: Escuela y comunidad en los Andes peruanos* (2002a), Virginia Zavala sees writing in Umaca (Andahuaylas) as an imposition rooted in the interests of the state and Evangelical church sectors but conveying little or no endogenous information. Linda King (1994) reports similar findings from Mexico. Others, however, see in village literacy a much stronger component of local genesis (Niño-Murcia 2004, 2009). A recent volume compiled by Zavala, Mercedes Niño-Murcia, and Patricia Ames—*Escritura y sociedad* (2004)—presents six works dedicated to the study of literacy in Peru, which show wide variation in degrees of endogeny. Three of these study Andean communities (Salomon, De la Piedra, Niño-Murcia), two concern Amazonian groups (Ames, Aikman), while one (Zavala) scrutinizes the state's National Program for Literacy.

LOCALE OF THE STUDY

The scene of this study is Huarochirí Province in the central Peruvian department of Lima. The department of Lima is a swath of the western or Pacific face of the Andean Cordillera. Its lands slope from the ice-crusted crowns of the mountains down to the desert beaches of the Pacific. Huarochirí Province forms a middle section of this large department (see map 1). Its lands consist of small watersheds that gather where glaciers meet high tundra 4,000 to 5,000 meters (13,123 to 16,404 feet) above sea level. Its rivers plunge through narrow canyons, and end in oasis-like valleys from an elevation of about 1,000 meters (3,280 feet) downward to the Pacific beaches and fishing coves. The capital of the province is a small city also called Huarochirí, located high on the headwaters of the Mala

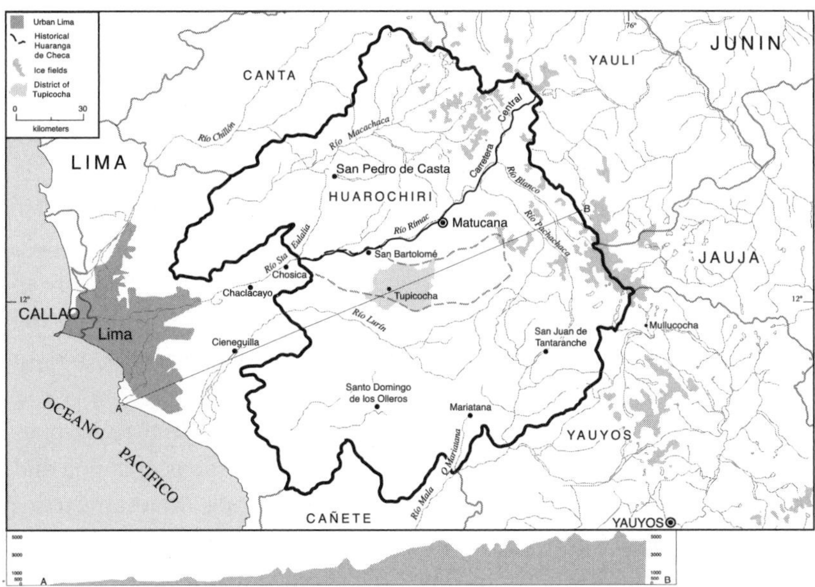

Map 1. Map of Huarochirí Province, with transect below illustrating elevations.

River. Tupicocha, like most Huarochirí villages, is located on a small ledge against the mountain wall. With its center at 3,606 meters (11,831 feet), its government encompasses 83.35 square kilometers (32.24 square miles), consisting mostly of rugged pastures at even greater elevations. It had 1,416 inhabitants in 2007.

Huarochiranos are mostly agropastoralists who live by pasturing on the high slopes near the lower edge of the puna (high-elevation grassland) and facing downward onto dry farming terraces and slopes around 3,000 meters (9,843 feet) above sea level. Villagers divide their time between herding Andean (llama and alpaca) and European livestock in high, seasonally rainy and snowy country of up to 4,600 meters (15,092 feet), and cultivating foodstuffs and truck crops in the lower tiers. These are steep and thirsty slopes whose natural cover bristles with cactus and thorny xerophytes. Village nuclei are located at 3,000 to 3,500 meters (9,843 to 11,483 feet), where the Spanish viceroyalty forcibly resettled the "people called Indians" in the 1570s and 1580s. On high holdings, villagers grow the Andean crops—potatoes, quinoa, and related plants—while farther down the irrigation system they produce beans, squash, maize, apples, peaches, and cactus fruit, and also harvest cochineal insects for commercial dye. Aromatic herbs for tea and medicine are the most profitable specialty. Sales of cheese and flowers also supplement a strained subsistence. Agriculture is a never-ending struggle to improve canals and reservoirs that capture the snow and melt off of the heights, as well as channeling scarce rain. The religious rites mediated through writing are usually efforts to cope with water scarcity.

But Huarochirí is not a remote or self-sufficient area. Even more than most rural Peruvians, Huarochiranos live in the shadow of a metropolis: the "Goliath's head" city of Lima, whose metropolitan population approached 9 million in 2010. Lima and Huarochirí coexist so closely that one of Lima's self-built peripheral boroughs (Lurigancho) now overlaps Huarochirí territory.

Villages such as Tupicocha appear intensely Andean in their agropastoral way of life, especially in their high reaches. But the people one finds herding alpacas under the glittering snow of Paria Caca Mountain almost always have close kin living as immigrants in the concrete labyrinth of central Lima. Many if not most Huarochirí highlanders travel there frequently to trade or to work for wages. Most families send as many children as they can to be educated in Lima, often by dint of great sacrifice. Many have relatives in farther diaspora. Huarochirí colonies thrive in Texas, Connecticut, New York, New Jersey, and California, not to mention Milan and Madrid.

Huarochiranos form only a tiny fraction of the nation. As of 2007 the Peruvian census counted 74,735 inhabitants of Huarochirí. One might expect the children of this province to disappear into the colossal maelstrom of Lima; 28.7 percent of the country's citizens by 1996 lived in Lima,[1] while projections from the 2007 census indicate that Huarochiranos make up only about two- to three-tenths of 1 percent of their country. But people from there are disproportionately visible because they fill roles that link urban and rural publics: market stall vendors, operators of tent restaurants in working-class neighborhoods, entrepreneurs in regional transportation, and truck-farm wholesalers. Despite suffering racially tinged snobbism, Huarochirí villagers regard themselves as progressive campesinos ('peasants') of Peruvian nationality, not as members of an indigenous "race." They regard those who speak Quechua as *indios*, an intolerably ugly term of stigma. They deny that any such people live in Huarochirí or that they are descendants of any such. The "indios," they say, were the builders of the archaeological tombs that dot the hillsides. These ancient people, they say, died by mass suicide in protest against the lash of Spanish colonialism (Salomon 2002a).

The village of San Andrés de Tupicocha holds lands from about 2,500 meters (8,202 feet) high to about 4,800 meters (15,748 feet) on the westward flank of the Andes. It lies a day's bus ride southeast of Lima, at the headwaters of the Lurín River, in the central part of Huarochirí. Of the village's 1,416 residents (according to the 2007 census) perhaps half live exclusively in the community nucleus, located on a difficult secondary road at about 3,321 meters (10,895 feet; Stiglich 1922:1084). Despite its closeness to the capital and its partly "semiproletarian" way of life (Weismantel 1988), the village is poor in modern infrastructure, having received electricity only in 2004. In 2010 the single communal telephone was just starting to be augmented with private land lines.

San Andrés de Tupicocha is the name of three superimposed jurisdictions. It is a district (the smallest unit of national government administration), a municipality, and a recognized Peasant Community. The last of these is the main concern of this study. Under Peruvian law, a Peasant Community (what was called an Indigenous Community until 1969) is a self-governing corporation endowed with control of "immemorial" communal titles to land and water. Communities are often the legal vessels within which traditional forms of power dating back much farther than the republic, or even the Spanish colony, can be conserved. They are governed by what villagers call *costumbre*, best rendered as "customary law." The intricate kinship-based rules of customary law and local ritual are matters of no interest to the state, as long as state requirements such as taxation and the cadastral roll are fulfilled. The majority of Tupicochan agropastoralists belong to households enrolled as *comuneros*, or community stakeholders. In 2007 the number of enrolled households fell below 130. Despite creeping privatization, the Community still owes much of its subsistence to an intricate system of canals, terraces, and walled pastures under the communal regime, begun in pre-Hispanic antiquity and forever in process of improvement. It is the Peasant Community's chief duty to administer them. This provides a domain in which vernacular literacy subsists unsupervised by state agents.

For administering the commons, the Community relies upon a very deep-rooted system of non-state-based institutions: a system of ten *ayllus* or *parcialidades*. These are corporate descent groups on mainly patrilineal lines, each with its own elaborate internal hierarchy of office and seniority, of ritual, and of recordkeeping. It is as if the village were a league of ten proud, self-conscious teams. Only ayllu members can be comuneros, and the only way to join an ayllu is to have birthright eligibility. The different ayllus act as parties working in fraternal rivalry to complete their respective shares of every communal task: mending the pasture walls, building the bullring, installing pipes in the irrigation ditches, and so on. Above and beyond the workdays the ayllus owe to the Community as a whole, members also owe many laborious duties to the ayllu itself. Tupicocha's ayllus are lineal continuations of the ayllus of Checa as described in the circa 1608 Quechua Manuscript of Huarochirí. It is the ayllus which hold as insignia Tupicocha's famous khipus. Modern ayllus, as they document their myriad internal obligations and their services to the larger community, figure as the most important collective actors in the production of endogenous writings.

LINGUISTIC BACKGROUND

Huarochirí is known among readers for its singular Quechua-language document, the Huarochirí Manuscript (Salomon and Urioste 1991, and other editions; Martínez Chuquizana 1996; Taylor 1999). This is the only known book from South America which might be compared to *Popol Vuh* of the Mayans. It explains Huarochirí's pre-Christian religious tradition in "pastoral Quechua" as written (with many nonpastoral localisms) by an unknown indigenous person in or close to 1608 (Acosta Rodríguez 1987). It contains a treasure of myths about the *wakas*, or deified places, and about the clans of the ancient inhabitants, their priesthoods, and their fortunes under Inka and Spanish rule. Translations have been published in many languages, including English (Salomon and Urioste 1991), and it has a large exegetical literature. A 1966 Spanish translation by Peru's bilingual literary genius José María Arguedas (Arguedas and Duviols 1966) gave it fame among Peruvian intellectuals. Many of the myths and rituals explained in it are still living culture in the higher parts of the province (Ortiz Rescaniere 1980), and these are among the practices that generate rural writing (see chapter 1).

The ancestors of Huarochiranos, including the creators of the anonymous book, spoke both Quechua and an ethnic tongue of the Jaqaru (Aymara-family) group, now extinct (Adelaar 1994). They used Quechua as the lingua franca of Inka rule, and continued to speak it as a colonial tongue. But they relinquished both tongues at a time they no longer remember. Today Huarochirí is monolingual in Spanish. Internal archives of communities in the region have yet to yield anything in either Andean language. The chronology of the shift away from American languages is unknown, but circumstances suggest a fairly complex process.

In 1839 a gazetteer-writing protosociologist, José María Córdova y Urrutia, perceived Huarochirí as overwhelmingly *indígena* (98.2 percent) and Tupicocha in particular as 100 percent "Indian" (1992:62, 72–73).[2] The national census of 1876 reported San Damián, which then contained all the villages studied intensively in this book, as 100 percent *indio* (Peru 1878:236). Although these studies are "language deaf," it is unlikely that during the nineteenth century Quechua was totally extinguished, because in the nineteenth century language was one of the markers (along with dress and bodily traits) of Indianness. Had such writers encountered bilingual or Spanish-monolingual campesinos, they would probably have perceived at least some of them as *castas*, or *mestizos* (people of mixed "race").

By 1940 the Peruvian state kept some linguistic records. In Huarochirí Province as a whole 88.2 percent of men and 91.2 percent of women were then reported as speakers of "Castilian."[3] Only 0.3 percent of men and 0.8 percent of women were Quechua monolinguals. Only sixteen people in the whole province knew "Aymara" (which may refer to the old, Aymara-like ethnic tongue). More recent censuses report nearly uniform Spanish monolingualism. The main period of language shift therefore probably was the later nineteenth century through early twentieth. Today's Huarochiranos think of Quechua as remote and foreign. They certainly share the Creole prejudice against it. When a stuttering man greeted Salomon at a party, the remark "He's saying hello in Quechua!" got a big laugh. Huarochirí local vernacular is rich in words of Quechua origin. Such words are felt to be "authentic" and local, but not indigenous. Nobody we met was aware that their own province once had an Andean language other than Quechua, although many know that a pre-Quechua language survives (tenuously) in the adjacent Province of Yauyos.

"THE ROMANCE OF THE PRECISE"

The numerous manuscript books that Tupicochans write are no literary treasure trove. Many would look tedious to outsiders. They are mostly administrative papers: *actas* (minutes of meetings), account books, receipts, and memoranda, plus some local histories. Nonetheless the popular attitude toward these writings differs from urbanites' indifferent acceptance of "paperwork." Modern campesinos bring to the bureaucratic-legalistic style of writing a devotion and enthusiasm that startle outsiders.

This has much to do with the corporate nature of the village. To be a comunero means to be a stakeholder in a legal entity, the *comunidad campesina*, which owns the pastures and canals on which villagers depend. Only children of the ten ayllus that compose the village have eligibility to become comuneros. Signing on as a comunero is a much weightier matter than just being a citizen. It entails thirty years of rigorous service, costly ritual obligations, and a succession of onerous terms as officer. Most of all, it demands work. Every comunero's livelihood depends on having the commons well maintained, for his or her family's labor and capital will be applied to them. To maintain and improve the shared infrastructure of pasturing and farming, including its administrative infrastructure, is to uphold both livelihood and solidarity. This is accomplished chiefly by *faenas* ('unpaid communal labor days'; Gelles 1984) levied on all the comuneros. Unpaid common labor is a reciprocity system, one in which a morally binding gift of labor is given to the community as a corporate entity and repaid by a combination of token ritual gifts (coca, etc.) with important use rights to the resources worked. In other places faena is usually called by the Quechua term *minka*, glossed as asymmetrical reciprocity (Mayer 2002:110–11).

A crucial point is that reciprocity hardly implies trust. On the contrary, Tupicochans are quite sure that if people can cheat they will. Moreover the administration of common resources inherently generates tension, because even without cheating, the village would still have sources of inequality and conflict. The root problem is that equal use rights in land and water are of unequal worth depending what private resources one brings to them. Some get extra value out of their membership because they own more livestock or can afford fertilizers, pesticides, and so on. "Have-not" comuneros feel the system is hard on them because it affords them bare subsistence resources while allowing some social peers to do better (e.g., by running small stores and extending credit). Until recently, it was routine for the men with the most cattle to hold the highest offices. Debts and grudges about bad marriages or failed business deals impede cooperation. Young men complain, with good reason, about being made to serve as officers before they have capitalized their households. Women are gradually winning stronger roles in governance but many still feel and resent female marginality. (For example, there are now female heads of ayllus, but this usually occurs because no plausible male is available for the job.) Game-playing vis-à-vis powerful outside organizations irritates those with only local networks. Villagers often say their peers are *vivo* ('crafty') and *egoísta* ('selfish'). Although the comunero way of life has provided a measure of safety amid the historic lurches of Peru's economy, it is overall a poorish life, and one that makes formidable demands on one's freedom of action.

Villagers' willingness to do their share in the common interest therefore depends on strict accountability. For this reason, villagers see record-keeping as the very linchpin of communal life. Accounting is not the boring matter urbanites take it to be; it is the very heart of the social contract. When done faithfully and skillfully, it makes everything else possible. Moreover, good records help to secure equitable treatment by outside authorities. The village's land titles and other foundational papers are revered and current papers scrutinized critically. In the village hall, the allegorical mural which symbolizes the community has at its very center a pen, inkwell, and open manuscript book. Strong literacy is associated with self-defense against fraud and abuse. Writing is even spoken of as the *arma* ('weapon') of the community. Literacy is closely associated with dignity and social respect.

Love of writing, then, has much to do with faith in the power of exact and permanent knowledge. *Constancia* ('document of record'), is an omnipresent word. If asked why one must write down so many details, Tupicochans usually answer, "Para que conste" ('So it will be on record'). The word *constancia* connotes durable knowledge, a defense against errors, falsehoods, and forgetting. Producing a constancia is the culmination of every collective function. The function is not considered done without it: the document is not *about* the deed but *is* the deed. Considering local usage, one might define constancias as consubstantial records. Constancias trump all oral testimonies in cases of dispute.

In short, intravillage literacy is a tough, practical matter of mutual social control. But villagers' relation with writing could also be called a romance, in the sense that it embodies admiration, a maximalist commitment, and utopian hopes.

To court exactitude, Wallace Stevens suggests (as reproduced in the epigraph to this book), it is not enough to abandon "the tired romance of imprecision" (1965 [1947]:353). Tupicochan writing indeed tolerates a modicum of "tired romance" in the form of civic bombast. But the core aesthetic of writing is an astringently plain one—"a rhetoric that convinces and appeals by adopting the language of antirhetoric" (Riles 2006:19, summarizing an argument from James Aho's 1985 book on the culture of accounting). The worth of precision comes into a villager's view when he scans the long record and sees the durable proof (constancia) of ever-emerging, enduring regularity and good faith. These moments are felt to have grandeur. Several Tupicochan rituals include the bringing together of objects understood as constancias: the joint presentation of all khipus on January 2, archival inventories at the ayllu and Community level, the joint display or all staffs of office on New Year's Eve, and the bringing together of all crosses on May 3. Jacques Derrida, in meditating on the nature of archives, called such events "consignations": moments when great accumulations of signs over time are gathered as "a single corpus . . . a synchrony in which all the elements articulate the unity of an ideal configuration" (1996:3).

Written records over the long haul manifest the cycles of production, construction, and solidarity in ritual. A complete year of recordkeeping, presented at the New Year's plenary meeting (Huayrona), is a beautiful thing, because it concretizes success in overcoming the myriad fights and hazards of the year to re-create the beloved virtual entity, the village. Huayrona, the highest annual day of monetary and moral reckoning, is "an appearance of Again." In it one glimpses the ever-returning, never-ending transcendent entity that endures even as fallible individuals come and go. If we suppose that ritual interaction with deities represents an idea of interaction tout court, the fact that such rituals are included in the accountable record shows how encompassing this idea is.

This book is primarily about what is Andean in graphic practice: habits developed outside immediate state and church supervision. For this reason we will give priority in these pages to the writings of the Andean kinship corporations, or ayllus (also called parcialidades). These small corporations exist below the threshold of legal recognition. The state, which recognizes the Community, takes no interest in its inner segmentation or its traditional rules about ritual and kinship. So when the ayllu or parcialidad laboriously creates a never-ending written simulacrum of itself, it does so out of a locally felt need. This lowest, unofficial tier of the graphic regime therefore is the best place to learn what is vernacular about Andean literacy.

To say that vernacular writing emerges at the margin of the state hardly means the state is irrelevant. As Veena Das and Deborah Poole (2004) emphasize, the mountainous regions that Peru's viceroyalty and republic long marginalized are not by that token outside the state. Colonial and republican governments have always been able to tax and coerce the margin. Flags fly and mayors get salaries even in the neglected outback. What in the past made the margin marginal, was the state's one-sided, unreceptive relation to its racially stigmatized highland peasantry: it ruled but excluded. Traditionally, campesinos who passed from margins to centers of the state (e.g., ministerial offices, courts) were made—by a precisely graduated, half-conscious etiquette of disrespect—to feel unentitled and unworthy. Their business was slow tracked to the point of oblivion. To live in the margins of the state was to live within the state, but in a particular way. Since 2000, popular participation in the state has improved markedly, and some Peruvian observers think marginality is becoming a thing of the past. But it surely was the condition that shaped rural writing habits.

In a sense, then, the writing of unofficial ayllu books is a state practice at the level of customary law. The emulation of state norms within the intravillage conduct of Andean institutions, even when no official demands it, is marginal citizens' manner of approaching state power. If ayllu records partake of parliamentary order while they honor the deified mountains, they do so in quest of access and intelligibility before both powers. Historic distance from the state and neglect by it afforded a space in which idiosyncrasies—including Andean cultural traditions—could continue to evolve. But when these peculiarities color peasants' approach to state centers, leaving "provincial" traces in their writings, the result has been that their writings and speeches were devalued.

In the first and second chapters, we will emphasize the development of Andean usages in writing along this margin (Larson 2004:54n29). In chapters 3 through 5, we will trace the particular ways such writings encounter—or rather, misencounter—the literacy of officialdom, and follow into the smallest details of language the discord between peasant and state uses of text. In the sixth and seventh chapters, we will concentrate upon texts of popular historiography: "homemade" texts through which

Huarochiranos look back upon their experiences, from ayllus to wider webs of power and loyalty.

METHODS

Grafismo is a handy Romance-language (Spanish, but also French, Italian, and Portuguese) expression with no English equivalent. It means a person's or a group's particular habits and orientations in using scripts. This study is intended as a historical ethnography of an Andean grafismo. The project consequently puts on the table a range of interests somewhat beyond those of the NLS debate proper. While sharing with NLS researchers an interest in the way the institutional vectors of literacy shape so-called literacy effects, we are also interested in the degree to which changing grafismo reflects and shapes broader cultural dispositions.

We adopt the pluralist premise of Keith Basso's 1974 proposal for an "ethnography of writing." We assume that some form of literacy exists whenever people use a signary (more or less widely standardized set of visible signs) to encode information, including the case of Tupicocha's ayllu khipus. We are interested in capturing a wide range of culturally programmed script-using behaviors; that is, in NLS terminology, *literacy practices*. In the field we sought to capture a wide range of *literacy events* and their products. From them we will advance generalizations about the informational exchange spheres which each practice of literacy mediates, or in other words, define each literacy practice's *domain*. Each sphere of information exchange, or domain, can also be characterized as a *network* or *graphic community*, by analogy to speech community. Like the concept of speech community, the concept of graphic community can be scaled up or down to adjust to the scope of a code's application, from broad lingua franca usage to the highly specific vernacular whose peculiarities mark local or other group boundaries. By filling each of these conceptual categories with ethnographic instances, it is possible to get an idea of the role of writing as the actual tissue of social exchange.

We have prioritized endogenous literate production, at different scales —from intrahousehold jottings and letters, through the business of corporate kin groups and rural neighborhoods, up to Community papers which concern self-government and often attest interaction with estates, merchants, the state, NGOs, and the church. Data collection as detailed below was conducted by agreement with village authorities and individual owners or authors of papers. Although Community-level archives are documents of record, and from Lima's viewpoint constitute official records, they are not locally considered public, because villagers are anxious about the security of their land titles. The tools of inquiry included interviews, inventories, photography, and observation, followed by paleographic transcription or audio transcription and systematic excerpting. Procedures for analyzing the corpus included genre "typologization" (categorization of writings by their genre templates); textual analysis for indices of articulation with nonwritten behavior; and dialectological and sociolectal study of fine-grain traits such as orthography, formatting, and syntax as well as research into indices of standardization or improvisation in literacy events.

We followed classic ethnographic fieldwork practices of anthropology and sociolinguistics in tracking writing through multiple functional domains. Sampling was not random but directed to selecting consultants with varied angles of view on literacy events: ex-Community secretaries, unofficial scribes, lay and official teachers and catechists, *camachicos* (an obsolescent term for past and present presidents) of the ten ayllus, "peasant intellectuals," and less-lettered peasants. Data collection proceeded by observation and semistructured interviewing, and regular attendance at events where writing acts are expected.

The fieldwork was done in discontinuous stints from 1994 through 2002 by Salomon, an anthropologist, and 2001 through 2006 by Niño-Murcia, a sociolinguist. The study began as a by-product of Salomon's inquiry into the alphabetic context of Tupicocha village's patrimonial khipus (locally called *quipocamayos*), published as *The Cord Keepers* (Salomon 2004a). The chapters developed mostly by Salomon are those concerning writing in self-governance and the interface between khipus and paper (chapters 1–2) as well as those on endogenous history-writing (chapters 6–7). In our search for alphabetic sources that might be functionally analogous to the cord records, or might comment upon them, it became evident that Tupicocha Village contained an immense deposit of endogenous writing, particularly at the ayllu level. The evidence also included, at lesser levels of detail, the archives of the provincial capital Huarochirí, the Checa Community of San Damián, the Concha Community of San Damián, the Community of San Francisco de Sunicancha, and the Community of Santiago de Tuna (the last at both Community and ayllu level). We also studied household papers, which sometimes treat noninstitutional family matters as being subject to the norm of constancia.

While many colonial and modern judicial or administrative papers have served as sources about ayllus, no previous study has examined ayllus' internal documentation. Within Tupicocha, all the archives of the corporate descent groups were inventoried. Key volumes were copied cover to cover, by permission, and selected passages were extracted. Extensive photographs were taken to illustrate the evolution of formatting and detailed writing practice. This material was studied by sociolinguistic methods by Niño-Murcia.

Niño-Murcia developed the sociolinguistic parts of the research (chiefly chapters 3–5). Prior to fieldwork in Huarochirí, Niño-Murcia carried out a quantitative analysis of documents from a copy of a Tupicochan manuscript of 201 pages previously photocopied by Salomon. This initial textual study was complemented with fieldwork (2001, 2003, 2004, 2005, and 2006) to obtain a clear understanding of the relationship that existed between its inhabitants' language use, social life, and literacy practices. Data collection on these points took place through varied techniques: participant observation in varied village activities (2001, 2003, 2004, 2005, and 2006); formal and informal interviews with different age groups, school and classrooms visits; informal interviews with school personnel; interviews with parents and observations in homes; observation of student-to-student, student-to-teacher, and student-to-group interactions; written annotations and audio and video recordings of writing events; study of interviewee comments on samples of written texts; study of school and newspaper records; and personal narratives of the literacy experiences that shaped adults' literacy practices. Spontaneous incidents of metalanguage also provided clues to local norms.

From the viewpoint of Tupicochans, the work of ethnographers is in some respects also a work of constancia. Following their preferences, we refer to people using their real names except where a legitimate interest might be prejudiced by mentioning them. In translating local writings we have respected the sentence boundaries and punctuation, and as much of the syntax as we could, together with original capitalization. The explanatory paragraphs discuss nontranslatable features that give the prose its peculiar savor, including local lexicon and nonstandard spelling.

ONE

An Andean Community Writes Itself

This chapter concerns the physical presence of texts in a modern village, the local way of producing texts, and the way local archives work. Visitors to Peruvian villages do not routinely see any of this. Indeed, they experience a first impression that these are alphabetically impoverished places. This mistaken perception results largely from misunderstandings about the role of literacy in campesino society. Writing lies at the core of community life, but local writings rarely speak outward to a general public. Rather, most writing safeguards an internal fund of knowledge. Nearly all collective action above the level of household intimacy, and even some intrahousehold business, is structured in such a way that the scenario for action itself includes making a record of the action. In the realm of the collective, nothing is "done" until it is written up. This does not imply a monolithic corpus, because a segmented society creates an archive with many segments. The products of incessant self-documentation rest in archives dispersed through the village, usually in confidential locations.

The way archives work has become an ever-widening theme. In brief, theorists emphasize four facets of "archivism." First, archiving—the systematic depositing of cultural traces—produces data structures of its own, which interest archivists and programmers. Second, each archival document is deposited with an intention or purpose of its time, and necessarily bears a trace of the interpretation and importance attached to some fact. An archive is therefore an "archaeological" deposit revealing the range of the thinkable under a particular cultural regimen. Third, archiving is the banking of effectual knowledge: the archived message speaks to the future and constrains it. Archiving is an exercise of power, and so is controlling an archive. Fourth, every actor thinks from and about some personal or shared "archive," namely, his or her fund of evocative or explicit past objects. Tupicocha is nothing if not an intensely archivistic society, and each of these concepts is germane to some part of its practices. We will return to them at various points in exploring its lettered sphere.

WHERE IS THE ALPHABET IN TUPICOCHA?

When it comes to well-known print media, rural Peruvians tend to be readers with not much to read. It is not that they lack interest. Among campesinos one never fails to meet a few people with avidly studious leanings: an all-night trucker who explains his readings on ego psychology while wresting a 1962 Dodge cattle truck around the hairpin turns of a cliff-edge road, or a peasant who trudges up the hill from his fruit trees, stinking of urea, telling what he has read about the diplomatic history of the First World War. Of course degrees of readership vary hugely, from the many who can only figure out items in simple formats (lists, headlines) to people who can expound dense legal prose or archaistic religious language. But in general villagers enjoy reading or being read to. They wholeheartedly second the internationally dominant ideology of literacy. Men who cannot write "well" (i.e., close to the metropolitan norm) are considered poor marriage prospects, because they cannot defend the household with tenable paperwork. Literacy for females is still somewhat controversial. Some men are not embarrassed to be heard scoffing that if women learn to write, they will just write adulterous love notes. Nonetheless in the younger generation of householders, who increasingly see urban employment as an option for daughters, female literacy is gaining support.

Yet the alphabet is not much on display. No neon signs with cheerful curlicues glow to greet the urbanite. Painted store signs are scarce. Hardly any commercial print can be found on sale, except required grade-school texts. Even missionary or NGO pamphlets are less than common. Tabloid papers that truckers bring from Lima pass from hand to hand for weeks until finally recycled as insulation for adobe houses. When travelers get off the bus, villagers often ask if they have brought anything to read. No less than fruit or bread, newsprint is considered a good visiting gift. Some mothers hope their *compadres* will bring their children books to strengthen them for school. Printed media are, however, counted as luxuries. They are in fact rather expensive relative to other products, partly because the Peruvian state does not provide subsidies such as media rate postage.

Where, then, is writing in this village? Over each door a careful glance allows one to see the faded trace of a census taker's chalk marks. Peering into the schoolhouse window, one sees shelves of government-approved texts under lock and key. The state puts its stamp on the most prominent buildings, namely, shields bearing patriotic insignia. Children have their say in scratched stucco: "The fourth graders are miserable dogs hungry dogs." Adolescents publicize who "is with" whom. Other graffiti announce a horse for sale or an opinion about an ex-lover. At the public health station a small sign announces the legal rates for medical help. "It's your obligation to vaccinate your child. Do it now," says the largest headline. A list tacked outside the irrigation office advises water users of their turns. Commercial container labels dot the village scene: Pilsen Beer, Inca Kola, Porky rendered lard, Full Speed cigarettes, Llama matches (see figure 4). Window grilles on the better-off houses bear ironworked initials of the couples that built them. Clippings of local interest or colorful calendars suitable for adorning walls are saved indefinitely. On adobe walls, each day's sunlight bleaches another infinitesimal shade from the palimpsest of political and election slogans (see figure 5).

The sphere of officialdom does send a lot of print to villages, but officialdom locks it away. The lion's share of Tupicocha village's total print assets have become concentrated, in two locations: the public school (the largest single building complex in this as in most villages), and the municipal building. Until 1998 the municipal collection consisted entirely of law codes, maps, and policy directives sent by ministries. The mayor, an ambitious champion of the village's claim to development, procured book donations by the National Library, the Instituto Francés de Estudios Andinos (a cultural affiliate of the French embassy), and certain banks which subsidize "cultural" publishing. Scholarly visitors including Gerald Taylor, a linguist distinguished for work on Huarochirí's colonial Quechua, have donated books too. This budding library grew to perhaps 500 volumes (see figure 6).[1] By 2010, it had been relocated to a rented reading room on the main street.

The public school has a reading room in its main building, stocked mostly with works distributed by the Ministry of Education (see figure 7

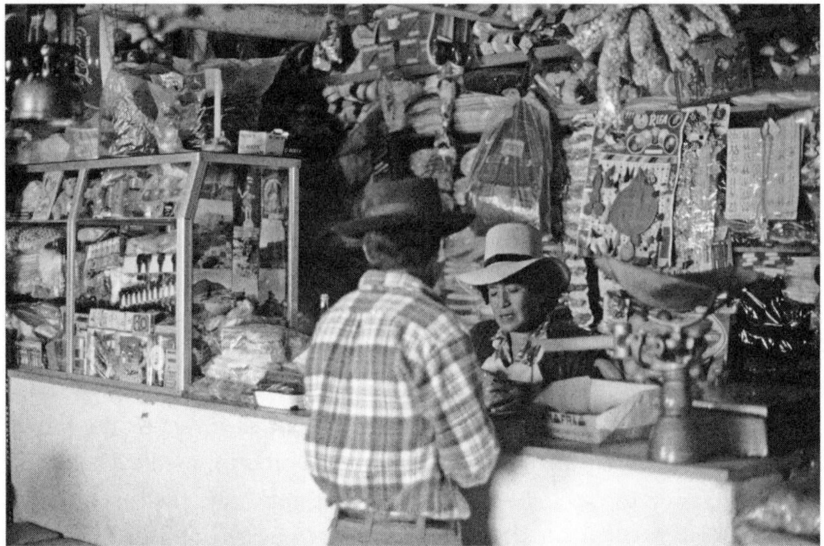

4. General stores such as Lidia Ramos's are second only to government offices and schools as writing-rich spaces in small towns. The snapshots in the showcase to her right are the ones her husband took when he climbed Shiucaña Mountain in the 1990s. This mountain is mentioned in the 1608 Quechua Manuscript of Huarochirí as home to Siua Caña Vilca Coto, the "most beautiful" of all the ancient gods.

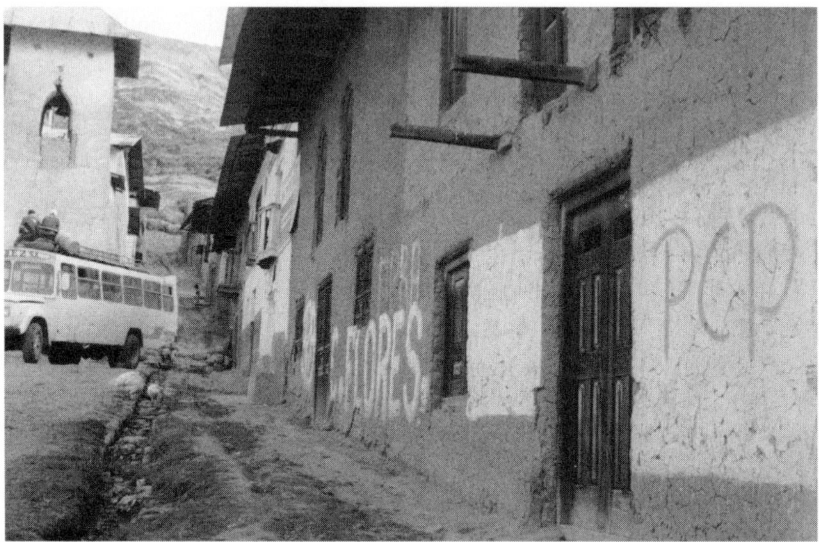

5. Up to 1992 San Juan Tantaranche was the scene of some Shining Path incursions. In 1994 Shining Path (PCP; 'Communist Party of Peru') messages still overlay the painted propaganda of legal parties.

6. The book collection in the municipal office in Tupicocha was amassed by the mayor starting in 1998. At left, a "retired" statue of Admiral Bolognesi which once stood in the main square.

7. The library of Tupicocha's public school (photographed 1999) was, as of 2005, the village's main location for print matter.

and chapter 3). The majority are grade-school texts in various editions and numerous copies.

Small municipal libraries exist in some other villages, but public access is hindered by the lack of salaries for staff to attend them. Libraries arise either by local initiative or by political patronage. Julio C. Tello, Peru's pioneer archaeologist, used his political connections to endow his hometown of Huarochirí (the capital of Huarochirí Province) with a library. In the 1990s it had about 44 meters (144 feet) of mostly full shelves. It holds many donations from Limeños who cherish Tello's memory, as well as from various NGOs, religious groups, and political parties. (Works of the North Korean leader Kim Il Sung occupied almost a whole shelf.)

The appearance of alphabetic deficit and urbanites' perceptions of campesinos as semiliterate come partly from the mistaken supposition that circulation of print is a true measure of literacy. The scripts that actually convey information vital to the community, and which *comuneros* consider vital, are not in print. Most are manuscripts, and some are typewritten pages. Letters that matter often appear as art: as epigraphy, as embroidery, and as carvings. Reading and writing are far from marginal to being a solid comunero. Ancestors who could barely afford schoolbooks rest in the cemetery under profusely engraved stones, and the wooden crosses that mark the graves of the poor are incomplete without at least their initials.

Tupicocha mounts an intricate cycle of fiestas and "customary" (i.e., distinctively Andean and local) dances, organized by voluntary societies who donate the proceeds to public works. On such occasions the society's members put their name and dates upon the monuments they create. When festival sponsors invested their proceeds in an iron gate for the Collca, or ritual plaza, they inscribed the inside (the part legible during sacred contexts):

work Of the
sponsors
of Corpus
Cristi of the
YEAR 1990
Help by the
comuneros and
the Council

and
the master artisan
Marcelino
Antiporta C.
And his fore—man Agapito R.R.
helper
SPONSORS
F[unda]dor FORTUNATO[2]
1st VICTORINO
2d DARIO
3d VICTORINO
4th MILTON
5th ALEJANDRO
6th VASILIO
7th EDILIO
8th MARCELO

Likewise, those who help in a roofing bee leave their initials on rafters, and donors of altar cloths have words of devotion embroidered with their names. Inscriptions on natural mineral surfaces are usually mementos of sentiment. Amused bus riders occasionally see cliffs and boulders oil-painted with fresh amorous spectacles:

LOVE LIKE MINE ISN'T SOMETHING
YOU FIND LYING IN THE ROAD.

These examples emphasize the in-group character of most local inscription. At the same time, public writing sometimes calls out to the cosmopolitan life which the electronic media glorify. One commercial sign in San Damián (1994) said *SASTRERIA MISTER.* At least one Tupicocha merchant cast his symbolic net across the Pacific, with a beer sign written partly in Japanese (see figures 8–9). And writing from afar that refers to the village is hoarded (see figure 10).

Diaspora and the deterritorializing way of life have increased communicative reliance on writing, especially during the almost twenty recent years when Tupicocha lacked a telephone. (Wires were stolen during the Shining Path conflict.) One particularly notices writings at the grimy storefront bus depots in Lima which serve, among other ways, as post offices and bulletin boards for villagers coming to market or city-dwelling

8. Global and local inscription (1997) at a Tupicocha merchant: "Have some delicious Tarmeñita beer," reads this hand-painted shop sign. The woman in full skirts is a stylized central highlander (*tarmeña*). "Namyejo rengue kyo" transcribes a mantra the shopkeeper learned from the proselytizing Nichiren Shoshu Buddhist sect, of Japanese origin, which he attends when visiting Lima.

9. The reverse side of the same sign shows the highland woman in her urban or traveling clothes.

BAJADA DE REYES

En San Andrés de Tupicocha

Fuera de Lima

CUENTAN QUE HACE MUCHÍSIMOS AÑOS, EN LA SERRANÍA DE LIMA, UNA JOVENCITA POCO PRECAVIDA FUE CON SU CÁNTARO EN LA ESPALDA A RECOGER AGUA DE UNA LAGUNA. AL INCLINARSE, EL PRENDEDOR QUE SUJETABA SU MANTA CAYÓ AL AGUA; ELLA TRATÓ DE RECUPERARLO, PERO DEBIDO AL OLEAJE SE HUNDIÓ MÁS, Y ASÍ QUEDÓ PARA SIEMPRE "EL PRENDEDOR EN LA LAGUNA": TUPICOCHA.

10. Printed materials from urban media that refer to the village are carefully hoarded. This article from a 1994 Lima Sunday tourism supplement describes the winter ritual cycle in Tupicocha. The sidebar at the upper right has the effect of "officializing" a dubious explanation, from folk etymology, for the village's name.

"children of the village." These spaces function like airlocks between two very different social atmospheres. One of these hidden "airlocks"—there are hundreds in the maze of working-class Lima neighborhoods—is the Expreso Pérez terminal serving central Huarochirí, a remodeled barbecue joint on the raffish fringes of the wholesale fruit market. Dance posters and bullfight posters in Day-Glo pink and green, proclaim hometown functions that, villagers hope, will stimulate urbanites to come home, spend money, and bestow donations.

> AN AFTERNOON OF BULLFIGHTS IN SUNICANCHA, HUAROCHIRI
> ORGANIZED BY THE BROTHERHOOD OF OUR LORD OF MIRACLES[3]
> HOMERO MACHUCA AND HIS CREW
> Bulls from San Damián will fight
> Represented by [the Brotherhood's][4] President Ruly Durán
> and its Secretary Oscar Anchelía Janavilca

Inside the bus terminal, over the benches where passengers nod, posters proclaim a regional conference sponsored by an NGO and a community mass in Lima for the deceased of the hometown. There are also

11. Rural bus lines carry Tupicochans in and out of diaspora, and also carry their correspondence. The bus, already battered when photographed in 2005, is still rolling in 2010.

calendars with fading panoramas of villages nestled in the skirts of mountains and flyers announcing "folkloric" dances in Lima's dance-and-stage show halls. The Virgin, or a polychrome saint, pronounces a written blessing on dangerous journeys.

Such bus lines function as rural society's post office (see figure 11). (The official post office only connects with large towns.) Villagers line up at the ticket window with letters for the drivers to deliver at different stops. As the bus trundles countryward through a maze of ramshackle factories and rough-built homes, "children of the village" flag down the driver, waving envelopes. Would-be letter senders hang from the doorway stanchion and yell, "Who's going to Pacota?" "Who's from Characuay-qui?" hoping to find a passenger willing to carry messages on foot to relatives in the outer hamlets. In highland towns, especially those containing the headquarters of more than one recognized Peasant Community, competitive monumentalism spawns elaborate hand-painted signs. These form a neat sampling of cultural capital's local verbal and visual currencies: modernism, Hispanism, indigenism, and nationalism. Such spectacular writing stands out in Huarochirí's provincial capital, the small city of the same name.

Llambilla (Yampilla Ayllu in the mythology from the 1608 Quechua Manuscript of Huarochirí) decorated its Community hall with a vast, gaily colored modernist-cubist mural, while Huarochirí Community preferred the bullfighting motif. Suni displayed the *wiphala*, or "neo-Indian" rainbow flag,[5] and a Quechua cliché, "AMA SUA"[6] ('Don't steal'), which public school books canonize from Inka Garcilaso's 1609 *Royal Commentaries*. Lupo squares off with military-style iconography and a Latin motto, "SI VIS PACEN [*sic*] PARA BELLUM" ('If you want peace, prepare for war'). Public works such as bullrings and cemetery gates also bear large, ornate legends. Catholic churches usually have no legends visible from the street but Pentecostal and Evangelical chapels, with their mystique of sanctity through scripture reading, almost always do.

One of the most important functions of rural writing is to performatively enact, and continually reenact, the birth of a new corporate entity. Graduating classes form significant durable age sets. Each year at graduation time the new cohort names itself after a canonized hero. (An example is the 1994 class of the San Damián high school, which hoped to be known forever as "The José Carlos Mariátegui Class.")[7] The new cohort takes a long journey together, and as it goes, paints its name on public surfaces. This custom, encouraged by public school teachers, is a troublesome source of vandalism at archaeological sites, where school youths hold parties (see figure 12).

Much as villagers prize inscriptions that performatively create and reproduce society, they equally prize inscriptions that attest its ancient legitimacy and antiquity. They regard inscriptions on church woodwork, church bells (Sunicancha has one dated 1675), and the huge retables of altars (Tupicocha's bears the signature of its maker dated 1762) as proofs of immemorial sanctity. *Peañas* (step pyramids built as sockets for the cross) that mark building entrances sometimes allude to ancient foundations, citing dates. Recent dates are no less revered, notably the dates of recognition of Peasant Communities, which are sometimes announced on costly brass plaques. Innumerable formulaic inscriptions appear on

12. The 1979 graduating classes of Huarochirí High School overnighted in a huge rock shelter under the snows of Paria Caca Mountain, where they oil-painted their names over a rich deposit of (probably pre-Hispanic) petroglyphs depicting the fertility of alpacas and llamas. Names appear on a scroll (at bottom), symbolizing academia and official learning.

display objects, such as *cajuelas,* or glass-walled religious show boxes; altar clothes; embroidered pillows for display of patrimonial khipus, among other uses; and the scarlet *banderolas,* or giant, hand-held parade banners which organizations carry as public regalia.

In Roman Jakobson's division of the functions of language, most of the inscriptions mentioned so far are "phatic," "emotive," or "conative": they exist to catch attention, to express feelings, or to make a reader do what the writer wishes (1960:357). All this could occur without writing's actually forming the spinal cord of an information system. How far does rural writing go as a rural order of information? The answer, as we will see below, is that it is far reaching and fundamental. But this can only be addressed empirically once one has looked further into writing as an institutional vehicle of action.

LEVIATHAN'S LEGENDS

At the beginning of his Huarochirí researches, Salomon surveyed all the public lettering visible in the village of San Damián, which is adjacent to Tupicocha and the largest in the central part of the province. In term of sheer numbers of inscription, the nation-state itself is by far the chief writer upon the public skin of rural society.[8] Posters from the Ministry of Health explain cholera prevention (see figure 13) and from the "Forces of order" (police, military) urge cooperation with antiguerrilla campaigns (see figures 14–15).

Stickers in 1993 from a Housing Census (donated to the state's Institute of Statistics by a brewing company) and older census marks constituted the lion's share of public inscriptions. The second largest body of public signs was electoral propaganda. State agencies also marked their works with wordy signs. But beyond inscriptions in public view, everyone carries the script of the state on his body. As Lund (2001) and Deborah Poole (2004:35–39) have observed, personhood itself is mediated through bureaucratic literacy, because one can do nothing without showing a national identity document. In presenting themselves bodily to the state and acquiring their documentary doppelgängers, people come to see themselves as part and parcel of the national project of literate bureaucracy. When formally introduced, many people spontaneously present themselves in the bureaucratic manner, surnames first ("Ricci Cajahuaringa, Florestán"), volunteering to show their identity documents or even reciting their identity numbers unasked.

Villagers can readily decode both the bureaucratic text and political subtext of a sign like

> MINISTRY OF AGRICULTURE-PRONAMCHCS PARTNERSHIP
> AGENCY: SANTA EULALIA
> MCCA: LURIN
> CC: CONCHA CHECA
> ACTIONS:
> Rural infrastructure.
> Soil conservation.
> Forestry development.
> 1994. "Seeking the development of peoples."

Comuneros are producers as well as consumers of text in state idiom, via correspondence and via occasional employment with the rural research teams ministries deploy (e.g., livestock and land tenure surveys). Young people experience learning the peculiar sociolect of government as advancement in citizenship. But the internalization of the state project hardly betokens placid acceptance of state messages. On the contrary, villagers criticize their government acidly. At least until the late 2000s, when rural administration began to improve, publicly inscribed pronouncements were taken as ironies because facts fell so far short of goals. For a

13. Detail of a Ministry of Health poster explains how to stop cholera contagion. Peru suffered a severe cholera outbreak in 1991.

14. Army helicopters scattered flyers like these (dropped in San Damián, probably in 1991) throughout areas of Shining Path activity. The fliers urged those implicated in terrorism to "repent" and avail themselves of safety from prosecution, but did not mention that turning in fellow combatants was the price.

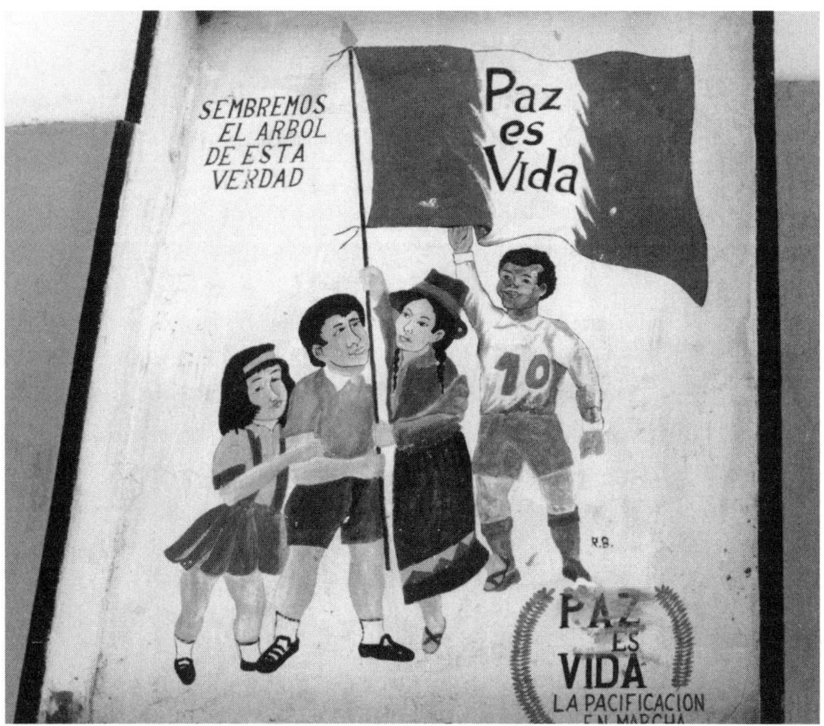

15. A political mural of the early Fujimori period (ca. 1992) urges citizens to join the armed forces in "pacification." Imagery showing nonwhite faces was at that time a novelty in government iconography.

time rural buses bogged down in mud right in front of the sign announcing state-sponsored improvements in drainage, a daily occasion for jeers.

LITERACY RATES AND WRITING TECHNIQUES

One might correctly guess from the above that Huarochiranos as a whole are deeply immersed in literacy. Huarochirí villagers do enjoy high literacy rates. In 2001 Peru's national census agency reported the country to be 87.9 percent literate for people over fifteen. The 1993 census returns put Tupicocha's literate population over 15 at 84.11 percent and in 2007 literacy surpassed 86%. Female literacy is lower than male, and the literacy of both sexes may be overestimated because census takers interpret "literacy" as very minimal competence. Most male comuneros can read newspapers and write readily within a narrow range of genres, relying heavily on types of formulism discussed below. In the 1990s girls dropped out of school—or, rather, were pulled out—markedly earlier than boys. Fathers justified this on the grounds that it is males, as privileged inheritors and defenders of landholdings, who must be versed in law. Adult women's fluency in writing is rising but still varies wildly, depending on how thoroughly chores, child rearing, and agropastoralism consume their time. Some all but forget reading. But a minority—often part-time traders, or activists in the Mothers' Guilds or the Association of Parents of Families (a parent-teacher organization), out-write their husbands. Newer, non-kin-based women's organizations in the village write their own documents (Niño-Murcia 2009), and teachers say that female drop-out rates, while still disproportionate, are decreasing.

Even though hardly a single store sells publications, many sell stationery in abundance. One can usually find spiral notebooks in three sizes, ledgers, pencils of varied quality, gritty cheap erasers and velvety expensive ones, ballpoints, envelopes with or without the red airmail edge, writing paper by the block, colored pencils. There are clean-cutting steel pencil sharpeners from Germany and Chinese Day-Glo plastic ones in animal shapes. Carbon paper and bound blank ledgers nestle under horse blankets and tarpaulins. Obviously somebody is doing a fair amount of handwriting.

Typewriters are rare, but one can sometimes hear the Community's ancient, candle wax-caked Underwood tap-tapping toward midnight as a secretary pounds out the endless paperwork of self-governance with cold-chapped fingers.

With the arrival of electricity in 2001, computers became a possibility. In 2006 we found two computers for official purposes, one in the *colegio* and another one in the municipal office. The municipality, unlike the Community, has a budget from the national government and has acquired ten computers purchased by the mayor for the purpose of providing the school with a computer facility. As of 2006, students in the fourth, fifth, and sixth grades and in high school receive instruction in word processing paid by the municipal office. One of the teachers owns a personal desktop. But Internet is still lacking and not likely to arrive soon, because the telephone company requires a large quota of expensive subscriptions. The manuscript culture of notebooks and ledgers remains as active as ever.

LABOR AND POLITICS SEDIMENTING IN TEXT

The overwhelming bulk of Tupicocha's writing consists of volumes of handwritten acts or minutes. These are usually hardbound ledgers preformatted for accounts but filled primarily with prose.

The genesis of the written record is invariably a literacy event bracketed by ritual events. And conversely any communal activity is by definition a literacy event; if a group event occurs and is not written down, it is almost as though it never happened.

Once a workday (etc.) has been proclaimed, Community authorities plant the small "work cross" and the staffs of office representing those in command. This creates a ritual space. For example, if the work takes place outside the populated center, the crosses of the Community and each participating ayllu, and the staffs of the *alcaldes campos* (rural constables) and their deputies, will be displayed.

All acts of a corporate body, whether it is an ayllu or the Community as a whole, must start with a coca-taking ceremony, called the *armada*. A common modern sense of *armar* is "to set up": the rite sets up a formal context. However, *armada* in Peruvian usage has other meanings. One is "a quota, usually monthly, which is fixed for the payment of a debt, a monetary obligation, or a purchase: He paid in six armadas" (Ugarte Chamorro 1997:34).[9] Throughout the Andean region the coca, liquor, and tobacco used in ritual are referred to as "payments" (usually with Spanish words assimilated to Quechua). So it is possible that *armada* should be considered in the same group as Andeanisms such as *cumplimiento, derecho, pago* or *pagapu*, all of which are etymologically Spanish words that mean "payment [to the mountain god]." These terms have a wide currency in the Quechua-speaking highlands, suggesting that areas far from Huarochirí also indigenized the colonial legal lexicon in order to address Andean deities.

During the armada, an usher distributes the inseparable ritual gifts of coca leaf, tobacco, and liquor at the hosting organization's expense. Coca leaf is indispensable. Each meeting's ritual module opens with a few minutes of meditative coca-sucking during which the members try to "find" through introspection answers to the day's issues. Sociable laughter is allowed, but body movements must be slow and unassertive. The officers also distribute cigarettes, and drinks of liquor, from which each must pour a small libation (*ch'alla*) to Earth. Long periods of silence are encouraged and provoke no discomfort. In the meditative quiet, people reach for more coca to signal that they are still "finding" the next turn of discussion. People who show up late are brought to the work cross and dealt some harmless but humbling blows of the *seplina* (braided whip or 'discipline').

The usher also gives each member a sprig of an herb or flower appropriate to the occasion, and the member tucks it in his or her hatband. (When working on pasture walls in the high slopes, e.g., members receive an herb that grows in such places.) The member is then said to be *enflorado* ('enflowered'). Each worker should wear the floral badge all day, as a proof of attendance. This ceremony opens the one and only formal context in which it is proper to write and sign documents of the collectivity.

Theoretically, secretaries are responsible for posting advance notice of *faenas*. The chanting of morning calls to labor over the village loudspeaker has become more important than postings, but public bulletin boards still do exist (see figures 16–17).

The secretary of any organization is responsible for immediately recording all deeds of the corporation during an armada or right after it. A party that has to go out in the rain or dark to do heavy, muddy canal work will unfailingly bring along a scrap of paper to jot down the exact extent of the job and the names of those who showed up, and especially of those who failed to. The scrap, a *relación* (list or report) will be given to the secretary.

The secretary may then copy the data into his notebook. The secretary's notebooks are his own private property, and not documents of record. A conscientious secretary uses notes to make interim drafts of all documents he intends to put in the books of record (see figures 18–19). At the next "hour of custom" with its armada, he will have it read out and ratified.

If the job is a scheduled faena, the group's scribe will arrive with both his notebook and the appropriate book of record on hand, as well as the rubber stamp of the sponsoring unit. During the *horas de costumbre*, or ritualized breaks, for enflowerment, coca, and so on, he will open his notebook to write a draft *constancia de trabajo*, which he reads to his peers even while they are still mopping the sweat of the last few hours' work or sucking the coca that consecrates it. If they approve, he will copy the text into the book as a *constancia* (act of witness). It becomes a record when it is stamped and everyone present signs it. Signing is highly formal; each must sign in the sight of all, and no signature can be retracted. The thump-thump of the stamps of the authorities marks the moment when it takes performative effect and is accorded constative value.

Any gathering that is enflowered and distributes the "rounds" can also be a business meeting. Substantial decisions may be taken, not in the

16. In San Lorenzo de Quinti (1994), a chalkboard at the plaza reminds members of Llacuaz Ayllu that it is their day for collective canal labor. Llacuaz is a name of pre-Hispanic origin, denoting herders of the high slopes.

17. In Tupicocha, a bulletin board announces irrigation turns.

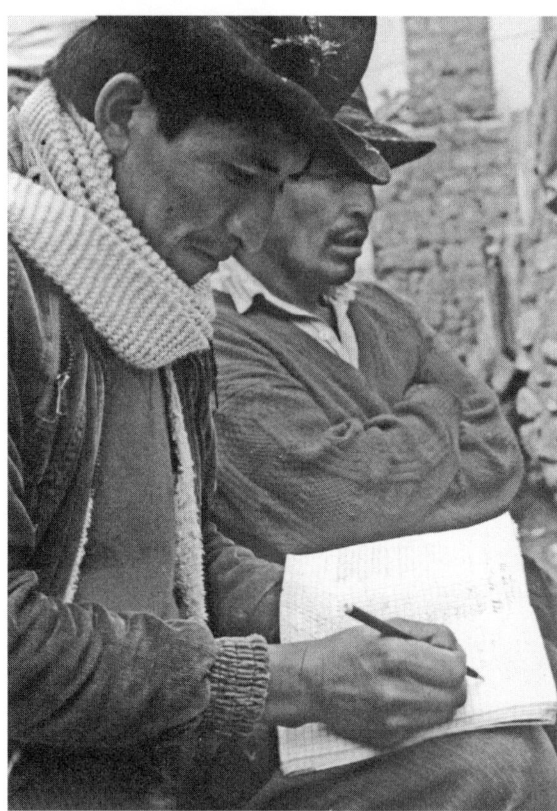

18. The first and most basic function of writing is to document fulfillment of reciprocity between community and "citizen." Segunda Satafasca's 1997 secretary tabulates it in his notebook.

19. "Hour of custom": At a faena to dig a filtration gallery (*amuna*) on the heights of Mayani, in 1997, secretaries of the parcialidades and the Community wrote contemporaneous records of the work as part of the same coca-taking ritual which consecrated the work.

Community Hall, but by people taking coca breaks on a remote mountainside, sitting on tufts of puna grass with their crowbars pointed at the sky. Any minute that records a decision, as opposed to a performance of duty, is called an *acuerdo* ('resolution') or *acta* ('act'). These writings follow the basic formulas of Latin American parliamentary procedure, with vernacular variations in lexicon and spelling. They are often bracketed, however, in an Andean fashion by mentioning the hours of custom or ritual intervals for enflowerment and coca taking (see chapter 4), and using them as section or paragraph breaks.

When multiple segments work together, as for example when the ayllus are all mobilized in a "general" Community faena, the respective secretaries should each write an acta and then consult with the all-Community secretary to be sure the respective groups' work is properly credited. If not, a dispute is likely to break out at the New Year Huayrona, or town meeting.

To formulate an acta is a somewhat delicate job. Tupicochan corporations rarely take votes, because they prefer not to put disagreements on record lest they rankle. Usually debate continues until it is clear which opinion has widest support, and the officers formulate a statement they hope the losing side can tolerate. An act that looks unlikely to pass by acclamation is redrafted. As a result, internal books tend to soft-pedal disagreements with phrases such as "after a light debate." But they do chronicle showdowns that lead to fissions, dismissals, or walkouts. Once in a while, indignation spills out in heated written language.

These facts refute any notion of coca taking and other Andean ritual as indexing distance from the state. Parliamentary formatting emulates state practices even though the ayllu has no standing as an organ of government. As will be seen below, deepening internalization of government norms reflects a characteristic posture: effort to gain position within the republican order by emulating it, while at the same time legitimating distinctiveness by attaching parliamentary approaches to Andean practices unknown in Lima.

Tupicochans value well-written actas highly, preferring handwritten ones because all the hands are well known and hard to falsify. Peasant Communities use typewriters sparingly, for exterior correspondence or for documents that must be submitted to the state (e.g., tax rolls, receipts for ministries, voter enrollment). The handwritten book of acts, crammed with signatures, is understood to be a concretion or distillate of the meritorious solidarity of its signers, and not just a constative reference such as a file of minutes.

HANDS-ON ARCHIVISTS

The all-Community archive of Tupicocha (as distinct from the ten separate archives of the ayllus) is a large, glass-fronted cabinet in the Community Hall, nearly filled with plastic-covered ledgers which contain the accumulated minutes. In 2006 their number was 107. In addition, it contains rolled maps and charts accumulated from surveying or litigation, and various folders of correspondence and receipts. Among the folders are the most treasured holdings: a collection of colonial documents and transcriptions of documents which villagers see as their foundational papers (see figure 20).

Inventorying the archive is a widely ingrained habit, perhaps with roots in colonial ecclesiastical practice (see figure 21). Every year's *cuenta residencial* ('general audit'; see chapter 2), whether at the ayllu or Community level, includes an inventory compiled by eyewitness inspection of all corporate property. The previous year's inventory is reentered, the property inspected, and a new entry written. The incoming and outgoing officers inspect the archive itself as the meeting's last order of business.

As a result all members annually lay eyes on every single volume of document patrimony. The job drains everyone, because it begins late in the day, after the exhausting audit of money, and also after many rounds of drinks. Nonetheless it follows a demanding procedure. All the volumes are stacked at one end of the authorities' long work table. The justice of the peace supervises. The outgoing vice president pulls out volumes in their sequence. He passes the volume across the table to the outgoing secretary, who checks the volume off against the previous inventory and hands it across to the new president, who in turn reads out the title, dates, and pagination. The incoming president hands it across to the incoming secretary, who inscribes it in the new inventory with any necessary updates (e.g., noting damage). When each volume has zigzagged through four inspections, it is stacked for reshelving (see figure 22).

Meanwhile, the other members mill about full of curiosity. They lean over the inspector's shoulders. They lift and riffle tomes, disturbing the sequence, revitalizing the bibliographic tradition as they exchange comments. These comments give an idea of how villagers think about ancient writings. They hold one text in special reverence: *El libro de la huaranga*,

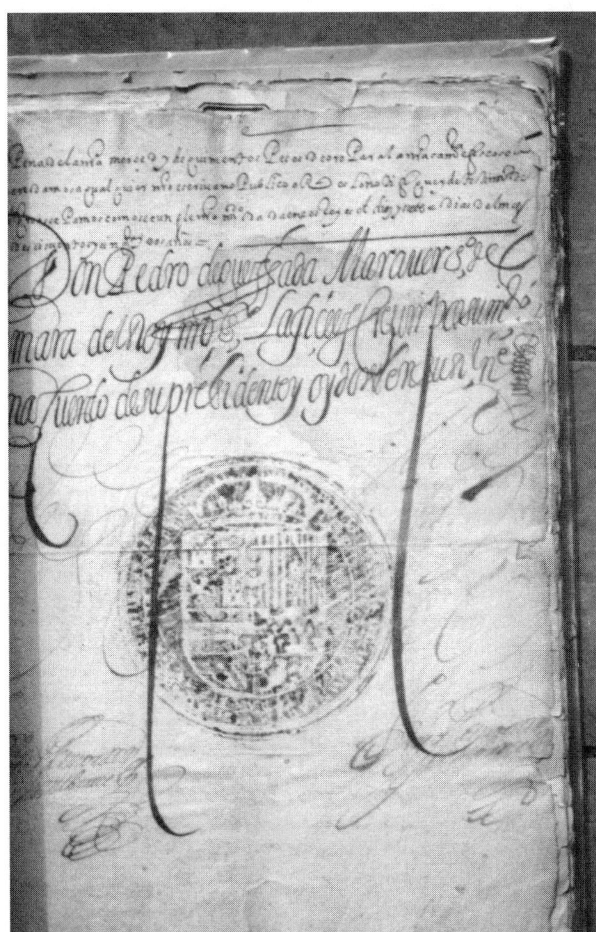

20. A document of 1652 in Tupicocha's Community archive has the trace of a viceroyal seal. It concerns the founding of a *cofradía* ('religious brotherhood').

which means 'The Book of the Thousand', using a Hispano-Quechua term for the Inka thousand-house census bloc. *El libro de la huaranga* is actually a 1748 *deslinde* ('boundary inspection') with earlier inspections incorporated. But to Tupicochans, it is a primordial charter (ACCSAT/SAT Folder 7). They respect it because it records the wholeness of a larger unit, embracing the old Checa ethnic territory approximately as recorded in the 1608 Quechua Manuscript of Huarochirí, and called the Thousand of Checa. The breakup of the 'Thousand' is said to be the source of long-endemic village conflicts, and the enduring 'Book of the Thousand' remains a sign of hope for a more coherent political future. (This aspiration is practical as well as nostalgic. The old 'Thousand' was coextensive with

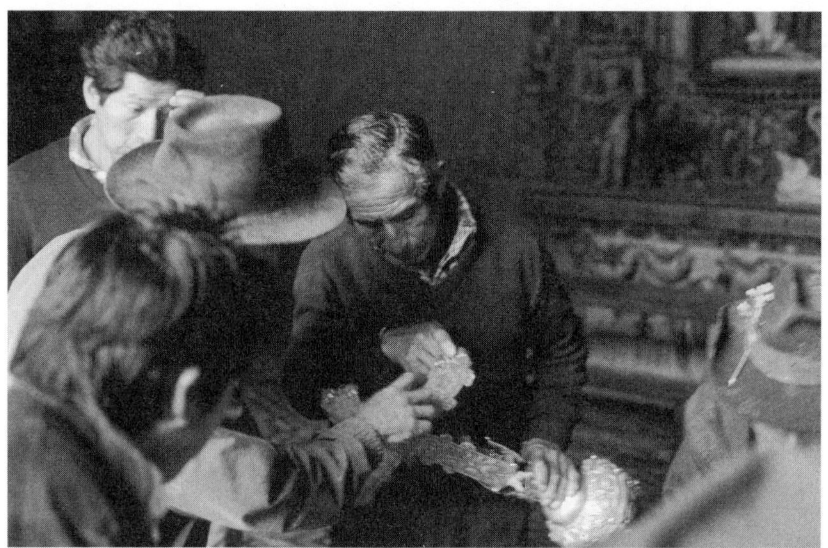

21. Officers charged with the care of Tupicocha's sacred property take inventory of church liturgical objects, 1997.

the upper Lurín watershed, affording a unit of governance that fit the necessary scale of water management. Later, smaller units do not, and this increases the tendency to fight over water.) The revered book is always the center of attention, but several other colonial "titles" also enjoy reputations as keystones of civic rights. They are always noted and discussed anew as the inventory handlers drag them up from the bottoms of stacks.

Various secretaries in various eras have re-seriated the collection, so volumes bear multiple conflicting numbers. Such numbers cannot be erased, because altering patrimonial documents, however minimally, is harshly forbidden. This causes confusion. Usually the members send a staffholder (minor officer) to call in a past secretary well versed in archival matters.

Tupicocha's Peasant Community has a large archive by rural standards (see figure 22). Its historical core consists of the thirty-eight folders, which contain important documents belonging to the Community but not generated by it. Some are prior to the modern record series, such as the colonial and early republican holdings including many viceroyal originals. Others were received from state entities, NGOs, or businesses. After the folders come the books written by the Community itself. In 1979 the number of bound seriated volumes was 70; in 1995 the number was 88;

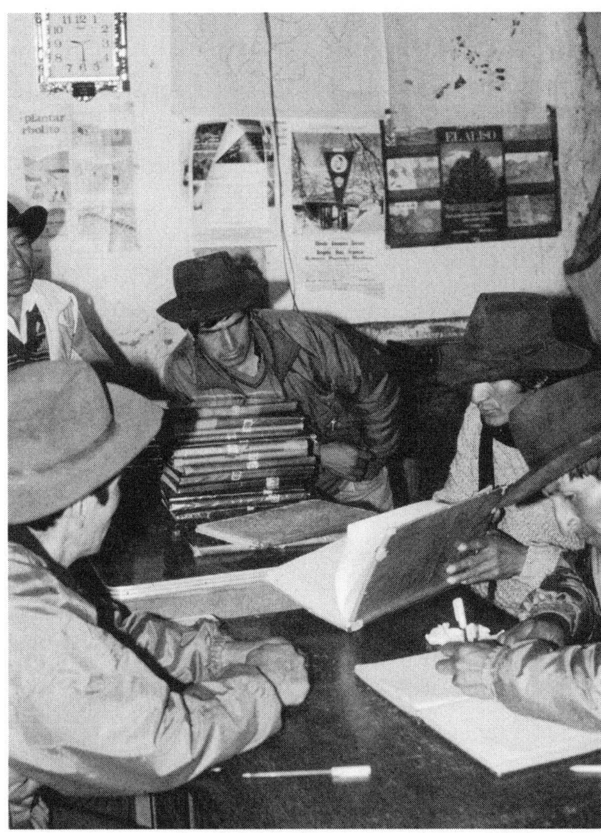

22. At the General Audit, the Tupicocha Community inspects its entire archive.

and in 2006 the number increased to 107. Most of them were 100-folio ledgers, but some had as many as 800 pages and many were 200-page lined volumes. The earliest books refer to ritual cargos and begin in the 1860s. It is likely that few if any bound volumes are missing, because an 1893 act observes that until the then-current series began, "no books existed" in the office (ACCSAT/SAT 05 1893:4–5).

The majority of volumes are supererogatory from the viewpoint of state legality. They establish folk-legal constancias concerning matters ranging from the ritual cargos for the Virgin of the Assumption, through the oil changes of "The Fuji" (Community truck of the 1990s) and "the Piónjar" (a jackhammer donated ca. 1970 by the Swedish government).[10] Much documentation concerns the innumerable days of collective work on canals and reservoirs. In addition the Community has a substantial collection of maps, blueprints, and bound sets of regulations from various ministries.

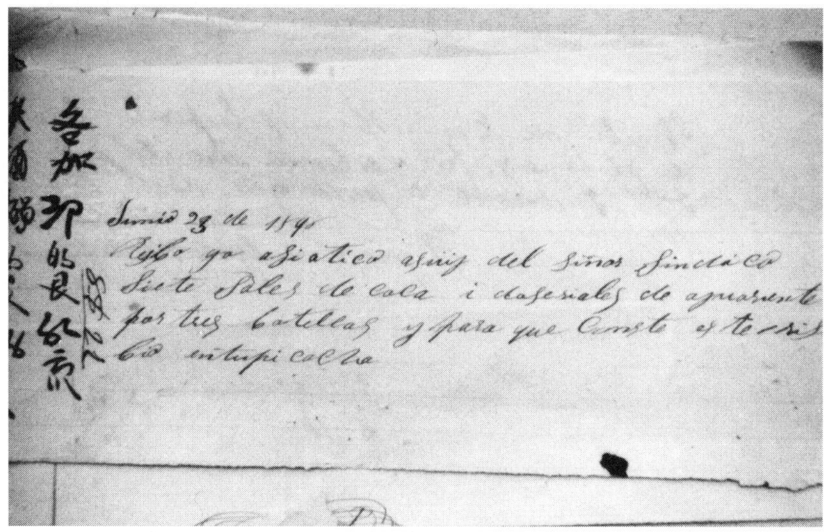

23. The Tupicocha communal archive contains receipts in simplified Chinese characters, issued by a peddler whose name was westernized as "Asian Asuij" in the 1890s.

Is Tupicocha representative? The neighboring Community of Santiago de Tuna has an archive that houses forty-eight manuscript volumes in four series, 1890–present. San Francisco de Sunicancha has at least seventy-one volumes, and retains a goatskin packet containing its eighteenth-century manuscript titles. On the basis of inspecting village holdings in many parts of Huarochirí and Oyón Provinces on the western face of the Andes; of doing the same in Azángaro, Chucuito, and Puno Provinces in the southern Andes; and of surveying Hostnig, Dongo, and Decoster's huge 2007 compilation from Apurímac Department, we conclude that archive keeping is usual among legally recognized communities and their satellites; that most house documents older or much older than legal recognition; and that on communal as well as household level, the historically Quechua- and Aymara-speaking populations have well-organized, strongly valued practices for preserving vital papers (Salomon 2004b). It must be admitted, however, that curation is uneven. In some villages archival manuscripts were lost through unexplained errors, or through fire (including arson, during the Shining Path war).

Colonial originals are sometimes referred to as *pergaminos* (parchments). Colonial handwriting is called *mosaico* (see chapter 3) or occasionally *latín*. "Mosaic" handwriting is considered illegible, but a few self-taught paleographers have learned to decipher it. The inspection process turns up many other surprises and intriguing memories. The wax seal of the viceroyalty, or even the waxy traces where one fell off, counts as a venerable charter of legitimacy. In 1995 someone spotted amidst sewn receipts a fascicle of papers in Chinese with translations on the reverse. This evoked lively memories of "The Chinaman": an intrepid southern Chinese who had come to Peru, probably as a coolie in the 1880s, and worked his way to freedom by traveling up the Sierra de Lima with a backpack full of tobacco, matches, and fireworks. He eventually married a local woman and became a villager of good repute until his death at an advanced age. His Chinese scripts are receipts and other business notes, written in a style of simplified characters characteristic of southern-Chinese merchants with modest education (see figure 23 on page 56).[11]

So much do villagers respect their foundational papers that some make an immense effort at learning to read obsolete scripts. This is no small matter, because until the eighteenth century scribes wrote an *encadenado* (chained) cursive now almost completely illegible to the casual eye. Later documents are almost as difficult because of careless handwriting, the percolation of ink from page to page, insect damage, and discoloration.

Tupicocha's most accomplished amateur paleographer is the campesino León Modesto Rojas Alberco. For many years, starting with his term as Community secretary, he was in the habit of rising at 4 a.m. to decipher and transcribe by candlelight. His private notebooks contain transcriptions of key documents from the thirty-eight folders. Different methods of transcription reveal a different theory of semiosis from the academic one, as we will see in detail in chapter 5.

Tupicochan interpretations of ancient writings differ widely from academic ones. Among the most respected documents in the folders are what villagers call *El auto de los muertos* ('The Act of the Dead'). It is a 1670 *real provisión* (administrative decree) from the viceroyalty (Lima, ACCSAT/SAT Folder 26), written in response to a petition from the village kuraka. He at that time asked for an opportunity to update tribute rolls so as to eliminate the unfair burden of being charged for people whom a series of epidemics had killed. To the academic eye it was a routine administrative episode, typical of the era. But Rojas Alberco interprets it in the light of a widespread legend from the central Andes. In oral tradition, highlanders account for the disappearance of "the people called Indians," that is, the builders of the pre-Hispanic tombs and ruins which dot every nearby mountainside, by telling of a mass suicide.

As a charter myth, the *El auto de los muertos* explains and justifies Huarochiranos' standing as free citizens. To understand this requires a sketch of their macrohistorical views. Rural villagers, unlike archaeologists and city-schooled Peruvians, do not regard the Spanish invasion of 1532 as the epoch-making division between ancient and historical Peru. They tend rather to conflate Inka government with that of the Hapsburg viceroys as an age of servitude, a time when the inhabitants were *indios*. Innumerable villagers were worked to death in mines or in labor levies on the roads. The villages stank with their corpses. Finally the "Indians" protested by hanging themselves or burying themselves together with their goods in caves. Some of these heroic suicides endure in the form of *los tapados* ('the covered ones,' i.e., the shrouded and tied pre-Columbian mummy bundles which turn up in remote places). Having lost their laborers, the oppressors at last lifted the cruel levies and the age of a free peasantry began. Bells tolled the end of servitude. Modern Tupicochans view the ruins and especially the "Indian" dead with complex mixed feelings. On the one hand, they are grateful to "the beautiful grandparents" for creating the age of citizen liberty through their self-sacrifice. On the other, they fear that the "covered ones" hold a grudge about losing their place on the earth. They might want to hurt modern humans by breathing poison on them. Rojas Alberco relied on this oral legend as a guide to understanding written colonial documents, sometimes using it to resolve doubts about the meanings of illegible words (Salomon 2002a).

OF SPOOFS AND MENUS: WRITING AS POPULAR CULTURE

Of course, a major aim of village literacy-learning from the start was to defend village interests by presenting cases before authorities in Lima. Today, as the urban diaspora becomes the inseparable complement of peasant life, the role of writing as a connection with the city goes beyond communicating with ministries where briefs and proposals must be delivered. Writing also serves to maintain ties with "children of the community" scattered around the giant metropolis. The saints' day sponsors in all Huarochirí villages have developed a genre of advertising directed to such expatriates. It is the festival program, printed in urban print shops using copy prepared by urbanite ex-peasants sensitive to their peers' tastes, and sponsored by successful members of the urban diaspora. Sponsoring village events heightens a donor's prestige and political potential, and consolidates loyalty. The most important urban sponsors of Andean festivals are, for example, a family which runs a chicken restaurant, a hardware dealer, and a locally famous "chicha music" disk jockey, Cool Jhonny León.[12]

This genre has a distinctive prose style mixing frothy pomp-and-circumstance ("the inexhaustible luncheon"; "the restorative breakfast") with allusions to old Andean customs rich in sentimental associations and comfort. They rehearse both old jokes and topical humor, referring for example to the donkeys that bring the sacred clowns from the mountain heights as "*cholo* taxis" or "Volvos," and the herbs they bring as "AIDS medicine." Usually programs are so finely tuned to local tradition that a person from even two districts away would fail to understand some references. After listing the members of the sponsoring society or volunteer network, they spell out the nonstop festival program. Two days' successive midday feasts are advertised as

> The bracing luncheon offered by Sr. Valeriano Llaullipoma at which exquisite little goats direct from the [legendary pre-Hispanic ruins of] Cinco Cerros will be savored and to settle the meal inexhaustible Crystal Beer, and imported wine and liquor . . .
>
> The succulent lunch offered by Sr. Blas Ramos and Sra. Dionicia Alberco in which various dishes prepared by a CHEFF from [the fashionable Lima borough of] Miraflores will be savored and to comfort oneself Polar brand stout and the whiskeys of Miraflores. [See figure 24]

Such prose, with its rhetorical allusions to elite pleasures, is a jocular way of exalting what are in fact down-home, rustic feasts where diners sit down to eat with mud on their shoes. The meals advertised are served on sawhorse and trestles in patios of peasant houses. Returning emigrants joyfully feast elbow to elbow with their hometown relatives. Members of the hosting society dash up and down carrying toppling stacks of plates. The favorite cuisine is steaming, smoky *pachamanca* (mixed food roasted underground in an earth oven) including mutton, bright-orange *oca*, green pea pods, and sweet potatoes, accompanied by steaming broth. Guests glorify their hosts by pinning money to their shirts. A successful host becomes a walking Christmas tree of cash, and a well-regarded benefactor of the Community when he donates it.

24. Flyers such as this one (from 1995) are circulated among emigrant "Children of the Village." They advertise urban fundraising festivals that replicate Tupicochan village customs. (The tree and the word *yunsa* allude to the widespread central Peruvian custom of cutting down a gift-laden "magic tree.")

Witty and extravagant writing also has its day in less outward-looking functions. Tupicocha, like many Spanish settlements, has picked up the originally Italian tradition of the *pasquín*, or barbed broadside, and charged it with Andean symbolism. On the Saturday of Holy Week, civil authority is in abeyance because *varayos*, the traditional authorities, leave their staffs of office in the church. This is the day when, in liturgy, God has died. The Devil walks the earth creating confusion and encouraging sin.[13] The *regidor* ('traditional-law constable') and his *alguacil* ('deputy') discreetly remove from the one-cell jail a battered and deconsecrated Christ image. It now serves as "Lucio" or "Lucero" (euphemisms for Lucifer). Lucio knows that Resurrection Sunday is coming, his time is up and he must make his will. The emaciated ex-saint is propped at the jail gate. Before the varayos get their staffs returned to them, they are treated to some pointed jokes, tacked onto Lucio's chest. This spoof is called "Lucio's Testament" (see figure 25). The following (1997) example is composed mostly of jabs at livestock-rich individuals, whose identities and misdeeds local men found it easy to decode (but did not want me to explain in print).

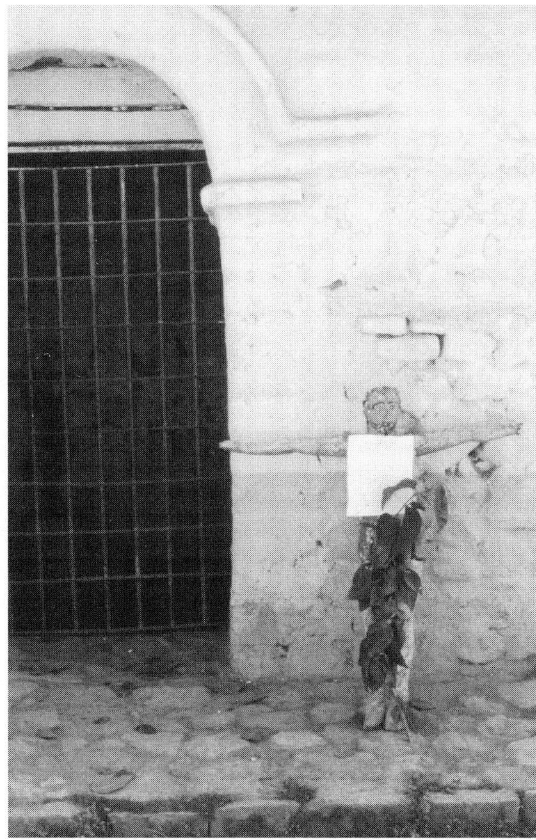

25. Outside the village jail, Lucio (Lucifer) exhibits his "Testament" in Tupicocha on Saturday of Holy Week, 1997.

TESTAMENT OF MY GOODS

In the location of this district of Tupicocha it being the hour of 9:00 p.m. of the day March 28th of the current year, I, Lucio, declare that I have a lot of properties of great stones and mountains and some tracts good enough to cure many cattle.

—In the present [document] I declare that my property called Tambina Macho is left for the benefit of my child called Erasmo Pulga Zamaniego whose boundaries are so huge that I don't even want to explain them

—In the present [document] I declare that I have a totally frightening tract called Punzucanza Chico, which I leave for the benefit of my child called Wuensislaho Pacheco Chico, so that it will bear him lots of fruit

—Item, I say that I have [object unspecified] on the tallest mountain, which is a branch office of Heaven with many black snowcaps, which I leave for the benefit of my child called Chapulín Ponguino Vueno[14] ==

In the present [document] it being 11 p.m. of the date already mentioned and not having anything else to declare I sign with my own hand, also feet

Don Lucio

THE LETTERED LIFE OF MODERN *AYLLUS*

The lettered tradition at the *ayllu* or *parcialidad* level has quite a different history from Community writing, but it also shows commonalities in technique and in rhetoric. The ayllu or parcialidad, as noted in the introduction (see also evolution of the usage of these terms in chapter 4), is a clanlike kinship organization, for which one has eligibility by virtue of one's father's (or sometimes mother's) membership. The ayllu has a political role as a constitutive segment of the Community; no quorum is present unless all the ayllu heads are present. It also functions as a "team" in the communal labor system. But at the same time it remains a familylike unit. Members are close kin, with complexly entwined careers, family ties, and emotional lives. Ayllu meetings are therefore at the same time intimate and bureaucratic. Ayllus are the owners of the patrimonial khipus, which formerly held their internal records. Today, they keep complete sets of records, similar to those of the Community. As noted in the introduction, they do so by their own will, since the state recognizes the Community as a whole and takes no interest in its inner segmentation.

Like Community writing, ayllu writing uses genres and formats modeled on modern bureaucracy and commercial law. Like Community usage, too, it tends to have a "zoom lens" construction, "zooming in" in some formats to cover minute transactions, and "zooming out" in others to evoke grander memorialism and ideology. However the microscale tradition of ayllu records constructs memorialism less on national or civic ideology and more on patrilineal lines.

When Ayllu Primer Allauca set out to write itself a reformed constitution in 1948, it reaffirmed Allauca,[15] the name from oral tradition, as "a name which we have known from our fathers and grandfathers, which they held in traditional custom since time immemorial, [and] which we have authentically [*veridicamente*] continued, from our childhood and very ancient documents" (AP1A/SAT 01 1948:2). Ayllu Primer Guangre wrote similarly when in 1945 it appointed its officers, "fulfilling the tradition and customs from our ancestors fathers who carry on" (AP1G/SAT 01 1945:119).

The ten corporations differ slightly in writing styles. For example, Primer Huangre tends to be franker about political disagreements; Primer Allauca is more reverential toward tradition; Cacarima is punctilious about documenting festivals, especially the Festival of the Crosses; Segunda Satafasca is more given to starting books about innovative topics; Unión Chaucacolca keeps more in step with national-level legal innovations and also tends to insist on ideology and internal justice. The ten corporations also enforce somewhat different auditing cycles.

Since ayllus in recent times did not have meeting halls of their own, the president or secretary stored the books in his home. (During the years since 1995 there have been increasingly serious attempts by ayllus to build their own lodges.) Usually the books rest in a chest that also contains sacred regalia such as khipus and the "clothing" of the cross. Security is tight. Not even the officer's wife or brother may loan out a volume. If one goes astray, there is sure to be consternation until it turns up. If it is still missing on audit day, the people present fan out in a sweep until they track it down. The books get fairly heavy use; on any given day, a few of the recent volumes are likely to be on loan to members. Some show wear and tear including dog-ears and marginal comments. At meetings members sometimes demand to "see the books," for example, when a person's eligibility for retirement is in question or when it is uncertain whether someone has complied with all faenas. At the annual audit meetings, all the books must be brought (see figure 26).

The insertion of Ayllu writing in the communitywide system has been changing during the century and a quarter since the kinship corporations took up the quill pen. The changes can be summed up on a three-stage additive model. The three stages actually overlap historically. In the first stage the relation between small and great corporations was one of *coordination*. The overall regimen probably reaches back to the pre-Hispanic term *llahta*, and its functions correspond to the khipu register. The pre-Hispanic and immediately post-Inka village consisted of a federation of ayllus under a *kuraka* (hereditary ethnic lord) belonging to the ayllu of highest rank. The lordship lost status and finally ceased to exist, circa 1800. The ayllus, however, continued as a federation under a village *cabildo*, or council, each segment being autonomous with regard to its

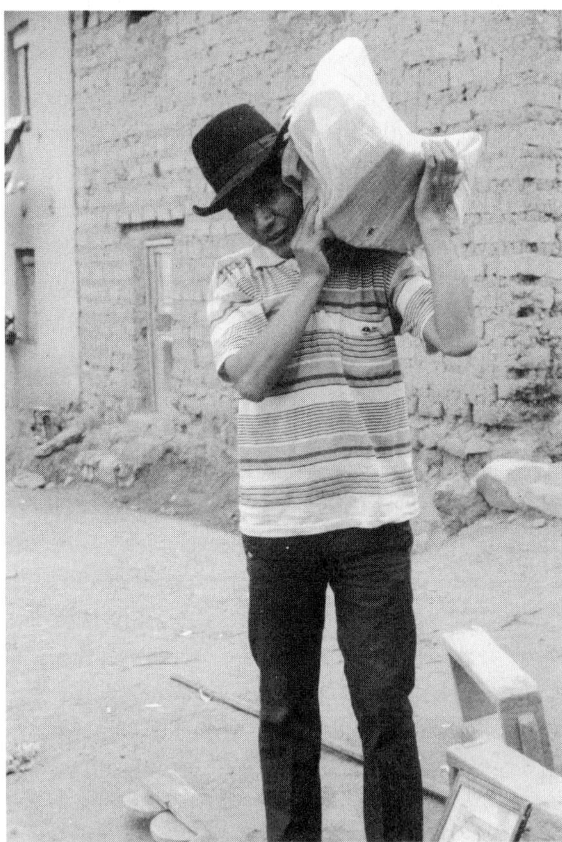

26. An ayllu secretary brings Segunda Satafasca's ayllu books to the inventory and audit meeting of 1995.

internal functions. Ayllu records concerned members' duties to each other and to the immediate kinship corporation. For example, they were bound to "walk" weekly collective work parties which successively served the household of each member. The ayllu also acted in coordination with other ayllus to build the llahta, or all-village, infrastructures. The earliest ayllu books record these duties. This constellation apparently endured through the later nineteenth century. At that time, the village as a political unit was headed by a *personero* and an *agente municipal* appointed by the state. These governed in concert with the customary-law cabildo formed by two *principales*, two *mayores*, and the six *camachicos*, or ayllu heads (ACCSAT/SAT 06). (Fissions in the 1920s increased the number of ayllus.)

The very old, federated-ayllu constitution is not an effect of incorporation in the Spanish state, nor, probably, the Inka one. The tellers of the 1608 Quechua narratives regarded it as a pre-Inka norm. Early Spanish rural governance was molded around it and left it substantially in place. The Toledan reforms of the 1570s aimed to undercut hereditary native nobles' command over ayllus, not to dissolve them. Toledan governance created a rival center of power: the cabildo, or village council. In sharply structured segmentary communities such as Tupicocha, heads of ayllus (camachicos, in Hispano-Quechua parlance) made the cabildo their forum. Although no set of colonial cabildo records has yet turned up in Peru, we suspect this was the arena in which "yndios" became adept at writing scribal formats.

By coordination, we mean the task of keeping the kinship-structured segments in step to achieve goals of the overarching village-level authority. The village cabildo was regarded as a confederation among preexisting, self-sufficient foundational units, all voluntarily cooperating to uphold common interests such as irrigation infrastructures and boundary defense. In the later nineteenth century, the *personería* apparently sought increasingly to orchestrate the *comunidad* functions. Heads of ayllus (camachicos) were expected to attend its meetings. When the legal authority sought to carry out tasks sponsored by the state—such as the building of a vehicle road to connect with the Lima-Huancayo Railroad under the *ley vial,* or highway labor draft—it used the traditional Andean authority structure to parcel out work. (José María Arguedas made an epic of a similar campaign in his splendidly ethnographic first novel, the 1941 *Yawar Fiesta.*) Many parts of this system still persist within the modified structures described in the remainder of this chapter.

The second stage in the evolution of Ayllu writing among the Communities might be called that of "homologization." It seems to correspond in Tupicocha with the 1920s. The ayllu continued to perform its internal duties, such as "walking faenas," but also came to conceive of the kinship corporation as being a microcosm of the nation-state and its component bureaucracies (see figure 27). It came to see itself as a module of the Community, more than a prior constituent of it. The term *parcialidad,* 'sector,' began to outweigh the term *ayllu,* which primarily connotes kinship. The "reform" statutes described in the next chapter are attempts to make each ayllu a miniature of state structure.

The inclination to homological organization as such may indeed be of ancient Andean origin. As many authors have noticed, Andean ideology tends to favor huge correspondence structures that posit likeness of form from the small household unit of two or three generations, upward to the

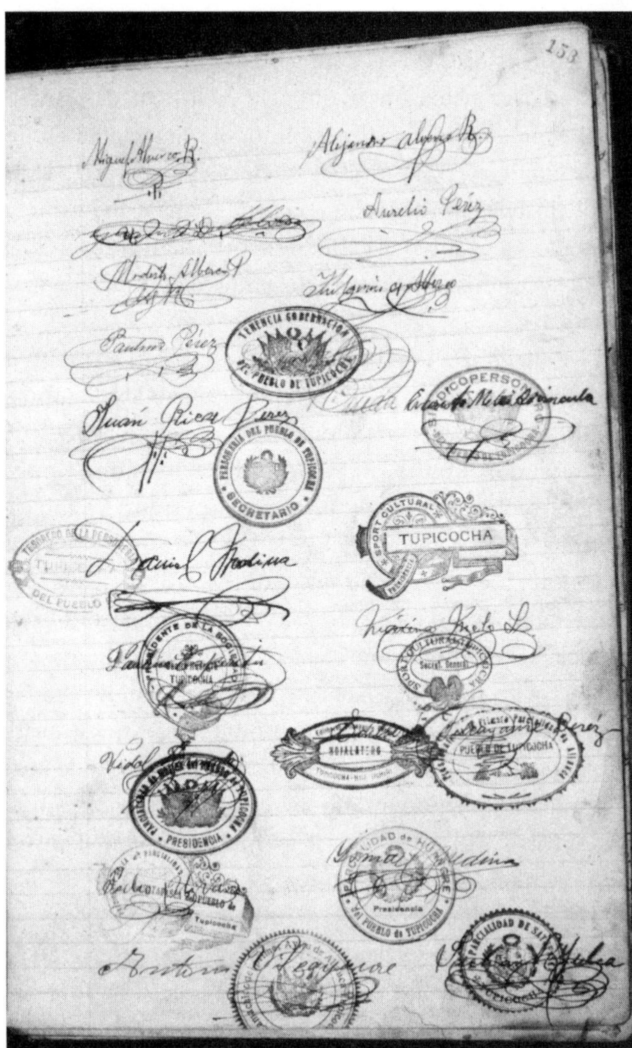

27.
Homologization: A 1936 page from the book of Chaucacolca Ayllu contains the "seals" of nonindigenous organizations, and, in the lower part of the page, those of the originally pre-Hispanic parcialidades.

larger web of corporate kinship, to large phratries like the "Thousand of Checa," to the exalted divine parents of apical ancestors, and finally to the forces of the cosmos itself.

In the era of President Augusto Leguía, the national state proposed to make "indigenous communities" organs of state. Tupicochans apparently were sharply attuned to this project. To them, "Reform" meant the need not only to exert citizen rights, but also to rectify what was felt to be the poor fit between small, preconstitutional structures and the national state, which was at last proclaiming the full belongingness of its "indigenous" people. In practical terms, this period saw an increase in the recording of faenas devoted to Community needs as opposed to *ayllu*-internal ones (AP1A/SAT 01; AP2A/SAT 02). By the 1940s, more intra-ayllu labor records deal with service to the overarching Community than to intra-ayllu service.

The third stage might be characterized by the word *introjection*. It includes the present. In this period, the ayllu not only resembles the state and other nationally chartered corporations in form; it absorbs into its own interior tasks of debating and executing policy from those exterior corporations. By 1926, Ayllu Mujica took on the celebration of *fiestas patrias*, the patriotic holidays, as ayllu-internal agenda (APM/SAT 02 1926:126). By 1939, Primer Guangre was disputing the power of attorney granted a certain man by the *municipio* because they saw it as "defrauding the rights of citizens" under the Peruvian Constitution (AP1G/SAT 01 1939:76). In 1941, Unión Chaucacolca, writing an act to pour everlasting ignominy on certain members who skipped faenas, added that these persons also "do not respect the norms of the Supreme Government" (APUCh/SAT 03 1941:162–63). When Primera Allauca wrote its 1948 internal laws, it asked the justice of the peace, an official of the national *gobernación*, to approve them (AP1A/SAT 01 1948:15). Ayllus even conducted some of the work of the national Census of Agriculture and Livestock (see figure 28). By the 1960s, the faena energies of ayllus were almost completely absorbed by communal business and service to non-community organs of government. This process fostered, among other effects, the growth of highly elaborate statistical self-study and self-recording.

We have called ayllu records nonstate writing because the state did not oblige ayllus to write, nor do state agents review the books. But in another sense ayllu records *are* documents of state formation. Coercion played little or no part. During nearly all of republican history, Lima ignored such rural governance as the *vara* system and confederated-ayllu polity. Rather, ayllus emulated forms of state organization because their members were themselves questing for a working relationship with the state.

One process visible throughout the ayllu's books is a long, slow self-redefinition as citizens. Andean institutions refashion themselves as they go so as to be more adequate for republican governance, to which the people called *indígenas* needed access for purposes such as schooling,

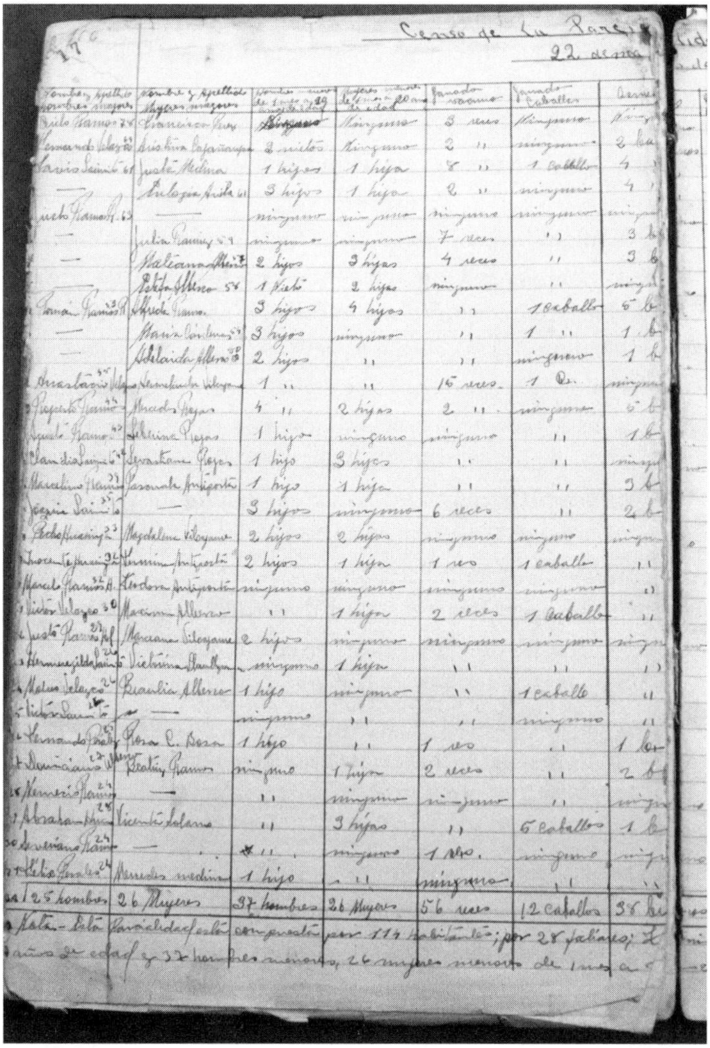

28. Introjection: Ayllu Cacarima in 1949 applied the state format for farm and livestock census to its own membership.

litigation, and public safety. While the republic neglected its countryside, villages carried on the construction of the republic at the (so to speak) cellular level. The many misencounters and conflicts between state and community reflect governmental unreceptiveness to the overtures of self-taught citizens. In chapter 5, we will emphasize a specifically graphic face of this situation: when campesinos approached the state in its own language—namely, legalistic script—the characteristics of writing that arose from endogenously republican processes are precisely the ones that have often marked rural writings for stigma and rebuff. Yet from the viewpoint of 2010, the homemade state-forming process looks more successful. The marked improvement in relations between the state and rural communities, which has impressed observers during the late 2000s is the product of many small-scale initiatives from the countryside, made fruitful by high mining revenues that enable the state to attend to long-neglected rural agenda.

For the most part, the processes reported in this chapter are fairly representative of Andean highland communities. Tupicocha, however, is in one respect quite exceptional. It is one of very few communities which retain alongside its books of acts a collection of khipus, the cord records, which once formed the backbone of Andean recordkeeping. The next chapter examines the relationship between these two profoundly different media.

TWO

From Khipu to Narrative

Most of the lettered life sketched in chapter 1 resembles that of similar villages. As in many villages, literate and numerate life had as its historical context a long coexistence with the ancient Andean medium, the *khipu*. Exceptionally, Tupicocha retains its khipus, at least those pertaining to the *ayllus*. This patrimony is studied in *The Cord Keepers* (Salomon 2004a), a companion volume to this one. The ancient Andean data medium, the khipu, had served Andean peoples for recordkeeping at least a half millennium before Spaniards arrived, and despite the growing power of the scribal establishment, Andean subjects of the crown kept on using it. During at least the first colonial century, the Peruvian viceroyalty's *ciudad letrada*, its "lettered city," existed within a country well supplied with masters of the old cord medium (Pease 1990; Salomon 2007; Sempat Assadourian 2002; Topic 2004; Urton 2002). Yet for reasons that remain far from obvious, no Spanish writer in all three colonial centuries seems to have learned and explained the khipu art.[1]

A "KNOTTED COUNTRY" UNDER SPANISH RULE

The present chapter will briefly review findings about the dual-media armature of the village, and make suggestions about the still surprisingly obscure matter of when and why the Andean medium died out. We will then touch on relations between khipu and narrative by consider possibly khipu-related properties of the written documents that supplanted ayllu khipus (Brokaw 2003).

Several general books explain khipu basics and research frontiers. Marcia Ascher's and Robert Ascher's *Code of the Khipu* (1981, republished 1997) presents a lively and accessible study of cord records' mathematical makeup. Jeffrey Quilter and Gary Urton's *Narrative Threads* (2002) thoroughly treats khipus in colonial context, and contains findings by William Conklin that are relevant to Urton's *Signs of the Inka Khipu* (2003). Brokaw's *A History of the Khipu* (2010) also emphasizes the post-Hispanic context. *Quipu y yupana* (edited by Mackey and Pereyra 1990) contains an earlier harvest of research, connecting the key findings of the 1920s with the current resurgence of khipu studies. Rich illustrations appear in Carmen Arellano's "Quipu y tocapu: Sistemas de comunicación inca" (1999), and also in a museum catalogue from Chile (Urton 2003).

The first interpretative task broached in modern times concerned the arithmetical structure of khipus. Leland Locke (1923, 1928) was able to establish base-10 positional notation as the numerical content of many knots. The plan is similar to Indo-Arabic mathematical computation, except that zero is represented by an empty place rather than a sign. Ascher and Ascher explain the basic "Lockean" conventions as in figures 29–31.

Figure 31 could, for example, represent a segment of an Inka census. It might describe a village from which some households had been removed for extraterritorial duty. Each pendant could stand for an ayllu, with its respective subsidiary signaling the number of its absent households. The topcord could signify the whole population with a subsidiary expressing the number of absentees. The Aschers detected more complex mathematical relations and also argued that khipu numbers can function as "label numbers." (That is, like a social security number, khipu numbers could register identity rather than quantity.)

But beyond numerical issues, there is doubt about how khipus expressed information. A field of basic dissensus lies wide open. In *Grosso modo*, three positions are in play. An eighteenth-century thesis (Sansevero di Sangro 1750) holds that besides the "numerical" code, a separate kind of "royal" khipu contained a Quechua-based syllabography (syllabic writing system). This eighteenth-century speculation parallels erroneous interpretations of Chinese and Egyptian scripts by the intellectual descendants of the seventeenth-century Jesuit scholar Athanasius Kircher and might derive from them. (Sansevero posits cord emblems which at once encode the elements of cosmology and the syllables of Quechua.)

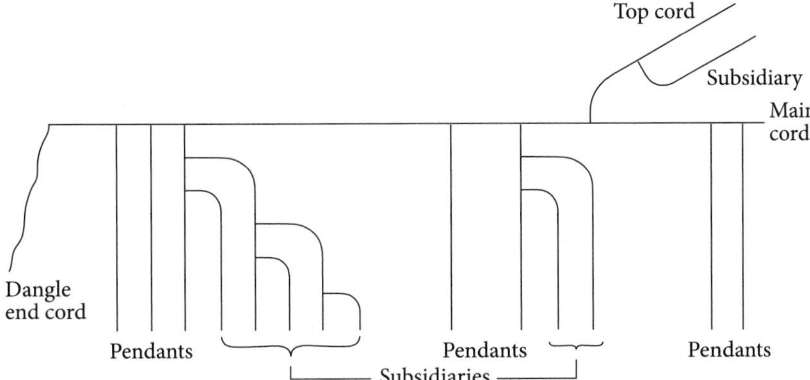

29. Robert and Marcia Ascher established basic terminology and structure of the Inka imperial khipu format (Ascher and Ascher 1997:12). By permission of Marcia Ascher and Robert Ascher.

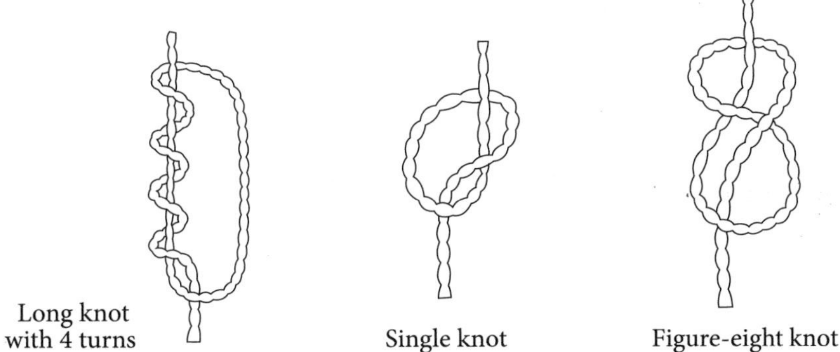

30. Three common knots were used in Inka khipus: Left: Inka long knot of value four, used in units place; center: simple (s) knot; right: figure-eight (E) knot (Ascher and Ascher 1997:29). The long knot registers units only, while the other two can register tens, hundreds, and higher brackets. By permission of Marcia Ascher and Robert Ascher.

Nonetheless it has gained new adherents through the publication of materials found in Naples in the 1980s and continuing to tumble forth in the 1990s from the private collections of Clara Miccinelli (Animato, Rossi, and Miccinelli 1989; Domenici and Domenici 2003; Laurencich 1996, 2005). Sabine Hyland (2003) has suggested that a neoplatonic reworking of khipu code by the early-colonial mestizo intellectual Blas Valera or his peers yielded real, but post-Inka, khipu phonography.

A second thesis is often linked with Geoffrey Sampson's (1985:26–45) revival of Ignace Gelb's 1952 term "semasiography." Semasiography is a name for codes whose signs are (in William Boltz's terms) semantically full

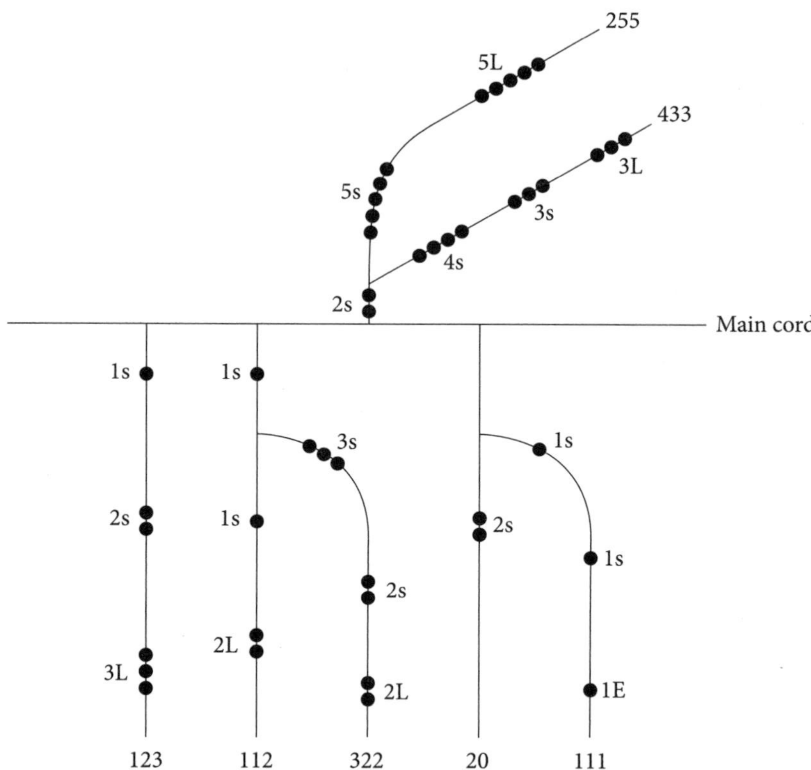

31. A khipu with arithmetical values: The topcord sums the values of pendants, and the topcord's subsidiary those of the pendants' subsidiaries (Ascher and Ascher 1997:31). By permission of Marcia Ascher and Robert Ascher.

but phonetically empty—codes such as sheet music or mathematical formulas (Boltz 1994:3–28). If khipu were of such nature, they would signify entities other than words: categories, acts, objects, or any culturally recognized entity. Boone and Mignolo (1994) have given such codes the nickname "writing without words." Finally, Urton (2003) has launched a third thesis—namely, that khipu signs are in themselves a neutral underlying code—each one being assignable to variable surface meaning according to contexts. That is, their status is similar to eight-bit ASCII sequences, which "stand for" nothing in themselves but are assigned to different surface entities depending on how they are deployed: a given eight-bit string of 0s and 1s could correspond to a letter in a text-processing program or to a color in a photo-editing program.

In studying the Tupicochan examples, Salomon (2004a) argues that they constitute a device comparable to the Sumerian "proto-writing" deciphered by Hans J. Nissen, Peter Damerow, and Robert K. England (1993) [1990]. The proto-Sumerian tablets consist largely of "noun-plus-number" sequences. Salomon (2004a) argues that Tupicochan khipus bear many resemblances to Inka khipus, but the "Lockean" arithmetical system is far less clear (perhaps absent) in their cords. If they functioned in a manner relatively independent of language—for example, by encoding particular deeds and objects rather than their verbal names—then the adoption of alphabetic writing represents a greater novelty than the mere substitution of an imported code for a preexisting but structurally comparable one such as a syllabary.

"Late khipu use" refers to the use of cord media from the end of Inka independence onward. Although Pizarro's armies entered Peru in 1532, the loss of independence is best dated to 1535, when Spaniards ransacked the sacred precincts of the capital, Cuzco. Up to this time, khipu trumped all other media as a source of authoritative information. But the khipu was not a strictly Inka medium. What little we know about the demography of Inka khipu use at the 1535 baseline suggests a large number of practitioners outside the charmed circle of Inka descent. The half-Inka chronicler Inka Garcilaso de la Vega wrote that each village had at least four khipu masters, keeping mutually verifiable records (Garcilaso de la Vega 1966 [1609]:331). If so, the all-imperial number of authorized masters would have been in the tens of thousands. The attested Inka manner of aggregating and verifying tribute rolls (Julien 1988) implies a well-developed "grass-roots" recording base.

It is unlikely, then, that later khipu use was a postconquest plebeian appropriation of a formerly aristocratic script. Rather, late khipu use probably represents an adaptive radiation of an already widespread skill. The decay of central authority made khipus useful as the private data reserve of indigenous polities, because khipus afforded a margin of data independence from the records of Spanish scribes and notaries. In this matter the distinction between speech and graphic communities is crucial. Spaniards (especially clergy, rural administrators, merchants, and would-be-feudal overlords of indigenous land and people) quickly acquired Quechua as a colonial "general language" (Itier 2002, Santo Tomás 1995 [1560], 1951 [1560]). Overlaps between Spanish and Andean speech communities were massive. But not a single person who claimed the status of Spaniard is known to have claimed khipu competence. "We [Spaniards] have been dealing with them [Peruvians] for more than seventy years without ever learning the theory and rules of their knots and accounts, whereas they have very soon picked up not only our writing but also our figures," wrote Blas Valera (quoted by Inka Garcilaso de la Vega 1966 [1609]:824).

The khipu information network had multiple colonial uses. People of Inka lineage used cords from the 1540s onward to claim noble status under Spanish law and to guard against tribute abuse (Garcilaso de la Vega 1966 [1609]:333). Viceroy Toledo, the architect of the "mature colony," consulted khipu masters to build an argument that Inkas were only "tyrants" and therefore unable to confer noble title (Sarmiento de Gamboa [1572] 1942:114–15). More consequential than these backward-looking uses, however, were khipus' ongoing roles in constructing colonial and even modern society. In nutshell synthesis, they can be reduced to three:

First, cords became systematically articulated with the world of legal paper. By the 1560s they began to figure as sources of evidence for litigation about tribute abuse (Loza 1998; Medelius and de la Puente 2004; Murra 1975; Platt 2002). Convinced of their accounting value, the colonial planner Juan de Matienzo (1967 [1567]:67) and the viceroy Francisco de Toledo (Levillier 1925:337–38), began in the 1570s not just to admit khipus but to demand that village scribes serving the *cabildo*, or village council, make continually updated transcripts of cord records of all village affairs related to the colonial state. Martti Pärssinen and Jukka Kiviharju (2004) have compiled a collection of the khipu "readout" documents that resulted from indigenous presentations within fora of the "lettered city."

By the mid-seventeenth century, nonetheless, the crown lost interest in khipus and also in Quechua. San Marcos University replaced its Quechua chair with one in mathematics in 1678 (Klaren 2000:74). By that time, notaries and scribes generating Spanish text via interpreters had become omnipresent in the countryside.

Indigenous authorities held onto the cord-plus-paper solution. A 1650 report on a textile plant in Andean Ecuador mentions that only the presence of a khipu master made it possible for workers and their bosses to agree on payroll amounts (Costales de Oviedo 1983:276–77). During the early independence era, the forms of khipu and rules for data exchange continued to mold themselves around administrative needs, but these were increasingly the needs of systems dominated by usurping private landlords. In the Puno, Cuzco, and Cajamarca highlands, the hispano-

Quechua word *quipo* came to acquire its twentieth-century rural meaning: a range boss who collected information on the herds under debt peons' care by inspecting cord records. Nelson D. Pimentel H. (2005) as well as Vidal Carbajal Solís, Mahia Maurial, and Elizabeth Uscamayta (2006) report patrimonial khipus referring to herds and their rituals in the regions of Oruro, Bolivia, and in Cuzco, Peru, respectively.

As to the second role of the khipu, the colonial church implanted (and later regretted, but could not uproot) the use of khipu as vehicles for catechism and confession. In particular, Jesuit missions to the Lake Titicaca basin experimented with khipu-based Christianity, but in 1583 the hierarchy in council banned catechetical khipus because they might contain "testimonies of ancient superstitions . . . [and] secrets of their rituals, ceremonies, and iniquitous laws" (Mannheim 1991:66–71; Sempat Assadourian 2002:134). Without permission, Andean parishioners, and, especially, women went on making cord memos of sins to confess, dates in the calendar of saints, and points of doctrine to memorize (Harrison 2002:267; Polia Meconi 1999:273). A few churchmen active in writing "pastoral Quechua" reported that by the first half of the seventeenth century, rural highlanders had developed comprehensive ways to encode Christian doctrine and confession on cords (Estenssoro Fuchs 2003:217–28). The most recent find of khipus collected in a church was reported in Bolivia in 1963 (Gisbert and Mesa 1966).

One important facet of church involvement with khipus is the invention of a hybrid medium, the *tabla quipo* ('khipu board'), which integrated alphabetic with cord signs in a single object. Two drawings, which seemingly show khipu boards used in the catechesis of women, come from the north coast circa 1789 (Martínez Compañón y Bujanda 1985:53). In 1852 the scientific traveler Mariano Rivero observed that "in some parishes of Indians, the khipu were attached to a panel with a register of the inhabitants on which were noted 'their absences on the days when Christian doctrine is taught' " (cited in Sempat Assadourian 2002:136). As late as 1968 another specimen of nineteenth-century origin was discovered, in disuse, at the church of Mangas (Robles Mendoza 1990 [1982]; see figure 32). Mangas is in Cajatambo Province, near the northern extreme of Lima Department. The tablet bears a legend meaning "Register [*padrón*] of the persons of the Town of Mangas, the registry began in the year of 1800" or "1880" (the doubt being Román Robles's). It contains the names of 110 men and women on front and back, and next to each a hole in which

FIG. 2

TABLILLA
DEL
PÁDRON DE MANGAS

Padron de las personas del Pueblo de Mangas;
se empezó a empadronar en el año de 1800.

Bartolomé Estrada
Paulino Félix Regalado
Jacobo Vanillas
Francisco Estrada
Lupita Estrada
María Fermín.
Gregoria Félix
Rosario Estrada
Silvino Marquez
José C. Estrada
Susana Alejos
María Flores
Miguel Flores
Espíritu Estrada
Paula Estrada
Leocadio Estrada
Andrea Flores
Bárbara Alejos
Nicolasa V. Márquez
Eugenia Flores
Nicolasa Regalado
Alejandra Rojas
Celedonia Alejos
Andrea Arcayo
Lorenza Ugarte
Luis Márquez
Bartola Ugarte
Toribio Villafuerte
Cipriana Villafuerte
José Rojas
Valentina Villafuerte
Manuel Martín
Dolora Meza

Elisa Martín
Ignacia Flores
Justo Sánchez
Vitoria Sánchez
Pablo Callampoma
Bartolomé Albornoz
Celestino Callampoma
Eugenia Callampoma
Juan C. Arcayo
Dominga Flores
Sabina Villarreal
Juan C. Zarabia
Plácida Flores
Matea Flores
Benita Flores
Manuela Albornoz
Cantaria Zaravia.
Anselmo Villafuerte
Ambrosio Estrada
Rufina Flores
Antonia Flores
Micaela Flores
Cirila Flores
Juana Estrada
Manuel Flores
Darío Ugarte
Erculano Félix
Manuel Fernández
León Flores
Ramón Aguado
Sebastián Meza
Eduardo Zaravia
Tiburcia Gonzales

Rosa Zaravia
Modesto García
Juliana Reyes
Cristina García
Pascual Natividad
Florencio Leonardo
Pedro Callampoma
Isabel Villarreal
Valentina Callampoma
Santa Callampoma
Santos Aguado
Juana Flores
Petrona Aguado
Josefa Rojas
Matiasa Reyes
Manuela Evangelista
Martina Aguado
Manuela Albornoz
Paula Aguado
Nicolasa Aguado
Nicolás Aguado.
Pablo Albornoz
Damasia Aguado
Florentina Albornoz
María Isabela
Margarita Isabela
Ursula Flores
Paula Estrada
Juana Reyes
Melchor Flores
Jacoba Aguado

32. Román Robles Mendoza drew the "Alphabetic *khipu* of Mangas" from Cajatambo for his graduate school thesis.

varicolored cords with lengths of four to twenty centimeters (1.6 to 7.9 inches) have been inserted. The cords are grouped by color, but since most are missing the color patterning is unclear. The knotting (if any) is not described in the report, nor the articulation of color elements in cords.

Third, and most relevantly for the present work, the "Indian" villages organized in the resettlement pattern called *reducción*, circa 1570–90, kept on using khipus for internal purposes, at least in Huarochirí, into much later times. As explained in *The Cord Keepers* (2004a:237–62), Tupicocha used them for recording intra-ayllu business below the threshold of state administration.

In short, in the period of late khipu use, the khipu orbit altered 180 degrees, from its pre-Columbian standing as the unified nerve system of cult and government, to a fragmented scatter of small local user communities no longer exchanging cord information supralocally. Not a single one of the modern khipu-holding or khipu-remembering communities which the researchers have visited was aware that other communities had also retained khipus.

COLONIAL LETTERS IN HUAROCHIRÍ

Huarochirí's insertion into the world of letters is notably old and deep. At the future provincial capital of Santa María Jesús de Huarochirí, in 1570, Peru's first Jesuits set up an experimental prototype for their famous schools to teach the sons of native lords literacy, music, and Catholic doctrine (Hyland 2003:37–47; Wood 1986:66). Because the interface between cord and paper is discussed at length in *The Cord Keepers*, only a few points of contact are noted here.

At the turn of the seventeenth century, Huarochirí was in the pastoral care of another brilliant clergyman, who, like Blas Valera, had enjoyed a bilingual upbringing of Quechua and Spanish in the shadow of the Inka palaces. Unlike Valera, this cleric saw nothing worth preserving in pre-Christian tradition. He was Francisco de Avila, a diocesan curate much influenced by Jesuits. Using as cat's-paw the minor native noble Cristóbal Choque Casa (Acosta 1979), Avila sleuthed out incriminating Andean cults and organized the series of persecutions called "extirpation of idolatries" (Duviols 1971; Mills 1997). The secret document he commissioned in order to do this has survived as the great 1608 Quechua Manuscript of Huarochirí.

The anonymous writer of this source was probably the same Choque Casa (Durston 2007). He was too young to study with the first Jesuits. But he was well versed in pastoral Quechua, and in scribal methods. He was apparently trained to work in the diocesan apparatus that the Lima archdiocese organized during the Third Council of Lima, which ended in 1583. Avila's biographer, Antonio Acosta Rodríguez, believes Avila charged his protégé with getting incriminating testimonies about the persistence of "pagan" worship so as to blackmail local foes. But the Quechua writer, for reasons unknown, chose a more complex approach. He conceived of his mission as a strangely subjunctive venture: he meant to write the book the ayllus would have written before 1532, had they been trained in the alphabet.

> If the ancestors of the people called Indians had known writing in former times, then the lives they lived would not have faded from view until now. As the mighty past of the Spanish Vira Cochas is visible until now, so too would theirs be. But since things are as they are, and since nothing has been written until now, let us set forth here the lives of the ancient forebears of the Huaro Cheri people, who all descend from one common forefather: What faith they held, how they live up until now, those things and more. Village by village it will all be written down: How they lived from their dawning age onward. (Salomon and Urioste 1991:41–42)

The writer knew something of khipus and mentions them twice, once as a resource of Inka administration and once as an internal record made by a community.

In 1750 some Huarochiranos rose up against Spain, an early episode in the wave of "neo-Inka" insurrections which shook various parts of the viceroyalty until the 1780s (Sotelo 1942; Spalding 1984:273–93). One episode of that struggle sheds light on the late colonial khipu-paper interface. Its source is the field diary of Sebastián Franco de Melo, a bilingual Spanish mine operator who fought down the insurgent Francisco Ximénez Ynga (Salomon and Spalding 2002). In rural rebellions, intercepted letters often provided the intelligence keys to tactical success. Franco de Melo invented a disinformation trick to disable rebel villages by setting them against each other: he disseminated twenty-two fake letters which would cause each rebel village to think its allied villages had switched sides.

The disinformation trick, however, depended on associated use of khipus. Franco had a herdswoman of his acquaintance, María Micaela Chinchano, make one khipu for each message, and tie the letter up in it. He wrote that the khipu "es el modo con que ellos se entienden" ('is the way they communicate'), using a distancing third-person pronoun that implies Franco, though bilingual, did not so communicate. As for what Chinchano knotted onto her khipus, doubt remains. She may have given a paraphrase of the letter's content, or some other signal falsely warranting its origin. It is also possible she made the khipus as address labels so as to avoid a disastrous misdelivery. What is clear from the incident is that circa 1750, khipu was a specifically "Indian," commonplace vernacular, among women as well as men, and not a specialist art.

In 1876 the Peruvian republic conducted a census attentive to literacy, in accord with the pro-schooling agenda of President Manuel Pardo y Lavalle (1872–76). It shows that Huarochirí's "Indians" had acquired a substantial command of the alphabet, even though the government at that time provided no schools in rural areas. A third of Tupicocha-area men, and in one nearby village 60 percent, could at least read. In chapter 3, which deals with the rise of schooling in Tupicocha, we will consider the obscure sources of this surprisingly early mass peasant literacy.

Not long after the census, in 1879–84, Peru warred against Chile. The Peruvian state was humbled and its central control over the countryside compromised by defeat. Tupicocha was one of many villages where peasant "patriot" militias fought Chilean soldiers; oral tradition records that in this era the village's khipus were cached in a cave.

The only explicit statement about the use of a cord medium between the war and the massification of state schooling comes from a village outside central Huarochirí, but close to it and comparable in most regards. In 1923 the pioneer archaeologists Julio Tello and Próspero Miranda described a *khipu-tabla* that administered intracommunal canal-cleaning and the veneration of non-Christian water-owning deities in Casta, Huarochirí (see figure 33). In many respects Tupicocha's New Year's administrative cycle and its plenary meeting, the Huayrona, closely resemble what Tello and Miranda saw:

> At Wanka Canal, where . . . all the men gathered, the [village] functionaries take attendance of the workers. They all sit in a circle, in the plaza that exists at this place, and the Headman notes the names of those who are absent. This operation is carried out through the use of the apparatus shown . . . , which consists of a rectangular board, equipped with a handle; on one of its sides appear the names of the workers, and by means of different-colored cords which pass through holes placed beside each name, and [by means of] knots, not only the absences, and the quality of work carried out are mnemonically annotated, but everything which the authorities demand from the worker as indispensable accessories for attending the work: special

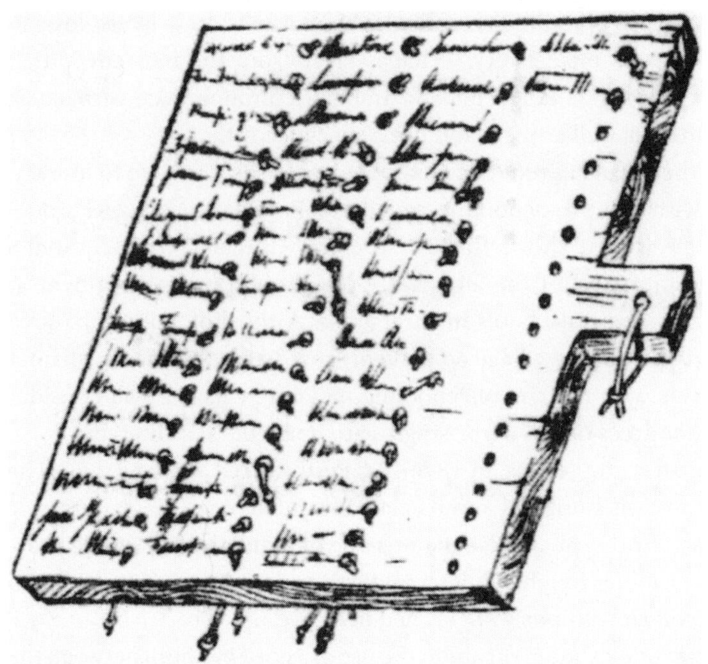

33. Celebrants of the canal-cleaning *faena* at S. Pedro de Casta, Huarochirí, registered participation on this tablet, according to the account in Tello and Miranda 1923.

> cothes, *wallkis*,[2] *shukank'as*[3] and *ishkupurus*,[4] tools, and even the greater or lesser enthusiasm of each person; with the objective of presenting it for the consideration of the elders, on the day of the Wari Runa.[5] (Tello and Miranda 1923:534)

If Tello and Miranda are correct, these cords encoded nonnumerical data. Wari Runa was a tribunal at which elders named incoming officers, judged and recorded the merits of everyone's participation in village duties, and discharged the dancers impersonating the Wari demigods. These are probable functions of the patrimonial khipus preserved until now by Tupicocha. Tello and Miranda specify Quechua as the language of ancient but incompletely understood song and invocation.

Census records from 1940 again show a high level of Huarochirí "Indian" literacy in relation to meager school resources. Very few of the ministry-sponsored schools now existing existed then. Yet of San Damián's 908 men over fifteen, 66.4 percent had *instrucción*; and of its 950 women, 40.4 percent had instrucción. Over 80 percent of the "instructed" had only primary schooling, but did know how to write (Peru 1941:68, 75).

Summing up the statistics discussed in more detail in chapter 3, male rural Huarochiranos seem to have been about one-third literate on the eve of the War of the Pacific, about two-thirds literate before the Second World War, and well over four-fifths literate on the eve of the military-nationalist revolution of 1969. During that interval, female literacy made major gains but did not crack the gender barrier in politics. Today both sexes are overwhelmingly literate. At every stage, peasant demand and initiative, only satisfied by state responses from the 1960s onward, were the driving force behind alphabetic learning.

THE KHIPU-ALPHABET TRANSITION AT AYLLU LEVEL

We have shown that the media history of rural Peru is one of complementary function and interaction between its two pristinely different graphic technologies: cord and paper. The final displacement of the former by the latter is a relatively recent phenomenon. What, then, undid the cord system?

Where the southern Andean highlands are concerned, Carol Mackey (1970) has provided a believable model. In the areas where she consulted senior herders, they knew the khipu as part and parcel of *gamonalismo*, the complex of land grabbing and debt peonage that made the Peruvian highlands a byword for violence and misery throughout the later nineteenth century and earlier twentieth. The retreat of the land grabbers amid worldwide depression and falling wool prices undercut that social order, and national agrarian reform (most active 1969–73) put an end to its remains. The sphere of exchange in which herding khipus had been key—that is, the articulation between herders intentionally kept illiterate and range bosses preparing ledgers for *gamonales*—died unmourned. Meanwhile, younger peasants were rapidly acquiring alphabetic literacy, which they saw as a potent weapon. They saw no reason why khipu should be learned any more.

But where Huarochirí and central Peru are concerned, the answers are different. Here, the khipu art belonged to the orbit of a deeply valued self-government, in a region with little land grabbing. Since the khipus had sacred value too, it is not obvious why people stopped learning to make them. Concerning the replacement of ayllu *quipocamayos* by writing, we suggest that

1. Writing did not replace Tupicochan khipus within the ayllu or *parcialidad* level until some time after the War of the Pacific (1879–84).
2. The initial reason for the transition had little to do with the "diffusion of literacy." It occurred at a time when writing was already an old tradition and literate men were already plentiful.
3. The late, slow replacement of khipus by books reflects the slow acquisition of written devices which could match the strengths of khipus.
4. Recognition of "Indian" communities by the national state from the 1920s on added impetus to the ayllus' absorption of book-writing norms.

In *The Cord Keepers* (2004a), it was argued that khipus served Tupicocha's ayllus in two ways. First, because a khipu is an assembly of separable data-bearing parts, it is useful as a simulation device. By simulating the arrangement of resources against the calendar and the social agenda, khipus served ayllus in reaching rational solutions to their complex organizational issues. Second, khipus served as updatable records of performance as the social agenda was fulfilled. Each ayllu applied the double potential of the medium—prospective or planning-oriented, and retrospective or performance-oriented—to create an overall system of social (not just monetary) accountability. By khipu, ayllu members kept plans and tracked their performance of duties to each other. By combined khipu and paper, the Community as a whole (i.e., the federation of ayllus) tracked each ayllu's contribution to the overarching whole—chiefly its shared canal infrastructure and the deities who owned water. On Huayrona day, the January *cabildo abierto*, or town meeting (Salomon 2004a:142–48), ayllus presented their cords for common inspection.

If we want to know how the khipu was demoted, a first question is when and how ayllus took up book writing. Ayllus, unlike the Community of which they are segments, do not own any prebook *fólderes*, that is, packets of colonial documents and unbound papers. Rare clues suggest the existence of intra-ayllu archives in other places before 1800, such as a 1723 "idolatry" trial in a remote part of Huarochirí which brought to light "a little chest of papers and a book of the Anan Cancha aillo" among the goods seized from the accused.[6] In Tupicocha, however, the self-alphabetization of ayllus begins with the practice of writing modern

TABLE 1
Initial Dates of Ayllu Book Series, by Ayllu

Ayllu Book Series	Dates
Allauca [undivided]	1923–[early volumes lost]
Satafasca [undivided]	1913–
Huangre [undivided]	1923–
Mujica	1876 [one act possibly dating to 1875]
Chaucacolca	1948 [earlier volume misplaced]
Cacarima	1905–[a]

[a]In nearby Tuna, Cacarima ayllu in 1930 made reference to a lost ayllu book of 1895. (APC/Santiago de Tuna 1905:3), suggesting a comparable starting date.

minutes, loans or IOUs, and receipts (etc.) into ledgers bought from Lima stationery businesses. The initial dates of these series, following the usual order of ritual precedence among ayllus, appear in table 1, above.

Were these books used simultaneously with quipocamayos? Unfortunately radiocarbon dating of fiber shreds fallen from quipocamayos (Salomon 2004a) gives only indecisive answers, due to inherent limitations of radiocarbon for the period 1650–1945, and also to the fact that the component cords of any one khipu may be unequal in age. The likeliest inference from the radiocarbon dates is that at least some cords were being made in the later nineteenth century and still modified in the early twentieth.[7] This is also the period when ayllus began to write books.

One clue to the relation between the media is the way ayllus inventoried khipus among their belongings in book entries. When Mujica and Cacarima started keeping books with inventories in them, they did not at first register the quipocamayos in the inventories. Mujica began writing its affairs in 1876, but did not inventory its khipus until 1897. These examples allow a guess that for the first decades after this ayllu began writing books, it considered the cords to be the record itself and paper a complement to them. Primera Satafasca's khipu has on some cords an ink stain matching an ink used in its early books, suggesting that books and cords lay together on the recording table. (They still do, at the New Year "family reunion," which is also the meeting for choosing ayllu officers.)

We have also seen that by the 1870s interaction with the lettered orbit was changing markedly, with wide, self-motivated literacy learning by "Indian" Huarochiranos. Applying the 1876 literacy percentages to Tupicocha's population, there would have been eighty-three males in Tupicocha (some perhaps minors) able to read and write. Presumably all the ayllus had at least a few. Community book entries from 1862 to the War of the Pacific are numerous, practiced, and conventional in format. Rarely was it necessary for a literate person to sign for an unlettered one (ACCSAT/SAT 06).

In short, literacy was probably not such a scarce resource. Why, then, did ayllus not generally avail themselves of literacy as a means of internal reproduction before the War of the Pacific? Apparently most ayllus, most of the time, were able to handle routine internal affairs by cord.

One ayllu, Mujica, decided just before the war that some kinds of business should be recorded on paper. One may get an idea about which kinds by noting the dates at which Mujica introduced various functions to its internal ledger (table 2).

The early books (see figure 34) stand close to the crabbed mold of official prose, and have no properties evidently analogous to khipus. Just to give a sense of their texture, here is the translation of a representative early entry:

> The *parcialidad* of Mojica finding ourselves gathered in the house of the *Camachico* [] for the purpose of entrusting the money to the treasurer D[on] Ermenegildo Antiporta in joint responsibility with his wife D[o]ña Estefa Vilcayauri Medina recognizes the sum of twenty one 21 sol 7 reales to hand over in one year when [they] have finished their duty with the interest calculated at ten per cent [.][8] This my document will be fulfilled without any margin for nonfeasance. My goods that I own will be the guarantee and as proof [*constancia*] of it I sign with my [writing? word partly illegible] with witnesses Tupicocha January 3 1893[.] With D[on] Rosendo Camilo being the Camachico. Ermenegildo Antiporta. [signatures of witnesses.] [Wavy overwritten lines signal cancellation]. (APM/SAT 01 1893:8v)

The document does not look a bit like those celebrated "paper *khipus*" discovered by John Murra (1975), María Rostworowski (1990), or Pärssinen and Kiviharju (2004). It looks like a rustic version of ordinary notarial writ. So ayllu books do not appear, at least in the beginning, a case of khipu carried on by other means. Seemingly, in the late nineteenth

TABLE 2

Matters Treated in Tupicocha's Earliest Ayllu Book, by Year of First Instance

Genre of Act	Year of First Instance
Acuerdo[a] por traspaso de tesorería (receipt for transfer of treasury)	1875
Acomodo de tesorería (alternate format for above)	1876
Acta de dentrantes (inscription of new members)	1884
Acuerdo de contrato o política (resolution on policy or contract)	n.d., 1897?
Inventario de bienes (inventory of collective goods)	1897
Acomodo de limanda (loan of votive pledge-token)	1897
Demanda de paternidad (paternity suit)	1897, unique
Vale de préstamo (IOU for loan)	1897
Recibo [por dinero u objetos] (receipt for money or objects)	1897
Acta de trabajo, acuerdo de faena (minute of collective labor)	1900
Acuerdo de amojonamiento (resolution of boundary inspection)	1900
Acuerdo de nombramiento (resolution of appointment to office)	1904
Vale por multas (IOU for fines)	1904
Acta de dejación (minute re. resignation from ayllu)	1904
Acta de arriendo de tierra (minute re. land rental)	1906
Acuerdo para celebrar fiesta (resolution to celebrate festival)	1906
Gasto [autorización] (authorization of expense)	1907
Lista de erogación de ganado (livestock assignment to pastures)	1914
Razón de las personas que faltaron (memo citing absentees)	1914
Acuerdo de los que guardan la mita (resolution re. excusal for community messenger duty)	1914?

Source: APM/SAT 01.

[a]Later done in *vale* or IOU format.

century ayllus began to think it prudent to write up certain matters in a fashion that the constitutional governments (municipality, justice of the peace, etc.) would recognize. In other words, they used writing for cases where imitating specific legal verbal formulas might be crucial to the collective interest. Among these, monetary transactions were preeminent,

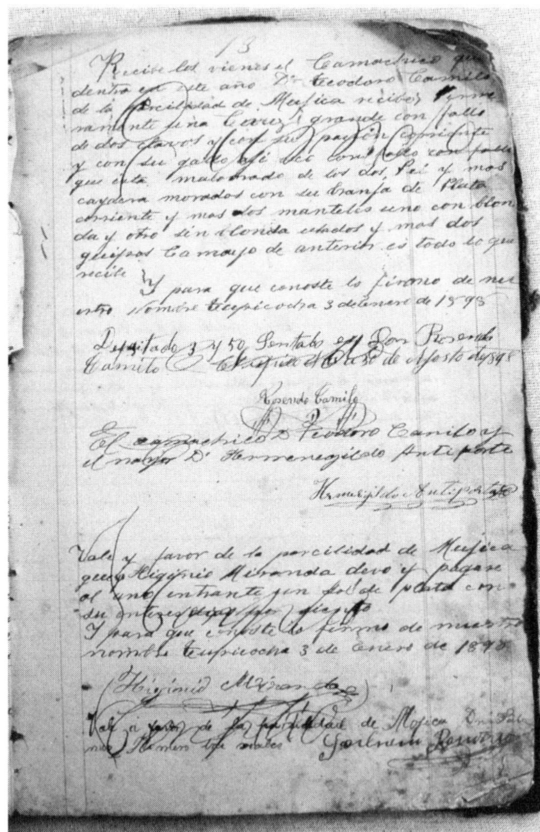

34. An 1898 page from the first internal book of an ayllu records the entrusting of Mujica's ritual objects to incoming officers, an IOU on its funds, and so on.

probably because they were liable to enter judicial fora. Wide alphabetic literacy by then would have given them means to do so. At the same time the already-alphabetic conduct of community-level business might have stimulated demand for more legally cogent records.

Table 3 summarizes the growth of intra-ayllu alphabetic writing. Growth was slow early in the twentieth century, followed by a major increase after 1940 and another major surge in the 1960s. It has stabilized at a high level. At the end of the twentieth century, the ayllus of Tupicocha owned more archival books than they had member households.

Tupicochanos say there are two ways of writing accounts: letra and paralela. *Letra* means the prose exposition of numerical data, as in the excerpt from Mujica's 1898 book above. *Paralela* means columnar or (later) grid or tabular reckoning. Oral tradition and ayllu books both confirm that letra dominated up to about 1935. Treasurers and secretaries did

TABLE 3

Manuscript Books of the Tupicocha Ayllus, by Decade of Volume Inception, 1870–1989

	1870	1880	1890	1900	1910	1920	1930	1940	1950	1960	1970	1980	*Total*
1r Allauca	0	0	0	0	0	0	0	3	2	2	6	2	*15*
1da Satafasca	0	0	0	0	1	1	0	3	0	2	1	1	*9*
1r Huangre	0	0	0	0	0	0	1	1	0	1	1	4	*8*
U. Chaucacolca	0	0	0	0	0	0	1	1	4	3	5	4	*18*
Mujica	1	0	0	0	1	0	0	1	0	3	5	4	*15*
Cacarima	0	0	0	1	0	0	0	1	1	2	3	2	*10*
2da Allauca	0	0	0	0	0	1	0	1	1	6	3	4	*16*
2da Satafasca	0	0	0	0	0	2	0	0	2	3	3	9	*19*
Centro Huangre	0	0	0	0	0	0	0	2	2	4	5	3	*16*
Huangre Boys	0	0	0	0	0	0	0	1	2	3	2	0	*8*
Total	*1*	*0*	*0*	*1*	*2*	*4*	*2*	*14*	*14*	*29*	*34*	*33*	*134*[a]

[a]Excludes lost and misplaced volumes (six identified), volumes in use and unobtainable (four identified), and blank volumes (two identified).

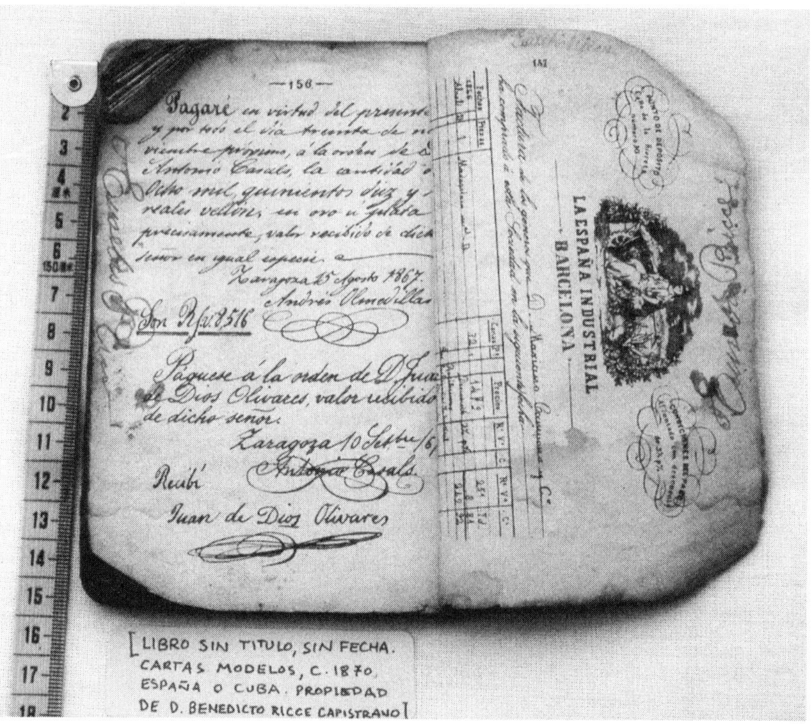

35. In Tupicocha before 1900, this book exposed some pupils to styles of commercial correspondence, including tabular formats (at right). Its title page is missing, but it appears to have been published in Cuba circa 1870.

columnar reckoning on scraps, but it was not considered appropriate to show columns in books of record. In this respect village writers stuck close to already-antiquated scribal models.

If villagers embraced tabular format only slowly, it was not for lack of acquaintance. One elder kept the book from which his grandfather learned to write business style, certainly before 1900, and it does contain models of tabulation (see figure 35). Although elders admit letra was overly laborious, they say it was more trustworthy because it required all receipts to be textually copied into books. Some even want to return to this tedious practice. (Lost receipts cause irritating delays at audits.) Ayllus used columnar displays by the 1920s. After 1935, when the Community won state recognition as a *comunidad indígena*, the "cuadricular" (i.e., columnar and eventually tabular) style used in government publications took hold everywhere. Veterans say that in this period the Ministry of Labor and Social Renovation taught some local people how to "square an account book."

Far from being khipus on paper, then, the early books served to dignify a small subset of internal ayllu business by expressing it in the archaistic, inconvenient, and privileged language of the law. In contrast to khipus, which (in Salomon's interpretation) share with Sumerian protowriting substantial independence from verbal language, these forms are maximally linguistic. They imitate sentences within the legalistic sociolect, even rendering numerals as words.

Letra writing as known in the early twentieth century thus carried the phonographic principle to an inconvenient extreme. First it required one to express every item as a complete sentence, arranging the referents according to syntactical rather than arithmetical relations. It also required one to express numerals in Spanish words rather than in their more easily calculated Indo-Arabic semasiograms. Because the medium was the prepaginated bound volume, in which erasure was prohibited, the finished series of sentences, like stretches of speech, could not be modified after utterance. It therefore lacked operability, the ability to simulate varying combinations.

The Tupicochan khipu as interpreted in *The Cord Keepers* (see figure 36) is held to contain more semasiographic elements. That is, it provided signs that nonlinguistically represented items of data. For example, a combination of knots on a pendant of a given color seems to have represented a number of items, regardless of how the items were spoken of (whether in Spanish, Quechua, etc.). The pendants' place in sequence along the main cord seems to have represented the temporal sequence in which works were realized. Discharged obligations could be un-knotted (see the diagram in figure 31). This record, unmediated by verbiage, had advantages which could be matched by books only after some decades of technical change. There is no proof to date that Tupicochan cords worked on Lockean principles. But even if they did not, they had some of the virtues of "data graphics," or as journalists now say, "infographics."

Edward Tufte, the author of three important monographs on data graphics, defines this medium: "Data graphics visually display measured quantities by means of the combined use of points, lines, a coordinate system, numbers, symbols, words, shading, and color . . . data graphics are

36. A Tupicochan khipu, Kh 1A-01 of Ayllu Primera Allauca, is similar in design to Inka khipus but its pendants are not grouped with spaces between.

instruments of reasoning" (1983:9). Tufte emphasizes that the goal of such graphics is a certain kind of "graphical excellence":

> A good data graphic show[s] the data; induce[s] the viewer to think about the substance rather than about methodology . . . avoid[s] distorting what the data have to say; present[s] many numbers in a small space; make[s] large data sets coherent; encourage[s] the eye to compare different pieces of data; reveal[s] the data at several levels of detail, from a broad overview to the fine structure; serve[s] a reasonably clear purpose [such as] description, exploration, tabulation, or decoration; and [is] closely integrated with the statistical and verbal descriptions of a data set. (1983:13)

Even without knowing what "things" the bands of color or the varied "bichrome" designs referred to, we can see that khipu had this sort of excellence: relations of contrast, equivalence, seriation, data hierarchy, and data versus metadata stand out as visual patterns in a way that they do not in scribal writing. It makes sense that these properties were cultivated, in a medium made for public display at the plenum, rather than for private scrutiny on a desk. Scribal letra, made for the desk, lacked Tufte's kind of "excellence." Scribal books are very hard to scan for overview, and they make it tedious to locate specific data or compare instances. But as the twentieth century advanced, two notable technical changes in ayllu self-notation occurred. These took the medium further from the old scribal norm, and brought it closer to the graphical array in which khipu seem to have excelled.

The first was the shift to paralela, or tabular format. A list as such, without associated data in columnar form, first occurred in Mujica in 1884, but the Mujica writers apparently felt uncomfortable with the format, because although they resolved in 1900 to keep a list to document labor debts, they did not actually start doing so until 1911 (APM/SAT 01 1911:53r). The first to make a list with associated numbers was Cacarima in 1906 (APC/SAT 01 1906:9). A 1918 page in which each entry carries two data items (AP1SF/SAT 02 1919:19) makes a weak example of a table, since one of the variables is the first name of the person concerned. Tabular format remained rare through the 1920s. Allauca (undivided) began writing lists without associated data in the 1920s (AP2A/SAT 02 1923–32), and Satafasca in 1921 obliged itself by statute to write "lists" (AP2SF/SAT 01 1921:12). In early lists one finds the word *primeramente,* a colonial prose mannerism introducing the list and reassuring the prose-oriented reader that although he is now invited to read vertically, the series of words will still obey the sentence syntax of prose. As for columnar data arrays—that is, lists with an item of data attached to each entry—they do not begin until 1912 (APM/SAT 01 1912:55r).

Today, each ayllu uses periodically accumulated *padroncillos* ('tables') and *padrones* ('multivariate charts or spreadsheets'). An example of a typical recent table would be a padrón of labor fulfillment, where the variables are *household, type of labor contribution, dates of labor within type,* and *completion or noncompletion of the task.* Since 1935, almost all ayllu books intersperse prose records with elaborate tables synthesizing their import (see figures 37–39).

Nobody today comments on padrones' and padroncillos' formal likeness to the khipu art. Indeed, they are not very much like khipus, except insofar as they minimize sentential or speechlike narration in favor of simple structures (chronological sequence, categorical identity, etc.) that simulate structured action. But tables stand in for khipu-style work better than prose does, and it is likely that in learning tabular formats villagers gave writing and books new viability as the vessel for an ancient order.

The second innovation in ayllu self-notation was the development of

37. In 1923 Ayllu Segunda Allauca performed among its members a round of mutual-benefit collective work days. This *relación* or *padroncillo* ('list' or 'table') records attendance.

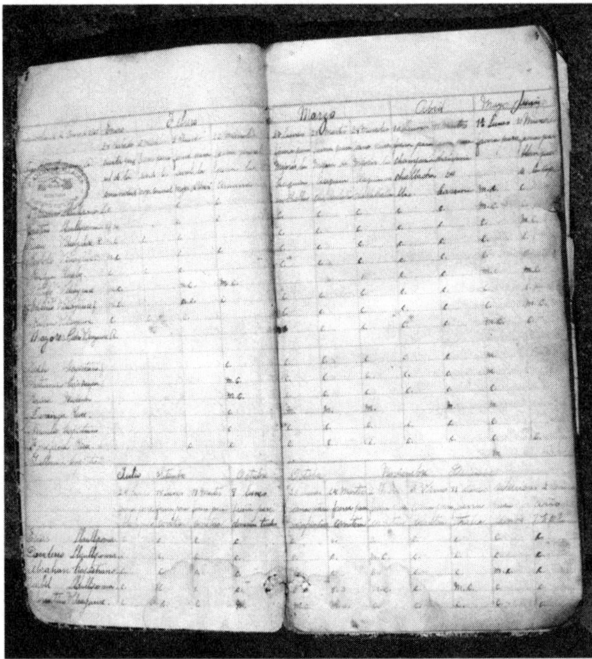

38. A 1982 padroncillo or table of Ayllu Segunda Allauca arrays the variables member, month, and work type within month.

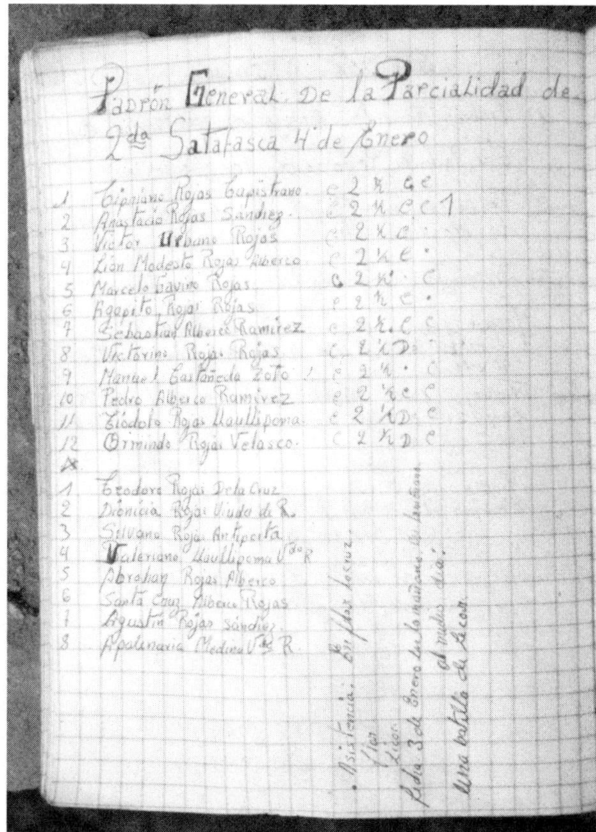
Padrón General de la Parcialidad de
2da Satafasca 4 de Enero

39. A draft 1996 padroncillo of Ayllu Segunda Satafasca is recorded in a secretary's notebook.

specialized concurrent volumes. Before about 1950, each ayllu gradually filled a single book with a miscellany of agenda, and when it was full, began another, equally miscellaneous one. This system made data retrieval time-consuming. (It would have been easier in a khipu, whose contents can be scanned for relevant color, markers, and so forth at a single glance.) In the 1950s some ayllus began keeping one book for work on the main canal, another for membership issues, a third for religious vows, and so forth. This practice was common by the 1960s, and proliferated almost crazily from the 1970s onward.

The combination of endogenous functional pressure with civic idealism certainly produced impressive bibliographies. Here are the translated titles of the books of a single ayllu (Segunda Satafasca) from the time it began keeping multiple concurrent books:

1. Book of the parcialidad Segunda Satafasca 1953–1968 [i.e., book of minutes of meetings]
2. Book of the parcialidad Segunda Satafasca of Placements [of pledge tokens] 1968–84
3. Book of the parcialidad Segunda Satafasca of [Public] Works [1965–81]
4. Ledger 1958–
5. Book of the parcialidad Segunda Satafasca 1979 Community (Works)
6. Book of the parcialidad Segunda Satafasca Wulkapampa [*sic*] 1965–84 [records of contribution to the building of a large new canal]
7. Book of Ururí [Dam and Reservoir] 1974–1991
8. Book Destined for the Chupaya Canal 1984–
9. Book of Inductions and Retirements of Members 1984–
10. Balance of Work [on Willcapampa Canal] 1984–
11. Soccer Book of Team Segunda Satafasca 1973–
12. Book of Inventory and Appointments to Office 1984–
13. On the Children [of the ayllu] Resident in Lima [1985]
14. Placements [of pledge tokens] 1982–
15. Book of the Delegate [i.e., counselor-spokesman] 1987
16. [Book] of Sessions [i.e., business meetings] 1988–
17. Book of Casama [spring, reservoir, and canal] 1988–
18. Lands in Hueccho [and] Masllaulli 1993–[concerns the ayllu's shares in lands Tupicocha won from a neighboring village in combat and lawsuit]
19. On the Ururí Dam 1991–
20. On Community Work [i.e., the Bullring] 1992–

These two technical innovations gave the book-writing art "seven-league boots" compared to its initial status as the laborious accumulation of letra. Today, villagers can readily draw up, with their multicolored ball-point pens, a four-variable chart comparable in overall data richness with Lockean khipus of the past. These charts are written in highly compressed notations that make little use of language mimicry. Their formal structure, like that of khipus, are visual arrays of data points rather than statements about them. (For example, one such chart is an array in which the horizontal axis is a series of successive collective labor days, and the vertical axis the sequence of members in seniority order. It would be easy to create a formally similar khipu.) The written symbols which fill cells are sometimes abbreviated words but are equally often semasiographs (numerals, dots, checks, question marks, *x*s, or other nonverbal symbols). So by a circuitous route, Tupicocha has recovered its semasiographic powers.

In sum, the first decades of intra-ayllu papers mimic the clumsy prose rendering of numerical matters characteristic of older Spanish convention —the conventions of the "lettered city" in its early phases. Only as the writers of ayllu books became familiar with tabular formats did their intra-ayllu accounts come to cover on paper the full range central to the *Huayrona* or civic khipu tradition. And only when the habit of keeping separate books for separate topics took root did paper overcome the clumsy omnium-gatherum format of early volumes.

Finally, it is fitting to ask how the transition from khipu to paper was related to power. Did it change the control of people via control of data about them? In the above pages we have emphasized how alphanumeric techniques on paper came to replace khipu as the way in which villagers controlled each other, and collectively controlled assets. In the early twentieth century *comuneros* found a way for constancias of local power to become commensurable with state records and yet faithful to local legality. The old function of cultural privacy was decisively sacrificed. In the next section, we will sketch the simultaneous development of literate "reform" as a part of peasant efforts to actively approach and influence the state. This part of the media shift was less autonomous, more responsive to large political demands. To the degree that it, too, influenced a media shift, one might say that khipus were as much displaced as replaced.

"INDELIBLE LETTERS ON THEIR HEARTS": AYLLU REFORMISM AND BOOK WRITING

In addition to the two technical factors of tabular form and specialized volumes, a third, more diffusely cultural factor has fostered the upsurge of ayllu writing. This was the promise of literacy as a way to erase the "Indian" stain and secure citizen dignity. Early in the twentieth century, well before state recognition of the community, several ayllus prepared for jural recognition by writing themselves reformed "constitutions," or organic statutes. Equipped with an ample supply of literate members, the ancient pre-Hispanic kin-structured corporations were now ready to introject state forms of organization arising from urban-based republicanism (see figure 40). The new social contract of modernity was understood

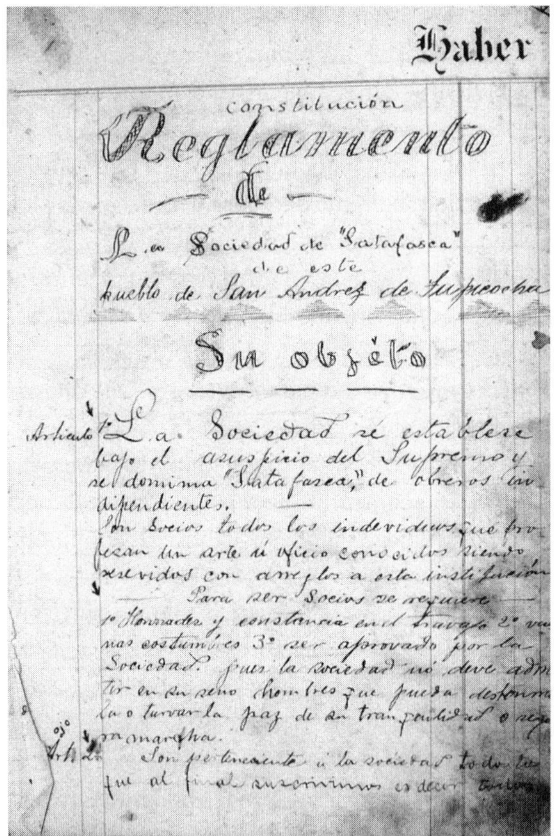
Haber

constitución

Reglamento

de

La Sociedad de "Satafasca"
de este
pueblo de San Andrez de Tupicocha

Su objeto

Articulo 1º La Sociedad se establece bajo el auspicio del Supremo y se domina "Satafasca," de obreros independientes.
Son Socios todos los individuos que profesan un arte ú oficio conocidos siendo servidos con arreglo a esta institución
Para ser Socios se requiere
1º Honradez y constancia en el travajo 2º buenas costumbres 3º ser aprovado por la Sociedad. pues la sociedad nó deve admitir en su seno hombres que pueda deshonrar o turvar la paz de su tranquilidad o regimen marcha.
Art 2º Son pertenecientes á la sociedad todos los que al final suscrivimos es decir todos

40. Still-undivided Satafasca Ayllu's 1920 book announces its reformed criteria for membership. The kinship factor remains tacit.

as meaning that all levels of governance should be isomorphic. Control over people, including local control, should be exerted through control over lettered information at *all* levels in *one* way: the constitutional one.

The national state never took note of kinship corporations below the threshold of juridical personhood. The standing of ayllus as constituents of the legally recognized community was not reinforced by juridical personhood. Even now it holds firm as a matter of "custom," that is, unwritten law, and kinship rather than citizenship defines eligibility. The mountains of intra-ayllu books, unlike those of the Community, have never been opened to "vertical" probes. Nongovernmental organizations, the Ministry of Agriculture and Livestock, or the various semiautonomous development corporations often avail themselves of communitywide data from the legal government, but never consult ayllu books. Indeed the present work is the first one based on an outsider reading.

Some ayllus that previously wrote no books of acts began writing them with their acts of "reform," and others inaugurated new series. Cacarima took up book writing as part of its 1905 reform. The first book of Satafasca (undivided) inaugurated itself with a fanfare of "Reform" in 1913, and at various moments in Satafasca's painful schism, members urged that the new organization reform itself by inscribing rules about cultivated manners in debate. From 1920 on, several ayllus began to style themselves reformed and wrote themselves new constitutions conforming to the models which urban and legal authorities were then promoting. Mujica included the word *reformado* in the title of its second book. Its members kicked off the year 1921 by reforming themselves in three ways: first, if a member's wife was in childbirth, the man was allowed an extra five days to make up any faena he missed while helping her;[9] second, the ayllu was to levy a fine for missing Community—that is, noninternal—faenas; and third, any substitute worker who attended a faena to do the work of an absent member would not receive the honorific gifts. Primer Huangre did the same in 1930. Another ayllu undertook to write itself a set of statutes because its members felt "totally demoralized" after an enemy faction had wrecked its meeting place.

"Reform" probably responds to the series of laws which the modernist Leguía regime promoted starting in 1920. Leguía's laws proclaimed the indigenous commons to be patrimony of their traditional owners (as against the property of latifundists who had encroached on such lands). It defined this right as a peculiar form of ownership, inalienable and collective. The law invited indigenous communities to petition for jural recognition, and thereby secure such property. Cacarima Ayllu in 1930 felt its indigenous heritage to be the wellspring of citizen liberty: the corporation, it argued, "should recognize individual liberty through the payment of the value of work or in other words through carrying on the ancient regimen of the grandparents" (APC/SAT 01 1930a:136). In 1936 Chaucacolca, though it regarded itself as "established" by written regulations in 1914, composed a new "Act of the Installation of the *Parcialidad*" in 1936 (APUCh/SAT 03:1). The concept of civic reform had durable appeal, especially as a way of salving the damage caused by factional splits. In 1948, Primer Allauca wrote itself an "Act of Organization of the New Reform," heavily emphasizing the ideology of progress through education, in which members promised "to write with indelible letters on their hearts the following phrases . . . said by the great thinker Marden.,"[10] "to sacrifice our personal interests for the good of the collectivity," and "seek by every legitimate means honor Glory and Triumph for Tupicocha" (AP1A/SAT 01 1948:2).

ROMANCING THE PRECISE ON PAPER

The immediate fruit of the rapprochement with Spanish-format tabular accounting has been an almost masochistic enthusiasm for accounting and auditing, not only in money matters, but in the record of labor and ceremonial participation. Let us take a synchronic look at the way the accounting register is mobilized in any recent year, and then consider how the reckoning of quantitative data is related to the emergence of narrative.

At the ayllu level, the *cuentas residenciales*, or annual public audit of the community authorities, begins by padlocking in the entire group of those to be audited (see figure 41). Their spouses or children throw bag lunches over the gate at midday. This financial and moral Dies Irae is also an ordeal whose many phases each impose their own stresses. The agenda is long: inventory of objects; inventory of records; collection of fines; induction and retirement of members; debits and assets of the ayllu fund based on pledges and festival income; debits and assets of the working treasury based on rentals, fines, and quotas owed; collection of fines; positions to be taken in all-communal controversies; and so forth. At the last audit of the year, the aim is to finish at a zero balance. Members divide up any positive balance in the form of a dividend, or negative balance in the form of an assessed per household quota. One reason for preferring to finish with zero is to have outgoing officers bow out with no lingering responsibilities, on which incoming officers might blame later trouble. The planning for the next cycle includes assessing the initial contribution which each household will have to chip in to restart the working fund. Sometimes, when a dividend has resulted, member households are required to immediately return it so as to form the coming year's ayllu fund.

Accountancy notwithstanding, an ayllu audit is also something of a party, and something of a sacred occasion. The usual "hours of custom" impart solemnity and help members achieve a pensive, collected state of mind. At major ayllu audits a musical duo (fiddle and wooden flute) is usually invited to give the function a tone of triumph and pleasure. At intervals, members take dancing breaks. They put their hands on each others' shoulders to stamp around in a circle, finishing each stanza with a whoop. There is psychological wisdom in combining "social dancing" (as

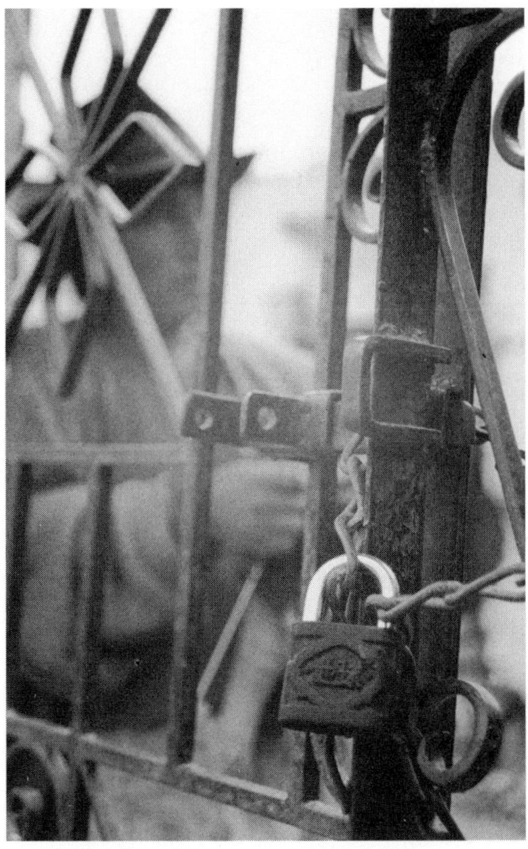

41. At the beginning of the 1997 General Audit, the directorate makes sure of the Community quorum by locking it in.

it is called) with accounting, because this dance—one of the very few occasions when ayllu mates touch each other—builds a feeling of warmth and discharges the tensions of tiresome, tense fiscal discussions.

As the treasurer or secretary lists the year's infractions, each member must review every glitch and lapse. The speaker recites the lapses in a measured, unconsciously versified diction:

> Patricio Caxavilca,
> one day of work
> for Masllaulli
>   when we planted potatoes,
>   and three bottles of grape brandy.
> Is everybody here?
> Aquiles Traslaviña
>   one day of work

on the filtration galleries
and two packs of cigarettes
and one attendance without tools.

Expenses, too, have to be recited in everyone's hearing, jotted and calculated by every member.

When we delivered the first harvest
a family-size soft drink
three soles.
And for the kitchen expenses,
ten soles.
And to contract the band,
three times,
seven fifty.
Yesterday,
in everyone's presence
we drank two bottles of anise
four soles.
Two anises in the night,
two small rounds,
for two who made pledges.
Here are the receipts, gentlemen.

As items are read, two ad hoc bookkeepers write them on separate blackboards (when available) and run subtotals. Each citizen present separately writes down the items and calculates on his own. If anyone's arithmetic disagrees, the whole subtotal is done all over again as many times as it takes to track down the discrepancy, however tiny. When asked why people are willing to tolerate the tedium, villagers emphasize the fact that unlike contracts with NGOs or affairs of the constitutional government, Community and parcialidad business is not overseen by any higher authority, so nothing except members' vigilance guarantees its solvency and honesty. The social contract is one of *absolute* accountability. As a result. the written simulacrum of communal life is judged by an almost impossible standard: one-to-one correspondence with the minutiae of a year's collective experience. At the Community level, most years, the general account ends with members all but literally staggering home.

At both ayllu and Community levels, despite the impressive array of

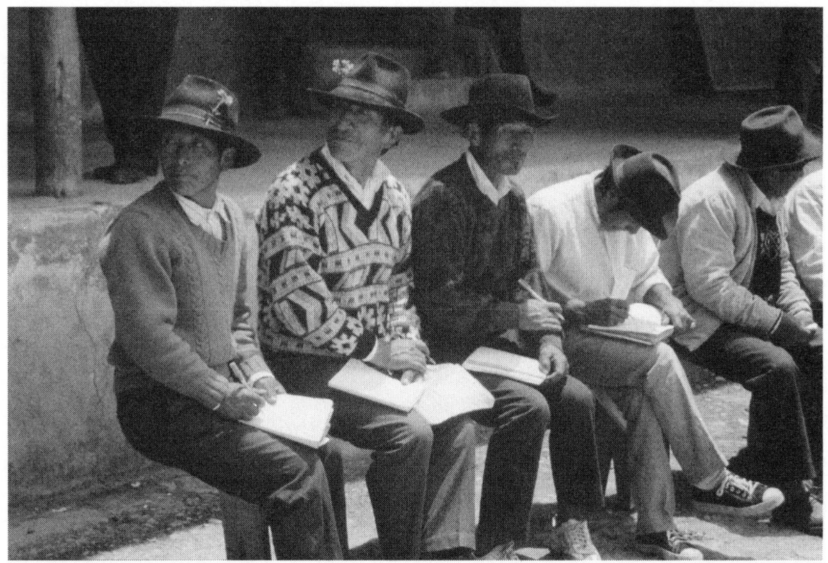

42. Participatory auditing: all members must reckon every transaction, and only when no discrepancies remain are the accounts cleared. This audit took place in Tupicocha, 1995.

"enflowered" males and their flapping white foliage of notebooks (see figure 42), women are vital to the process. Some pass the time spinning with drop spindles, periodically loosing zingers about what they consider bad expenses. The actual collection or disbursement of cash in and out of the strongbox is often entrusted to the treasurer's wife. Because women are not obliged to accept the rounds of drinks which accompany all ritualized business, they are considered the best fiduciaries. They are also consulted for memory of details not on the written record. Women have license to prod the process with mild satire—"Well, everybody owes, so nobody owes, right?"—and to "cool out" men upset over petty blame.

An observer with a conflict-oriented theoretical inclination would notice that auditing enforces an unsatisfactory status quo. The community is not as egalitarian as it means to be, because communal entitlements of land and water are more valuable to those members with more capital they can apply to them. But accounting also yields a vital reward. The end of the accounting—often after two whole hard-to-spare days—brings a special euphoria. Accounting is the exertion that retrieves from the "tired romance" of bombast and insincere cliché, the underlying regularity and perfectibility of the common venture: the beauty and exactitude of action in groups, and the convincing "worthwhileness" of getting things right for the sake of the virtual being—called community or ayllu—that sustains the members. "To act as if we were one person" is a common rhetorical stimulus. Reaching resolution is a moment when one can almost experience that great fiction, the "ever-never changing" social whole, as something real and palpable.

MINUTES OF A MEETING WITH THE DIVINE LOVERS

We now follow the "romance of the precise" to its summit: the businesslike documentation of an encounter with the divine. It is a summit not just in its metaphysical premise, but also in the organizational and even the geographical one.

The most elaborate records of work are those written at the climax of the cycle of labor on the irrigation infrastructure. The climax is the *champería*, or canal-cleaning "water festival." "Water festivals" at the high sources of irrigation are almost universally central to Andean ritualism, and they form a *locus classicus* for ethnography. In Tupicocha, as in most high villages, the canals that feed the fields suffer collapses and algal congestion during the rainy season (or did until their recent rebuilding with PVC pipes). At the end of the rains, in late April or early May, the entire village mobilizes as a general faena and ascends the Andes to the inlet where their canal catches water melting off the sacred snowcaps. This place is understood as the intersection of divine and human society. They then work their way down the whole branching system. Maintenance crews form ayllu by ayllu to clean their respective traditional "stretches." When all are clean, a message is carried to the top of the system. The intake can be opened and the water joyfully greeted as it rushes to the fields. The management of these ayllu crews is the immediate motive for bringing books along and narrating each champería cycle.

Because it is work and ceremony at the same time, canal labor is sometimes commemorated in special maplike landscapes like figure 43. These are historical mementos, not administrative documents, but their content matches the content of the corresponding document. In figure 43, the small figures—such as the surveyor beside a ravine or the hunter going after deer to feed the work party—correspond to events also recorded on paper. The drawing as a whole could be taken as a visual chronicle of the days of work.

Tupicocha is presently losing its "water festival" complex because the plastic pipes replacing stone channels make annual cleaning unnecessary.

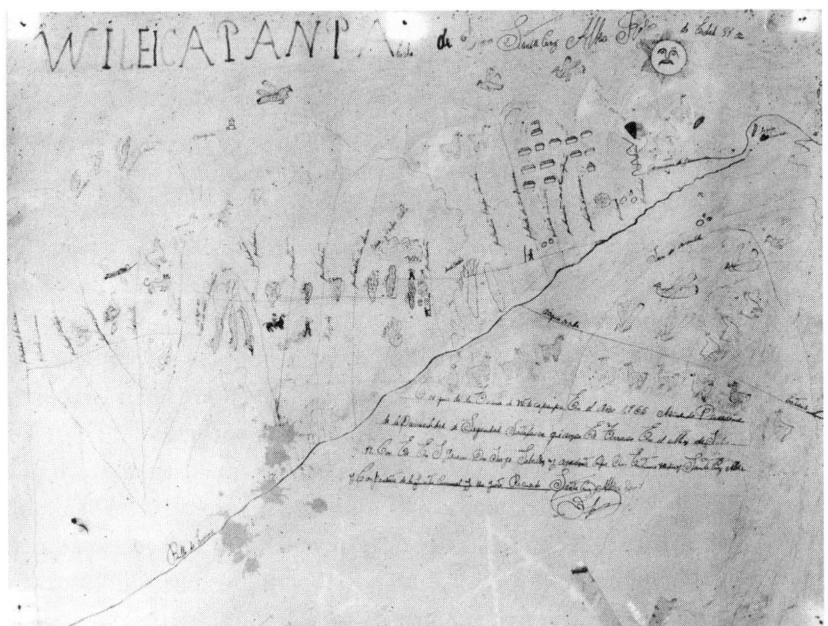

43. In this 1965 *croquis*, or drawing that combines a map and landscape, Santacruz Rojas, an elder of Segunda Satafasca, commemorated his ayllu's part in a series of faenas to improve the Willcapampa Canal.

But canal cleaning, and specifically the gathering at the headwaters, was from pre-Hispanic times on the moment of dialogue with the divine mountain "Owners" of water. The Tupicochan water deities (every village has its own) are a couple who live in a secret place above the water intake, on the snowy, wind-lashed heights of Germania. They show themselves to humans in the form of two skulls. (Perhaps these are remains of one of the many pre-Hispanic mummy shrines despoiled by seventeenth-century clergy and later grave robbers.) Manuel Ráez Retamozo's 2005 compendium on ritual in the Lima highlands has a cover photo showing the skulls being venerated. The "beautiful grandparents" are called Pencollo and María Capyama, or Catiana, the latter name also being a pre-Hispanic legacy. Capyama's myth appears in chap. 31 of the 1608 Quechua Manuscript of Huarochirí (Salomon and Urioste 1991:136–44). Pencollo is also known as Chupaquino. They are imagined as glamorous creatures in love, enjoying pleasure and power among the streams and glaciers of the heights.

The ritual cycle—with its masked and brightly costumed celebrants, the Huaris (or Huares)—intensifies social and ecological bonds with great expressive force. But the bonds among people, water, and land are felt to be actually ratified and implemented by an elaborately legalistic—in fact, by local criteria, legally binding—code of exchange and recordkeeping. Tupicocha's interpretation of Mama Catiana and Señor Pencollo as "water Owners" is quite literal. The climactic ritual in which the Huaris with their musicians mediate between the Owners and the irrigators sums up the state of village water law in a single exchange of messages: a petition for water use, and a concession to the users.

The excerpts which follow are ayllus' own accounts of combined work and ritual at the intake of Tupicocha's great Willcapampa Canal. To understand it one must know a few details about the ritual program.

When the villagers reach the highest slopes, they make their overnight encampment. There they appoint four Huaris, and attendants for them. The word *wari* in Quechua means primordial. The Huaris are costumed dancers who impersonate the ancient ancestors of the village. In preparation for this role, they undergo a short ritual that temporarily removes their baptism, so they can be in uncompromised relation with the old gods. This necessitates an act to take away their Christian names and confer poetic or comic ritual names. In 1991 and in 1993 Primer Allauca registered the names of those who impersonated sacred personages (see table 4).

The costumed ancients intercede for their "children," that is, the modern villagers. They deliver to the deities who own the water a written request in the genre of a formal legal petition, asking permission to continue drawing off irrigation water. During the morning after arrival, the Huaris ascend to the secret place on the heights where the water-owning deities live. Musicians and the water-control officials accompany the Huaris. Mama Catiana and Señor Pencollo receive them at their secret home. The Huaris then lift the skull deities in a fine textile and address them with gifts. As soon as the Huaris have delivered the offering and the message to the divine couple, they hear the deities' reply "by telepathy," as one said, and write down their will. The party then descends to the assembled workers at midday carrying Mama Catiana and Señor Pencollo. There they "telepathically" read aloud the "letter" from the deities to the villagers.

The records of any given champería are extensive, and the following translation, though extended, has ellipses as noted. It is Mujica Ayllu's record of one exchange with the Andean gods:

TABLE 4

Ritual Names of the Huaris (Delegates for Transactions with the Deities Pencollo and Mama Catiana) of Primer Allauca

Dance Order	Christian Name	Poetic/Comic Name	English Translation
		1991 Name Registration	
1st Huare	Nilton Segura	Cutito	[?] [diminutive]
2d Huare	Dario Rojas Ll.	Pugartiago	'Santi-flea-go'
3d Huare	Sabino Alberco	Cumbre Solín	'Solín Peak'
4th Huare	Mateo Espiritu	Chulla Llaqui	'Sad without Mate'
1st Trumpeter	Mariano Laymito	Picaflor de Cueto	'Cueto's Hummingbird'
Drummer	Marcela Llaullipoma	Flor Huarochirana	'Flower from Huarochirí'
		1993 Name Registration	
1st Wahre	[not available in registry]	Wahre Chico Catahua	'Little Ancestor Catahua'
2d Wahre	[not available in registry]	Nevado de Tocto	'Snowcap of Tocto [Lake]'
3d Wahre	[not available in registry]	Suira Cocha Nunca Te Olvidaré	'Milk-white Lake, I Will Never Forget You'
4th Wahre	[not available in registry]	Culy Cucha y Curie	[?] 'Gold Lake Golden'
1st Trumpeter	[not available in registry]	Mando Agua Todo	'I Command All Water'
2d Trumpeter	[not available in registry]	Ecos Banda Banda	'Echoes Band Band'
Drummer	[not available in registry]	[female; name not written]	

Source: The names from 1991 are from AP1A/SAT 02 1991:28; 1993 names are from AP1A/SAT 02 1993:40.

ACT OF WORK OF THE CANAL CLEANING OF WILLCAPANPA 1994

Willcapampa jurisdiction of san miguel de viso within bounds of the province of Huarochiri dept. of Lima it being 8:30 of the day Monday 16th of May of 94 the members of the parcialidad of Mojica found themselves gathered in the presence of the president Ormindo Antiporta Vice president Edelberto Advincola S[ecretary] Alejandro Advincola a member at large absent.

1. The members of our parcialidad were present at the said place with the purpose of fulfilling the said general faena decreed by our community's authorities.

Our members were at the orders of the president right away at 9:00 in the morning of the day for the beginning of fulfilling the dispositions of the president of the Community directorate [roster of the directorate follows] . . . and also in presence of the Irrigators' Committee and its directorate [roster follows] . . . and also in the presence of the Campos and Alguaciles [i.e., staffholding officers with rural jurisdiction; roster follows] . . . and also accompanied by the political Authorities namely the Governor [and his staffholding officers; roster follows] and also the Regidor [head staffholding officer] . . . and also the presence of the Justice of the Peace . . . and also we take note of the presence of a visit by some university students from [the National Agrarian University of] La Molina Upon having the presence of the Authorities and comuneros both men and women and retired people being 9 AM on the day 16 of May 1994 the custom [i.e., ritual] of the champería was begun according to the authorities' proclamation.

The President of the Community Sr. Tiofilo A[lberco] S. welcomed the comuneros and comuneras and the retired as well as active comuneros in general giving his words lucidly throughout the great crowd. To the champería, may it every year be fulfilled to carry water to the district of S[an] A[ndrés] de Tupicocha. Next likewise the President of Irrigation [i.e., of the Irrigators' Committee] Sr. Agustín Rojas gave a welcome to everyone present in general, in order to save time and next

2. 2d the naming of the Huares was carried out namely the following 1st Huare Gavino A. Rojas 2d Manuel Espirito 3d Jhonson Laymito 4th Huari.[11] . . . . [suspension points in original][12] and next came the nomination of the music [i.e., musicians] The following by appoint-

ment of the President of our Community the cornet player [i.e., player of the seashell trumpet, or in some cases ram's horn] Ormindo Antiporta Rueda and the drummer [i.e., player of the *tinya*, or small, female drum] Lidia Avila de E.[13] Next the herb bearers [i.e., carriers of the sacred plants of the heights, which are felt to be tokens of divinity] the following 1. Eber Llaullipoma 2. Sr. Amancio Javier 3. [The youth] Armando R.C.

2. [error in numeration] Next the Campos [i.e., staffholding officers of the countryside] were present doing their duty according to their good will among their Alguaciles. 3d [error in numeration] Next the Treasurer of the Community gave his disbursement reserved for the champería of Wilcapanpa to Chupaya [a lower part of the hydraulic system] the sum of 10,000 new soles already realized in the form of expenses for the good of the comuneros and comuneras and retired members[.][14]

3. Next the President of Irrigation took the stand in high emotion before his comuneros and comuneras and retired members and congratulated us on our general faena of champería for our peasant community of the district of S A de Tupicocha for their [i.e., our] great interest and good will and sacrifice which this great attending crowd displays for the Work in the Location of Willcapampa.—

4. The Governor of our district making our reference that our comuneros might take good care of their health and life in the face of our Work so as not to compromise the authorities and comuneros[15]—

5. Next the Treasurer of Irrigation being represented by the comunero Cipriano Rojas his father Cilvano Rojas was present with the sum and quantity of 40 bottles of coca [probably meaning rum, but perhaps Coca Cola][16] and 1 kilo of coca [leaf] and also 10 packs of cigarettes[.] 2d Hour[17] 1. Being 12 o'clock midday the Huares were officially received by the comuneros in a group and the others present with the purpose of receiving their reply and message from Mama Catiana and Sr. Pincollo so that the irrigating comuneros recognizing thus their good will for this year 1994 what will be their offering of good will.[18] And in a short time we had the pleasure of their letter from Mama Catiana and Sr. Pincollo of giving us water and with the purpose of being sure the comuneros of Tupicocha fulfill their promises. And so they will give water to Tupicocha. *2d*

the authorities and the *Campos*, the Irrigators' Committee authorized the Huaris to say goodbye to the crowd[19] thanking them by the will of the multitude of Tupicocha's comuneros.—–

When it was 2:30 in the afternoon we the comuneros by order of the authorities have proceeded to carry out the canal cleaning where we arrived at Biscachero[20] where the Community gave a general rest and give permission for resting according to customary law by the good will and discipline of the workforce and next the measurers [*toperos,* i.e., those who assign *tupus,* or stretches] and receivers [i.e., parcialidad representatives acknowledging the apportionment] gave assurances that they would fulfill their duties. And the people [*masa*] agreed to it. and Next the President of the Community announced that the Monday faena was completed, stating that they [comuneros] should be ready at 8:00 on Tuesday. [The comuneros then sleep the night in their encampment, using blankets that are brought along.]

At 8:30 of the day Tuesday the 17th of May the work from Biscachero to Chupaya with the purpose of furthering our *champería* and fixing the collapsed part at the place called Montepato where it is Chaucacolca [*parcialidad*]'s job to work and finally we reached Pampa Calato.—–(APM/SAT 07 1994:89–91)

The record continues at the same level of detail through the succeeding three days. It includes thoroughly political and secular matters such as disputes over the assignment of difficult stretches, the disciplining (by whip) of those who fall short, the statistics of attendance (170 comuneros on most occasions), and the penalties to be inflicted on those who refuse ad hoc assessments to cover canal repairs. As in all other faenas, the *horas de costumbre,* or daily ritual periods, count as *sesiones,* or business meetings, with power to make decisions at parcialidad or Community level. They are also the occasions for writing the record. The champería quoted above ends with a dry summary of what is in fact an expansively joyous celebration. Toasting and dancing welcomed the first of the water which would carry the village through its long dry months.[21]

To villagers, this jointly religious and bureaucratic constancia needs no further comment. Records such as the above are used primarily to verify details about who performed which offices, paid expenses, and so forth, or what precedent was set concerning some contentious detail. The more studious members of ayllus spend private hours reading over them. People greatly enjoy finding mentions of their deceased relatives in honorable roles.

The connection between divinity and writing is close but not obvious. When the Tupicochans ascend en masse to the divine sources of water, they renew a social contract with the water gods, and implement the mutual promise—superhuman water in exchange for human devotion and good social conduct—by means of a strictly bureaucratic regimen. Only a person who is up to date in faenas and sacrifices or ritual roles, receives a ration of irrigation. That is why the ostensibly secular Irrigators' Committee finds itself deep in the ritual action as the collectivity approaches the divine couple who "own" the water supply.

In another publication, Salomon (1998) shows how colonial law and water ritual were articulated in the neighboring village of Concha. The Concha example is worth a moment's attention because it shows with special clarity how the village contract with divinity is transmitted. Concha happens to get its water from a high lake, the one called Yansa in the 1608 Quechua Manuscript of Huarochirí and today called Yanascocha. When Concha villagers perform their analogue to the Pencollo-Catiana cycle, their water authorities prepare a document they call the *recado*. The recado is a formal petition for irrigation, addressed to the lake-owning couple, whom they call Pedro Batán and María Capyama. By way of signature it bears a roster of household heads of Concha Peasant Community, in numbered list format (see figure 44), with the rubber stamps of the respective authorities. The finished list, speared on a stick, becomes the sail of a tiny sailing raft which the local equivalents of Huaris launch onto the waters of the lake (see figure 45). The raft has a hold, stuffed with coca, tobacco, petals, perfume, and other gifts. When the raft reaches the middle of the lake and sinks (see figure 46), villagers say that the Owners have accepted their petition. The Concha villagers greet the beginning of the irrigation cycle jubilantly.

The term *recado* is of interest. In modern urban usage, it often means a casual note. But its usage here connotes anything but informality. Rather, it harks back to one or more colonial-era usages. *Recaudo* meant a legally forceful document offered in support of a motion or petition. Joan Corominas (1976:496) shows that *recaudo* is related to *caudal*, meaning 'goods' in the sense of 'capital', and he adduces early modern usages proper to the business sphere. So *recado*, meaning a document for the water gods, is likely to be another of those Andean ritual terms—such as *armada*,

44. The sail of the raft which carries Concha Community's offerings to the divine couple residing in Lake Yanascocha consists of an official list of the comuneros who wished to irrigate with lake water in 1994.

45. Dancing celebrants launch their boatload of coca, tobacco, and other gifts to the lake deities Pedro Batán and Mama Capyama, asking their favor for the 1994 irrigation cycle.

46. As 1994's "boat" floats to the center of the lake, Concha Community members anxiously await the moment when the underwater deities will reach up and accept it.

cumplimiento, *derecho*, and *pago*—which migrated from the language of Spanish accountancy to that of Andean religious reciprocity.

The logic of transaction demands a written answer from the divinities. On this facet, the closely related Tupicochan practice is more explicit. The 1994 champería act cited above mentions that the Huaris return not only accompanying the Owners in physical form (skulls), as visitors among living humans, but also bringing a letter from them. As the minutes say, "We had the pleasure of their letter from Mama Catiana and Sr. Pincollo of giving us water and with the purpose of being sure the comuneros of Tupicocha fulfill their promises." This letter forms the apical link in the whole web of self-inscribing action. Yet this highest of all writings is *not* copied, shown, or archived. It is above human capacity.

When the Huaris commune with Catiana and Pencollo at the divine home on the barren, icy heights, they jot down what the Owners tell them on a piece of paper. At the midday climax of the villagers' encounter with the Owners, the Huaris read it out publicly. However. they are not in possession of a fully inscribed legalistic text like all the texts discussed so far. Rather, they have in their hands a roughly scribbled, frequently not even legible, simulacrum of writing: bold wavy lines and elliptical scribbles made with a wide-tip felt pen.

The actual performance is improvisational in its exact wording. On July 6, 1999, when Tupicocha was beginning the conversion of Willcapampa from ditch to pipe channeling, the words Pencollo and Mama Catiana sent were "Congratulations on eliminating leakage and not wasting; may [the canal] yield well, and may everyone feel joy in seeing it produce" (see figure 47). Depending on the morale of the village at a given date, the "letter" may be gentle and cordial as in 2000, or it may include pointed reminders about failures of duty and reciprocity.

Andean peoples have an undeserved reputation for solemnity. In fact, laughter is a big part of this celebration as of others. In 1992, after millennia of cohabiting in the waters, the pre-Hispanic lovers finally announced their marriage:

> The [Huaris] delivered a letter addressed to the President and it was read out, it was for a matrimonial act and that they have as their godfathers and godmothers 1st godfather Alberto Vilcayauri Medina and godmother Sra. Cipriana Espíritu 2d godfather Tito Rojas and doña Rosaura Rojas, all assembled in the Municipal Palace of Chupaya. (AP1A/SAT 02 1991:29–30)

47. This snapshot was taken by a participant in the encounter with the "Owners" of Willcapampa's water on July 6, 1999. The deities, Pencollo and Mama Catiana, are incarnated in the crania partially revealed to view in the carrying cloth. The improvised sanctuary consists of an "arch" of irrigation pipe, with a bottle of consecrated liquor suspended in a pipe-joining gasket. *Cushuris*, or coca bags, are festooned with puna grasses from the heights where the "Owners'" have their secret residence.

To be the godparents of a divine marriage is, of course, recognition of high honor. The message brought jubilation and laughter. Chupaya refers to a high and wild stretch in the freezing upper slopes. Its "Municipal Palace" would be the glacier-crowned cordillera itself.

The fundamental message of the letter from "the grandparents" is always that despite everything, the Community remains the Owners' beloved, and that if they promise in good faith to abide by the customary law, the canals will fill with water for one more year. The physical scrap called the "letter" is intentionally destroyed. There is, as one might expect, a taboo on treating the superhuman script as if it were just any text. The "letter" from Mama Catiana and Señor Pencollo is never archived.

FROM ENUMERATION TO NARRATION

Does Tupicocha generate any narrative history, in the usual sense of backward-looking synthetic narrative? It does, but not quite as urban writing arts do. We have already described how historical records accumulate at an hour-by-hour scale. In most cases such work testimonies are entirely prosaic, serving to document accounting of labor. When Mujica was helping build the Willcapampa Canal, a routine 1982 faena left the following imprint:

> We put it on record in the present Book of acts; before the following [members] of this parcialidad of Mojica . . . that we don Cipriano Advincula Capistrano; don Leonidas Dias Romero owe on the work of Anchachi Cliff and Pampa Calato We will come with a peon to the Tuco Cliff stretch—also don Clemente Dias Romero and don Martin Camilo owe just on Pampa Calato—Also Silvano Urbano Alberto Advinculo—A list was taken in the following form—
>
> 4. Clemente Dias Romero   2 stretches Ancachi Pampa
> 5. Cipriano Advincula   2 stretches " "
> 6. Leonidas Dias   1 stretch pampa calato
> 7. Martin Camilo   1 stretch pampa "
> 8. Silbano Urbano Ramos   1 stretch — "
> 9. Alberto Advincula   1 stretch — —— ——
>
> for a faithful record of which we sign to fulfill faithfully [signatures] . . . at Piedra Turco. 8th of September of the year 82 (APM/SAT 07 1982:65)

Multiplied by thousands, such acts make up the largest share of primary sources for the communities and all their corporations.

MEMORIALISM AND THE WRITING OF "LITTLE HISTORY"

The conviction that each increment in the canal system binding society to land and water must be remembered forever is the axis of a "little" local historiography that sticks to a microscopic view. By "little history," we mean an obstinately particularist past-knowledge. It relates to "national history" in a particular way. Tupicocha's microscopic canal histories are independent in origin from the grand narrative (having grown from pre-Hispanic irrigation and khipu technologies). They could have multiplied indefinitely without producing any grand national narrative. And yet at the same time, they are told within context of the national history in a way that informs the meaning of both. "Little history"—what Dipesh Chakrabarty calls "History 2"—"interrupt[s] and punctuate [s]" the grander history of nation and development (2000:64). Making "little history" of canals and the like in the context of introjected legal genres is itself Tupicochans' way of living out state formation.

For example, when Ayllu Segunda Satafasca did a collective workday on a plot, which one member had generously loaned for the good of the common fund, the scribe coupled the work record with a highly colored passage linking the Andean ideology of ancestry with patriotic sentiment:

> We will pay the fines according to the articles of the forward-looking people [*progresistas*] of the fatherland; and the soil we tread today we remember our grandparents the blood loyalty [*sangreatad*,[22] a nonce word] and we are here, the descendents who [go] behind in the shadows of our grandparents; and this job of sowing was scheduled for the date eighteenth of February. (AP2SF/SAT 01: 1935:81–82)

Memorialists sometimes painted on a larger canvas. In 1965, during the early stages of the Willcapampa Canal project, at a moment that was exciting because the Community was about to open the longed-for new water intake, Segunda Satafasca spent July 20 on the freezing heights. The secretary chose a slightly heightened diction:

> On this day Tuesday we woke up and most of us greeted the day with its strong wind as the new dawn arrived, after our breakfast we began our stretch of the place called Panpalancha toward the [canal] intake the place called Ullullcapampa and likewise we broke camp under the immediate order of the President Don Eusebio Ricce Camilo the Vice-president Don Julian Antiporta Rojas the treasurer Saturnino Urbano A. and the other members of the Community directorate, united with the [directorate] from Tuna, and following our stretch we have had lunch in the place Montepate at its foot with the people from Tuna in this way we finished this day with all [crews] just a very small distance short of the intake and when it was five in the afternoon we have rested at "Wullcapampa" site and we sent a committee to bring *guamanripa* [*Senecio tephrosioides*, a valued high-altitude herb] and the ones elected to do it are Don Aníbal Medina and Don Pedro Alberco and Don Antonino Ramos. (AP2SF/SAT 08 1965:6–7)

Even the men sent to gather herbs for tea were elected by formal procedure. Ink was drying on the record of their service before the tea boiled!

A few meters away, on the same day and hour, the people of Mujica wrote in their book:

> On this day Tuesday we have passed the rations around at eight in the morning together with the comuneros of Tuna, and began the stretch of Pampa chancha, to Tucoto. The comuneros from Tuna took responsibility for the meals for the [contracted hydraulic] engineer, and at twelve midday we broke camp under the orders of the Community, Don Eusebio Ricce, Vice-president Don Julián Antiporta Rojas, Treasurer Don Saturnino Urbano, and the other members, after arriving at the intake with our encampment we went back with our crew in the customary way to [join] the members who were following the staked path, and we arrived to the same place, we were only 120 meters short of finishing, since it was already 4 in the afternoon the engineer ordered us to rest, at 5 in the afternoon we and the comuneros from Tuna toasted each other with several cups of nectar [i.e., liquor] and we rested. (APM/SAT 05 1965:81)

No matter how elaborate the prose sections grow, narration and tabulation always proceed in parallel. The secretary who wrote Mujica's detailed act based the names, measures, and hours on the preliminary *relación* in his notebook. At irregular intervals, when he was sure of their correctness, the secretary—shivering as he sat on a boulder—compiled daily checklists in columnar or tabular breakdowns of attendance.

The upshot of the constancia complex is that enumeration and narration go hand in hand. It is easy for any eyewitness to draw from tabulated numbers a narrative of events, the more so given the opportunity to go back and refer to daily minor acts.

Those who have puzzled over how khipus of the Inka Empire recorded *chansons de geste*, or historical summaries, may be pondering a problem that is only problematic if we assume that the art of reading equals the exact sound-for-sound reconstruction of a fixed utterance. To Tupicochanos, the important matter is to express enumerated data in relation to public or moral concerns. The order of deeds and not the sequence of speech sounds is the object of concern. Accuracy can be attained by combining tabular summaries and rearticulating them in a characteristic verbal style.

This art is, of course, no longer practiced with cords. But there is a genre with some parallel properties, the *recuerdo histórico*, or 'historical keepsake.' Recuerdos históricos are composed narratives read out by secretaries and ratified into ayllu books not as a record to establish the facts of the past—that is already done, of course—but of conveying its moral import for the future. Cacarima Ayllu produced a particularly large one when, on February 7, 1949, it "enflowered" itself while working on the walls of Canchuray pasture, and decided that it needed a history of its participation in the then-new Casama dam. Cacarima had been devoting labor days to it intermittently for three years when it wrote:

> The said Casama Dam was begun in the year nineteen forty five . . . on the date fourteen of May of the same year, uniting all the authorities, citizen members, they saw that the old reservoir was very small. [The Community] decided to buy land from Don Mauricio Vilcayaure to do as had been resolved, and so they did it, on the very same day the letter of sale was finalized and took judicial possession to build our Dam.
>
> [An intervening passage describes the meeting at which work rules were set.] They began to make the first wall for the plan in the month of May and next to do the excavation in different ways we as children of the parcialidad of Cacarima began in the same month and [finished?] in the month of June in five days of work, and the people who cooperated in it are: the 1st first day was Monday the twenty first of May. Flavio Laimito, Lidio Huaringa, Justo Ramos Rojas, Cirilo Ramos, Manuel Perales, Augusto Ramos, Marcelino Ramos, Pedro Huaringa.
>
> In the second faena which was Monday the twenty eighth of May of the same year, they were: Manuel Perales, Cirilo Ramos, Agusto Ramos, Fernando Perales, Lidio Huaringa, Justo Ramos Alberco, Pedro Huaringa, Flavio Laimito.
>
> [Similar paragraphs narrate the third through fifth days of faena.]
>
> During this time the Camachico, who was Don Anastasio Velazco, did not accompany us.
>
> At that stage the work was paralyzed for about two months and hardly had it gotten underway again when it ran into the biggest obstacle of all which was the death of the President of the Community Don Lidio Huaringa R.I.P.
>
> Lying abandoned for some years and in what followed the said work began again on the fifth of January of nineteen forty eight and was finished, that is to say our stretch of it, in the way that follows.
>
> On the date fifth of July of the present year all the authorities members and citizens of the Casama dam gathered seeing the disapproval of the President of the Community Don [name omitted] and the lack of

confidence in him they elected a committee called The Committee for the Casama Dam, the citizens elected were as President Don Pedro Alberco Rueda . . . [and other officers, listed]. And thus getting work underway the excavation of the level [bottom] began by squads or crews and it fell to our first crew to work the day Thursday fifteenth of July . . . [additional workdays similarly narrated].

The said work was advancing very slowly and those who were discouraged felt they had to quit the Committee for the Casama Dam. The only one who kept working on it was the Treasurer [i.e., Don Gaspar Laymito] and the *personero jurídico* [i.e., legal spokesman of the corporation] Anselmo Medina Lasca [Lacsa] Ñaupa and the Secretary of the Town of the Community Don Paulino Perez in a meeting with the members of the aforesaid dam on the date of 25 twenty fifth of August and all the citizens in the first round [i.e., of coca, at the morning "custom hour"] requested out loud as if they were one single person that the work be assigned in stretches, and that is how it was done immediately, and our stretch was received by a son of the parcialidad of Pedro Huaringa because the Camachico Don Moises Velazco was not present, and at midday the work began as soon as our stretch was known which measured Two meters forty centimeters in width by twenty three persons at which work only eight persons were present, and the rest not [present], but seeing that it is important all the rest found the energy to arrange it, and so it turned out just as if nobody had been missing we followed on with our stretch . . . [Nine days of faena are narrated.]

During the days that [the sentences] above indicate [the workforce] was employed only on the excavation of the [bottom] level. And not all of the fulfillments were in the form of labor but many of the members gave each other tools such as wheelbarrows, combos [steel digging/cutting tools], and others this was our way of working the days that they sent their tools the personnel did not go as well as some who paid fines on the work day in lieu of work and so it was arranged and the work days fulfilled.

On the date twenty second of October this stretch was received to build the ditch to place the first stones of the foundation, the member Don Agusto Ramos received this stretch because the Camachico Don Moisés Velasco was not present and on this day the ditch was begun and finished and all the members fulfilled their obligations . . .

[A further paragraph narrates the building of the reservoir floor and walls with the help of a contracted master mason, listing dimensions of the "stretch" Cacarima ayllu built.]

After we finished the said work another stretch of the inflow and outlet channels was received the member Don Roperto Ramos received the said stretch and this is on top of the reservoir, it is a total of six meters twenty one centimeters on this stretch

We have spent two days of work which were the days Thursday the eleventh Friday the twelfth of November and seeing that we were only a little bit short of finishing the level we agreed to postpone it in favor of the stretch [of the channels] and this we decided the day Thursday seventeenth of November of the present year, with seventy seven centimeters of width and two meters forty of length toward the cliff pending for each person on the said work of the wall and the channels we have used up nine small sacks of cement for the buying of the cement, explosives, and requests for permission all the comuneros instituted a quota of ten soles of gold and the Treasurer Don Gaspar Espiritu received it. The dimension of the reservoir is twenty five meters length, seventeen meters wide, and the height of the wall is two meters fifty centimeters the canal is sixty meters long. . . .

[The equivalent in money of the supplies and labor is itemized. A list of the names of Cacarima members follows.]

For its validity we sign with our own hands and letters as a sign of truth [rubber stamps] [signatures]. (APC/SAT 02 1949:106–12)

Such keepsake histories are not read out to the public very often, but officials consult them as a basis for their own orations. At the ceremonies to clean Willcapampa Canal in 1993, the president of the Irrigators' Committee gave a speech called "Historical Sketch" in which he remembered early pioneers of the Willcapampa project going as far back as 1892 (APM/SAT 08 1993:41).

COULD CORD RECORDS HOLD THE "LITTLE HISTORY"?

It is not too hard to understand the construction of this "little history." The overall scheme is chronological. The writer relied on padroncillos, or tabular data, summaries giving the apportionment of "stretches" and recording the attendance of members. The raw data have been divided as episode types. Repetitive formulas glue the raw data together, some of these being locally common ideological motifs ("as if we were one person"). Some episode types require statement of multiple variables: for example, the passages which record assignment of stretches contain three physical dimensions, the divisor (i.e., number of "personnel"), the name of the person who received the notification, and an expression of enthusiasm. Similarly, episodes of the labor-day type contain the calendar date and the record of participants, with an optional ordinal number. However, not all contents are stereotyped episodes. The recuerdo histórico also includes explanations of political events which interrupt the regular patterning of work, and explanations of procedures that might not be obvious. The writer did paragraph the narrative, but it is also interesting to break it up by episode type. Since ceremonial enflowered episodes initiate periods of action, they are used here as the major divisors. The episode-type structure is the following:

- Meeting and roster of officers (Community)
  - Political history (land purchase)
  - Dimensions of project, initial
  - Meeting and assignment of "stretches," 1: for excavation
  - 5 labor days or faenas
  - Political history: absence of Camachico, death of Community president
  - Meeting and roster of officers (Committee for the Casama Dam)
  - 3 labor days or faenas
  - Political history: languishing of committee leadership
  - Meeting and assignment of "stretches," 2: continued excavation
  - 8 labor days or faenas
  - Political history: explanation of Cacarima's rule for alternate fulfillment
- Assignment of "stretches," 3: ditch
  - 1 labor day or faena
  - Political history: foundation stone, technical leadership
  - 9 labor days or faenas
- Assignment of "stretches," 4: foundation (refers back to some of preceding faenas)
- Assignment of "stretches," 5: channels and walls
  - 3 labor days or faenas
  - Detail on "stretches"

Materials consumed and per-person payment quota

Final dimensions

Value in labor

Total value in labor and materials

List of participants

Closing formula

Signatures

Stamp

Can one imagine such a body of data being formatted as a Tupicochan khipu, or as one of those famous but ill-understood "historical khipus" of the Inka? Yes, if one is willing to assume mechanisms by which (1) a cord sign indicates an individual, and (2) a cord sign indicates a break in patterned action, including possibly a sign as to what sort of break it is. The narrative is regular enough so that one can imagine a historical khipu being made by some procedure such as (a) assigning physical property to an episode type, for example, gray cord = meeting and assignment of "stretches"; (b) a standardized array of variables including, for example, the date of a labor day and the identities of those present; (c) conventions indicating the presence of a nonpatterned event such as the death of a leader or the breakdown of a directorate. Tupicochan khipus do contain what appear to be "special" notations like a tuft of unspun wool inside a knot or a bright-colored ply. This description approximates the notional "formula" khipus which Ascher and Ascher (1997:75–76) suggested as cord vehicles for episodically structured narrative. If we are ready to suppose that an episodic structure of events, and not a verbal structure describing it, was the object of khipu making, then it is unnecessary to suppose that "historical" khipus would use signs drastically different from those in the "statistical" sort whose numerical properties Locke reconstructed.

The difference between purported "statistical" and "narrative" khipus is likely to lie in, first, the re-sorting and condensing of raw statistical-chronological data, and second, in the enrichment of devices that comment on or allude to the political or moral *singularities* of events. In other words, a historical cord record might likely have retained the basically patterned or preformatted "annals" of "raw data" records, condensed it, and built upon it a more complex qualitative likeness of events, perhaps with showy physical signs such as "marker" tufts. In sum, the narrative work that emerges by recasting numerical data and listings into a prose "keepsake" enshrines past work in a distinctive "romance of the precise."

Along the way, three data-handling habits come into play: First, as already noted, the scribe aggregates data or groups discrete items into series, creating the pattern of regularly accruing events. Second, he adds to the pattern the idiosyncratic and the nonobvious—a death of a leader, an unusual custom—in such a fashion as to alter the texture from the uniformity of the filled grid to the punctuated uniqueness which "histories" peculiarly possess. This process also entails adding in morally dramatic rhetoric, making explicit the homily future generations are supposed to learn. Third, the writer is engaged in a series of "re-entextualizations," as Richard Bauman and Charles L. Briggs call them (1990): transcriptions ascending a gradient of fixity from the provisional list, to the draft table, to the padroncillo of record, to the recuerdo which addressed posterity after the yearly audit has cleared all previous tables.

THREE

A Tale of Two Lettered Cities

Schooling from Ayllu to State

Across the dusty patios of rural schools all over Peru, in the 1990s, platoons of gray-uniformed infant soldiers goose-stepped in wavering squares. From toddler age upward, young villagers acquired the alphabet in what looked like a child-scale boot camp for citizenship. Since 2000, the Education Ministry has deauthorized military drill and promoted a less authoritarian pedagogy. Yet by tacit accord among parents and teachers, marching continues in many places—an ingrained practice rooted in unspoken premises about community and state. "Alphabetization," the never-ending project by which the Ministry of Education conquers and eternally reconquers the purported illiteracy of the countryside, is one of those premises (Portocarrero and Oliart 1989).

So it is interesting to learn that ministerial "alphabetization" is actually a late chapter in the story of rural schooling. The rural school as known today came into being *after* Tupicocha had already developed a substantial written practice, and schools to impart it. The oldest generation still alive remembers how Andean communities made writing their own through autodidact resources, and how they developed a local school system, for both sexes, on the structure of their ayllu organization. The ayllu and community of the early twentieth century called upon the state for support ex post facto, seeking response from what seemed a remote and indifferent center. Only later did the state impose itself as the unique source of literacy. In the schoolhouse of today, teachers trained to see their work as the literary enlightenment of a benighted countryside remain unaware that state schools have marginalized and submerged an older lettered establishment.

In the pages that follow we will trace how Tupicocha village first built schools upon the ancient armature of ayllu organization, then obtained and paid for ministerial education. Ethnographically considered, literacy in Tupicocha becomes a tale of two lettered cities: on one hand the durable legacy of the older scribal model, gradually becoming more democratic and vernacular; and on the other, "standard" literacy projected from the capital city as a project of modernization-from-above. Both projects, of course, carried political freight too important to ignore.

CAPTURING LETTERS: AUTODIDACTS, AYLLUS, AND EARLY SCHOOLING

It was apparently in the later nineteenth century that villagers began to see generalized citizen writing, rather than the services of scribes and notaries, as the answer to their documentary needs. In that era the national state had yet to intervene in the way the village trained its members. Yet Tupicocha and similar villages already had some freestanding schools of their own. When the incomparable field geographer Antonio Raimondi made his detailed survey of Huarochirí in 1862, he found a school already functioning in Tupicocha (with sixty students), and another in San Damián, as well as a *preceptor*, or tutor, in Langa (1945 [1862]:19, 25, 27). In 1892 the prefect of Lima Department observed that the district which includes Tupicocha had four schools for boys and two for girls, and that the residents themselves financed and ran them with only a minor contribution from a nearby municipality (Zavala 1892:138).

In 1876, Peru took a census of its territory with attention to education. In this year, public instruction in rural zones was nonexistent. However, the results showed that one-third of the male indigenous population of Huarochirí already knew how to read and write in 1876 (Peru 1878::253–56). The 1876 census is "pre-Lancasterian." That is, it contains separate reckonings for those able to read and those able to write (and presumably also read). Pre-Lancasterian pedagogy considered reading the prior and elemental skill, with writing an optional advanced course of study. In table 5, the columns labeled *literate* contain the sum of those able only to read, plus those who could read and write.

San Damián district covers the ethnographic area studied intensively here (Tupicocha, Tuna, and adjacent villages). The one-third estimate of

TABLE 5
Huarochirí's 1876 Rates of Literacy, by Districts, with "Leer" and "Escribir" Summed as "Literate"

District (Page in Census)	Literate Men (%)	Literate Women (%)	Literate Total (%)
Carampoma (201)	25.6%	0.3%	11.8%
Casta (206)	15.5%	0.6%	7.3%
Chorrillos (211)	40.8%	12.3%	26.4%
Huarochirí (217)	26.6%	1.3%	13.4%
Matucana (228)	38.8%	7.6%	24.5%
Olleros (229)	16.9%	0.8%	8.1%
Quinti (234)	60.3%	19.1%	28.6%
San Damián (239)	36.9%	1.4%	18.6%
San Mateo (245)	29.6%	4.0%	17.0%
Sta. Eulalia (251)	27.2%	8.7%	19.4%
Province (257)	34.1%	4.1%	18.9%

Source: Peru 1878:201–57.

literacy is an understatement, since the census did not filter out children too young to read. Of the 238 *instruidos* ('literate' men) in San Damián, 210, or 88.2 percent, could write as well as read. The extreme gender inequalities in reading indicate restrictions on literacy instruction, but the span of male literacy seems wide enough to suggest a pervasively literate political process. Strikingly wide variations among districts suggests that their respective internal decisions—to hire teachers, and, in some villages but not others, to teach girls—made them self-governing in their relationship to the written word.

It was amid this scene that the ayllus in Tupicocha started sponsoring a village free school. The village moved to establish a communal school in 1903, and still has receipts for the small sums it paid its contracted teacher. On May 16, 1907, it legislated "to make a school facility in the public plaza" (AMSAT/SAT 06 1907a:14).[1] Before 1910, the Tupicocha community paid San Damián District to let some of its sons go to school there. Although San Damián had higher rank, being a head of district, between 1920 and 1925 it had only minimal schools: a *fiscal* ('government-sponsored') school) offering the first three years, and a short-lived convent school run by the church.

The oldest generation of Tupicochanos now living remembers that before the arrival of ministerial teachers, those who knew how to read and write taught others. Even those who served as teachers were usually autodidacts and quite poor, living on the bare margin of respectability. "Contracted teachers" often worked for a few sacks of potatoes and other payment in kind. Andean villages welcomed and treasured comuneros who brought literacy back from their military service, or who learned it as helpers to the clergy or to merchants or landlords. A few learned writing in prison. Sometimes, on a benevolent whim, townspeople who employed "Indian" servants or house porters allowed them to sit in on their children's tutoring. When such pupils returned home, they too were able to teach. Huarochirí was not one of the regions where repression by hostile latifundists made it necessary to smuggle the alphabet in as contraband and "read by moonlight" (Salomon and Apaza 2006:313). But it did rely on its own resources in the first stages of schooling.

Tupicocha's first school was an extension of ayllu organization.[2] Mobilizing these kinship corporations, with their ancient roots, as "teams," the village established a school in the traditional ritual and assembly precinct called the Collca. The term Collca is a Hispanized form of the Inka-era word for storehouse. The Collca is the place where the ayllus still display their khipus in the annual Huayrona, or town meeting. Situating the alphabet literally in the place of the khipus may reflect the post–War of the Pacific generation's feeling that schooling should carry on the colonial-Andean mode of ayllu documentation in a new medium. These self-built schools eventually did obtain recognition by the Ministry of Education. On November 2, 1907, municipal papers report a visit to *Escuela de Niños* ('Boys' Primary School') No. 4432 directed by Sr. Felipe Sotelo. In August of the same year the corresponding girls' school is reported closed (AMSAT/SAT 06 1907b:17, 1907c:22).

In the 1920s through 1940s, many decisions about the school were taken by the village council acting as "indigenous community." The census of 1940 reflects important gains in literacy (Peru 1941:68, 75). At community level, debate constantly centered on the building of a new mixed school or, alternatively, the building of twin classrooms for girls and boys (AMSAT/SAT 06 1907b:17–18). From 1928 on the papers refer to two schools—the male Escuela Elemental de Varones No. 4432 and the female Escuela de Mujeres No. 4433—with both directors signing (AMSAT/SAT 06, 1940:190). But their activities were planned in common, and usually the same homework was assigned in both. A *patronato escolar* ('school trusteeship') was organized on July 3, 1942 (ACCV/SAT 1942:5), and it acquired a lot in Cosanche (immediately outside the village) to build a demonstration farm for teaching agronomic technology. The next year the "Indigenous Community," now a recognized corporation, donated a lot to build a school gymnasium.

The school for girls was functioning toward 1927, when a committee was formed to organize a book fair for November 10, 1928. This celebration inaugurated the school library (AMSAT/SAT 06 1903–44:f. 113).

The ayllus or kinship corporations provided the armature of school support. When a teacher had to move house from a neighboring village, the ayllus were to provide the mules and workers. The work was divided according to the traditional rank order of the ayllus, as already described in the 1608 Quechua Manuscript of Huarochirí. Ayllus Allauca, Satafasca, Huangre, and Mojica agreed to supply a donkey, while Chaucacolca y Cacarima ayllus were to guarantee enough workers to carry out the move to Tupicocha (AMSAT/SAT 06 1903–44:f. 87). Such logistical matters were no small obligations. In more recent times, when severe rains caused flash floods closing the road, teachers were forced to walk "ten hours to reach Tupicocha to carry out their turns by the roster" (ACCV/SAT 1972).[3]

THE LORE OF LITERACY: MODEL BOOKS, CALLIGRAPHY GUIDES, AND PRIMERS

In the era of autodidacticism and village-built schooling, where did campesinos get their ideas of correct writing? They tapped into a tradition of model books and pattern guides rooted in the oldest strata of the "lettered city." Manuscript books produced in ayllus and other institutions predating state schools long continued to show traces of colonial influence: peculiarities of rural writing are often demotic variants on the scripts of the lettered city.

The deeper history of Spanish colonial writing, therefore, shaped rural writing habits. The most influential print prototype for colonial calligraphy and scribal form was Juan de Iciar's 1550 *Most Subtle Art, through Which One Learns to Write Perfectly* (1960 [1550]).[4] Phillip II of Spain (reigned 1556–98), who presided over the Toledan reform of Peruvian government, promoted scribal standards and archiving so doggedly as to be remembered as the *papelero* ('paper-shuffling') and *escritófilo* ('script-loving') monarch. By enforcing with suffocating rigidity the production of records about every transaction of state, church, and commerce, his regime set early precedents for Tupicocha's intensely documentary habits (Castillo Gómez 1999a:25–27).

The American diffusion of Iberian primers was massive by any standard and spectacular for its era:

> Fortunately, we know the press runs of the primers sold by the Cathedral of Valladolid from 1588 to 1781. The total—54,250,600—is astonishing. Given that a large share of them, perhaps the majority, were taken to America, it is impossible to know how many stayed in the [Iberian] peninsula. Nonetheless two things are clear. One is their short use life, because of loss, damage, wear and tear or dismemberment. The other is that the average of 28,091 primers sold yearly from 1588 to 1781 hides important differences between periods of rising sales (1624–1659, 1660–1696, and 1724–1781) and stagnant or falling years (1600–1623, 1697–1723).[5] (Viñao Frago 1999:65–66)

As writing grew in visibility and potency, formal traits began to receive wider attention. Everything that could contribute to fixing political meaning in script, such as styles that manifested elite origin or the visible identity signs of those asserting power, became iconic of royal power (as architecture did also). Details of handwriting, the style of composition, formulaic protocols, and the aesthetic *afeytamiento* ('grooming') of script came to be matters of substance. They still are to a substantial degree in rural society. It was correct, though unusual, to tear up immediately any written provision not in good handwriting (Castillo Gómez 1999a:28–29).

Handwriting styles in Spain caught the interest of the various royal courts, which over time showed preference for different forms. While Aragón preferred a more legible style, like the one fashionable in Italy at the time and known to modern readers as italic, Castile adopted the less convenient styles called *cortesana* ('courtly') and *procesal* ('procedural'). These made the reading of Castilian texts more difficult for outsiders to the state's subculture. Emilio Cotarelo Yori defines the procesal text as "a round hand written somewhat capriciously, with notably little care, and with an extreme tendency toward ligature" (cited in Viñao Frago 1992:66).[6] When written quickly, procesal yielded texts with all the words on a line ligatured to each other, making reading harder. Indeed the very tendency toward difficult writing fomented the ever greater production of manuals from 1548 on. Writing became the well-defended province of instructors and scribes (Gimeno Blay 1999; Viñao Frago 1992). By the second half of the eighteenth century, it proved difficult to satisfy demand for primers and school readers, and to satisfy it the Royal Press itself undertook production of primers (Viñao Frago 1992:55). Among the most influential guides to graphic protocol was the *Manual de escribientes* ('Writers' Manual') of Antonio de Torquemada (ca. 1552).[7] It laid down practices that became standard for the internal work of the emerging modern state. It imposed remarkable uniformity all the way to the remote outliers of the empire (Egido 1995; Gimeno Blay 1999). Other manuals also seem to have contributed to the durable setting of imperial graphic norms. One of them was made especially for notaries by the Mexican Nicolás de Irolo Calar 1996 (1605) and entitled *La política de escrituras* ('The Proper Use of Writs').

Because of anxiety about their titles, tribute rolls, lawsuits, and accounts, rural Andean people have historically been attentive to the multiplying material stigmata of authenticity in documentation. Tupicochan villagers command a wide variety of formulas derived from these old scribal arts. They are particularly demanding about seals (today rubber stamps), signatures, *rúbricas* (complex flourishes beneath signatures, which are taken as signs of authenticity), kinds of paper, and handwriting styles. Although schoolroom handwriting has now become common, villagers are still fascinated by these older signs and when handling old volumes during inventory enjoy poring over them.

Attitudes about writing still bear the impress of one norm-setting book which proved immensely influential in many Spanish-speaking countries: *El Mosaico* ('The Mosaic'; Bastinos and Puig 1927 [1866]). This amazingly durable classic (the 1941 version being its fifty-seventh edition, according to Spain's National Library) is a compendium of sample manuscripts designed to show how one reads and accurately copies various genres of texts, using different commercial and legalistic hands and styles. The copy which Tupicocha used and still possesses bears on its title page the imprint of "54th edition," and the legend "Literary Letter Book for Exercising Children in the Reading of Manuscripts . . . A Collection of Autograph Texts by Certain Famous Men of Our Time and by Distinguished Literary Figures, Teachers, Businessmen, Industrialists, etc. A Work Declared as [instructional] Text in the [Iberian] Peninsula, Cuba and Puerto Rico, and in the Republics of Eastern Argentina, Peru, and Guatemala."[8] It consists of a section of letters, a literary section, a commercial section with model letters and business documents, a part on accounts, and finally a miscellany of geographic, historical, and commercial information with letters that describe such cities as Rome, Paris, Hamburg, Havana, and Manila. It bears an 1870 nihil obstat of the archbishop of Lima. Copies of *El Mosaico* are treasured as heirlooms. Elderly people tell us that after beginning with the alphabet, they developed their abilities further by copying texts from it.

In contrast to cosmopolitan and academic society, which sees paleography as a byword for esoteric and impractical interests, Andean villagers see paleography as a useful achievement well within the sphere of public interest. Because command of local titles and lawsuits was the path to leadership for villagers in an age when peasants were first learning to defend their own writs, legal and archaic literacy counted for more than did contemporary literary genres (Chartier 1999:103). *Pasivos* (that is, semiretired community members) recall, emotionally moved, how "before the school was official (with instructors sent from Lima), someone who knew how to read the *Mosaico* would teach the others to read and write it. Some who knew how would even teach the others how to decipher and copy very ancient [colonial] documents" (Don Alberto Vilcayauri Medina, born in 1924, speaking in August 2004).[9] At least one woman, Isabel Llaullipoma, is remembered affectionately as one of the early experts and teachers of *Mosaico*. Today, in Tupicocha the word *mosaico* means any archaic writing. Tupicochans say that "learning mosaico" became their ancestors' main resource for learning to manage "Latin" and old Spanish, and thereby enabled them to create forceful documentation about their village's land rights.

Members of the elder and the middle generation speak of *El Mosaico* almost with reverence, as if it were one of the sacred writings (like the "Book of the Thousand" and the Christian scriptures). This may have to do with the fact that people see the learning of literacy as related to catechism. The Community's copy of *El Mosaico* (see figure 48) is held by an elder who in the past taught catechism.

A few other books are held in special esteem for having helped villagers learn to write in more recent times. Everybody remembers clearly the

48. In 2005 this 1927 copy of *El Mosaico* was in possession of a Tupicochan elder.

texts with which he or she was taught, and people smile as they recall passages from them. Among those which Tupicochans remember and still own is a copy of *El Libro de la Escuela Elemental Peruana* ('The Book of the Peruvian Primary School'; Guzmán y Valle 1923) which served the early teacher Don Modesto Alberco. His descendants regard it as an heirloom. In a handwritten note he says he started to use this textbook in 1930. *El Libro de la Escuela Elemental Peruana* served to teach initial reading by syllabification, and to impart moral, religious, and nationalist messages.[10]

Alberco's volume or one like it may have influenced the only important primer written by a local man. It all but saturated the early literacy experience of the generation which now holds senior village posts. This is *Espejito* ('Little Mirror'), composed by a teacher from the provincial capital of Huarochirí, Don Sixto Cajahuaringa Inga (1907–2003). A son of the province, Cajahuaringa began to teach in the provincial capital in 1932–37. He served a long career as a teacher in rural schools, during which he took some part in the scholastic-indigenist current chapter 6 discusses. His book *Espejito* appeared in several printings without dates, but they appear to be from 1940–50. A second volume of *Espejito*, for second grade, was also printed without date, but allusions and symbols in it, particularly images of the "rebel Inka" Túpac Amaru II and a mention of President Juan Velasco Alvarado (1968–73), indicate the period of military-nationalist "revolution from above."

We interviewed Cajahuaringa Inga near the end of his life. Lodged with his emigrant children in a smoggy district of inner Lima, he roused himself from his sofa to riffle old pages and recall that he saw teaching as a vocation to enable nonviolent rural self-defense. He could not remember how he chose the title—nor is this explained in his printed memoir—but it seems related to the long popularity in Peru of devotional books using the mirror metaphor.[11] The archives of Cajahuaringa's publisher show that *Espejito* enjoyed long success.[12] Why? Both the first-level and second-level *Espejitos* tell children that literacy is a service to the country and, at the same time, that literacy will strengthen them against a crooked society: "My son, now that you can read and write, nobody will be able to fool you" (Cajahuaringa Inga and Teresa de Cajahuaringa n.d.:[pages not numbered]120). The second *Espejito* said "Our slogan is STUDY IN ORDER TO NEVER LET OURSELVES BE FOOLED" (Cajahuaringa Inga n.d.[pages not numbered]:25). These regionally produced books remained very popular until the ministry imposed *Coquito* as the only approved text. *Coquito* is a primer for reading and writing widely marketed all over Latin America and edited so as to be "neutrally" middle-class and urban, without any manifest national, ethnic, political, or religious bent.[13]

Huarochirí is not among the Peruvian provinces that have experienced epidemic agrarian bloodshed. Its ideology of literacy never bonded with insurgency as did that of Azángaro and other provinces of the southern highlands, where local icons include a roaring puma holding a schoolbook and an infuriated peasant crowd brandishing books instead of rifles (Salomon and Apaza 2006). But Cajahuaringa's ideology of writing as a weapon of self-defense proved persuasive. Even now it outshines any association with literary pleasure or cultural distinction as a motive for study.

STATE PROJECTS FOR "ALPHABETIZING" THE COUNTRYSIDE

Cajahuaringa was a countryman who made his career in the state. He brings us to the other half of the story: the state as protagonist in the shaping of rural ways with letters.

Both the centralist ideology of the newborn republican state (1821–25) and its meager budgets pushed it to prioritize urban schools, meaning those of the capital and the then-small cities from which the departments were governed. José de San Martín proclaimed Lancasterian (concurrent reading and writing) curricula to be a republican agenda (Fonseca 2001). But in rural archives, it is hard to find any actual traces of rural public schooling before the War of the Pacific (1879–84; Encinas 1986 [1932]:62). "Slow, extremely slow, was the educational process of our country" wrote R. Mac-Lean y Estenós (1944:293). The war of independence produced such chaos it was impossible to advance any kind of education in the short term. Simón Bolívar merged two existing schools in Lima under the name of Convictorio de Bolívar with the intention of offering the old indigenous elites education, and he also set up a "Lancasterian School" for women (Guerra Martinière and Leiva Viacava 2001:11–14). Yet only after 1850, when President Ramón Castilla's government produced a general regulation for instruction, did the state take responsibility for standards and levels. The 1872–76 presidency of Manuel Pardo set rules for school infrastructure, but construction was never well funded (Guerra Martinière and Leiva Viacava 2001:19, 45, 48, 61, 80, 94).

In 1879 Chile attacked Peru and inflicted a crushing defeat. Peruvian elites suffered consternation over the "national question," that is, the realization that the "national" state born out of the Spanish Empire's richest and most prestigious province had crumpled under military pressure from a less richly endowed republic. Many thought the heart of the problem to be an "Indian question." The Indian question was formulated as the presence of immense "backward" masses unequipped to contribute to the "nation." This debate coincided with the heyday of scientific racism.

Much Lima opinion quickly embraced the idea that a racial deficit dragged the state down. A few, notably among Cuzco's provincial elite, argued that the deficit was institutional rather than racial. Early indigenists, from 1903 onward, maintained that the state inherited an obligation to redeem "Indians" from their "degenerate" condition and restore Inka greatness. This debate resonated throughout the twentieth century.

During the last two decades of the nineteenth century and the first two of the twentieth, the heirs of a government restored to sovereignty amid postwar ruin prioritized education as a project of unification destined to overcome the racial "handicap." But it was slow going. In 1890, when law theoretically required schooling in all municipalities with 200 or more inhabitants, the actual number of schools registered nationwide was 844, including night and Sunday schools (Mac-Lean y Estenós 1944:319). The "aristocratic republic" of 1899–1919, so named by Jorge Basadre in recognition of its domination by moneyed civilian lineages, promoted the project of a "modern" and "civilized" Peru, defined as one equipped with widespread education, a unified judiciary, and a national system for hygiene and sanitation. Town schools multiplied rapidly in the early twentieth century, and some young villagers traveled to them. In 1913, a ministerial report claimed 56,879 "indigenous" primary school students (31.97 percent) out of 177,941 children matriculated nationwide (Mac-Lean y Estenós 1944:553). Instruction came to be the cornerstone of civilian patriotic ideology. National education budgets grew by 700 percent between 1900 and 1919. In three decades education expenses grew more than sixteenfold (Contreras 1996:6–8). To be educated meant, of course, to partake only of "white," urban Catholic mores.

Building of schools in small towns by the ministry did not become widespread until the 1920s. Even then, the policy of building schools in municipalities with "head of district" rank meant that children from outlying villages, who were perceived as racially unacceptable, had less access. Elders who remembered the era said "Indians" were unwelcome in such schools. Although President Augusto Leguía's two presidencies set about to modernize "Indians" through separate paternalist entities, such as the Patronato de la Raza Indígena ('Trusteeship of the Indian Race,' founded in 1922), fast-growing school enrollments during his regime (from 195,000 in 1920 to 313,000 in 1930; Klaren 2000:242) reflected his policy of serving the emergent commercial middle class, much more than peasant schooling.

Daniel Hazen (1974) has shown how in Puno Department, these same years so favorable to town schooling, produced rage among rural people shut out by class and racial exclusions. The 1900s through 1920s witnessed waves of fierce agrarian uprisings against expanding estates. Demands for public schooling almost always figured in these battles. The rebels' sympathizers in the southern Andes—socialists, anarchists, syndicalists, and leftist indigenists, but also Adventist missionaries (Teel 1989)—propounded universal rural literacy in a way that brought it uncomfortably close to agrarian radicalism, and indeed both Peru and Bolivia saw the growth of experimental rural schools explicitly dedicated to revolution. Regional elites and their agents blamed *indios leídos* ('reading Indians') for fomenting fights about land titles. Lima's "political class" saw rural education as a double-edged sword. Praised as the vehicle of economic modernization, it was also feared as the harbinger of defiance. Already in the 1920s, and even more so as the Right seized the tiller of state in the late 1930s, "indigenous education" became acceptable to Lima only under less destabilizing premises. Ministers of education vacillated between programs for segregated, culturally differentiated indigenous schooling and programs for uniform indoctrination, but saw both as paths toward the production of "citizens" who would absorb "mestizo" culture and Spanish language at the expense of Andean lifeways that educators saw as primitive and violent.

How to square the circle of educating the countryside without agitating it? At the national level, the Ley Orgánica de Educación ('Educational Organization Law') of 1940, and Manuel Prado's 1939–45 presidency redefined the "Indian Problem" away from the whole matter of indigeneity. No longer were "low cultural level," racial inferiority, and degraded habits the main concern. Rather the problem could be redefined as part and parcel of an economically inadequate premodern rural order. Neither undercapitalized, predatory estates nor neglected villages seemed capable of productive growth. "Indians" became a regional pariah class to be redirected toward development and modernity. They were described as culturally archaic populations in need of utilitarian enlightenment, and misperceived as isolated folk disconnected from the state. "Alphabetization" (in Spanish, of course) would redeem the Indian as person and as citizen. During and after the Second World War, presidents gave at least lip service to building a school system which would saturate the whole of society. In the poor and turbulent department of Puno, for example, at the end of Prado's mandate in 1945, public schools numbered 450.

As Brooke Larson (2003) has emphasized, educators fired up the old indigenist idea that Indian peasants needed a remedial, and separate educational regimen in the 1940s and '50s because they perceived urban-oriented education as an invitation to cityward migration and to politicization, rather than to rural development. Alphabetization figured as a sort of secular conversion. For regions where Quechua or Aymara was spoken, the Prado regime mobilized *Brigadas de Culturización Indígena* ('Indigenous Culturizing Brigades') modeled on Mexican prototypes. These educational caravans traveled the Quechua countryside preaching developmentalist modernity. Trucks crisscrossed the high plain booming from loudspeakers sermons against coca-leaf chewing and in favor of mechanized agriculture (Hazen 1974:263, 292–302). From 1944 to 1945 Brigadas Alfabetizadoras ('Literacy Brigades') replaced them, attempting to speed up learning through bilingual night school short courses, to little effect.

The United States embassy shared Lima's anxiety about situations of potential revolution. In Peru and neighboring countries, this brought about a strange alliance between North American "progressive" education and assimilationist indigenism. In 1945 President José Luis Bustamante followed a Bolivian example (Larson 2003:197–203), inviting intervention by educational reformers from the United States. A United States–Peruvian advisory commission called Servicio Cooperativo Peruano Norteamericano de Educación (SECPANE; 'Peruvian–North American Cooperative Education Service') made its home in the Education Ministry. The commission drew on North American personnel ranging from Protestant Evangelical missionaries to progressive pragmatist followers of John Dewey and Columbia Teachers' College. Its sponsors intended to dilute the association of rural education with radicalism and out-migration by introducing development-oriented and technocratic training in the bosoms of villages. Its most ambitious program proposed a whole new kind of school: Núcleos Escolares Campesinos (NEC; 'Peasant Schooling Centers'). These agricultural-technical and "home economics" boarding schools were to be inserted directly inside "indigenous" settlements. The NEC would upgrade the peasantry in its place, focusing pupils on immediate productive and sanitary improvements rather than remote revolutionary utopias. Transitional bilingual teaching would wash out Quechua in favor of national "mestizo" culture. But some Peruvian educators had other aims, and they too made their mark within SECPANE: when Bustamante chose as his education minister Luís Valcárcel, indigenism's most prestigious spokesman, Valcárcel in turn opened ministry doors to pioneering Quechuists such as Julián Palacios Ríos and Manuel Núñez

Butrón. In some villages one can still see the ruins of NEC pharmacies, classrooms, showers, and guinea-pig hutches. Those who knew the NECs remember them as problematic because they required parents to take part in ways that disrupted the agropastoral round.

In the later cold war era, agrarian turbulence forced centrist politicians to at last attend to some peasant claims. Fernando Belaúnde Terry's first presidency (1963–68) is not remembered by urbanites as a radical one, but agropastoralists in the Sierra de Lima recall it as a time of immense change. Belaúnde at last negotiated the dissolution of some giant estates, and he financed a surge of rural school-building (Viza Yucra 1977). His regime took no interest in any distinctive "indigenous education." Linguists who called on educators to acknowledge multilingualism were treated as dreamers. But in villages to which the state had long turned a deaf ear, the arrival of these cookie-cutter schools counted as an answer at last. Many people in middle age at the time of our fieldwork went to such schools and remember their foundings as benchmarks for rural progress.

Universal compulsory education for rural residents did not come into effect until 1969, the beginning of the military-nationalist revolutionary regime of President Juan Velasco Alvarado. At that time, Tupicocha's men were already about four-fifths literate. Aiming to co-opt the "classist" social theory of Velasco's leftist rivals, as well as to supplant any residue of ethnic ideology, *velasquista* educators suppressed the term *indigenous* and installed *campesino* as the prescribed identity. Ministerial teachers imbued with Marxist social theory at teachers' colleges and led by the Communist union Sindicato Unitario de Trabajadores en la Educación del Perú (SUTEP; 'Unified Syndicate of Education Workers in Peru') took to heart the idea of schools as transformative vanguards. From 1973 to 1976 Velasco's successors, barely keeping the bridle on rebellious SUTEP, attempted a shock-worker plan for rapid educational growth called ALFIN, but it proved disappointing. Then the economic slump of the 1980s dropped schools and teachers into poverty. Ever more numerous schools with ever poorer and more disillusioned teachers provided fertile ground for the Shining Path insurgency of 1982–92. Tupicocha's school itself was never in combat. But Shining Path guerrillas with help from teachers seized a school in a nearby hamlet, Guangri. It overlooked a narrow defile of the main road to Lima and figured in Shining Path's "ring of iron" campaign to assault and choke off Lima-bound commercial traffic.

After the highland insurgency was crushed in 1992, during Alberto

49. In the 1980s, leftist-nationalist teaching glorified insurgent "Inka" patriot-peasants. Francisco Inca was a 1750 neo-Inka rebel active in Huarochirí. Note the *khipu* near his head. The blood-dripping legend says, "In memory of our martyrs of Huarochirí." In his right hand, he grips the pre-Hispanic star-headed war club. The rainbow flag (left) is an "invented tradition" known as the "Inka Flag." Under it is a Quechua cliché quoted from Inca Garcilaso de la Vega. This mural was painted over about 2000.

Fujimori's authoritarian presidencies (1990–2000), fading school murals on revolutionary themes (see figure 49) lingered while educational doctrine shifted to the production of more individualist and upward-aspiring, technologically minded students. President Alejandro Toledo (2001–6) aligned himself, up to a point, with the new, culturally pluralist program called "intercultural education," developed with able help from Germany's aid agency GTZ. But his reforms did not extend to disturbing centralist administration of schools.

THE SCHOOL AS VISIBLE BODY OF THE STATE

And how did villagers engage these shifting state projects? Two or three generations ago Tupicochans, like many villagers, responded to antirural education priorities by sending delegations to make functionaries notice their self-propelled schooling efforts (Degregori 1994). Seeking out the state, when the state did not want to hear from peasants, was a matter of networking, fundraising, small-scale lobbying, and knocking on doors. In 1943 three expatriate "children of the village" mobilized the Cultural Club of Tupicochans Resident in Lima to procure Ministry sponsorship for Rural School 457, offering five years of instruction. The first teacher appointed in Lima, Misael Rosado Anchilía, arrived in Tupicocha in 1944 with his wife, Rosa Tello de Rosado,[14] who also taught there. (Their surnames suggest they were from nearby places.) Manuel Prado's presidency, as noted, had proclaimed attention to rural priorities, and in 1945 *El Comercio*, the most influential of Peruvian newspapers, together with villagers, gave Prado exaggerated but politically opportune credit for Tupicocha's new "Rural School."[15] The local municipality also joined in, with forty soles for each of the twin schools, while the Indigenous Community promised a counterpart donation to be determined later (AMSAT/SAT 07 1944:f. 25). Because it signified long-awaited attention from the national state, this ceremony was much remembered.

Don Alberto Vilcayauri Medina, who was an early ministerial teacher in Tupicocha and in the nearby villages of Antioquía and Carampoma between 1943 and 1951, recollected that in these years of scholastic poverty classes gathered in Collcas, or Andean ceremonial centers, and in the community assembly room. The books of acts from that era evoke rugged learning conditions: "the community hall, where the Boys' and Girls' Schools numbers 457 and 464 are now functioning [is] not yet finished because our community and municipal income is insufficient and [needed] only for other expenses, of lesser size." (AMSAT/SAT 07 1955:70).[16] The ongoing work of building schools continued to be carried on by the ancient ayllus. Records of 1943 show the ayllus assuming "stretches" of work on the walls of school no. 457 (APUCh/SAT 03 1943:199). It took a long time for state inputs to match proclamations.

The physical infrastructure here as elsewhere grew, in effect, as the community's gift to the state, insofar as unpaid common labor days erected them. In 1949, the provincial government set aside 1,000 soles to buy these school's desks and supplies. But from 1970 to 1974 earthquakes wrecked the provisional schoolhouse, and it became necessary to discuss building an "Education Center" (meaning a single large precinct to contain schools of all levels). The committee to realize this plan started work in 1976. In 1977, again recurring to the pre-Hispanic system of *chuta* or *trecho* for parceling collective tasks among the ayllu segments, the Community (now styled "Peasant" rather than "Indigenous") set about to build what has remained the village's largest single public work (APM/SAT 04: 1977b:51).

From about 1970 on—that is, from the era of military-nationalist "revolution from above"—direction of Tupicocha's schools by Lima functionaries became increasingly unilateral. In 1971 Tupicocha was directed to combine the boys' and girls' schools. In 1981 it acquired the name it still bears, César A. Vallejo National Mixed School, in honor of a poet (1892–1938) who is justly considered a glory of the nation. Parents who had hoped to express more local allegiances by naming the school in honor of the village's patron Saint Andrew were frustrated when ministerial authorities invoked a law making names of saints or living persons ineligible (ACCV/SAT 1983). The ministry upgraded Tupicocha's school to include secondary levels (1977), and also installed *prekínder,* or day care, for children three to five years of age. (Day care is considered important because long "vertical" treks to high pastures or canyon-side terraces keep agropastoralists away from the village during daylight hours. State babysitting combats the allegedly harmful practice of bringing toddlers along.)

Peru has no legal entity such as the self-taxing school districts of the United States, but villages do in effect tax themselves to support schools. While the government payrolls the school, provides supplies, and intermittently pays engineers for building work, villagers in *faenas* still do the actual construction and maintenance. There is also an undeclared monetary levy: festival sponsors (*mayordomos* of the patron saints) pay for the expensive components (window frames, plumbing, etc.), using donations from devotees. Parents wield no institutional means to influence the conduct of schooling. Many take part in a parent-teacher association called the Asociación de Padres de Familia (APAFA, 'Parents' Association') which is administered as a school fundraising network.

Toward 2000, schools were poorly funded, but hardly short-staffed. In 1994 San Damián—with 1,990 inhabitants, of whom 684 were between five and nineteen (INEI 1994:201)—had 18 primary school teachers and 13 *colegio,* or middle-high school teachers, yielding a class size of about 22. The ratio of students to teachers is falling even lower as children of peasants migrate to Lima. Peru's public-sector teachers as of 2006 numbered about 320,000 employees in some 60,000 schools.

Rural teachers, badly paid, routinely suffer privations. A young couple who teach with idealism and brio at San Damián School lived in the 1990s in a building the villagers had abandoned because they foresaw that the next earth tremor would knock it into the abyss. Teachers usually request urban assignments, so small towns get the least experienced, and often least talented, teachers. Unpromoted teachers who work in villages they dislike tend to show their feelings. Villagers complain bitterly of bad classroom behavior, including drinking on school days, absenteeism, sexual misconduct, and ethnic abuse ("disrespect"). During the licensed rule of folly that comes with the rainy-season ritual cycle, costume dancers stingingly satirize teachers for bribe taking or sheer dumbness.

The governmentalization of education has put great social distance between teachers and comuneros. Despite their poverty, rural teachers feel a strong sense of urban selfhood. They segregate themselves in almost caste-like ways. Most do not socialize with campesinos except when the school itself is the host. Teachers tend to see themselves as a selflessly austere corps of leaders on missions among "illiterate," racially and culturally deficient people. Most pointedly absent themselves from festivals or Andean rituals that are important to peasants. Through their powerful union, SUTEP, teachers long gave at least verbal obeisance to a sectlike antique Marxism which campesinos regarded as self-serving and obsolete. A substantial number of teachers individually reject SUTEP's subculture and discipline, sympathizing with either leftist-populist or neoliberal programs. In the 2000s, a series of much-resented and mostly failed strikes weakened SUTEP's grip on education.

Unmistakably, teachers have become the most visible body of the state throughout the countryside. In many villages, teachers live in special hostels which help them cut down on costs but also cut down on contact with pupils' families. Teachers dress differently, in a hyperurban style, striving to keep shoes glossy and neckties straight amid mud and dust. Some female teachers topple along on high heels, struggling with uneven cobbles. Nearly all married teachers leave their spouses and children in Lima, and unmarried ones conduct their entire social lives in Lima. Their epic commutes are exhausting and costly to all concerned. But teachers see them as logical extensions of their vocation, which is to embody and enforce in the countryside the cultural model set by the capital.

On Fiestas Patrias, the national patriotic festival whose climactic day is July 28, the school becomes the focal institution of the village, much more so than the *gobernación*, which officially represents the state. Teachers become temporary leaders, somewhat as the Curcuches, or sacred clowns, do when they act as lords of misrule in the rainy season festival. School officials make stern speeches about the unity of community and nation, hurrying about in suits as they muster children in military procession. That the proposal for "unity" means unity on urban terms is accepted as part of normality, neither resented nor applauded.

Thus state unilateralism has lodged official literacy at a great social distance from peasantry. But the teacher corps contains a few figures with local commitments. Some teachers (mostly female, and mostly at grade-school level) request assignment to their hometowns so they can care for their elders. With advancing seniority, these educators become deep-rooted, influential local citizens. Such rooted teachers are the ones able to build up parent-teacher solidarity. Some, especially those who rise to become school directors, achieve local eminence. Educator-returnees are an unrecognized mainstay of whatever legitimacy the Ministry of Education enjoys in the countryside.

Teachers' dramatic self-differentiation is intended to convey a tacit message about hierarchy: "this is the better way." Textbooks also convey explicit icons of racial and class codes (Portocarrero and Oliart 1989). Older ones (Castillo Morales n.d.:203), still in the school library, feature illustrations of Peruvians classified by race in a pyramid of civilization, with "Indios" and "Negros" shown lowest and nude. More recent books, however, focus less on phenotype and emphasize hierarchies of achievement. Some treat the impoverishment of the countryside with sociological candor, and others accommodate regional cultural practices. Under the presidency of Alejandro Toledo (2001–6) approved "intercultural" material in Quechua began to appear in some regions. Current curriculum norms (2008–2010) afford a module in which teachers are asked to teach about the local culture. Most teachers say they are willing, but hard put to do so, because they lack prepared relevant materials.

The schools' grip on villages derives less from their educational function than from another, unacknowledged function: schools are what archaeologists call "ceremonial centers." School spectacle is more effective than curriculum in giving the state cultural presence. Teachers put an enormous share of their time and supplies into patriotic pageants, folkloristic shows in honor of civic holidays, and soccer tournaments. Parents labor and pay devotedly to make sure their children march with splendid paper lanterns or dance in adorable mock-traditional costumes.

Outside evaluators look askance at the resulting shrinkage of curricular hours. But critics are unable to account for the fact that ceremony is the part of school life comuneros most enthusiastically approve. If it were not for the legal obligation to school their children, many families say, they would spend little time in such settlements as Tupicocha. The corporation of the commons would then be neglected, and small towns would depopulate more than they have done. School festivals turn this obligation into pleasurable solidarity and indirectly help the commons.

Overblown graduation ceremonies form the climax of ceremonial cycles at the schools. Kindergartners or even preschoolers completing their first year are honored with full academic pomp, including caps and gowns, urns of festive food from each home, portraits and costly diplomas in fake-leather binders, and dance costumes for infantile replicas of regional or local "customs" (see chapter 6). Parents invest extensive work decorating the schoolhouse, and spend burdensome sums on photos, diploma frames, and regalia. School pomp also entails all-night partying for adults, including grandparents. These events are popular and prominent in village life. They function as the first step bonding the children into age sets. By the time children graduate from primary school, their school cohorts take shape as social networks cross-cutting the ayllus and easing cooperation among them. School-based age sets also network the village's diaspora with its stay-at-home campesinos. And the sight of toddlers in tiny suits and gowns clutching diplomas delights parents as a visible promise of their future in a more prosperous, less stigmatizing urban milieu.

Still teachers, like most state personnel, shun the actual traditional governance of the village. They tend to drastically underestimate the vitality of its writing culture, or if they do notice it, belittle it as idle, backward-looking *papeleo* ('paper-shuffling'). Imbued with the rigid prescriptivism of the older Spanish linguistic establishment (see chapter 5), they take the nonstandard spelling and syntax characteristic of village papers as proofs of educational failure.

Sometimes they vent damning public judgments. In a village bordering Tupicocha, a public health nurse, indignant about local reception of her teaching, posted a flier calling the community "80 percent illiterate." She was, of course, mistaken; the census at the time registered about 10 percent illiteracy. The resulting furor was so hot the mayor had to shut down the health post temporarily and petition for her replacement.

BOOK OWNERSHIP AND LIBRARIES

How much of a village's "bibliosphere" belongs to the state orbit, and how much to other circuits? Encounters between readers and the printed sources which embody normative writing habits have different results depending on who owns the books and where they are.

The privately owned book, as Jean-Marc Buigues points out in studying early-modern libraries, was often a working instrument but even its mere presence conferred symbolic distinction (1995:405). This effect lingers. In the Peruvian countryside, to keep more than a few cheap and basic or officially required books at home is a peculiarity that peers will notice. Book ownership indicates disposable income. But income is not the main social signal it conveys. It betokens, as well, an unconventional readiness to spend on building one's personal abilities and distinctions. Heavy reading seems to Tupicochans at once admirable and suspect, because it implies ambition in bad as well as good senses. Also, because voluntary solitude is off the normal behavioral track, solitary reading may be misinterpreted as snobbish rejection of sociability, or private scheming. Of course skeptical neighbors sometimes suspect book buyers are buying the prestige of literacy more than its utility, but at the same time they credit a private life of reading as a source of strength for those who can practice it. Readers acquire a knack for talking with people of power and wealth. They are able to help their children or other people's win the diplomas which have become a necessary, though rapidly inflating, kind of social capital (ibid.:404, 410).

Most Tupicochan households, however, hold scarce published print. Most have bright-colored wall calendars. Many keep some school texts, farmers' almanacs, songbooks, loose sheets with announcements about agropastoral matters, programs from festivals, religious booklets (and, among Protestant converts, Bibles), recipes distributed by the local public health center, rural magazines such as *Agronoticias*, old Sunday supplements, and the odd heirloom book from a beloved relative. Some households keep copies of "monographs," which are usually photocopies of typewritten *licenciatura* theses by teachers. Such productions are held in high esteem, and if a visitor asks about their history it will immediately be proffered (see chapter 6). Some households also have copies of homemade, job-printed articles, booklets, and commemorative publications which often come from the "provincial clubs" formed by "children of the

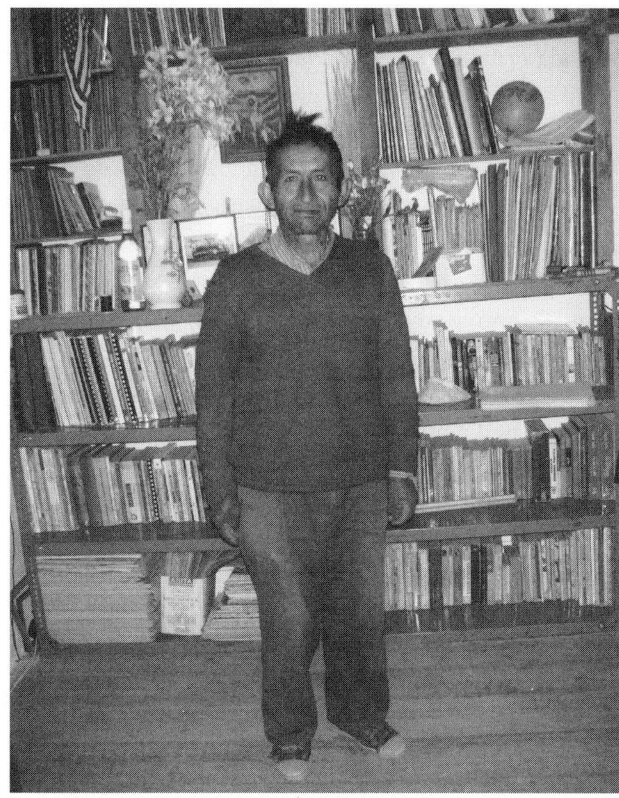

50. The village's foremost private book collector is León Modesto Rojas Alberco (1947–), a campesino who lived briefly in Lima in his youth, and who has a self-taught vocation for document work of all kinds, including the paleography of colonial *mosaico*.

community" in Lima (see chapter 7). In 2001 three families still held their copies of *El Tupicochano, Organo de difusión del Comité ejecutivo central de Tupicocha Residentes en Lima metropolitana* ('The Tupicochan, Outreach Organ of the Central Executive Committee of Tupicochans Living in Metropolitan Lima') dating from 1975. Finally, some houses have brochures handed out by international NGOs.

The most bookish villager, León Modesto Rojas Alberco, owns some 400 volumes, mostly from the myriad kiosks that sell used books in central Lima (see figure 50). Men of bookish bent become the mediators between the world of official letters—the law, schools, the church, NGOs—and the internal documentary circuit of the village. They are called on, for example, to correct papers that must go before outside authorities (e.g., voting rolls, testaments). In some ways they are modern successors to the colonial *letrado*. Such *peritos* ('writing experts') in certain regions become folk scribes. They develop a clientele seeking confidential consultations, counseling and drafting, and ritual observances to infuse documents with the power to endure and persuade (Salomon and Chambi 2006).

What about state-linked, as opposed to household or communal, ownership of print? The municipality built up a small public library in the 1990s, but no systematic public access existed, and the comuneros shrugged it off as a political vanity. A later mayor merged it with the school library, and since then it has been relocated in a rented space on the main street, still lacking staff to facilitate access. Like the school itself, the school library originally evolved from a communal organization. The initiative to create it arose in connection with the *fiesta del libro* ('book fair') which the ayllus organized in 1927 (AMSAT/SAT 06 1927:113). Over the years an association of emigrant villagers supported it and procured government donations.

School library inventories give an idea of recent state scholastic discourse. The lion's share consists of ministerial readers and classroom magazines for pedagogy. Storybooks, reference works, children's encyclopedias, texts on commercial practice and political economy, Catholic religious instruction books, and guides to good (i.e., urban) manners supplement them. The school also accumulates outdated self-help titles. Some titles try to impart old-fashioned urban female gender roles, "las labores propias del sexo" ('tasks proper to the sex'). These are surreally irrelevant to the actual work of farmer-herder women, a pointed reminder that teachers see peasant girls as people of "low cultural level." Volumes of state-directed "development" pedagogy from the 1960s onward urge technical "capacitation," while titles from the 1990s (some translated from English) exhort villagers to become competitive career-makers through "realizing personal potential."

A 1987 inventory showed increases in Catholic catechetical holdings and in "premilitary" instruction materials (i.e., plans for uniformed drilling and other armylike school practices). Between 1987 and 2001 basic English books piled up in startling numbers of copies, the English language being a required, but utterly ineffectual, part of grade-school curriculum. The offering of Peruvian literary prose by 1987 reflected aspirations to follow Peru's rising reputation in the cosmopolitan literary orbit: among the authors were Manuel Scorza, Ricardo Palma, Ciro Alegría, Alonso Cueto, Martín Quintana, José María Arguedas, and César A. Vallejo.

But the library is more a showcase of literacy than a reading workshop. Clean and comfortable, it is well liked by children. Yet it is not very accessible to them. Hours are rationed and access to books strictly regimented. Teachers constantly nag students with warnings that their peasantlike habits (dusty clothes, Andean-style bag lunches, wisecracking while reading, etc.) are the enemies of literate culture, to be curbed when one enters the library. The physical cleanliness and newness of books is such a fetish that most of them remain underutilized. Teachers fear they would be criticized for letting their pupils dirty the pages. The upshot is an unspoken but unanimous sense that books are one of the good things in life which sit just out of reach.

The school library contains not a single example of or allusion to the manuscript books which the Community, the ayllus, and village civil society produce in the course of their own activities. The two literate orbits function side by side, separated by a categorical difference so deep and unquestioned that inquiries about it are not easily understood by teachers or pupils. Questioned whether schools ever teach children about the ancient writings that the village regards as foundational, teachers (other than the local-born) responded that such scripts have no place in curriculum.

"WISE JOHN," OR, MYTHS AND SENTIMENTS ABOUT THE PRINTED WORD

As we have seen, the encounter with authoritative sources of writing has been an equivocal one during the whole of post-Inka history. Almost without exception, our conversations with campesinos about their experience with writing evoked first of all the proverb "La letra con sangre entra." This cliché could be rendered "No bleed, no read" or "Blows drive the letters home." Often, too, people say "Para aprender es menester padecer" ('You have to suffer to learn'). The notion that literacy is a painful kind of learning, intrinsically connected to violence and suffering, has deep roots in many Spanish-speaking regions. Diego Saavedra Fajardo (1584–1648) was speaking not for peasants but for elites, when, in the seventeenth century, he wrote that "Letters have bitter roots, even if their fruits are sweet. Our nature abhors them, and it feels no other labor so keenly as their first rudiments" (cited in Cortés Alonso 1986:6).[17]

When Tupicochans who had reached adulthood by the 1990s recalled learning to read and write, almost all of them talked about corporal punishment, humiliation, and anxiety:

> At that time they were so strict in school! They used to punish us if we didn't know something. They'd whip the little girls with nettles, what

> we call *chinga* here. It hurt, it hurt a lot! But it was worse for the boys because they used to put them through what was called "the dark alley." The boys and the teacher formed a double file, like a tunnel, and the punished boy had to pass through it while they hit him with their belts. They hit him hard. It hurt a lot, and it went on till all of them had hit him with their belts. But one learned! [With a tone of nostalgia.] They used to beat us because "No bleed, no read." And even if it was out of fear, we did learn.[18] (A woman born in 1950, interviewed in 2004)

In a more Quechua-speaking and more impoverished part of Andean Peru in the 1960s, Alejandro Ortiz Rescaniere (1973:134–41, 146–49) found oral versions of a narrative dating at least to 1570. In this (as in innumerable oral and documentary sources) the Inka king's misunderstanding of what a book is triggered the first act of the colonial tragedy. He also collected "the school myth," a now-famous tale about why children hate school. The reason is that a demon who lives in "a cave called school" is always trying to trap and kill the young descendants of the Inka. These texts have been misinterpreted (Classen 1991; Seed 1991) as expressing an essential antiliterate bias in Andean cultures.

In fact, Andean people everywhere treasure literacy and feel the lack of it as a terrible affliction. In Quechua, the unlettered are *ñawsa*, 'blind'. There is no such thing as Andean antiliteracy. It makes more sense to understand these searing myths and memories as traces of the punitive teaching Saavedra Fajardo knew among Spaniards, further embittered by the marginalization and racial stigma meted out in the past to "Indians" by the ethos of Lima and its school system. The sociolinguist Virginia Zavala, studying a Quechua-speaking district, reported that parents experience schooling as an arena of conflicts and pressures. "We used to live a tranquil life without knowing how to read nor write,"[19] said the elder Don Cecilio when Virgina Zavala interviewed him in Umaca (Andahuaylas) (2002a:105). But the source of pain is the social relation around text, not the text itself. Rural Andean appreciations of authoritative books and the learning encounter are ambivalent rather than negative. As we have seen, much of this ambivalence results from the historic process of school governmentalization. In a little over a century, the state provided massive scholarization, but in the same process wrested schooling from local initiative and made it unilateral.

The story of "Wise John" collected by Abilio Vergara and analyzed by Juan Ansión (Ansión et al. 1992:153–55), gives a clearer idea of modern sentiments about schooling. The hero is an anonymous schoolboy, who falls into the power of a monster named Wise John. By memorizing secret spells from his book collection, Wise John has learned to command fierce animals. They snarl and claw at the boy. How can the child escape from Wise John's lettered mantrap? The schoolboy really does know how to read, but he pretends to be a foolish illiterate. Secretly, he steals into Wise John's library and studies it. By reading he learns spells to turn the tormenting animals against their master. The boy corners Wise John and beats him with his own power. Text exists in this imagined world as the property of predators. But a youth who approaches predators astutely and studiously masters the source of their powers fares better than one who flees. The story is faithful to rural sentiments about learning, which do include fear and pain, but also aspiration and the pride of the underdog meeting a challenge.

What one might call the Wise John ideology of literacy has driven the encounter with authoritative writing for many generations. Interactions with so-called correct, that is, legal or academic, writing always involves disadvantage. Yet this situation is itself the stimulus by which rural people see themselves as becoming intellectually strong and able. For better or worse such thinking has become the unquestioned attitude of rural majorities. Their personal narratives assume that unpleasant, violent, authoritarian schooling is inevitable and normal. And despite everything, it is desirable; as one popular *huayno* song puts it, "I want to read and also / To write so that our / People may at last stop suffering" (Zavala 2002a:97).[20]

It was in this spirit that Cajahuaringa Inga told his young readers the great reward of literacy is to be protected against cheating. Documents of the communities repeatedly speak of literacy as a defensive weapon. One ayllu book says, in distinctly nonscholastic Spanish, "By general agreement in support of our community's rights and we have seen fit, the citizen Don Antonio Avila, a fellow of this ayllu, as a person versed in the titles that protect our rights and is able to defend us for which reason we named him Delegate before the representative [of the state]" (1940; APUCh/SAT 03 1940a:108).[21]

Meanwhile, the ground is shifting underneath the order that the "Wise John" story allegorizes. For one thing, as Tupicocha and hundreds or thousands of other villages shift to a deterritorialized way of life, the role of literacy changes also. When comuneros send their children to school, they are mindful of the next generation's chances for employment in Lima, no less than of the need to continue defending old communal titles. Tupicocha and its diaspora have become a single interdependent web of livelihood. Within it the peasant, even the lettered peasant, may no longer figure as the key earner or defender. With its high chronic underemployment and frantic competition for jobs, Lima produces an ever-growing swarm of private technical academies into which young ex-villagers plow their own and their peasant parents' earnings. Some ex-villagers or children of recently arrived migrants enroll as part-time students in nonelite universities. As they become actors in their home villages, they will alter literate culture in ways just now becoming visible.

And the ministerial regimen of literacy is also changing. Teachers' colleges today propose less authoritarian pedagogy, and tone down *mission civilisatrice* rhetoric about the countryside as the "Intercultural Education" model spreads. Slowly too, the vice-grip that the fossilized teachers' union SUTEP held upon personnel rules is being pried loose by pressures toward competence rating of instructors (Degregori 2008). Peru's chronically poor performance in international comparative surveys of educational achievement (Economist 2007) has embarrassed recent presidents in dealings with the World Bank, and has put steam into critiques of education. In 2009, after numerous and violent strikes, SUTEP made its first small concession toward performance-based evaluation of teachers. But "performance" of what? Will "reform" mean anything more than pressure to become more efficient in imparting ministerial doctrine? It remains to be seen how the state can interact with demotic literacy practices—and someday, perhaps, hasten Wise John's retirement.

FOUR

"Papelito Manda"

The Power of Writing

The sun rises on a day of *faena* ('task, assignment'), that is, a collective workday ordered by the Community authority. Everyone is getting ready to answer the call. While some workers ready cement, sand, lumber, shovels, and pickaxes, one member in every ayllu packs notebooks, pens, a big bag of coca leaf, tobacco, bottles, and rubber stamps. Not one of the innumerable ayllu or community tasks—canal cleaning, cattle branding, road mending, fence mending, building a reservoir, or even playing a game of soccer—is considered done unless it yields a document. In Tupicocha and in countless other Andean communities, the document is a coequal part of the social fact, no less than its ritual or its labor.

Indeed one could define a faena, or any community action, as the union of three things: rite, work, and script. Scripts of work and ritual govern the building of a small world. But how does such power get into scripts in the first place? What is it about a text that makes it compelling? One may rightly point to the power structures that impose authorized signatures and audits, and so on. But at the actual moment of inscription, none of that avails if the right phrases are not used in the right formats.

Tupicochans, like any letter-bound people, build up the overarching virtual entity called society in the putting together of words. The edifice of customary law is, irreducibly, a series of language events. The language event that transforms work and ceremony into script is one in which the words of familiar peasant neighbors become transmuted into utterances of an impersonal collective power. This chapter clarifies the rules of such language events: "literary processes . . . behind the constitution of authority in texts" (Messick 1993:1). It explores the finest-grained manufacture of power. The path involves showing rules and reasons for choosing words as authoritative, and forms for deploying them in genres. Along this path we find that archaistic and legalistic forms are only one ingredient in the manufacture of authority. To be powerful, formulas of law and tradition must join with words that express experiences and feelings shared among ayllu mates in their ever-changing civil and political lives. For this reason we are concerned first of all with word choice, taking lexicon as a sensitive indicator of the encounter between continuity and experience. But we are also concerned with the more rigid genre vessels into which words are fitted. Old forms provide that "appearance of Again" which makes written records the visible embodiment of the enduring collective, but newer words recreate it for actuality.

First, we will look into the pragmatic movement of verbal action from speech toward writing as it occurs within the invariant ritual-literate surround described in chapter 1 (see the section "Labor and Politics Sedimenting in Text"). A particular kind of conversation, dialogically managed, distills ayllu or community talk toward a moment of inscriptive decision. At the signing, a document comes into existence as the writ of an author transcending all those present. Second, we take note of some theoretical contributions about the sociocultural nature of word choice and the reasons why, at the moment of inscription (however conservative its ideology), mutations and changes occur. Third, we document in detail a few case studies in the building of authority through choice of words, showing how and why certain key usages gain or lose power. Last, and more summarily, we turn to genre: the structuring devices which turn pragmatically novel literate events into instances of recurring types.

The examples in question are routine and unexciting documents. We set them forth in a skimmable format, but conserve their texts exactly because one needs at least a compact *corpus inscriptionum* to demonstrate in detail how the power of writing is interminably regenerated.

GENERATING PERFORMATIVE POWER IN THE RITUAL SURROUND

Peruvians often quote a Latin American cliché about written authority: "papelito manda," meaning "paper is boss," or more literally, "little paper commands." The diminutive ending *-ito* suggests ironic surprise that a scrap of cellulose can trump human agency. In almost any setting—whether academic, political, legal, or athletic—one mutters this remark as in wry acceptance of a perversely inevitable fact. The gist of papelito manda is close to J. L. Austin's sense of performativity: the act of writing of a paper does not simply refer to something but changes the world in a way that affects things and people referred to. When I sign my license, this becomes a world where people must let me drive. When a performative is written rather than spoken, it becomes a fact rather than an act: no longer an event in context, but a timeless thing with an existence independent of human discourse. The old lettered city established included a high regard for an enduring performative force seen as uniquely present in writing.[1]

In the "lettered city" as Rama conceived it, the power of writing derived from the power of command: ultimately, divine command, but immediately that of people in privileged statuses. To impart force in writing one had to delegate one's words to a specialist (scribe, notary, lawyer) who, with a great show of social distance, transformed them into text that the unprivileged could only ratify (Chartier 1999:117). These distances have nearly disappeared. Tupicocha has no scribe or notary. Is the secretary post, then, a center of power? Each secretary who writes for an ayllu is just its amanuensis, and as such he (or increasingly, she) carries out an obligation that will ideally devolve on all. Secretary duty is considered onerous, confers no immediate privilege, and is positively shunned by many campesinos who experience paperwork as tedious or frustrating. (At a minimum, it costs them sleep.) Men who have lived in cities tend to get called on disproportionately, more to their annoyance than profit. Authorship and authority inhere rather in the ayllu as a corporation, embodied by the sum of the signatures.

The manufacture of authoritative language through writing in the ritual-literate surround takes place via a structured scenario guiding speech toward inscription as text. As it enters this passage, discourse includes more than the strictly verbal. Paralinguistic elements such as specific gestures, turn taking, the curtsey to the "work cross," silences and meditative intervals, rhetorical warmth or coolness, intonation, and even insignia (staffs of office, herbal ornament in hats) are structured and structuring features of the writing context. They all have to be deployed according to strict local convention to imbue a text with full performative and "constative" values.

The verbal action follows a funnel-like path, from wide-ranging, semi-structured speech—a loosely parliamentary register of speech, with shows of respect but also sprinkled with local jokes and emotive expressions—inward toward the more and more restrictive formulation of an *acta*. For Tupicochan purposes it helps to conceive the literacy event and its practices as a dialogical theater, in the Bakhtinian mode, because the documents produced there are literally constituted by a diversity of voices.

The stage has its rules. Barbed comments, heavy irony, loud voices and laughter, heartfelt protest, and even tears of frustration can play parts, but their part is largely cathartic. In some kinds of meeting, the president or *camachico* periodically decrees musical breaks, during which members dance to an archaistic Andean tune, in a circle, with hands on the shoulders ahead of them. Drinks and stamping rhythms foster feelings of closeness. In other ritual-literate intervals, the "hour of custom" near midday doubles as lunch break, when people share treats with kin and friends. These routines generate enough warmth for people to speak candidly.

Only toward the end of a module, when the secretary is sure of being able to formulate a sense of the meeting, does he or she begin offering suggested wording for an acta. While the resulting papers are sometimes garnished with rhetoric about unanimity—"as one man"—and always speak in undifferentiated first-person plural or in an impersonal third person, they are understood as condensing and containing the polyphonic hubbub that generated them. What appears as a chorus may have started as a cacophony. When villagers return to a page, they often read it together and take the occasion as a moment to reconstitute from memory or even from speculation the dialogical context that produced it, as if rehearsing its constative genesis. A book of acts is not a report merely *about* a series of transactions. (By analogy: an account statement is merely *about* transactions but cancelled checks *are* the transactions.) The heart of the matter, from the Tupicochan viewpoint, is that partaking with others of a literacy event creates or reproduces a bond. This includes latent as well as overt strands in it: not just fellow membership of an ayllu, but the kinship and in-law relationships entwined with it. Even facts that are not of the group's own agency need *constancias* if they have implications for ayllu action; on May 24, 1940, only three hours after an earthquake damaged the church and school, Chaucacolca Ayllu had already written an act about it (APUCh/SAT 03 1940b:126). Signing together is a ritual of consubstantiality in the collective domain. It produces a conjoint incarnation of the actors. When campesinos put their heads together over the community or ayllu acts of a hundred years ago, they pore over signatures of ancestors, noticing who signed next to whom (suggesting they sat together). They take the whole as a sort of charter, but also as a sociogram of old bonds and ruptures.

Signature is understood as consubstantial with the person; rumor says one can harm a person by practicing magic on his signature. Signing is the crucial index of personal agency, and for this reason much care surrounds signatures representing persons of diminished agency, namely, the unlettered and some women. In documents from 1903 through 1987 proxy signatures could establish nonliterate persons as agents.[2] The first female signature in Cacarima's ayllu books, that of Faustina Alberco, occurred in 1950 (APUCh/SAT 03 1950a:337).[3] Today female signatures are not rare, but only a few senior *comuneras* are heard at full volume on the dialogical stage.

ON CHOOSING WORDS OF POWER: THEORIES OF LEXICAL CHOICE AND CHANGE

Ayllu texts are the words of the group, and the addressee is a reader qua member of the group. Skill in producing text that convinces as a corporate voice is a core competency in the local idea of literacy. New Literacy Studies have paid great attention to the North Atlantic ideology of literacy as a "state of grace" in the individual (Shirley Brice Heath's phrase). But for Andean village situations, it is equally important to notice that although literacy is lodged in the individual, it is also an attribute of a collectivity and members are required to use it as a sign of their collective identity. Because it functions this way, it tends to acquire some locally special traits.

Let us look at what makes the appropriate special quality. V. N. Vološinov emphasized that a "*word is a two-sided act.* It is determined equally by *whose* word it is and *for whom* it is meant" (1973:86; emphasis in original). It has to be not only appropriate to its referent, but also to its speaker and to its addressee. If they want to talk effectively, a given speaker and a given listener should use certain words and avoid others, even when the options are denotatively synonymous. A usage that is off-key in either of these respects will fail to generate reciprocity between speaker and listener, however referentially precise it may be. "A word is a bridge thrown between myself and another," as Vološinov put it. For the written record, choosing an innovative word is a weighty matter. Yet it has happened many times. When and when not?

Every time verbal "bridges" are built, the writer must come to grips with unforeseen contingencies, from the ephemeral to the momentous. So authoritative writing entails tension between conservative and innovative verbal representations. On the one hand, from one historic period to another, writing retains its cogency and the overarching community retains its putative reality because people and deeds are denoted by long-lived terms. This tendency is so strong that many terms remain constant even as their referents change. Old toponyms come to refer to different land features. Old lexical bottles (such as the word *ayllu*) come to hold new semantic wine (folk-legal attributes of this originally pre-Hispanic institution having changed). To read constancias with historic intent is to contemplate an enduring whole where old words stand for partly imaginary continuity. But on the other hand, at the moment of creating new utterances, one must *also* achieve performative relevance to emerging conditions and surroundings. To be "conatively" felicitous—that is, to influence listeners to act as the performative change requires—speakers must create verbal acts that are congruent with realities of the moment, with changing structures of power and circumstances. Lexical change is the trace of the renovation of the virtual entity, a civic corporation, amid social change.

Regarding lexicon we concentrate on what the sociolinguist Anna Wierzbicka calls "key words . . . words which are particularly important and revealing in a given culture" (1997:15). Using Japanese examples, Wierzbicka writes that

> a key word such as *enryo* (roughly 'interpersonal restraint'), *on* (roughly 'debt of gratitude') and *omoiyari* (roughly 'benefactive empathy') . . . can lead us to the center of a whole complex of cultural values and attitudes, expressed, inter alia, in common conversational routines and revealing a whole network of culture-specific "cultural scripts." (1997:17)

Although less clear in definition than Sherry Ortner's famous 1973 term "key symbols," Wierzbicka's definition surpasses it in quantifiable applicability. We will track the rise and fall in authoritative potency of a few characteristically Tupicochan terms, each loaded with consensual experience and feeling—but experiences and feelings changing in their historical contexts. The Tupicochan words studied are not chosen arbitrarily but are the most frequent substantive terms (words and set phrases) in the subcorpus quantitatively analyzed (the internal records of Cacarima Ayllu).

Ayllu documents, as noted, are intrakin group business, and words in it are a good sample of language taken as locally felicitous: good bridges among the members. Some of their terminology changed during the twentieth century while some did not. Some lexicon of ayllu writing remained anchored in local cultural classifications, while some replaced local terms with words from national discourse.

There is important rhyme and reason to such change. Contrary to the stereotype of word-level analysis as "atomizing" study or as cultural butterfly-collecting, it is indispensable for understanding just how global and local codes influence a community's way of working with language, and in the long term shape what it becomes as a cultural collectivity. A word can be replaced when another word is recognized as similar enough in its semantic scope to work as its denotative equivalent, *and* when it is accepted as appropriate to the roles people are playing when speaking or writing it.

As Tupicocha's ayllu-structured governance came into close articulation with the national state, villagers came to perceive some local words as standing in comparable condition with national words. They became candidates for replacement. They actually were replaced when the novel alternative seemed more appropriate to local roles. Meanwhile, other words did not change, because nothing in the avalanche of incoming, innovative language equated semantically to local terms or to the roles that fit around them.

For example, terms about local ritual tend to fall mostly in the latter class: words not replaced. Some exalted Andean regional deities have acquired alternate names from the Catholic lexicon (the mountain Quyllur Rit'i 'Starry Snow' being glossed as 'the Lord [*Señor*] of Snows'), but not so for Tupicocha's Huaris or Huares ('primordials'), the costumed villagers who act as mediators between the village and its water-owning divinities. For a term to be interesting as an index of social change, it has to fill three conditions: First, it must present some cultural elaboration and not be a mere connector or formal device. Second, it must be a key term in the local sociolect. Third, it must be in fairly frequent use.

As we track examples through time, we will refer to a three-part historical periodization from chapter 1 (see the section "The Lettered Life of Modern Ayllus"). The earliest set of relations among ayllus, dominant in both Inka and colonial times, was that of *coordination* within a federated community with shared infrastructures. Ayllus created ritual-political and religious structures organizationally like each other and mutually comparable, though linked to different deities, ancestors, land rights, and so on. We spoke of homologization, when Republican-era ayllus perceived themselves as parts of a higher, more inclusive formation demanding pervasive uniform structure, so that small ayllu and larger community organizations should stand in a formal microcosm-to-macrocosm relation. For the most recent period, we spoke of introjection: ayllu units saw themselves as organs of the community, and the community as an organ of state, so that each ayllu saw itself as obligated to internalize and carry out within its own domain the state's organization and agenda.

As we read Tupicochan texts through time, particular lexical items stand out because their variations correlate with social changes. The seemingly dry terminology of quotidian records forms "a subtle arrangement of boundaries and connections, contrasts and parallels. . . . These patterns can . . . be unraveled, revealing the regularities on which meaning in public life depends" (Wuthnow 1992:13). We are interested in how the written text reflects both national and local sociopolitical conditions—not because we suppose big institutions simply stamp their lexicon on smaller ones, but for more interesting reasons. The corpus suggests that the selection of terms was and is negotiated within the discursive polyphonies of their times.

TUPICOCHA'S CHOSEN WORDS OF POWER: CASE STUDIES IN LEXICAL CHANGE

The crucial time for the next few examples of change and nonchange is the beginning of Augusto Leguía's second presidency, the *oncenio* ('eleven-year era') of 1919–30. Proposing to harness the insurgent dynamism of peasant and ethnic organizations to state projects, while at the same time favoring modernization through increased foreign investments (Kristal 1997:186; Poole and Rénique 1992: 101–6), Leguía expanded the bureaucracy to intervene in many matters that touched peasants directly: road building, mining, and (for the first time) *asuntos indígenas* ('indigenous affairs'). His *patria nueva* ('new fatherland') was in time to prove a politically incoherent project, but in the short term it brought abrupt changes in rural governance such as the replacement of old municipalities with new forms (Basadre 1931:186, 216–17). Most crucially, in 1920, it allowed traditional-law institutions of the commons to petition for recognition as *comunidades indígenas*. In July of the same year, the First Congress of Indigenous Communities took place, and this unprecedented event resonated throughout the country. These moments stimulated radical self-reorganizations by villages, increasingly convinced that they would be more able to win the aid of ministries if their local institutions were better matched to national ones. Change was now to be codetermined by intracommunal and large-scale dynamics (Roseberry 1994; Thurner 1995:293).

Communities saw reason to homologize their customary law with "statutes" of the state, sometimes drafting the local "constitutions" described in chapter 2. Ayllus followed suit, "reforming" themselves homologically even though no law asked them to. The ayllus had already begun to formulate written internal statutes around 1905, and these were redrafted repeatedly over the next thirty years to improve articulation with national institutions (e.g., by guaranteeing the land-tenure interests of peasants drafted for the army, or by authorizing absences to learn the "artisan industrial" livelihoods that Leguía's regime promoted).

Lexical changes putting old Andean practices on a verbal par with modern national ones followed close at hand. We can see in verbal microcosm what Messick called "literary processes . . . behind the constitution of authority in texts."[4]

CAMACHICO > *PRESIDENTE*

The Quechua word *kamachikuq* derives from a verb root *kama-* which is exceptionally hard to translate, because it denotes a pre-Hispanic metaphysical notion. A nominal form, *kamay*, meant the specific animating essence of a species, including its form, idiosyncrasy, energy, and vitality. A particular constellation (in chapter 29 of the 1608 Quechua Manuscript of Huarochirí) looked like a llama, and had the power to *kama-* earthly llamas: it animated them and made them flourish. To the verbal root *kama-*, the noun *kamachikuq* adds a causative, a dynamic, and an agentive: 'one who imparts species order and energy.' In political usage, *kamachikuq* was the person who imparted in a political unit its particular identity, power, and organization. *Kamachikuq* seems to have been a term of Inka administration, but it endured centuries after Spanish conquest as the Hispano-Quechuism *camachico*. It denoted ethnic "Indian" authorities of lower rank than *kurakas* or colonially recognized native noble heads of polities (Guaman Poma 1980 [1615]:53, 121, 190, 302, 486, 556, 633, 696, 815, 909; Salomon 2004a:60; Taylor 1974–76). Hereditary native nobility was extinguished in the repressive aftermath of the eighteenth-century neo-Inka revolts, and never stably resuscitated in the republics borne of Bolivarian army intervention. But the minor, nonhereditary Andean offices, known as *camachico*, persisted through the twentieth century in many rural areas. In Huarochirí, the word *camachico* flourished into the twentieth century as the title of a head of an ayllu. Some villages still use it in the twenty-first.

Tupicocha, however, replaced *camachico* with the Spanish *presidente*. Modern Tupicochans are no longer aware of the Quechua root *kamay* nor of the etymology of the traditional title derived from it, but they do remember it as the old word for an ayllu head. Elder members still use it orally. We will analyze the evolution of the lexical binomial *camachico/presidente* as it is demonstrated by texts from the first half of the twentieth century. The quantitative base is from Cacarima Ayllu's *Libro No. 1 del Año 1905 Perteneciente A la Parcialidad de Cacarima*, a series of ayllu acts that covers the years 1905–39 (APC/SAT 01). Cases from other ayllus have been cited for comparison.

From 1905 through 1921, only the terms *camachico* and *camachico cesante* ('outgoing camachico') appeared in Cacarima's book. Examples include

> En la casa del Casa del *Camachico nuevo* . . . tomaremos cuenta al *sisante camachico*.
>
> [In the house of the new camachico . . . we will audit the outgoing camachico.] (APC/SAT 01 1905a:1)

> Entregando al *Camachico dentrante*.
>
> [Handing over to the incoming camachico.] (APC/SAT 01 1905b:5)

> Y para ello lo firman el *camachico sesante y entrante* como se dice con responsabilidad, según el inventario y aci lo firman el *sesante* y el *intrante.*
>
> [And for this (purpose) the outgoing and incoming camachicos sign as is said with responsibility according to the inventory and thus sign the outgoing and the incoming.] (APC/SAT 01 1910:19–20)

> Recibo estos vienes yo *camachico numbrado* de la parcilidad. Dejando en su rresponsabledad del *camachico sesante.*
>
> [I the designated camachico of the parcialidad receive these goods. Leaving it in the responsibility of the outgoing camachico.] (APC/SAT 01 1911:24)

By the early twentieth century the number of Spanish speakers was large, and many of them are likely to have been Spanish-dominant bilinguals or monolinguals. For them, the religiously grounded derivation and the august connotation of kamachikuq would have become obscure or unknown. The semantic space of the term would have shrunk to administrative meaning: head of an ayllu. The idea of labeling such a person as an executive officer in the style of the Constitution became thinkable. When in 1920 the Leguía government allowed indigenous communities to petition for recognition as organs of constitutional government (rather than to be made over as municipalities or municipal annexes), it became possible and ideologically appealing to conform the community to the state. Quickly, ayllus also began to homologize.

The term *presidente* came to Cacarima ayllu as an innovation from the capital, and through a very special medium. It first appears on the rubber stamp, bought in Lima, with which the ayllu leadership sealed its acts from 1916 onward. Rubber stamping, understood as the successor medium to the highly prestigious colonial wax seal, was at that time a token of administrative modernization. When Cacarima's members resolved to buy a stamp, they also "bought"—but only tacitly—the equation between *presidente* and *camachico.* (In 1916, with homologization in the air, it would have seemed counterproductive to ask a stationer in Lima to make a stamp with such an "Indian" word as *camachico.*) The legend on the rubber stamp reads *Presidente de la Parcialidad—Cacarima—Tupicocha.* Five years later, in 1921, Cacarima's leaders began to emulate it with their own hands:

Reunidos en la Casa del Sr. Camachico Don Aurelio Ramos es para el nombramiento como es costumbre de nuestra Parcialidad de Cacarima se nombro por *Camachico o presidente* de la parcialidad a Don Roman Ramos, por mayor á Don Gaspar Laymito por secretario a D. Cornelio Florencio Por alguacil Roperto Ramos.

[Gathered in the House of the Honorable Camachico Don Aurelio Ramos it is for naming as is the customary law of our Parcialidad of Cacarima Don Roman Ramos was named as Camachico or president of the parcialidad, as *mayor* Don Gaspar Laymito as secretary D. Cornelio Florencio as *alguacil* Roperto Ramos.] (APC/SAT 01: 1921:68)

The innovative term *presidente de la parcialidad* at first went side by side with *camachico o presidente*, as if to suggest that they were complementary rather than synonymous terms. They usually appear with the older term first, but sometimes with *presidente* first. A double usage in the sense of a complementary binomial would have followed the logic of the institution, because of the ayllu's Janus-faced character. *Ayllu* was and is a kinship term, evoking the inward-looking, intimate quality of membership. Seen from within, the corporation is a kindred united in mutual service. But seen from without it is a component of a larger, explicitly political organization. Considered as a parcialidad, the kinship corporation is an outward-looking "team" in the political union and fraternal rivalry of federated segments. The fact that *presidente* lacks the connotation of kinship but accents those of citizenship and political dignity made it a congenial name for one aspect of the corporation.

Para que conste lo firmamos el *camachico o presidente* en la parcialidad.

[To make a constancia we signed, the camachico or president in the parcialidad.] (APC/SAT 01 1922a:75)

En casa del *Presidente o Camachico sesante.*

[In the house of the outgoing President or Camachico.] (APC/SAT 01 1923a:82)

The unitary term *presidente* first appeared as intra-ayllu usage in Cacarima in 1922. We can see that its ascent owes much to homologization

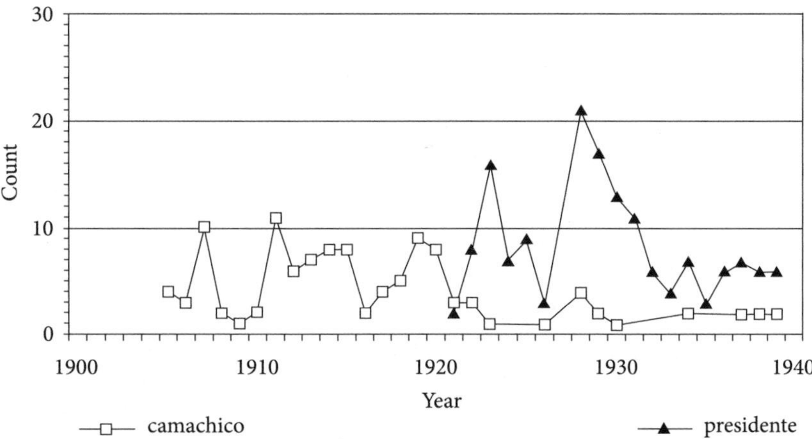

51. A diachronic comparison of frequency between /*camachico*/ (the older Quechua-derived term) and /*presidente*/ (a Spanish-derived term for the same office), as found in records of Cacarima Ayllu.

from the fact that municipal (state-staffed) offices made the shift before ayllus did so internally. In April of 1923 the six *camachicos* appeared before the municipal authorities as *presidentes* promising that their respective parcialidades would help bring a contracted teacher to Tupicocha (AMSAT/SAT 06 1923: 87).

Presidente took clear intra-ayllu dominance in 1928 and never lost it, although *camachico* did persist at low levels (see figure 51). At this period the word *presidente* came to seem not only semantically congruent with *camachico* but also sociologically appropriate, because the role of the ayllu leader was increasingly becoming that of a chair in parliamentary process and leader in a state-like organization. The word *presidente* appears superimposed over the word *camachico* (APC/SAT 01 1922a:72), suggesting hesitation to let a native lexical item coexist with a neologism that has started to be naturalized in discourse. This hesitation reveals a lexical change underway but still not naturalized in habit.

It was in the 1930s that ayllus began to heavily introject the agendas of higher governmental units (district, province, and national state). From then onward, most ayllus executed more faenas on behalf of the overarching community than in benefit of their own members. *Presidente* continued to be the dominant term. But the semantic and sociological victory of *presidente* did not erase the term easily. Still in 1952 Chaucacolca listed its officers with binomial titles alluding to older regimens: Camachico or Presidente, Vicepresidente or Mayor, Tesorero, Capitán, Vocal or Alguacil (APUCh/SAT 03 1951:388).

CAMACHICO CESANTE > EX-PRESIDENTE > DELEGADO

Another example in which local Andean semantic precedents influenced the language of power occurs within the same domain as *camachico/presidente*. It concerns terms for outgoing leaders of ayllus. The outgoing ayllu head was long called *camachico cesante*. When *presidente* came in, the journalistic usage *ex-presidente* quickly followed. But *cesante* and *ex-* turned out not to be interchangeable in Cacarima's eyes. Only once did Cacarima apply *cesante* rather than *ex-* to a *presidente*.

Reserve about equating *cesante* with *ex-* reflects a semantic and sociological difference.. The implication of *camachico cesante* is not simply retirement from responsibilities, because former camachicos were expected to take on a further positive role. Camachico cesante refers to the responsibilities of the *anciano de la comunidad* ('elder statesman'). In the collective memory of the group, the camachico cesante functioned as the institutional memory of the ayllu and as the voice of the group's conscience. It was his job to deal with sensitive matters that the camachico/presidente might not dare to mention lest his political future be damaged. The elder was also expected to be the arbiter of customary law, and to keep watch enforcing the customs:

> Nombramos de *camachico* al Señor Fabio Laymito en mayoria de botos y como tambien por boto del *Señor Camachico sesante* Don Aurilio Ramos este nombrado es *para que cumpla con las costumbres del pueblo y de su parcialidad.*
>
> [We name as camachico Señor Fabio Laymito by majority of votes, as also by vote Don Aurilio Ramos is named *Señor Camachico sesante* so [the group] may comply with the customs of the town and of their parcialidad.] (APC/SAT 01 1913:31)

The term *ex-presidente* may have been an adequate "dictionary" match for *camachico cesante* but it did not feel sociologically comfortable because of its suggestion of being hors de combat when in fact the *cesante* was (and is) supposed to be an assertive member. Most ayllus stopped writing *ex-presidente*. Today they title their elder statesmen *delegado* (delegate) because as a prestigious person he can be the group's spokesperson in public fora.

The lexical change from *camachico* to *presidente* and its corollary from *cesante* to *ex-* to *delegado* illustrate communal changes in relation to local, regional, and even national political agendas, much as Wierzbicka aptly suggests (1997:5):

> Culture-specific words are conceptual tools that reflect a society's past experience of doing and thinking about things in certain ways; and they help to perpetuate these ways. As a society changes, these tools, too, may be gradually modified and discarded. In that sense, the outlook of a society is never wholly "determined" by its stock of conceptual tools, but is clearly influenced by them.

MAYOR > VICEPRESIDENTE

A comparable change emerges, but with less clarity, in regard to the term for the camachico's complementary officer. We do not know to what Quechua or Spanish colonial term it corresponds. Perhaps it is related to the Inka and broadly Andean institution of "diarchy," (Duviols 1979) under which the Inka had as his *inkap rantin* ('Inka's stead') a complementary lord of royal rank. This institution conforms to a pervasive Andean preference for dual structures. It forms a deep-rooted local precedent, an element of "History 2" in Chakrabarty's sense (see chapter 2), a persisting local precedent conditioning the appropriateness of one political term.

What is clear is that in the early twentieth century, each Tupicochan ayllu or parcialidad had two top authorities called *camachico* and *mayor*. These two positions had complementary functions, apparently without either one being supreme. The camachico had charge of the internal affairs of the ayllu (as the Quechua etymon suggests), whereas the mayor was the ayllu's outward-facing spokesman in the councils of the village as a whole. However, the mayor was generally supposed to be more senior than the camachico; in ambassadorial status, his gravitas mattered as much as his administrative skill. *Mayor* means "elder" in metropolitan Spanish.

In 1919 Satafasca Ayllu wrote: "Han venido las autoridades en vecita y han tenido el honor de nombrar de *mayor* a D. Salomeo Rojas por ser mas mayor de edad de D. Pedro Rojas" (The authorities have come on a visit and have had the honor of naming Don Salomeo Rojas as *mayor* because he is older than Don Pedro Rojas) (AP1SF/SAT 02 1919:23). While the historic role of the mayor does not come fully into focus, records from the old municipality (which alone exerted state authority before legal recognition of the Indigenous Community) show that both the camachicos and the mayores of the ayllus attended meetings presided by the municipal agent (Salomon 2004a:192–93). Numbers of mayores fluctuated, but in 1912 six mayores appeared, matching the number of camachicos.

As *presidente* came to replace *camachico*, the term *vicepresidente*, vice president, was introduced as the equivalent of *mayor*. In semantic space the two terms are even less close than *camachico* and *presidente*. *Vicepresidente* lacks the exterior/interior contrast, and it implies subordination rather than complementarity. It may have been received as the necessary verbal complement to *presidente* because it is morphologically like it, and therefore apropos for the *camachico*'s functional complement. Also, a national vice president is the stand-in for the president if the latter is unavailable, so the term is not wholly inappropriate. But the transition from complementary to hierarchical terms introduced arbitrariness. One can see how arbitrary it was from the fact that certain other villages chose the reverse option. They made their *vicepresidente* the heir of the *camachico*'s responsibilities, and assigned to the *presidente* outward-looking duties proper to the *mayor*.

AYLLU > PARCIALIDAD

The terms for the kinship corporation, *ayllu* and *parcialidad*, stand in a historic relationship somewhat like that of *camachico* and *presidente*, albeit with different chronology. *Ayllu* is a word known to the Inkas but usually referring to non-Inka, kinship-structured social groups. (Different terms denoted kinship corporations of the blood royal.) As a verbal root, *ayllu-* could mean 'to tie.' As mentioned above, *parcialidad*—sector, social segment—is among the earliest and deepest-rooted colonial terms for indigenous institutions; it was in use by 1550 and omnipresent by 1600. So its appearance in the context of ayllu reform circa 1920 was anything but innovative. The surprise is that it took so long to enter the intravillage lexicon. *Parcialidad* is semantically similar to *camachico/presidente* insofar as the Quechua term highlights the fraternally "tied," intimate, kin-based and hereditary face of the institution, while the Latinate one highlights its function as a segment within a larger, political structure. Because the Spanish-derived term is sociologically felicitous—it corresponds accurately to the "team" function of the group—it has thrived. Tupicochans always use *parcialidad* when in the presence of outsiders, unaware that it belongs to the colonial age of servitude rather than to that of citizen dignity. But *parcialidad* does not altogether displace *ayllu*. In the plenary session where the heads of the ten ayllus assemble, the terms *ayllu* and *camachico* are still used. These terms evoke camaraderie and feelings of closeness (Salomon 2004a:57).

HORA DE COSTUMBRE

With this example we shift from the interpretation of terms that did change away from "indigenous" usage to those that did not. As we have shown, the conditions for a word (and its written likeness) to be recognizable as performatively forceful include semantic scope that covers with sufficient precision the cultural entity in question, and that also fits the current constellation of power relations by standing in cogent relation to that system's other terms. We emphasized that a term becomes vulnerable to replacement when a different term applying to the same cultural entity fills both these conditions.

In some cases such a rival term never appeared. As introduced in chapter 1, *hora de costumbre*, "hour of customary law," denotes the intervals during which a group activity is framed by ritual and transformed from mere action to written performance and constancia. It is the deictic anchor of ayllu writing in time and social space. Indeed, a repeated word boundary error may subliminally reflect a feeling about deictic anchoring in the moment which par excellence *is* the event: scribes sometimes write "la *ahora* de costumbre" ('the now of customary law': APM/SAT 04 1975d:37; APM/SAT 04 1986:119). Since about 1970 it has been common to make the ritual surround explicit by mentioning the hora de costumbre.

The potential alternative term to *hora de costumbre* is *hora de descanso*, 'hour of rest.' It is sometimes heard spoken, and it does occur once in Mujica Ayllu's long series of acts (APM/SAT 04 1978:55). It is of course true that one of the things people do during this interval is rest. In this respect one might compare it to the descanso between halves of a soccer game, which is probably the source of the gloss. But descanso is a poor semantic likeness to the domain of costumbre. "Rest" implies inactivity, while "customary law" implies a concentrated activity that is moral rather than physical. Occasionally, prose elaborations emphasize this dimension:

> Siendo en la *Segunda ahora de costumbre* dio el enfloro el Señor precidente con mucho emoción por los asistentes
>
> ['Being in the second hour of customary law the Honorable president with great emotion gave the enflowerment to those attending.'] (APM/SAT 04 1986:119)]

And when using the word *descanso*, the scribe emphasizes that the "rest" is at the same time a matter of customary law: "Descanso como es de costumbre de nuestra parcialidad" ('Rest as is the customary law of our parcialidad'; APM/SAT 04 1983:80).

Hora de costumbre receives significant special treatment insofar as it can often be written with uppercase initial letters. The closest analogical examples are terms for Catholic ritual, as, for example, *Santa Misa* ('Holy Mass'), *Cruz* ('cross'), *el Santísimo* ('the host'), or terms for revered places or institutions such as *the Collca* (the ritual precinct of the community). Even if the whole phrase is not capitalized, the word *costumbre* usually is. This treatment is not common when *costumbre* occurs in other contexts. The deferential usage proper to sacred or patriotic contexts may act as an additional deterrent to replacement; terms such as *descanso* do not provide sociological cues to sacred behavior such as libation and "enflowerment," but *costumbre* does.

"HIJOS (O HERMANOS) DE NUESTRA PARCIALIDAD"

Another modern usage which occurs stably, but not without alternatives, is the one denoting ayllu members: "*hijos (o hermanos) de nuestra parcialidad*" ('children [or siblings] of our parcialidad'). It often appears at the end of a constancia just before the signatures. In Mujica Ayllu, the norm for writing is to inscribe and sign as *hijos* or *hermanos de la parcialidad* unless some of the people taking part are nonmembers. In that case, a more bureaucratic usage occurs: *firmamos los asistentes* ('we who are present sign'; APM/SAT 04 1975b:28–29).

The kinship idiom is only partly metaphorical, since ayllu mates are in fact in patrilineal consanguineal relationships, or (as is usual for women) affines with multiple links to the member patrilineages. The ayllu figures as an abstract parent, as do the community and other virtual entities in other contexts. But the ayllu's claim is more cogent because the actual genealogy is common knowledge. Ayllu meetings, especially the major one on January 2, are sometimes called *reuniones familiares*, 'family reunions'. They are occasions for hugs and tears, not common in a generally reserved society such as Tupicocha. The appeal to filial loyalty is a card often played in the language of power, both in high-register formal speech and in writing. A particularly poignant aspect of the power of writing is the fact that constancias of past gatherings are keepsakes of the beloved dead. When an ayllu or the community takes inventory of its books, people usually stop to pore over pages where their ancestors signed. Old affectionate nicknames are recalled and endearing incidents are retold. Such conversation functions to keep alive copious knowledge of chronology and genealogy.

Since the 1920s, the ayllus have also used other terms. These lexical rivals to kinship rhetoric play rather on the rhetoric of partnership (*los socios de esta parcialidad*, 'the partners of this parcialidad,' also translatable as 'the stakeholders') or of citizenship (*los ciudadanos de esta parcialidad*, 'the citizens of this parcialidad'). These forms express homologation with categories from business law or civil society and from politicolegal movements. They are common in ayllu "reform" statutes. In high-register speech or in writing their semantic burden differs from kinship rhetoric in figuring the corporation as businesslike, civic, and law bound rather than intimate and sentiment bound. These terms, too, seem to be in stable employ.

These two ways of writing about membership coexist by virtue of the paradox of "brotherly bureaucracy" inside these core corporations; the model of kinship intimacy and the model of citizenlike or businesslike commitment are both necessary to successful ayllu conduct. Women's attachment to ayllus has traditionally been seen as an affinal link less politically compelling than patrilineal consanguinity. But there are female members with genealogical entitlement (notably single mothers who stay with their natal ayllus and endorse their children as future members). A few women hold ayllu office. It remains to be seen whether the language of power will eventually recognize gender and affinity.

A VOLUNTAD, SU VOLUNTAD

Voluntad, most narrowly translated 'will,' can mean 'goodwill, enthusiasm' in most varieties of Spanish. Though foreign to national-style bureaucratic language, voluntad is frequent in ayllu papers. Voluntad is a "good vibe" word, imparting emotional warmth and a reassuring feeling of fellowship, even when, as in this example from 1979, the context is distressing:

> También se hase costancia en esta parsialidad de la sequía de la devina probidencia que nos esta castigando probidinsialmente que lo resibimos con *cariño i buluntad* i Tambien se Acordo sobre las multa sera la suma 200 soles. Para su costancia firman los hijos de la parsialidad.
>
> [Also we put on record in this parcialidad the drought by which divine providence is punishing us providentially (and) that we receive it with affection and good will (*buluntad* = voluntad) and Also it was Agreed about the fine it will be the sum of 200 soles. For constancia the children of the parsialidad sign.] (APM/SAT 04 1979b:60)

Here (as in the ritual of the sacrificial boat on Yansa Lake, described in chapters 2 and 6) it is assumed the divinity is a party to the power of writing and a putative reader of it. The passage assures the superhuman powers which give drought or flood that Mujica has steady goodwill toward them even when they punish humans.

But apart from the emotive power of the word, voluntad has a specific regional use not found in dictionaries. It belongs to the lexicon of Andean reciprocity. Enrique Mayer's well-known ethnography of the named canons of reciprocity in the central Peruvian highlands (1980) includes voluntad as the least measured, most committed form of mutual giving:

> Voluntad was [in Tangor village] an obligation that a person fulfilled because of an underlying relationship—most notably, kinship—that bound two people together. The service had to be provided at times specified by custom. . . . Usually the event itself involved a ritual in the family that was to receive the contribution, such as a baptism, a first hair cutting, a house roofing . . . or the death of a relative. The appropriate return was automatically made when the other family celebrated the same ritual. . . . approaching a more "generalized" reciprocity. (Mayer [1980] 2002:110–11)

Voluntad is general reciprocity, the material enactment of a standing relationship wherein interreliance may deepen without limit. The term is used in much the same way in Tupicocha. In ayllu writing, it signals an act of giving which goes above and beyond the strictly measured requirements of administrative reciprocity. A voluntad is a gift offered to demonstrate broader generous disposition and readiness to deepen a relationship. Giving voluntad is an act of merit worth recording not because the giver is thereby entitled to a return but because, on the contrary, the gift imbues an ayllu transaction with trust and open-ended commitment, so that participants need worry less about exact returns.

> Que dicho carretillas a puesto don Julian Antiporta Javier: su voluntad y mas medio botella de pisco para todos los presentes.
>
> [That don Julian Antiporta Javier contributed the said wheelbarrow-loads: his voluntad and also half a bottle of grape liquor for everyone present.] (APM/SAT 04 1975f:39)

> También una pequeña voluntad del propietario de camión.
>
> [Also a small voluntad from the owner of the truck.] (APM/SAT 04 1977a:50)

Donación and *contribución*, both terms that members know, could be lexical rivals to voluntad, and do occur in some ayllus' books. But *contribución* has in the past often been used as a term for involuntary levies. It tends to connote obligation rather than generosity. (In the early Republican era, *contribución indígena* was the euphemism for a resuscitated colonial tribute system.) *Donación* is best known as NGO rhetoric: faraway international entities, not dear neighbors, do this kind of giving. Neither is a name for the special kind of merit ayllu books record. Precisely because items of voluntad do not create an accountable claim on anyone, they add strength to the social contract among all those partaking, and lend prestige to the giver: the giver has made the regime of sharing easier for all. The books' dry, modest way of recording this merit is to local eyes a more convincing support than the bombast of holiday rhetoric.

GENRE VEHICLES

If lexicon has to respond to experience, it also has to fit into verbal forms that uphold the illusion of permanence in powerful institutions. Nearly all pages of ayllu books have as a framework one or another kind of formulaic boilerplate. Boilerplate is not a bad metaphor for what genre formats do: a rigid, durable container controls the heated, dynamic flow of verbal steam, so as to regularize motion.

Sociolinguistically, genres can be defined as sets of organizational and grammatical features that identify discourse as being of a sort that takes place repeatedly. "A communication situation that occurs regularly in a society . . . will tend over time to develop identifying markers of language structure and language use" (Ferguson 1994:20).

In genre, of course, there is an element of sleight. As Barbara Johnstone points out, "The biggest obstacle to describing recurrent situations is the fact that exactly the same situation never actually recurs" (2002:149). Formulism in genre has an affinity to the ritual surround that invokes it: both narrow the unrepeatable flux of action down to hyperstructured forms, which consist of sharply delimited successive blocks. Boilerplate formats are apparatus for identifying these building blocks, putting in their respective places the verbal acts that constitute (for example) a work constancia.

Sociolinguists see boilerplate building blocks as cluing the reader or the hearer into the particular significant data embedded in the recurrent event, while at the same time legitimating the whole language event as equivalent to a delimited class of similar events. They term the identifying tags "pragmatic expressions" (PEs; Carranza 1997) or "textual cues" (Widdowson 2004). These are the phrases which identify parts of a document and articulate them into a standard pattern. Such guideposts also tell readers how to use the information contained, which is to say they structure its authority. They often represent, on the tiny stage of phrasal choices, large phenomena which we discussed above under the rubric of state and community.

What ayllu scribes actually produce is documentation with identifying structure and usage corresponding to specific kinds of acts. This applies to whole ayllu books as well as to their document contents. Each book begins with an "act of installation" in which it performatively bootstraps itself into being. Books of mixed contents (which tend to be earlier tomes) compile the following genres: (1) *constancias de trabajo* ('work acts'); (2) *relaciones, listas* ('lists'); (3) *inventarios de enseres* ('inventories of belongings', incorporating catalogues of the books themselves); (4) *balances de caja* ('balance sheets', including expense reports); (5) *acuerdos de faenas* ('plans for future workdays'); and (6) *acomodas* ('writs of religious vows'). Some also contain "historic keepsake" narratives which, as analyzed in chapter 2, are secondary syntheses of the above primary records. In recent decades, ayllus have organized separate series of books for different genres, such as one for inventories and another for work acts.

A WORK ACT

We take as example a work act. In the example, PEs that introduce "building blocks" are italicized. A documentary appendix in the rear of the book exemplifies other genres. In any genre, the PEs tend to be traces on paper of discussion rounds during the dialogical making of the text. These structuring devices are not usually peculiar to the Tupicochan corpus. Most belong to parliamentary or legal jargon used throughout the Spanish-speaking world, and are current instances of a very old tendency to appropriate forms from the lettered city.

The following is the kind of act that ayllus write with coca in their mouths, with their crowbars planted in the soil like standards, in their high fields and pastures during the ritual "hour of customary law." At such moments the work party becomes an ayllu quorum. The italicized phrases are the PEs its secretary must write to establish the genre. Without all of these, there would be nothing to talk about—no constancia—in future recall of the event.

(1) *En el lugar de* Mayani	(1) *In the location* Mayani
(2) *fecha* 20 de Enero de 1930 segun acuerdo en primera seción se dio el devido cumplimiento en *la faena del serco dela moya* y asistimos a dicho trabajo	(2) *date* 20th of January of 1930 in accord with an agreement reached at the first meeting due fulfillment was given in *the faena of fencing the pasture lot* and
(3) *los hijos de la parcialidad* de Cacarima *don Valentin Ramos precidente de dicha parcialidad Don Lidio Huaringa Don Bernardo Velasco Don Aurelio Ramos Don Cornelio Florencio Don Eulalio Laymito Don Fabio Laymito Don Serilo Ramos Pascual Velasco y Marselino Ramos* y a petición del acuerdo de primer sicion	(3) *we children of* the parcialidad of Cacarima attended *don Valentin Ramos president of said parcialidad Don Lidio Huaringa Don Bernardo Velasco Don Aurelio Ramos Don Cornelio Florencio Don Eulalio Laymito Don Fabio Laymito Don Serilo Ramos Pascual Velasco and Marselino Ramos* and at the petition of the agreement of the first meeting
(4) *se acordo* poner en tasación de la moya del sitado y	(4) *it was agreed to* put the pasture lot of the cited [place] at rate and

(5) *se resolvio por mayoria* que no se bende ni se pone en tasación de lo contrario impulsar y seguir adelante el progreso y seguir tal y conforme como anterior y el que uno de los hijos de esta parcialidad quieren disestir de ésta moya en bes de tener derecho de lo contrario lo perdiran sus derechos corespondientes de la parcialidad y los dimas acuerdos como hase de los dentrantes se discutira en secion entrante y	(5) *by majority it was resolved* not to sell it nor put it at rate [but] on the contrary to push progress onward and continue just as before and [if] one of the children of this parcialidad should want to give up on this pasture lot instead of having a right [to it] on the contrary he will lose his rights corresponding to the parcialidad and the rest of the agreements such as about the newly inducted members will be discussed at the next session and
(6) *lo firmamos*. Siguen 8 firmas.	(6) *we sign*. 8 signatures follow.

Source: (APC/SAT 01 1930b:37)

The gist is that Cacarima, in accord with a planning decision taken at its New Year meeting, is improving a pasture lot which was to be rented at a fixed rate for income. During this job, the "children of the parcialidad" decided not to rent it after all but rather to go on improving it for the benefit of their own animals. They warn that any member who declines to work on the improvements will be denied its use.

The necessary ingredients for a writ in this genre are commonplace bureaucratic ones. But, as we mentioned in the section "On Choosing Words of Power," not even boilerplate is immune from incremental changes that grow amid unrepeatable events. Tupicocha has its own habits in using genres. One is special concern for maximum detail in defining the *We-here-now* of the utterance, that is, the deixis. (Deictic terms anchor the text in space, time, and society.) The items a work act must contain are the following: (1) A statement of place in detailed local toponymy. The *Here* must be a unique action setting, usually expressed as an activity joined to a location. Examples are "wall of our stretch," "road-mending of a place," "improvement of the plaza," or "fencing Mayani pasture lot." (2) A statement of date and hour. The *now* is often specified as first, second, or third "hour of customary law." (3) A statement of those present, with ayllu officers coming first; then officers of other ayllus and local officials who may be attending; and finally, the comuneros, or "children of the ayllu."

The *we* usually states the titles of office of at least one member and the honorific *don* of all senior members. Verbs are usually in the first-person plural, deviating from the impersonal third-person constructions normal in state papers. (4) Resolutions, each starting with *se acordó* . . . indexing consensus. (5) An optional item headed "resolved by majority," registering additional agreements. (6) Signatures, led by formulas meaning "we sign," or "for constancia and validity we sign." Proxy signatures must be tagged with formulas such as "en remplazo de mi padre" ('as my father's stand-in'; APM/SAT 04 1979a:7), or "su peón de Martín Camilo A" ('as peon of Martín Camilo A.'; APM/SAT 04: 1974b:3, 1974d:8). Finally, the signatures and the rubber stamps of authority complete the document. Ayllus have at various times had unspoken rules about order of signing: in some times and places, they signed in seniority order, in others by groups with shared patronymics.

OTHER GENRES

For other genres, a brief summary suffices.

ACOMODAS, OR VOWS. Writs of religious promises form the one exception to collective-oriented *we-here-now* deixis. An acomoda is the constancia of a promise to donate to the saint image belonging to an ayllu, or a community, or to donate to a religious confraternity. Acomodas are written in the first-person singular. The corporation raises money for its common fund by receiving vows, but it does more than this; the circulation of pledge tokens also functions as a way of organizing and displaying a network of allies who belong to other such segments. When a person who has voluntad toward an ayllu or a community or confraternity makes a promise, she or he usually deposits a down payment when signing the acomoda. The ayllu or community then shows gratitude and bestows some of its prestige by lending the donor a portable sacred object, such as (for major pledges) a *cajuela* (glass-sided diorama; see figure 52). These tokens are called *limandas* or *demandas*: "Percibo una *demanda* de plata que es una cordón de plata" ('I receive a *demanda* of silver which is a silver cord'; LCSI/SAT 1905:7). One year later, the *devoto* ('devotee') makes good on the promise at a *ricuchico* ('public ceremony of acknowledgment'; from Quechua *rikuchikuy*, 'to make seen, to show off'). Then she or he enjoys the kudos of newly won prestige: toasts, hugs, shouts of acclaim. During the twentieth century the limanda complex became more and

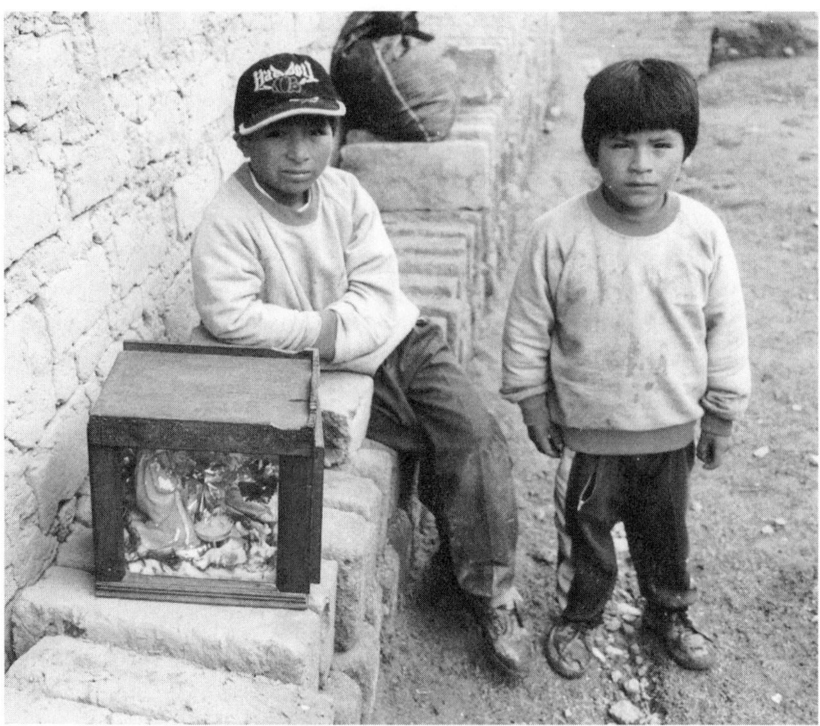

52. The cajuela, or religious diorama, is an important pledge token (as here, in Tupicocha in 2008).

more lucrative to ayllus, and many kept separate inventories (APUCh/SAT 03 1950b:368) or even whole books about them.

RELACIONES, OR LISTS. Attendance lists are the bare bones of documentation, lacking richly connotative rhetoric and highlighting nothing but the agency (i.e., responsibility) of members. But these humble vehicles have force. They are the easiest of all ayllu papers to read, and they jump out to the naked eye. The making of a list at an action setting puts members on the spot and will do so again when it is referred to at audit time.

PLANS. As emphasized in studying Tupicochan khipus (2004a) villagers try to lay down detailed plans for the use of work power, materials, and money. The appendix includes an act which committed Cacarima Ayllu to its 1923 plan for *tornamano*, that is, a cycle of faenas in which the group applied its labor first to the goods of one member and then the others successively.

INVENTORIES. Taking of inventory forms part of every accounting session. Every portable belonging must be physically brought to the session, an exhausting procedure. Inventories not only specify all objects but also identify details such as color, number of tassels, textile quality, and marks of wear and tear. The example in the appendix shows how, in an economy of material scarcity and moral strictness, tiny property details (such as the fringes and tassels on an altar cloth) acquire moral implications and this routine genre swells in importance. One cost of ayllus' ultraconservative accounting rules is that it becomes extremely difficult to get rid of anything. Even if a proper act is written, officers fear being accused of releasing belongings improperly, so inventories tend to lengthen with broken junk as well as new acquisitions.

EPIGRAPHY. The unity of rite, work, and script reaches its perfection when the *acta* is physically one with the ceremony and the work product. This is the case with epigraphy on monuments and sacred gifts. It is almost universal for donors to inscribe their names on donations. In Andean style one writes an entire genre act on it. This example from 1936 is painted onto the litter that carries Tupicocha's patron Saint Andrew. The "building block" signals (PEs) run in a different order from other genres but are close enough to make the lovely polychrome woodwork a clear three-dimensional acta. Such epigraphic acts have tended over time to develop in a regular local register, and can be seen scratched into recent cement work.

RECUERDO
En el Pueblo de San Andrés de Tupicocha esta Obra perteneciente, al Patron San Andres sea constroydo.
Siendo de "Personero de la Comunidad de Indíginas" el Señor Don Santos T Capistrano y Perez. y el Secretario General, el Señor Don Gervacio Medina dicha Obra lo han trabajado el Carpintero Don Feles Urbano y Don Florentino Sanches proficionales de esta localidad. la indicada Obra prencipiaron el 26 de Octubre y lo de terminaron, el día Sábado 28 de Nobienbre del año 1,936.

COMMEMORATION
In the Town of San Andrés de Tupicocha this Work belonging, to the patron Saint Andres was built.
Being the "Spokesman of the Indigenous Community" the Honorable Don Santos T Capistrano y Perez. And the General Secretary, the honorable Don Gervacio Medina the Carpenter Don Feles Urbano and Don Florentino Sanches professionals of this locality made the said Work. they began on October 26 and they finished, Saturday the 28th of November of the year 1,936

y como también, sea comprado, una "Capa" para el imagen, del Patron San Andres con los fondos del mismo patron. acuerdo el Señor Personero con los nuebos precidentes de la Comunidad.	and as also, a "Cape" for the image, of the patron Saint Andrew was bought with the funds of the patron himself. By agreement of the Honorable Spokesman with the new presidents of the Community.
Tupicocha 29, de noviembre del año 1,936. Firmas: Santos Capistrano Florentino Sánchez Felex Urbano Gervasio Medina y C.	Tupicocha 29, of November of the year 1,936. Signatures: Santos Capistrano Florentino Sánchez Felex Urbano Gervasio Medina y C.

THE "TASTE" OF LETTERS

During the peer-review process for this book, one anonymous critic asked whether it could really be true that "the rule of 'papelito' goes uncontested." The question is a good one. Many rural groups experience written process as beholden to unresponsive or even abusive external power structures and liable to internal abuse too. Yet to a remarkable degree, the power of writing does go uncontested. Although we heard plenty of protests about bad paperwork, we never heard protests against paperwork as a system. And although Salomon heard reports (in another province) about incidents of archive burning during the Shining Path war of 1982–92, the reason was not revolutionary fury about the tyranny of paper. On the contrary, villagers burned what they considered precious records because they feared—with good reason—that if guerrillas captured them, pages identifying holders of traditional or communal authority would make officeholders targets for murder.

How does "papelito" maintain such compelling legitimacy? The making and shaping of the collective enterprise consist, inherently, of a chain of verbal events channeled by a characteristic dialogical "funnel" into writing events. The ritual surround which invokes Andean or Christian divinity, the cultural discipline of coca-taking meditation, formal register, semiparliamentary rhetoric, and political prudence all guide language toward utterances suitable for a secretary to turn into performative accomplishments by writing them. In such structured situations (some of them centuries prior to the scope of this study) repeated protocols, with their characteristic turns and breaks, generated mutually similar verbal likenesses—generic likenesses, which in time become consciously enforced formats. Part of the respect that the result receives is the effect of genre as such: the work act, for instance, becomes instantly recognizable as an occurrence of a permanent, everlastingly recurring feature of society. Genre can easily be naturalized as part of order itself: "an appearance of Again."

But genre alone cannot command. An act could appear in perfect format and yet look wrongly worded. Conatively effective writing has to deploy mots justes. We have explored what makes a particular word "right," in the sense of condensing just the right semantic shades to render it persuasive as a representation of the general will. Mikhail Bakhtin eloquently summed up the matter: "each word tastes of the context and contexts in which it has lived its socially charged life" (1981:293).

Over the very long span of Tupicocha's lettered history, traditional practices and deeds have been called by long-lived terms. Their august aura evokes assent even after their actual referent has shifted. Thus *ayllu* and *parcialidad* have both remained names for something people do want to enact, even while their referents have been mutating for at least four centuries. But at the same time, to be persuasive a word also has to engage with the world as it emerges at the moment of performance. The word *presidente* as the title of an ayllu head is the trace of a certain moment: the moment when, due to a national political change, political homologization with the state trumped archaic legitimacy as the semantic core for an appropriate leadership term. Lexical change, then, is anything but random. Words arrive and depart the linguistic stage by the logic of actuality, as Tupicocha finds new ways to renew the virtual entity—community—that members rely upon to sustain them.

These precedents and semantic imperatives belong to the big picture but also smack of what Chakrabarty (see chapter 2) calls "History 2"—local narratives which derive from local experiences prior to, and independent of, the grand narratives of nation and development. "History 2" is not a mere matter of survivals; it is through "small" history that people connect to states, churches, and economies. Word alterations show on the microscopic scale how "small" histories played a part in Andeanizing the colonial scribal legacy, and thereby infusing into the stiff and specialized scribal sociolect some demotic recognizability. They have reinforced the power *of* writing among neighbors. But as we will see in the next chapter, these and other small innovations at the same time put Tupicochans into a problematic position where power *over* writing is concerned.

FIVE

Power over Writing

Academy and Ayllu

In chapter 4 we concentrated on the power *of* writing. Power *over* writing is a different matter. As Roger Chartier argues, performative power, such as the force of an authoritative text, becomes a fact through special linguistic rules and conventions that invoke power (1999:25–27). But where do such conventions come from? Power *over* writing is the ability to prescribe forms of writing: to define norms and classify usages as legitimate signs of position in hierarchy. This chapter concerns power *over* writing as exercised institutionally. We argue that a rural writer works in a field over which multiple institutions set rules, and that contending rules force choices with real consequences.

Holders of power over writing include metropolitan-based academics, grammarians, lexicographers, editors, educational policy makers, software writers, and journalists among others. The grand imagined community of people who use a given written language consists in practice of populations with unequal relations to these holders of power over writing. Populations who share a language have differing habits in using and writing it. In most countries, one variety and its graphic code are exalted as "standard." Descriptively considered, the "standard" is just one norm among many. It is not a better, richer, purer, or more complete version of the language, only a privileged one.

Neither does a variety become canonized as standard by virtue of any intrinsic property, such as possessing the highest degree of communicative efficiency in a given terrain (because it has more speakers or a more homogeneous form than rival varieties). When Spanish clerics toward 1600 sought to establish a Quechua for Christian usage, they bypassed the most widespread interethnic dialect in order to canonize the one associated with a narrow Inka elite, even though this greatly impeded efficiency.

By definition, standards are at war with variability. Standardizers seek "invariance or uniformity in language structure" (Milroy 2001:531). "Standard" is always a more explicit norm than the vernacular norms that people know unconsciously, because "standard" is expounded by metadiscourses such as textbooks, grammars, and dictionaries. These tools make invariance visible and practical in a way that vernaculars rarely attain. Sociolinguists, by contrast to standard-setters, seek to treat the many varieties of a language and their varying scripts on an equal analytical footing. Rather than classifying writings in terms of their differences from "standard," we treat standard as one of various coexisting language norms.

But a standard is a very odd kind of norm. A "standard language," with its written version, is an imaginary language. It is an ideal code or supranorm, not ever fully realized by anybody. And yet imaginary as it is, it becomes a weighty social fact. A standard is projected with the purpose of governing diverse, real, implemented norms. Standardizers usually concentrate intensely upon writing, partly because of writing's capacity to "freeze" usage in artifacts that have an existence independent of the ongoing language life around them. Standard texts become models, even fetishes. The fact that writing holds still and lets itself be analyzed makes it a particularly intense theater of metadiscourse, evaluation, and social judgment (Cameron 1995:2). As we will see, even tiny discrepancies between habitual norms and standards—enforced via education, editing, lexicography, or law—are consequential. Vernacular traits suffer damning classifications from those authorized to judge what is standard. Many common graphic habits (to be detailed below) are classed as stigmata of "illiteracy" and "low cultural level." How does Tupicocha, as a writing community, practice, interpret, and respond to rules prescribed by a "higher" authority? How does the resulting textual practice play out in wider arenas?

As we saw in chapter 3, schools position themselves as fortresses defending ideal, canonical writing. In the name of supplying citizens with this precious resource, they try to "correct" the "damage" that people on the periphery of the republic of letters allegedly inflict on the language. As we approach the actual rural texts that teachers criticize, we will identify the pool of resources that writers in Tupicocha have learned from colonial models, *ayllu* ritual language, old legal documents, and earlier, more autonomous schooling. The texts they have produced implicitly demonstrate changing ways to work on the uneven terrain of power over writing.

Institutions that promote "standard language" as the permanent benchmark of cultural competence—ministries, national academies, universities, publishing houses—leave out of account the shifting, dynamic nature of language. Education imparts amnesia about how languages, such as Spanish or English, first arose as marginalized varieties branching off from self-consciously "correct" ways of speech (Niño-Murcia 1997; Pérez Silva 2007). The structural changes whose inner logic historical linguistics reveals also have an outer, conflictive dimension: language change is not purely random drift, but regularly grows from "agency of subaltern groups in important historical junctures" (Das and Poole 2004:19). Today's Spanish models of correctness were considered yesterday as vulgar deformations of the Latin language. Historical linguists who want to know the directions language was taking on the Iberian Peninsula late in Roman history, today look to homemade tomb inscriptions by people too poor to hire "proper" Latin writers. As Romaine (2000:136–37) points out, "Histories of languages are usually written from the perspective of the standard variety, and processes . . . are treated as faits accomplis" if they are treated at all. Let us have a look at process closer up.

DIGLOSSIA

C. A. Ferguson (1959) first described the sociolinguistic condition known as diglossia as a form of bilingualism where one of two closely related languages, coexisting in a single speech community, has high prestige, and the other low. Since that time, the concept has grown greatly, admitting new axes of variation besides prestige: acquisition, standardization, stability, lexicon, and functional scope. One can add another variable: medium. Oral/written diglossia with its ideology of "high" versus "low" plays out differently in school and ayllu settings, for reasons we have suggested. But in both arenas, diglossic difference is "a *gradient, variable* phenomenon, which cannot easily be boxed into an either-or binary system of categorization" (emphasis in original; Schiffman 1997:208). In this section we will concentrate on the arena of ayllu and community.

SPEECH AND WRITING AS DIGLOSSIA

While various linguists have suggested that written Spanish is diglossic in relation to spoken language, textual diglossia is especially sharply marked and relevant in the peasant setting. In an ayllu or a community context, the most important source of norms for high-prestige, authoritative writing is legal genre text. Legal correspondence has long been the most vital written business of village councils. But mimesis of legal language also has to do with conferring prestige, as Rama argued (see the discussion in the introduction). When language variance becomes a resource and a status sign—as legalistic language did early in the colonial era—specific variations stand under judgment as discriminants of social standing. If language is cultural capital (as Pierre Bourdieu held; 1984, 1991), then learning the legalistic way of writing was and still is a low-risk, high-yield investment. And it is a strong card in peasants' claim to "cultural competence" conferring citizen dignity (Hymes 1974). The better it is imitated, the better the chance that villagers' papers will hold up in court should they prove relevant to a suit.

The urban prestige and legal power of letters in the scribal tradition is not all there is to it. Diglossia between spoken and written language has to do with deeper-rooted, more general cultural norms about the relation between language and practice. As Rama observed in 1984, Latin American literacy was diglossic from the colonial start. Colonial society "exhibited a sharp and habitual distinction between two separate kinds of language. The first of these was suited to public, formal, or official occasions. Its baroque mannerisms were carried to an unparalleled extreme. Above all, it served for writing, and it was practically the only language to find its way into the written record. The other half of Latin American diglossia was the informal speech of everyday life" (1996:31). Writing was glorified as the visible source and essence of "order." Ordinary speech was felt to embody exactly what should *not* be written. Spoken language is felt to be the domain of the pragmatic, contingent, and ludic; while writing is felt to be the domain of the permanent, obligatory, and serious.

This ideology has persisted with incredible vigor in the rural Andes.

Locally written Spanish is not a general-purpose medium. It is tightly tied to a narrow range of speech registers and written genres. For intravillage purposes, the language of literacy is tilted toward extreme formality, archaism, and legalism. In Latin America, far more than in English-speaking countries, ordinary citizens are expected to be able to read the actual texts of statute and law codes. New regulatory codes are hawked in public squares, sell like hotcakes, and make their way quickly onto the shelves of Peasant Community offices. To be handy with such language is, second only to actual politicking, *the* vital single skill for defending Community or any other interests. It is the most immediately efficacious part of being an "educated" person—the threshold of real solvency where cultural capital is concerned.

What has occurred as a result is not a versatile articulation of language as writing, but a rather popular inclination to pull the narrow register and genre of legalistic language into wider usage, and thereby make solvent a wider range of local institutions. That is the path to effective citizen dignity. Language as spoken undergoes not transcription but something approaching translation as it enters writing. This inclination readily spreads to nonlegal genres, including letters written among family members and internal papers of teams and clubs.

As a result, Tupicochans view writing as inevitably serious business. Villagers, aware, in an intuitive way, of slight but socially radioactive differences between their habitual speech and urban-norm Spanish, often feel anxious about having their speech written down or otherwise recorded. "Don't, it might come out badly spoken," said an otherwise self-confident man when asked if we might transcribe what he told us. The scruple is not about the interethnic acceptability of rural Spanish; in this respect the Huarochiranos we met, unlike rural people we encountered in the Titicaca basin or Cuzco, are uninhibited and even playful (Salomon 2004b). Their scruple is about *permanence versus transience*: writing, with its distinctive speech registers, produces *language of record*. Its registers are felt not only to be "high," "difficult," or "educated" but also *durable* and *consequential*, while the vernacular is keyed to transience, rapport, negotiation, play, change, humor, and the provisional. For this reason people feel the normal way of speaking is not the kind of language that should be written down. That would imply freezing what was meant only as contingent or processual utterance. Writing is anything but the art of capturing speech. It is the art of transforming speech—that is, social process—into a specialized language of record which is as maximally different from speech as its authors can make it.

TRANSCRIPTION IDEOLOGY

Tupicochans are acquainted with legal paleographers who retype colonial papers for court use, but they also do their own paleography. The way Tupicocha transcribe old documents demonstrates an interesting dimension of diglossia: a concept of documentary semiosis different from urban or academic ones.

With the exception of signatures, with their distinctive deictic anchoring in the bodily person of the writer, metropolitan standards of writing treat the letters as a suite of symbols which signify by virtue of the significant contrasts among them: there are many ways to write an *A*, but they are all equivalent as long as they stand in the conventional array of contrasts with other letters. So legal and academic transcription is simply a matter of replacing obsolete alphabetic signs with newer signs that stand in the same contrastive array. Of course this norm does not take full account of all writing's attributes as a kind of language. Given instances of the letter *A* do have significance through other properties than their mere stance in the code array. They have an aesthetic function comparable to the poetic function of language (calligraphy), expressive properties insofar as, for example, a line may exteriorize haste, vehemence, or timidity, a phatic function in size or boldness, and so forth. They often bespeak a period, and indeed transcription is needed chiefly because of obsolete forms. In the metropolitan norm, all this may be washed out without calling into question the authenticity of the transcript.

It is otherwise in villages. For León Modesto Rojas Alberco, the self-taught paleographer we mentioned in chapters 1 and 3, the physical characteristics of each letter are part of its meaning. For example, the obsolete character legible as an initial double *R* should not be replaced by *Rr*. Rather, it should be drawn in its characteristic shape but somewhat assimilated to the modern capital *R*. Other retentions include large rubrics under signatures and the curlicues colonial scribes drew on blank areas to prevent falsification. Overall, Rojas seeks to write a hand resembling old hands, so that the page resembles what villagers call *mosaico* (see figures 53–54). The product is not a transcription in the abovementioned Saussurean sense, but a reproduction.

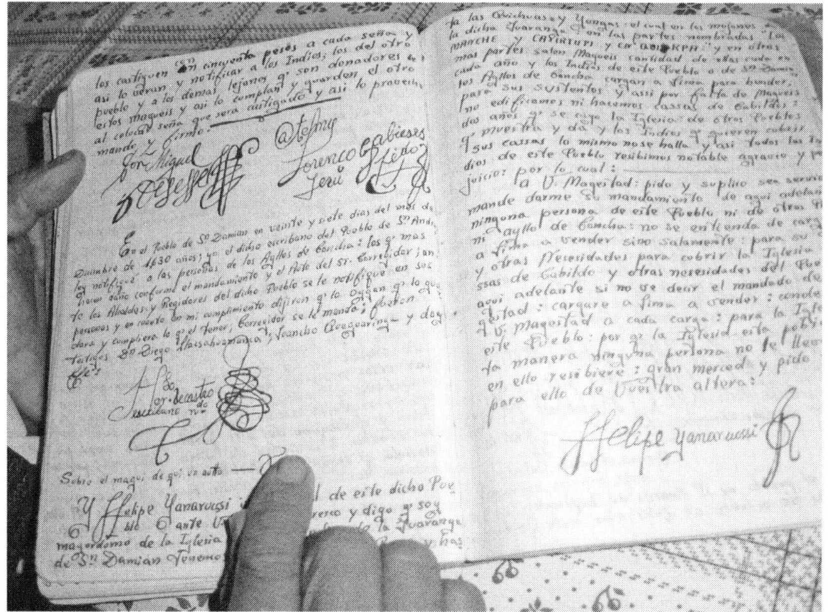

53. León Modesto Rojas, a self-taught paleographer, made this likeness of a 1630 petition to the viceroyalty. It asks for protection against forced sale of straw and other goods that were needed by the *yndios* of the *huaranga* to maintain their homes.

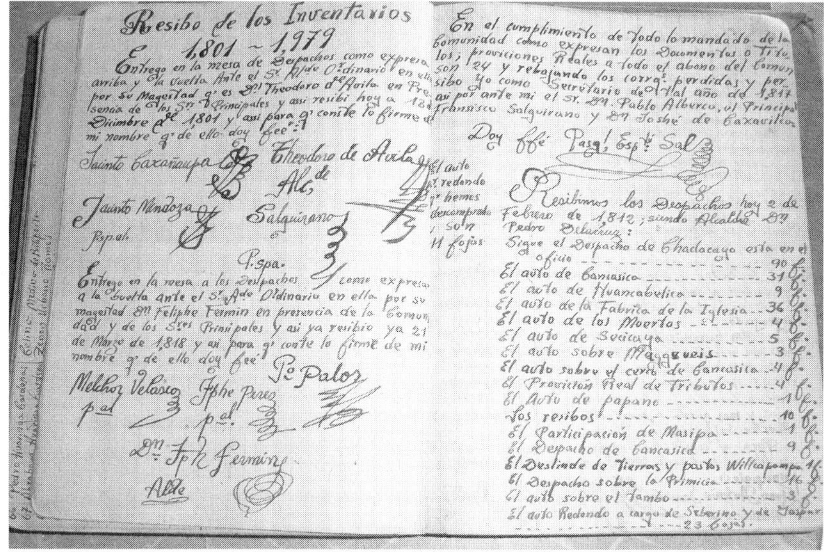

54. Another work of local paleography: The series of inventories transcribed here (one dated 1801 is on the right page) counts as a master document insofar as it attests the integrity of Tupicocha's foundational archive.

One might compare folk paleography with the halftone process used to reproduce a painting on paper. The actual elements imprinted are not similar to the original. But they are disposed so as to let the current reader experience the artifact in as much as possible of its original nature. This proceeding makes good sense within the local understanding of what a *constancia* is. It is the visible precipitate of a literacy event that had many attributes besides alphabetic ones. Traces of the state of society at the moment of inscription—for example, the expressive, aesthetic, and phatic dispositions of people present—are of the essence. As much as possible transcription is intended to allow modern readers to inhabit once again the event that generated the document. Independently, a similar practice evolved on the plains of Mojos in eastern Bolivia in the nineteenth century (Saito 2005:40). Archaism is a frequent attribute of "high" language in diglossic societies; what is interesting here is the peculiar potential of a visual medium—handwriting—for realizing it.

WRITING NORMS IN SOCIAL PERSPECTIVE

Amid a social setting that assigns writing the role of "high" language in diglossia, folk legality and its indigenous roots pull on literate practice from one direction, but prescribed "standard Spanish"—the highest-prestige variety, and the one whose proponents have the say-so on what constitutes literacy—inevitably pulls even more strongly in another. In Peru this imaginary ideal language is called *lengua culta* or *la norma culta* ('cultured language' or 'the cultured norm'). Rural people, especially highlanders, receive less training in it than urbanites, and pay the price. In the academic context in Lima, student writings that deviate from the norma culta are marked down as "deficient," "inadequate," "weak" or "insufficient," exposing students from the provinces to discrimination and scorn (Zavala 2009). Inés Pozzi-Escot in 1975 noted that one Lima university had an official Spanish checker (*revisor*) to catch nonstandardisms written by Andean-born students. The *revisor* was authorized to enforce the "cultured norm" on pain of withholding the degree (1975:323). These are weighty matters for migrants especially. "Differential access to linguistic codes affects . . . ability to exercise influence" (Graham, forthcoming; Howard 2007:143).[1]

Likewise papers that rural scribes and secretaries submit in Lima, reflecting rural norms and often deviating from standard Spanish usage, can evoke the scorn of notaries and ministerial clerks, who turn them back for costly editing. Rarely do objections concern morphology, syntax, semantics, or pragmatics of the text, still less its logic or relevance. Rather, objections allege faults in the mechanical application of conventions about spelling, handwriting, and genre formula.

Common sense might suggest that mechanical conventions would be of least consequence, because they are the least meaningful parts of writing. The informational value of a sentence is theoretically unaffected by small variations in the representation of words, as long as the script can be taken as an unambiguous equivalent for an utterance. But in practice mechanical details gain immense importance (Clark and Ivanič 1997:214). The reason, of course, is that they provide information about the creator of the text. Bourdieu (1991) points out that the standard is at once the means and the product of forms of social evaluation. Approximations to the norma culta (spoken or written) constitute the unmarked, routinely acceptable way to speak or write. The more standardlike usages are, the more they accredit the text as coming from an entitled source. Since written communication is usually read in the absence of its author, readers rely on minimal graphic traits for clues about whether the writer is a person who must be taken seriously. The pickier the arbitrary mechanical discriminators are, the more effectively they serve instituted hierarchy.

So why does a community which faces all these hazards, and which receives quite a lot of instruction in "standard" (compared to villages where Quechua or Aymara is spoken), produce what urbanites see as deficient writing? Starting fieldwork, we entertained a two-part hypothesis. First, informally acquired vernacular literacy follows particular norms of its own; and second, these local norms of written language grow from judgments of "correctness" based on written models at villagers' disposition as well as local and extralocal language norms. Village documents take up and conserve differences in norms of speech, differences in rules and habits for applying writing to speech, and differences in local theory of the writing act itself.

To speak of local and extralocal language norms with which the Tupicochan writer is familiar is to imagine him or her as standing within various overlapping zones of authority. In the next pages we will trace that multiplicity. Spanish standard writing is taught as the transcript of an internationally standardized speech. But villagers' experience of oral language also includes nonstandard (regional, local) norms of speech, while their experience of writing is mediated by nonstandard access to writing models. We will move inward from the more inclusive norms toward very local ones, attending first to the standard ideology and then to local habits of language.

LANGUAGE IDEOLOGIES AND THE CONSEQUENCES OF STANDARDIZATION IDEOLOGY

Of old, the term *standard* (in both Spanish [*estandarte*] and in English) meant the banner of a king, or the commander of an army or a fleet. A standard served to group forces around their authority. "Standard" also means a fixed measure of weight or value, or a professional rule, a benchmark, or the default item in a class of items. In sociolinguistics, too, the term fuses the notion of a center of authority with those of a leadership to be followed, an unmarked normality, and a measure for gauging difference (Crowley 1989).

Although standardization opposes linguistic reality rather than embracing it, we cannot dismiss standardization ideologies as illusory because they operate powerfully in every society where a standard language is the official language of the state. They are immensely consequential. "Proper language" amounts to a regimen of symbolic domination in which an educationally privileged class or ethnic sector with favorable access to the recondite canons of standard language are licensed to assign values to others' linguistic forms and usages (Bourdieu 1984, 1991; Cameron 1995; Crowley 1989, 1991; Heller 1999; Silverstein 2000).

LINGUISTIC HIERARCHIES

In typical language communities language varieties, often called "lects," stand in a hierarchy. (The term *lect* was coined to defuse the pejorative connotations that *dialect* has in common usage. *Lect* and *variety* are near-synonyms.) An average user of a language has "polylectal competence rather than just competence in their own lect" (Romaine 2000:139–40). That is, she or he knows sets of rules for speaking his or her language in more than one way and maneuvers pragmatically among lects.

The most educated speakers in a language community speak an "acrolect" or "high" variety, that is, a variant of the language modeled upon literature or other canonical writings, prescriptive grammar, and style manuals. Written language is especially influential in this sector. Its members prize the ability to speak in forms that resemble respected prose styles. Standard languages are explicitly (though incompletely) governed by acrolects. Those with less formal education speak a "mesolect" or a "basolect." All of them form a continuum of differences. Basolects have their own vernacular peculiarities. But basolect speakers at least some of the time imitate speakers with more formal education and higher social standing: professionals, teachers, priests and pastors, government officials, social workers, health personnel, and businesspeople. Notions of "correctness" are imposed by such status figures, whose credibility depends on their command of standard language canons.

In Spanish-speaking Latin America today, educated speakers' acrolect is conditioned, especially in their writing, by the standard of the Real Academia Española (RAE; 'Royal Spanish Academy'), which claims centrality in defining the tongue. The community of written Spanish is also much influenced by a few internationally marketed dictionaries and grammars. Institutions continually push their productions toward this "center," more so for written products which seek a multinational market. Elite publications and elite electronic media are the closest practical approximation to standard. The countryside, however, produces writings reflecting more diverse norms because rural populations are in less frequent and less cordial contact with the wellsprings of standardization. The standard ideal, which works in favor of the most educated, works against campesinos.

CONSEQUENCES OF STANDARDIZATION IDEOLOGY IN PERU

Peruvian public discussion about language reflects hypersensitivity about "correctness" and unwanted diversity. Perhaps half the national population lives in regions that are bilingual or multilingual on unequal terms rooted in colonial domination. Throughout the country there is a deeply rooted belief in language hierarchy. Indigenous languages are seen as inherently inferior to Spanish. One corollary is rejection of any Spanish usage that bears the imprint of interaction with Quechua or Aymara. Entrenched semiofficial academies of the Quechua language in various highland cities only reinforce purism and the ideology of language hierarchy by promoting counterpurisms and reversed hierarchies. Serafín Coronel-Molina (2007) comments that the purism and antivernacular standardization favored by the Quechua Academies are mere mirror images of Lima-based Spanish prescriptivism.

There are some countercurrents to hierarchical purism, such as literary canonization of famous authors who use Quechuisms freely. In recent years the movement called Bilingual Intercultural Education has striven to change public perceptions. The "political class" and educational elites in the 2000s expressed hope about shaking off colonial inequalities at last, while at the same time hoping somehow not to disturb the privileges of acrolect and standard. In 2005 the new Peruvian National Curriculum for Basic Education proclaimed a more tolerant view of language diversity. But the new platform tries to have it both ways:

> Considering that our country is enriched with cultural and language diversity, schools should teach students to understand language diversity and promote respect for indigenous languages and Spanish regional vernaculars, so that they realize that there is more than one legitimate way of speaking Spanish. However, schools should not give up the teaching of proper and correct Spanish. (cited in De los Heros 2009)

Susana De los Heros (2008, 2009) studies language ideologies in Peruvian education. From Ministry of Education documents and nationally assigned textbooks as well as from teachers' testimonies, focus groups, questionnaire responses, and statistics, she confirms that strong hierarchical-purist pressure toward a single "proper and correct" way to speak and write Spanish still exists. She also detects awareness of the cost of such pressures. Of the teachers in Lima questioned in De los Heros's study, 34.93 percent felt that standardization is necessary for Peruvians to relate to each other in effective communication. Most teachers believed that knowledgeable upper-class Limeños are the models of standard Spanish. But ambivalence and confusion emerged too. Some who said standard Spanish should not be imposed at the same time said they constantly correct students' Spanish toward standard. Many or most teachers are themselves speakers of lower-prestige lects (De los Heros 2009; Pozzi-Escot 1975), and some told De los Heros they self-monitor their own language anxiously as they try to become models of "proper" usage.

After analyzing the textbooks selected to be used nationally, De los Heros (2008) concluded the Ministry of Education was "still aligned with a standard ideology which may be also reinforcing the teachers' hegemonic views on language." The official textbook for the first year of high school until 2008 was *Talento: Lenguaje-comunicación.* (Pando Pacheco and Pando Merino 2004). It is based on then-current ministerial doctrine. Figure 55 is taken from it. (An English translation has been inserted in the speech bubbles.)[2] The page depicts children chatting about a highland

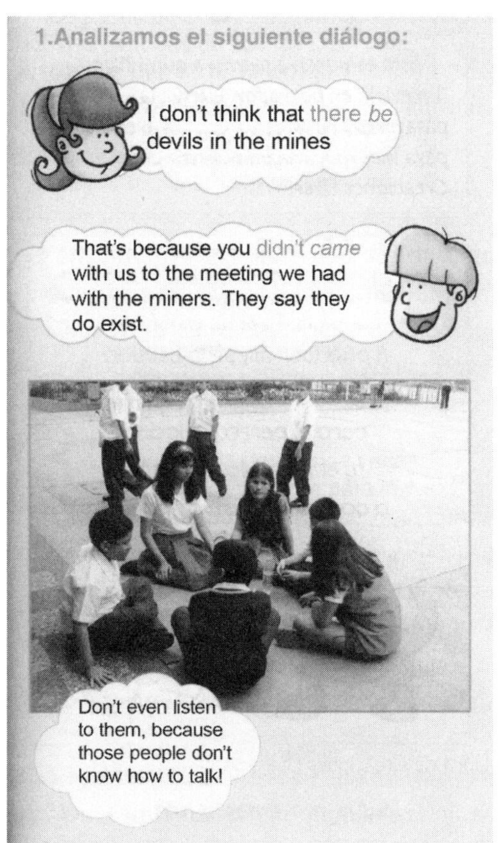

55. A national high school textbook (Pando Pacheco and Pando Merino 2004, no longer in official use) contains this warning not to listen to people who use "barbaric" verb forms.

belief that demons inhabit mines. It identifies as "barbarisms" two extremely common colloquial verb forms, *haiga* ('there might be' in subjunctive) and the colloquial past second person suffix *-stes*. The legend warns pupils not to even listen to people who use them, "because they don't know how to talk."[3]

A bitter controversy in 2006 brought standardization ideology and Peru's uncertain pluralism into the headlines. The linguist-politician Martha Hildebrandt by 2006 had greatly influenced metropolitan ideas of language through her books and media talks, advocating self-improvement through learning of the norma culta. A champion of standardization (secretary of the Academia Peruana de la Lengua from 1993 to 2005) as well as a powerful figure in Congress, she frequently polemicizes in the media against "barbarisms." In 2006 Hildebrandt publicly lambasted two congressional deputies from Cuzco—Hilaria Supa and María Sumire—for taking their oaths as congresswomen in their native Quechua. They were entitled to do so; Quechua is legally Peru's second "national" language, and the Congress did accept their oaths. But Hildebrandt, who does not know Quechua, blasted the deputies for indecorous behavior by violating Lima's taboo on Amerindian speech in public places.

Linguists and sociolinguists took the occasion to polemicize eloquently in the press about language choice rights. Hildebrandt insisted that the norma culta is not itself hostile to Quechua. But in practice it is hostile, because teaching about "barbarisms" consists in substantial part of damning Spanish expressions that show Quechua or Aymara substrate effects. Popular mentality associates such usages with lowly race; Spanish-monolingual urbanites find it hard to believe that speech or script in such language can encode intelligent cognition. In this way the norma culta movement encourages presumptions of stupidity or "low cultural level" in evaluating peasant writings that show Quechua influence, however indirect or minor. Hildebrandt's supporters alleged as proof of Supa's incompetence the many Quechua-influenced quirks visible in her personal notes from congressional sessions (Mariátegui 2009). A sarcastic headline urged Supa to consult *Coquito*, the grade school primer.

The 2006 fight over Hildebrandt's insult to the Quechuaphone congresswomen was experienced as a far-reaching sign of the times, because as Deborah Cameron puts it, linguistic struggles invoke a "symbolism in which language stands for other kinds of order—moral, social and political" (1995:25). Although the Quechuaphone congresswomen legally won the day, public linguistic bullying such as Hildebrandt's efficiently renews a cycle of discrimination. Precisely because they do not want their children exposed to rejection by the powerful, parents who habitually speak low-prestige varieties of Spanish feel a need for public school to enforce "correct and proper" Spanish. Villages' demand for standard language reflects the educational self-defense ideology Cajahuaringa (see chapter 3) preached, but, because the demands of standardization are inherently unsatisfiable, the defense remains self-punishing and only partly effective.

SOURCES OF WRITING NORMS FOR SPANISH WRITING

We turn now to specifically graphic aspects of language inequality. Because establishing a standard written language for Spain was a long and central project of what eventually became the Spanish empire, the *longue-*

durée political momentum of state-sponsored writing norms is worth tracing. The Christian academy of Toledo (eleventh century) acquired great importance in fixing language norms and unifying Spanish writing. The chancery of Alfonso VI (1040–1109) brought into Spain a script already dominant in much of Europe by replacing Visigothic minuscule with Carolingian minuscule, and diffusing it to other Spanish chancelleries. The commanding figure in the definition of Spanish writing was Alfonso X "the Wise" (1221–84), who codified a Toledan scriptorial style as the standard for all official documents. The Alfonsine legacy shows conscious reflection on popular ("vulgar") language and the fixing of orthography. This period saw the appearance on the page of the central-Spanish tongue, or "romance," as the vernacular was known, which later came to be called Castilian. It also saw conventions emerge about the sort of prose called *castellano drecho* ('straight' or 'correct Castilian'; Fisher 1996:74–75; Niederehe 2001). Toledo's School of Translators led "the intellectual world in matters of *scientiae linguae*," until in the early thirteenth century France began to take the vanguard (Niederehe 2001:ix). Through the eleventh and twelfth centuries Toledan Spanish predominated in deeds, military papers, and registries (Percival 2001), growing in functional reach at Latin's expense. Yet the enduring prestige of Latin as the language of education, law, and faith was to remain a powerful force in literacy ideology, intermittently influencing the standard through periodic harking back to Latin's erudite glory and imperial prestige.

The decisive step for the Americas in the fixing of Castilian norm as ideal standard was the opus of Antonio de Nebrija, still rooted in Toledan language. His *Gramática de la lengua castellana* ('Castilian Grammar,' 1492; Nebrija 1980 [1492]), and *Reglas de orthographía en la lengua castellana* ('Spelling Rules in the Castilian Language,' 1977 [1517]) were the first grammatical corpus for a neo-Latin language. Many of the rules he set still define the standard ("The past of *ando* [I walk] is *anduve* and not *andé*"),[4] but not all endured ("*Escrivo las letras ami amigo*" ['I write the letters to my friend'] has a preposition and possessive adjective fused in a way no longer permissible).[5] Nebrija was conscious of the graphophonemic dilemmas that his system would create. In a preface he wrote, "But I say that today nobody writes our language purely for lack of some letters: [the ones that] we pronounce and do not write; and others that on the contrary we write and do not pronounce" (Nebrija 1977 [1517] :111).[6] Nebrija's work enjoyed wide diffusion in Europe and the New World.

"Nebrija, with his *Artes* and *Diccionarios* [i.e., Latin-Spanish, Spanish-Latin] was the most widely diffused Spanish author in the Indies. In all the colonies the doctrines of the Spanish master were followed" (Rivas Sacconi 1949:143).[7] After Nebrija, from the sixteenth through seventeenth centuries there followed over twenty new Spanish grammars (Ramajo Caño 1987).

The Real Academia Española was founded in 1713. It chose a crucible on a fire as its emblem, and blazoned it with the slogan "Limpia, fija y da esplendor" ('Cleans, fixes, and lends radiance'). As its symbols proclaim, RAE sought to govern language with a rigor now unfamiliar to the English-speaking orbit. While Iberian hegemony in linguistic matters has receded, the general notion that a central institution should publish and enforce standard language took deeper root in the Spanish-speaking New World than in Anglophone America. The academy produced as a collective work a *Diccionario de la lengua castellana* commonly nicknamed *Diccionario de autoridades* (1726–39) and a *Gramática de la lengua castellana* in 1771 (facsimile edition, 1984). The RAE's supremely influential dictionary and grammar receive continued updates and are available on its institutional website.

Elites in Spain's ex-colonies, like those in England's, debated "linguistic Americanism." The crucial works date from 1840 to 1880. Andrés Bello, an important Chilean politician in the Junta Revolucionaria, or political insurgency against Spanish rule, favored protecting the unity of the Hispanophone orbit by fixing uniform standards that would reinforce Iberian norms in the ex-colonies. He published a *Gramática de la lengua castellana, destinada al uso de los americanos* ('Grammar of the Castilian Tongue Dedicated to the Usage of Americans,' 1850 [1847]) and a system for spelling reform (1884 [1844]). Bello anticipated the descriptivism of modern linguistics, perceiving that the differences between Chilean Spanish and that of Castile were "accidental divergences" and not degenerations (1850 [1847]:34). Bello's proposed reforms (like those of Noah Webster, with whom he is sometimes compared) did have some effect, as, for example, in his durably influential rules for the use of the gerund (Niño-Murcia 1997). As we saw in chapter 4, some Tupicochan "errors" are actually acts of belated loyalty to his "Chilean orthography."

Since the post-Franco RAE accepted descriptivist linguistics, dogmatic Iberocentrism in transatlantic Spanish linguistics has wilted. During the 2000s, the RAE took on a vast agenda of documenting language variation in the Spanish-speaking world. The *Nueva gramática de la lengua española* (Real Academia Española y Asociación de Academias de la Lengua Española 2009), approved by the language Academies of Spain, the Philippines, the United States, and nineteen Latin American countries, in 2007 received the blessing of Spain's king and queen in a ceremony at Medellín, Colombia. It adds to Iberian-oriented rules variant rules to accommodate norms of the ex-colonial countries (Reinoso 2009). The RAE's internal debates have been more resolutely pluralist than Peru's. The Peruvian linguist Jorge Pérez Silva (personal communication, February 16, 2009), who represented the Andean region in the Inter-Academic Commission charged with grammatical research, told participants that the terms *lengua culta* and *lengua vulgar* were inopportune because they legitimate linguistic discrimination. Ignacio Bosque, the editorial director of the *Nueva gramática de la lengua española* defended *variedad culta* as merely descriptive, and it is defined so in the introduction to the work.

In time the resulting reference works will influence Andean editorial practice and literacy teaching. But at the time of our ethnography, prescriptive sources about writing constrained teachers to a standard different from the Tupicochan vernacular. This, as we will see, placed village writers in an area of intersection among plural norms.

NORMS AROUND A LOCAL SPEAKER/WRITER: THE NATIONAL AND THE LOCAL

No matter where or how a standard has been set, it remains an abstract type, a celestial ideal. It takes effect, as we have noted, through being invoked as a weapon in earthly contention among groups with rival norms or linguistic habits. Any given speaker or writer perceives the recommended ideal through correctness as she knows it: that is, through concentric layers of practice around her, embodying various norms.

Where do norms come from, besides central authorities? In contact zones between Spanish and indigenous American languages, hybridization in language becomes a constitutive element of identity (J. Hill and K. C. Hill 1986; Howard 2007). Even in regions without currently active bilingualism, hybrid influences arrive in indirect ways (Pérez Silva, personal communication, February 16, 2009). Since language use is a social practice, acquired in a particular community, features specific to such a community "sound right," or "look familiar"—the more so because local features are realized and reinforced within warm, local relationships

(Cameron 1995:6; Coseriu 1982:11–43, 97–98) such as Tupicocha's ayllus. With the passage of time, any local community's usages contribute to forming its local norm or habit. Whether or not such usages match standard, they seem right and are accepted. Speakers grow up acquiring elements of a local norm among various norms, varieties, or lects.

One well-studied example of diverging norms in Spanish concerns object pronouns in Amerindian language contact zones among other places. The Madrid usage *la dije el recado* ('I told her the message') marks the indirect object pronoun with female gender. It is a nonstandard habit to use the gender-inflected direct object pronoun *la* instead of the gender-neutral indirect object pronoun *le*. This habit is called *laísmo*. This usage is widespread in Castile. Correspondingly, *leísmo*, the use of gender-neutral *le(s)* as an accusative corresponding to feminine direct objects (*Le vi*, 'I saw her') is also considered nonstandard. *Le(s)* used with a human male direct object as referent is accepted as a standard construction. The variety spoken in Lima differentiates case, gender, and number. By contrast, in Andean Spanish *leísmo* and *loísmo* are constant features, taking no account of grammatical gender. The variety spoken in Tupicocha is a local variety of Andean Spanish. Tupicochan examples are *Le vi a la señora* ('I saw the lady'; with a gender-neutral indirect object pronoun used as accusative pronoun), *Lo hierven el agua* ('They boil the water'; with a masculine direct object pronoun where the standard Spanish and the Lima norm would require a feminine; see Klee and Caravedo 2006:105–6).

These elements of Lima and of Tupicocha norms—divergent within one day's bus ride—do not come from separate worlds. A Tupicochan hears and more or less consciously knows both object pronoun rules, and myriad other "diatopic" (place-linked) details of plural norms. As much as institutions strive to impose conventions and lessen diversity, the variety of relationships a person engages in continually gives occasion to use varied norms pragmatically. Users of language draw from the available "pools of linguistic resources," to use an expression of George Grace (1981:264). These resources are what we now focus on.

Lima, a city to which nearly all Tupicochans travel, is today largely a city of ex-peasants and their offspring. Lima adds urban usages to villagers' "pool of linguistic resources." The Lima urban variety of Spanish, in all its "diastratic" (class-linked) versions, coexists with the Andean variety (which itself is somewhat diverse). It has been thirty years since Inés Pozzi-Escot (1975:322–23) began documenting cohabitation between Andean and metropolitan Spanish. Recent years have produced generational changes which show immigrants in the capital moving from an Andean norm toward the *norma limeña*,

> a direction compatible with a tendency towards standardized or prestigious forms in line with the process of globalization. Andean immigrants tend to abandon the features of their native varieties, even though they maintain strong family ties, and end up acquiring forms that are more commonly used by the Limeños with whom they have the most frequent contact. (Klee and Caravedo 2006:111)

Once again, loísmo will do for an example. The first generation arriving in the capital retains a pronoun system that is simplified in terms of gender and number and that uses *lo* as object pronoun, while the Lima-born mark objects with a system of clitics marking gender and number. City-bred children of immigrants use a hybrid system with elements of both Andean and Lima Spanish (Klee and Caravedo 2006).

So a Tupicochan, like anyone, is constantly choosing from the "pool" of resources that may or may not prove pragmatically "right." One way to track awareness of intra-Peruvian clashes of regional norms and the genesis of judgments about particular forms' acceptability and prestige is to analyze spontaneous conversations on the topic (which are rather frequent). Here is a fragment of a 2001 conversation between two public health workers stationed in Tupicocha. Neither of the two had roots there. One was a Limeña (L), and the other hailed from the coastal province of Ica (I). (I) had lived in Tupicocha for four years, while (L) was in her first year.

L: Tú tienes más o menos como tres cuatro años aquí. Ayer estábamos hablando [de] . . . cómo hablan así *voltiado* las palabras, y ya. Y: yo te he escuchado porque a veces tú también hablas así y eso es pegajoso ¿no?	L: "You've been here about three, four years. Yesterday we were talking [about] . . . how they [Tupicochans] talk with words turned inside out [*voltiada*], like. And: I listened to you because you sometimes talk that way too, and that's sticky, no?"

I: Eso sí se pega. Osea por el mismo tiempo que tú más paras en un pueblo, se te pega sin querer. Ya, tú lo dices, ni te das cuenta.

I: "That sure does stick. I mean, just because of the time you stay in a town, it sticks to you without your wanting it. Soon you say it [yourself], without even noticing."

L: No te das cuenta pe, no te das cuenta. ¿Cómo era esa palabra, este, *voltiada*?

L: "You don't notice, right, you don't notice. What was that word, um, 'inside-out'?"

In saying *voltiado* ('inside out', which is *volteado* in norma culta), the two women were referring to intonation patterns and word order unlike their own or those of places they had worked before. By "stickiness," they meant the tendency to involuntarily acquire "undesirable" norms if one stays too long among basolect speakers. In this conversation the Limeña was somewhat snidely criticizing the woman from Ica for not resisting this tendency enough.

THE LIMA NORM AND THE TUPICOCHAN ANDEAN NORM

Traditionalists of Lima's elite Creole culture remain intensely conscious of the city's inheritance as capital of the viceroyalty of Perú and academic home of the norma culta. Propounding "correct" Spanish in the manner of Martha Hildebrandt is no longer a matter of enunciating propriety from a safe stronghold, but rather defending a highly valued Creole heritage amid a hubbub of other varieties (see table 6). One hears many norms spoken cheek by jowl, from the most *castizo* ('blue-blooded,' acrolectal) to the most *motoso* ('peasant' or "cholo" sounding). Because Tupicochans travel often to Lima, most of them are also aware of this variety and have status concerns about it.

Tupicochan Spanish, on the other hand, is a kind of Andean Spanish. The term Andean Spanish, coined in reference to Peru, has more recently been applied to highland varieties in Ecuador, Bolivia, southern Colombia, and northwestern Argentina (De los Heros 1999; Klee and Caravedo 2006; Escobar 2007). It is a geographical dialect and at the same time a contact variety, sometimes counted among the "indigenized varieties" of colonial languages (Escobar 2007:236). Andean Spanish forms a continuum connecting Spanish with Amerindian languages, local varieties being closer to one or the other. Julio Calvo (1995), Rocio Caravedo

TABLE 6
Examples of Grammatical Discrepancies between the Lima Norm and Other Regional Norms

Norma Limeña	Other Regional Norms	English Translation
Te fuiste	Te fuistes	'You went'
Nos levantamos a las 6 A.M.	Levantamos a las 6 A.M.	'We get up at 6:00 A.M.'
Le vende carne a Manuel	Lo vende carne a Manuel	'She [or he] sells meat to Manuel'
Luis compró un radio	Luis un radio compró	'Luis bought a radio'

Source: From Pérez Silva (2004).

(1990), Rodolfo Cerrón-Palomino (1992, 2003), Juan Carlos Godenzzi (1991), Klee and Caravedo (2006), and Jorge Iván Pérez Silva (2004) have all documented Andean Spanish among Hispanophone monolinguals, and Escobar (2007) has documented it among bilinguals. Although Tupicocha was called an "Indian" and later an "indigenous" community well into the twentieth century, at least some Tupicochans of the 1920s seem to have already spoken Spanish freely (as we judge from their papers, e.g., AP1SF/SAT 01 1928:76, 78),[8] which waive the right to translation. Lima-dwellers stigmatize Andean Spanish traits calling such speech "motoso." (The derivation of motoso is obscure. It may derive from a medieval word which Joan Corominas knew as a "Gallicism" in Iberia, cognate to French *mot* [personal communication, Steven Dworkin, May 6, 2007]. But others suspect Peruvian allusions to *motas*, meaning hanging threads on a threadbare textile, or to Quechua *muti*, 'hominy,' a peasant food par excellence.) Despite the stigma, some "motoso" traits have become stable parts of the Andean Spanish regional norm (Cerrón-Palomino 2003; De los Heros 2008; Granda 1999:48).

The Tupicochan norm as of the 2000s is nowhere near the strongly indigenous pole of Andean Spanish usage. Though different from the norms of educated Limeños, it bears resemblance to a popular Lima norm evolving amid contact between the Creole or Afro-Peruvian working class and ex-peasant *serranos*. Nonetheless in both writing and speech, Tupicochans do utter Andeanisms. Any Peruvian would instantly recognize their speech as a highland variety. The high articulation of the middle vowel /e/,

56. *FUNERARIA* ('funeral parlor') was written *FUNIRARIA* on this Tupicochan funeral parlor around 2000: This is an example of hesitation regarding vowel uses.

an Andean shibboleth, persists, particularly in a female gender sociolect: "Curri ps hijito, trí agua, ichi a la olla!" (*Corre, pues, hijito, trae agua, echa a la olla*, 'Hurry up, son, bring water, throw it in the pot'). The maker of the painted sign in figure 56 carried the same articulation into writing.

A few notable traits of Andean Spanish as spoken in Tupicocha are as follows.[9]

1. In phonology, the mid-vowels */e, o/* change to the corresponding high vowels [*i, u*]. For example, *hermano* > */irmanu/* 'brother' (see figure 56). This trait is one manifestation of what is called trivocalism, because it derives from Quechua's trivocalic system in contact with pentavocalic Spanish. Trivocalic tendencies in populations without Quechua are not rare. Tupicocha's trivocalism is probably a remaining trait formed in the times when Quechua or the older regional ethnic language (related to Aymara) was spoken; alternatively it might be an indirect influence (personal communication, Pérez Silva, 2009).

   When Tupicochans write, their spelling clearly shows trivocalism in perception of Spanish words such as *mesmo/mismo, nengún/*

ningún, prisedente/presidente. Hypercorrections often seek to adjust it to the norma culta. These Andeanisms have not changed much since the bilingual or trilingual mid-eighteenth century (*Migil,* cf. Limeño *Miguel; disimos,* cf. Limeño *decimos; quibrados,* cf. Limeño *quebrados* [all from 1751]; ACCSAT/SAT Folder 26 1670:f. 3r). The late nineteenth century shows similar trivocalism: *manuanse,* cf. Limeño *amanuense,* 1875 (APM/SAT 01:1875:1r); *dintrada,* cf. Limeño *dentrada; rial,* cf. Limeño *real,* etc. in 1890 (APM/SAT 01 1890:[unnumbered page]4r); *piscau,* cf. Limeño *pescado* (ACCSAT/SAT 05 1909:135).

2. Another feature shared with Andean Spanish in Tupicocha is the use of the doubly marked possessive, as in *su casa de Juan* or *de Juan su casa.* This Quechua-like usage would be something like saying in English "of John his house," rather than "John's house," marking both *John* and *house* for possession. Double possessive marking, though present in Tupicochan speech, is rare in ayllu books. Writers—some of them very young people, drafted as ayllu secretaries when only recently inducted as members—seem to maintain a competence in a variety suitable for writing, separate from their oral habits.
3. In morphosyntax, as noted above, Andean speakers generalize the use of *lo* as third person clitic without taking account of the antecedent's gender, number, or case. For example, *La leche no lo toman* ('Milk they don't drink') overrides the feminine gender of *leche.* Andean Spanish also lacks gender concordance between a noun and its modifier, as in *camisa negro* compared to Lima *camisa negra* ('black shirt').

   A sign in the Tupicocha plaza reads:

Esta pileta es tuyo	This fountain is yours.
Cúidalo	Take care of it.

   The use of what Lima norm and the standard treat as a masculine direct object pronoun (*lo*) when the antecedent (*pileta*) has feminine gender is correct only in Andean Spanish. (In Limeño it would be *cuídala.*)
4. Andean Spanish allows subject-object-verb (SOV) syntax, as in *Juan una gallina compró* ('Juan bought a hen'), which in Lima would be *Juan compró una gallina.* This is no longer common in Tupicocha.

5. Andean Spanish tends to reduce Spanish diphthongs to monophthongs, as in *ruego* > *rogo* ('I beg'; Calvo 1995; Escobar 2007; Godenzzi 1991; Pérez Silva 2004; Pozzi-Escot 1975; Rivarola 1995, 2000). This is found in older Tupicochan writings but rarely in current usage. All of these have been explained as tendencies to conform Spanish with Quechua and Aymara systems.
6. Quechua distinguishes two past tenses, the "surprise" past tense (a past event of which the speaker was not aware at the time) as opposed to "contemporaneous knowledge" past tense. This obligatory distinction in Quechua is calked in popular highland Spanish: "Esta cerveza ha sido [or había sido] rica" ('This beer has [had] been delicious' means 'This beer was delicious [all along, but I only just found out]'). In other norms it would be "esta cerveza es rica."
7. Tupicochans consistently use second-person verbs with the formal second-person pronoun *usted. Usted* is grammatically third-person (because it etymologically meant 'your mercy'). "Usted piensas así" (instead of "Usted piensa así" or "tú piensas así"), which is the norm in Tupicocha, sounds to Limeños something like 'That's what you thinks.'

One can get an idea of local norms from metalinguistic judgments about correctness. A worker at the public health post said that he never used the Andean Spanish double possessive, but minutes later in the same conversation said, "de mi esposa su familia" ('of my wife her family') and "de su familia su chacra" ('of his family their plot'). Under pressure of standardization, people profess norms that unselfconscious behavior contradicts (Fasold 1984:158, 165–70). The writing of ayllu papers, and so forth, is a context evoking high linguistic self-consciousness and adjustment toward urban norms as far as people know them. But unconscious habit can guide the pen as well as the tongue.

Finally, Tupicochan vocabulary was collected by asking people from other places, such as schoolteachers and health workers, what words they had heard here but not in other places. Their responses included terms from their professional contexts. The health workers interviewed in June 2001 were surprised by local terms meaning 'to give birth' (*dar a luz* in Lima), namely, *pasar* ('to pass' as transitive verb) or *salvar* ('to bring to safety, to save').

L: Por ejemplo acá no dicen "ha dado a luz" o "va a dar" o "está dando a luz" ¿no? sino dicen "ha pasado."	L: "For example, here they don't say, 'she's given birth' or 'she will give birth' or 'she's giving birth,' no?, but they say 'she has passed'."
I: "Ya pasó."	I: " 'She already passed [the baby]'."
L: O "ha salvado."	L: "Or, 'she has brought it [the baby] to safety'."
I: Osea ya pasó el bebe, ¿no? algo así.	I: "That is, she already passed the baby, right? Something like that."
L: Ayer el señor, el abuelito, decía pe cuando atendimos un parto, "ya había salido el bebe," entraba el abuelo decía "¿ya salvó?, ¿ya salvó el bebe?"	L: "Yesterday a gentleman, the grandfather, was saying y'know, when we were attending to a birth, 'the baby has already come out,' he came in, the grandfather and said, 'Has she brought it [the baby] to safety? Has she saved the baby?' "

The sentence "Ya había salido el bebe" uses the Andean Spanish "discovery past" tense as mentioned above.

Other lexical examples seen as peculiar by outsiders to the village include rustic, archaic, or indigenous terms. In 2001 teachers at the village school mentioned those listed in table 7. (Later, villagers were interviewed to see whether they in fact use and accept them.)

SPELLING AND WRITERS

The single aspect of Tupicochan writing which falls furthest from the Peruvian standard is orthography. Since spelling is so sensitive a matter in the politics of literacy, and so sensitive an index of hierarchy among norms, it is worth looking in some detail at Tupicocha's choices of "linguistic resources" for facing the small but socially loaded doubts that arise in Spanish spelling (Schieffelin and Doucet 1994).

Some Tupicochan spellings that urbanites see as wrong are simply

TABLE 7

Examples of Discrepancies between Lima Usage and Tupicocha Usage

Lima Term	Tupicocha Term	English Translation
Recoger la fruta	Pañar la fruta	'Pick the fruit'
Vivir en Lima	Parar en Lima	'Live in Lima'
Se está oscureciendo	Ya no miro	'It's getting dark'
Acá cerca	Aquisito	'Nearby here'
Al frente	Frentecito	'Facing'
¿Cómo te llamas?	¿Y te llamas?	'What's your name?'

belated retentions of forms that have gone out of date in official channels. For example, writing the preposition *á* ('to') with the acute accent was correct according to the Royal Academy standard of the eighteenth century. Villagers may have learned it from scribes of that era. They still saw it in *El Mosaico* during the 1920s and kept using it. The conjunction *and* is spelled *y* in standard Spanish, but Tupicochan records often use *i*. This too is only an anachronism. The *i* form was a fashion promoted by nineteenth-century proponents of spelling reform. In 1925 legal documentation from Lima still used it: "28 de agosto i 11 de setiembre." So did the revered 1935 document by which the state recognized Tupicocha's "Indigenous Community" with its "tierras i título de dominio" ('lands and titles of dominion,' Resolución Suprema Lima, August 31, 1935). *Setiembre*, a common spelling of the standard *septiembre*, is another belated retention of Bello's independence-era spelling reform.

The Spanish orthographic system now taught as standard has been considered among the more "transparent" ones in worldwide comparison (Besner and Chapnik Smith 1992), but still it hardly reaches the ideal of one grapheme per phoneme. Orthographic doubts, and prestige-loaded arbitrary solutions, arise, especially when one phoneme has two or more graphic counterparts. Prestige-variety education requires intense teaching of these cases. Intellectuals, no less than school-weary pupils, have long wished for a more predictable orthography.[10] The Peruvian anarchist Manuel González Prada (1848–1918), who now is revered as patriot and social critic, held out for *i* instead of *y* (*hoy* > *hoi*), wiped out *x* in some usages (*exceptuando* > *esceptuando* 'excepting,' *extranjeros* > *estranjeros* 'foreigners'), and altered standard *<j>*/*<g>* usages (*refugian* > *refujian* 'they take refuge'). Lima presses today print him "respecting his peculiar spelling" (Contreras and Cueto 2004:175). All these solutions also occur in campesino writings. So it is ironic that lettered Limeños disdain the "rustic" writings of peasants. Only those whose sociolinguistic distinction is high beyond reproach can safely toy with the arbitrary literate conventions that mark distinction.

One hazard is *<v>*/*<b>*. Spanish represents its voiced bilabial by two Spanish characters, so writers are troubled by choices like *bender*/ *vender* for standard *vender* ('to sell').

A similar choice is *<j>*/*<g>* before *<e>* or *<i>*: *gente* /hente/ ('people') versus *jebe*/hebe/ ('rubber').

A third and very common hazard has to do with *h*. In all lects, *<h>* is always mute, usually because it is the visible but inaudible ghost of Latin or latinate *<f>*.[11] When a word starts with a vowel, one needs to know by rote whether a silent *<h>* precedes the vowel. This produces errors of omission, such as *acia* for the standard *hacia* ('toward'), as well as such hypercorrections as *hera* for standard *era* ('was'). The *<h>* seems maddeningly arbitrary to all Spanish writers, and *<h>* nonstandardisms are of course omnipresent in Tupicochan papers.

A fourth, also very common multiple-grapheme hazard concerns sibilants. Sibilant variance has to do with dialect difference. In Spain *<s>* represents /s/ while *<c>* and *<z>* stand for the unvoiced /θ/, as in English *Thursday*. But all Latin American sound systems are *seseante* ('essing') and therefore in New World Spanish writing communities, *<s>* and *<z>* appear as arbitrarily distributed signs for /s/. Moreover *<c>* represents the same sibilant before *<e>* and *<i>*. A word like *ciencia* ('science') presents three-pronged *<s>*/*<c>*/*<z>* doubts. (In the quoted examples in chapter 4, we saw spelling variations in the locally common word *cesante*, 'outgoing': both *cesante* and *sesante*.)

A different difficulty arises where one grapheme can correspond to plural phonemes, for example, as *g* does: *<g>ganado*/ganado/ ('livestock') versus *<g> gente*/hente/ ('people').

These variants are of no communicative importance. Anybody would understand *peses*, *peces*, or *pezes* to mean 'fish' (plural). A few such alternations might affect lexical minimal pairs (e.g., *taza* 'cup' or *tasa* 'rate'), but context resolves them. Tupicochans use *<s>*/*<z>* almost interchangeably in internal papers at no cost to clarity, but regard s/z as an important contrast for spellings of proper names, perhaps because of the bureaucratic messes that result from mismatches with one's national identity card, or perhaps because the written name is regarded as a visible icon in a one-to-one relation with personal identity. Like instances of missing or superfluous *<h>*, confusions of the type *<b>*/*<v>* and *<s>*/*<z>*/*<c>* are viewed by acrolect speakers as signs of "low cultural level" (though in fact even the most bookish writers do choose the wrong grapheme occasionally).

POOL OF ORTHOGRAPHIC RESOURCES

Using these observations, we can characterize spellings found in the corpus of Tupicochan ayllu documents with a view to comparing the written lect with written standard. The examples demonstrate varied ways of writing single words. They come from a corpus of 37,115 words in papers from 1905 to 1939, that is, an entire book not counting signatures.

Let us illustrate with a couple of examples. First one may examine variants arising when there are plural options for representing a given phoneme. For *faena*, ('task, work day'), a word that appears 53 times in a sample of 37,115 words, there are three nonstandard variants. Singular and plural forms have been merged in one figure since they are not considered graphic variations.

1. Faena (34—64.15 percent of 53)
2. Fahena (4—7.54 percent of 53) (hypercorrection)
3. Faina(s) (10—18.86 percent of 53)
4. Fayna (5—9.43 percent of 53)

Three variations of the word *faena* represent all the possibilities for divergence from the canonical convention: *<ae>* ~ *<ai>* ~ *<ay>*. This is a general tendency in all the varieties of the Spanish language. The hypercorrection *<h>* is not a conventional use.

The following twenty-five variations of *novecientos* ('nine hundred'), which appears 144 times in the corpus, represent all the possible permutations resulting from *<b>*/*<v>* and *<s>*/*<c>*/*<z>* plus some trivocalism and diphthongization */o/>/ue/* associated with *nueve*. But as is usual for Tupicocha, the highest percentage is the conventional form *novecientos*. None of the variants impairs the legibility of the text.

1. Novecientos (61—42.36 percent of 144)
2. Nivecientos (1—0.69 percent of 144)

3. Nobeciento (2—1.38 percent of 144)
4. Nobecientops (1—0.69 percent of 144)
5. Nobecientos (9—6.25 percent of 144)
6. Nobeicieto (1—0.69 percentof 144)
7. Nobesientos (4—2.77 percent of 144)
8. Nobiciento (1—0.69 percent of 144)
9. Nobicientos (6—4.16 percent of 144)
10. Nobicieto (1—0.69 percent of 144)
11. Noveciento (1—0.69 percent of 144)
12. Novesientos (3—2.08 percent of 144)
13. Novicientos (2—1.38 percent of 144)
14. Novisientos (4—2.77 percent of 144)
15. Novivientos (1—0.69 percent of 144)
16. Nubecientos (1—0.69 percent of 144)
17. Nubicientos (1—0.69 percent of 144)
18. Nuebecientos (2—1.38 percent of 144)
19. Nueveciente (1—0.69 percent of 144)
20. Nuevecientos (34—23.61 percent of 144)
21. Nuevecietos (1—0.69 percent of 144)
22. Nuevecintos (1—0.69 percent of 144)
23. Nuevesientos (1—0.69 percent of 144)
24. Nuvecientos (2—1.38 percent of 144)
25. Nuvicientos (2—1.38 percent of 144)

Many other cases demonstrate doubt about multiple graphemes that represent single phonemes, as in all Spanish speech communities. The sample size from which the following examples derive were *avanzada* (7), *alguacil* (40), *voluntad* (50), and *cruz* (146).

1. Abanzada (6—85.71 percent of 7)
2. Avanzada (1—14.28 percent of 7)

1. Alguacil (32—80 percent of 40)
2. Alguasil (4—10 percent of 40)
3. Algucil (4—10 percent of 40) (segment or syllable */a/* omitted)

1. Voluntad (15—30 percent of 50)
2. Vulunta (6—12 percent of 50)
3. Vuluntad (3—6 percent of 50)
4. Buluntada (1—2 percent of 50)

5. Buluntad (1—2 percent of 50)
6. Bolontad (1—2 percent of 50)
7. Bolundad (2—4 percent of 50)
8. Bolunta (3—6 percent of 50)
9. Boluntad (17—34 percent of 50)
10. Bolutad (1—2 percent of 50)

1. Cruz(es) (123—84.24 percent of 146)
2. Crus(es) (15—10.27 percent of 146)
3. Cruces (6—4.10 percent of 146)
4. Crúz (2—1.36 percent of 146)

Another such case is *parcialidad*, a very common near-synonym for ayllu. In our sample it occurs 282 times and other variants, such as *parsialidad*, only 27. *Crus* for standard *cruz* ('cross') is a common error everywhere, but the Cacarima authors got it "right" more often than "wrong" (126/146). Other variations occur when a writer perceives a pair of morphemes as a single morpheme that sounds like the paired ones. These might conceivably impede intelligibility but in local practice they do not.

Se ha ('it has') > *sea* ('let there be')
Se ha dicho ('it has been said') > *sea dicho* ('let it be said')
Se ha mandado ('it has been sent') > *sea mandado* ('let it be sent')

In short, for the most part, Tupicochan writers have succeeded during the last century in distancing their writing from the Andean Spanish norm and pushing close to the Lima norm. In a corpus of 37,115 words the following percentages confirm as much.

Sesión (Lima norm 16—1.36 percent of 20), Sicion (3—15 percent of 20), ~ sision (1—5 percent of 20)
Limosna (Lima norm 96—91.42 percent of 105), Lemosna (9—8.57 percent of 105)

In all Tupicochan cases the canonical spelling taught in school is far more frequent than the noncanonical forms that come second in the above comparisons. Derek Besner and Mary Chapnik Smith (1992) commented that such results occur in words that are very frequently written because they often become fixed iconographic gestalts irrespective of phonological components. This certainly seems to apply here because the words are all common ones in an ayllu's agenda.

Other very common phrases may be used in stereotyped fashion such that the senses of their component words give way to a perception of phrase as a semantic unit. Such usages yield local variant writings: *Haciendo conocer* ('making known') > *ciendo conocer* (APM/SAT 04 1974c:5); *Habiendo termiпádose* ('it having ended') > *viendo termiпádose* (APM/SAT 04 1974a: unnumbered front page); *Habiendo presentado* ('having presented') > *dando presentado* (APM/SAT 04 1975:5).

Research on language usages suggests that speakers do not divide words into phonological segments unless they have been explicitly taught to do so and even then only if training is long enough (Faber 1992:111). But once people write vernacularly, their spelling reveals how they perceive their tongue's phonology. For Edward Sapir (1949:56) writing is an acting of introspection which manifests language awareness (Aronoff 1992:75). Alice Faber argues that the perception of language as sound segments is a consequence rather than a cause of phonographic writing and not, as some have thought, a precondition for its evolution.

Texts from Tupicocha form a valuable sample of popular writing in which writers have replaced some conventions with homemade cognitive solutions. Desiring a Lima-norm product, village writers apply the norm as they know it through experience that is largely regional and local and for this reason reach nonstandard conclusions, but only in a minority of cases.

A SAMPLE OF TUPICOCHAN TEXT

The 1975 document reproduced and translated below allows us to review the "coherence, cohesiveness, and adequacy" (Cassany 1999:78–87) of a rural script. Written in a narrative style typical of ayllus' minutes of their own proceedings, it performatively decides what fine to impose on those who fail to do assigned labor or arrive late for communal work. It created a binding constancia. Two proper names are altered to make anonymous the mention of a discreditable fact.

CONSTANCIA DE TRABAJO DE LA PARCIALIDAD DE MOJICA
(1) FECHA 18 DE AGOSTO 1975 (2)
Encontrandonos (3) en trabajo de la muralla de nuestro trecho correspondiente (4) bajo la junta directiva Presidente don Pedro Romero Alberco, Vice presidente don Hilario Urbano Avila secretario general don Fortunato Antiporta Medina vocal don Avel Urbano estando en

esta segunda hora de costumbre (5) en el trabajo para la Terminacion de anivelacion de semiento (6) de piedra y barro, y preparación de tierra y remojar para hacer árboles de 45 centimetros y en esta hora se acordó *en voz de todos* (7) por la inacistencia (8) de dos quienes son don Adalberto y Ricardo Cajías Miño [seudónimos] que diberán (9) pagar su multa de cien soles por día (10) porque asta (11) el momento estamos sacando sus trecho para no quedar mal y que este todo correcto en caso contrario que no se arregle a esta parcialidad, se pasará a disposición de la autoridad política para que haya mas normalidad en nuestro trabajo Tambien se acordó estar en la hora exacta para el trabajo, en caso contrario será castigado por disposición de la junta segun su demora (12) y para constancia y valides (13) *lo firmamos los asistentes* (14)
Tupicocha (15) 18 de Agosto 1,975" Siguen *20 firmas*. (APM/SAT 04 1975b: 28–29).

The translation below does try to convey the nonstandard syntax and stylistic flavor of the original. We introduced somewhat arbitrary English nonstandard spellings to show where spelling variants occur in the original.

RECORD OF WORK OF MOJICA PARCIALIDAD MADE ON
AUGUST 18, 1975.
Finding ourselves in the work of the stretch of wall corresponding to us under the board of officers President don Pedro Romero Alberco Vicepresident don Hilario Urbano Avila general secretary don Fortunato Antiporta Medina and member at large don Avel Urbano it being at the second hour of customs in the work for the aleveling of the fundation of stone, and clay, and the preparation of the earth and its soaking for making 45 centimeter [18 inch] trees and at this hour by common voice it was agreed that because of the unauthorized absince of two who are don Adalberto and Ricardo Cajías Miño [pseudonyms] that they shed pay their fine of a hundred *soles* per day because until the present we are carrying out their stretch so we do not come out looking bad and that it should be set right in the event that it turns out otherwise and not be regularized with the parcialidad, recourse will be taken to the political authorities so that there may be more regularity in our work Also it was agreed to be at work at the exact time, in the contrary case [the infractor] will be punished by disposition of the board ac-

cording to the lateness and for *constancia* and vallidity the people attending sign.

Tupicocha, August 18, 1975. [20 signatures follow.]

Some characteristics of this text as a trace of a literacy event are as follows:

DEICTIC ANCHORING IN TIME: time of action is defined not only by date "8 de Agosto 1975" (1, 15) but also by ritual time (5) identifying the "segunda hora de costumbre," or second coca/ritual break. Calendric time is registered both at beginning and end of text. It is usual for Tupicochan documents to be extremely explicit about time, registering it not only in terms of public or calendric time but also by the private internal time of ayllu coca and enflowering rituals. It is during these rites that writing occurs. The standard deixis of ayllu writing recursively legitimates itself by referring to its origin in the rite which legitimates the work.

DEIXIS IN SPACE: Space registry is also always extremely explicit. It may refer to the very detailed toponyms of local usage (this text does not) but whether it does or not, it qualifies space in terms of group social duty the actors have acquired in relation to it. "Nuestro trecho" ('our stretch') (4) means the stretch which the community has assigned to the ayllu. In any community work, the community assigns each ayllu a stretch sequenced by its ritual rank and proportioned to its manpower so that ayllus, as rival "teams," have equal duties per member household and equal chances of fulfilling to the credit of the ayllu.

LANGUAGE FUNCTIONS: The document is at the same time a constancia of work actually done, and a performative utterance that changes the nature of the work group by altering some of its rules (10, 12). The phrase "para constancia y valides" ('for constancia and validity') (13) plus the signatures mark the writing as effectual. As well as being referential in the first respect and performative in the second, it shows conative heightening in its exhortation and warning. As is characteristic of ayllu writing, dryly legalistic writing nonetheless yields some expressive flavor for those who know the community. The feeling expressed is complex. The writers are displeased about the lateness and absenteeism of some of their peers (who are also close relatives; 8, 9). The document ventilates anger. At the same time it comforts those who sign it by convincing them that they are not without recourse against these weaknesses, and that their submission to strict order gives collective strength (12).

WRITING CONVENTIONS AND ALTERNATIVES: In the word *diberán* ('shed', standard *deberán*) Andean trivocalism <*e*> > <*i*> has influenced perception (9). *Cimiento* > *semiento* ('fundation') (6), *inasistencia* > *inacistencia* ('absince') (8), and *validez* > *valides* ('vallidity') (13), result from the above-mentioned doubt about multiple graphemes for /s/. *Semiento* is also influenced by trivocalistic hypercorrection. *Hasta* > *asta* ('until') (11) is the common dropping of a mute grapheme. The acute accent mark is repeatedly omitted: *encontrandonos* (3), *terminacion* (6), *mas* (12), *segun* (12), and *tambien* (12) lack it, a deviation from the Lima norm. The text's sufficient clarity shows how little such variations affect communication.

Some Tupicochan written forms reflect popular etymologies based on rural experience. This category includes words and concepts crucial to the technological and folk-legal systems of the countryside, some not found in dictionaries. Popular etymology, of course, is anything but peculiar to the rural settings. Reforming unfamiliar words by assimilating them to apparently relevant familiar ones is a normal process of all language change, visible in the early evolution of Spanish as much as in its modern dialectal diversification. For example, early Spanish modified a Latin word **verruculu* to yield *berrojo,* ('bolt') which speakers then remodeled as now-standard *cerrojo* because of semantic attraction toward *cerrar* ('to close') (Penny 1991:265). An English analogue would be *penthouse,* which entered British usage as *pentice* from a French usage meaning 'addition' (cognate to *appendix*). It was later assimilated to *house* by semantic attraction, and around 1600 even remodeled as *paint-house.*

Ralph Penny (1991:262–67) notes that word remodeling is influenced both by associations among meanings, which he calls metaphoric and metonymic change, and associations among sounds, which he calls popular etymology and ellipsis. The common Tupicochan example *parcialidad* > *parcelidad* demonstrates both. From the sixteenth century onward, Spaniards used *parcialidad* ('sector') to mean a segment of an Andean polity, sometimes applying it to corporate descent groups (ayllus) and sometimes to moieties (*sayas*). Colonial change toward ideas of land as property tended to give it a territorial referent. The more recent word *parcela* means 'plot.' Tupicochans have metonymically linked "names of things which are already linked in the real world" (ibid.:264): ayllus and plots of land, that is, *parcialidades* and *parcelas.* Popular etymology playing on the sound likeness completed the remodeling with forms such as *parcelidad.*

Several other Tupicochan usages are peculiar modifications of usages common in other parts of the Spanish-speaking world. As remodeled, they have entered the local norm for writing.

Unánimamente (= de modo unánime) > *en voz de todos* (APM/SAT 04 1975e:38). Villagers are familiar with the *cultismo* ('erudite form') *unánimamente* and write it. Their spelling *unanima mente*, born of common doubts about word boundaries, morphologically resurrects what is in fact its Latin-into-Romance etymology ('with single-spirited mind'). But *en voz de todos* ('in everyone's voice') is a more compelling synonym because it reflects the actual practice of giving assent by many audible voices when a gathering takes a decision.

De su puño y letra 'by his or her own hand' > *con puños y letras* 'with hands and letters' (APC/SAT 01: 46, 1916; APM/SAT 04 1975e:38) is a very old scribal locution more literally meaning 'from his/her hand and letter.' It is modified in Tupicocha from singular to plural, probably in recognition of the fact that ayllu/community writing is by default considered a group enterprise and signatures always occur in clusters. The author is not the scribe but the totality of members who sign.

Bienio > *benio* ~ *venio* ('biennium'): "su *venio* de seguir" ('his following biennium'; APC/SAT 01 1905a:1). This word denotes the two-year term of office in traditional governance: "siendo en mi *benio*" ('being in my biennium'; APC/SAT 01 1929a:131); "en su *benio* como de mayordomo" ('in his biennium as majordomo'; APC/SAT 01 1929b:132; APM/SAT 04 1977c:52; APM/SAT 04 1976:44); "Cumplido los tres *benios*" ('having finished the three biennia'; APC/SAT 01 1939:99).The Tupicochan version reduces the diphthong and thereby assimilates the word to *venia*, ('genuflection'). The common alternation *<b>/<v>* allows writers to bring it still closer to that gloss. The semantic association is with the curtsy (*venia*) to the cross, a gesture which every officer makes on entering or leaving a meeting.

Probationary members, meaning younger entrants with pending requests to become full ayllu members, are called *próximos* ('next ones'). This word undergoes a shift *próximo* > *projimo* as in the example "También se acurdo de acer trabajar los proxcimos por la mitad, progimos que no cumple un trabajo serán sancionado por la suma de 5.50 sole" ('Also it was agreed to make the probationary members work a half task, [and] the probationary members who do not finish a job will be sanctioned with a fine of 5.50 soles'; APM/SAT 04 1977b:51). The word *próximo* ('next', in space or time) has been influenced by *prójimo* ('fellow man'), with suggestion of familiarity and solidarity. *Prójimo* also has a faint religious halo because of the phrase "ama a tu prójimo" ('love thy fellow man'). The metonymic component would be the fact that probationary members physically sit next to full members and arrive next in time to full members. Feelings of hope and kind regard are extended to these, the group's future successors.

WRITING BETWEEN CENTRIFUGAL AND CENTRIPETAL

The diglossic situation between rural speech and rural writing has changed little since ayllus began to put their records on paper. Despite the increasing availability of alternative models such as magazine interviews and popular nonfiction, it is unlikely to change because rural lettered practices arise quite separately from contexts where one might want to transcribe the colloquial. Writing begins when the pragmatic work of speech is finished.

Studying, copying, and adapting endogenous texts produces changes within this canon of formality, not an exit from it. Where the external and mechanical properties of the texts are concerned, village writing conforms most of the time to the urban norm in structure, style, and lexicon for genres such as minutes, resolutions, vows, memoranda, or orations. Concurrent, overlapping nonurban norms such as Andean trivocalism show that the urban norm has been filtered through provincial and village culture. Ayllu writings also show in marked degree the graphophonemic nonstandardisms typical of any writing community tenuously connected to standardizing resources (dictionaries, editors, spell-checkers, etc.). But Tupicocha succeeds in its purpose not to stray far from the precedents of the lettered city. From the mid-nineteenth century onward, its characteristic vacillations and fluctuations are rarely peculiar enough to impede understanding by a metropolitan reader.

It used to be commonly thought that writing, through both its centralized institutional control and its physical durability, fixed a standard and slowed or stopped variation. To put it differently, it seemed that writing favored centripetal power over language, while speech favored centrifugal dynamics in language. This study has shown that it is not the medium as such which decides the balance between fixity and mutability, but the total context in which speech or text are produced (Roberts and Street 1997).

For this reason a great growth in literacy such as Huarochirí experienced in the twentieth century does not by itself make production uniform. Nor does majority popular literacy, already an accomplished fact, undo the relation between linguistic production and social discrimination, as much as the millions of rural devotees of literacy hope for that result. Efficacy does not affect the tendency to evaluate utterances and the people who make them by checking mechanical features of text against codified standards. To the commonsensical question of why spelling matters so much, Romy Clark and Roz Ivanič (1997:96) respond that its handy, though spurious, accuracy as a measure of social competences is just irresistibly easy: it matters because "spelling can be unequivocally judged right or wrong."

"Linguistic practice (and symbolic practice more generally) under standardization is an essentially contested order of sociocultural reality," writes Michael Silverstein (2000:124). The "imagined community" (Anderson 1983) of the nation-state, in one stage almost coterminous with "print culture," usually arises accompanied by proposals to fix in print a uniform way for its members to talk to each other. Because the state proposes standard language as a form of unification, all who speak as citizens are expected to show at least gestures of loyalty to the "national" standard language and its script. In Tupicocha people do so readily and enthusiastically. Yet Tupicochans bring with them writing precedents and practices derived from experiences older than the republican project. Language practice, as it brings together local and metropolitan norms, is inherently productive and innovative. Willy-nilly it generates challenges to conscious models. Tupicochans became literate in large part out of desire to be served by the state, and imitated state forms far beyond the call of duty. Yet in applying these forms to their own needs, especially internal needs, they became unintentional innovators.

From the viewpoint of the elite custodians of literacy, it appears a problem that rural people write prose "plagued" with so-called spelling errors. Some of their errors are ethnically or racially stigmatized motoso ones, but at least as many are the mechanical irregularities produced by writers of all ages and educational levels everywhere Spanish is spoken (Matute 1998; Polo 1974).

As Bourdieu put it, "The language of authority never governs without the collaboration of those it governs, without the help of the social mechanisms capable of producing . . . complicity, based on misrecognition, which is the basis of all authority" (Bourdieu 1991:113). The misrecognition of the abstract standard as the living essence of language has enormous influence on all parts of the Peruvian literacy community. It costs all parties much effort and anxiety, and it postpones the claims of communities that are more than imaginary. Rural people have nonetheless consistently chosen to write in ways they consider proper to customary law and to identity, producing for their own purposes the distinctive accounts of themselves, which form the subject of the next two chapters.

SIX

Writing and the Rehearsal of the Past

When a lettered *yndio* picked up his quill to write a preface for the great 1608 Quechua Manuscript of Huarochirí, he started by asking what difference it would have made "if the ancestors of the people called Indians had known writer[s]" (Salomon and Urioste 1991:41). Today (2010) in Tupicocha, the people who descend genealogically from the 1608 narrators have known writers, and some indeed have been writers, for over 400 years.[1] So they can affirm as roundly as anyone else that their ancestors did know writing. What difference has that made?

This chapter "zooms out" from the microprocesses that generate the record whose details are studied in chapters 4–5, and asks how Andean villagers synthesize and interrogate their likeness of the past. What do all those *constancias* add up to? The chapter addresses ethnohistory in the sense of ethnohistoriography: given certain media, a folk theory of legibility, and vernacular habits of recordkeeping, what ways of handling the record constitute a usable representation of the past? What is it useful for?

Ethnohistorians have studied vernacular "past-knowledge" in many peasant societies. The discussion, which Bernard Cohn started with his 1961 article "Pasts of an Indian Village," snowballed so much that in 1995 his admirers made vernacular history the theme of his festschrift (Hughes and Trautmann 1995). This vast field has a thriving Andean component (Glave 1991; Mallon 2005; Rappaport 1990; Rivera Cusicanqui, Conde, and Santos 1992, for example). Within Andean literature, the relation among writing, non-Western media such as *khipus* or local icons, and oral lore is by itself a substantial theme (Abercrombie 1998; Condori 1992; Rappaport and Ramos 2005).

Ethnographer-historians who study what Raymond Fogelson (1974) called "ethno-ethnohistory," meaning local theory and interpretation of the past, emphasize a few characteristic themes. One is the intimate relation between popular historical sensibility and political selfhood, that is, the ways in which recitals of pasts generate imagined collective subjects felt to transcend individual lifetimes and exert permanent group interests. (Combès and Saignes 1991 offer a telling South American example.) A second is the plural and disjointed nature of past-knowledges. A single collectivity's statements about the past are hardly ever unanimous; nor are all parties in a peasantry equally authorized to voice them. Rather, they tend to be distinguished horizontally as proprietary knowledge of social segments (i.e., paradigmatic sets of similar corporations, like the ten *ayllus* of Tupicocha; see Urton 1990), or vertically, as bound to strata in social hierarchy (such as the superordinated state sector, i.e., teachers, social classes, clergy). They may also be bound spatially to geographically separate populations (like neighboring groups anchored to different water sources). Narratives are no less varied in context. A particular version is "right" in one context even if it substantively contradicts one belonging to a different context. A third axis of discussion is the inexhaustible debate concerning the irreducibly different (or not) epistemological footings of "past-discourses:" do "other histories" imply "other" premises about time and change? Is practical reason a common ground among all? What is locally considered knowable about the past? (Bender and Welberry 1991; Bloch 1989; Friedman 1985; Hill 1988; Krech 2006; Munn 1992; Turner 1988).

We will glance at some of these theoretical axes. But that is not the main objective. This chapter, rather, is guided by Stephen Gudeman's and Alberto Rivera's (1990:4–7) suggestion that anthropological fieldwork is done within a community of inquiry long before it is sent "home" to begin its rounds in academe. A fieldworker necessarily documents a society's ongoing self-interrogation and its internal dialogues, "a long conversation in which folk, inscribers, readers, and listeners are all engaged" (1990:189). Gudeman and Rivera focus upon "models" which have been shaped and reshaped by centuries of discussion. By "model" they mean far-reaching metaphors, such as economy being like a house or a polity being like a body. While sharing their notion of conversation, we would put at least as much emphasis on *inquiry* as on modeling. The record of the precise is accumulated in order to control certain social situations, and interrogated to answer questions about past situations. In using its fund of constancias and memory, a village is engaged in a sort of research.

The ethnographer becomes a specialized listener-in on "conversations" from which his/her own account can never be independent. We have already considered how Tupicochan writing generates "the precise," that is, a corpus that in villagers' view closely matches and codifies the whole sum of the deeds on which its existence as a collective subject consists. But what questions bring the record into broader use? How are the constancias of infinitesimal deeds and the tiny traits of writing that make constancias believable, then aggregated to form a village's sense of itself in time? Given the fact that coexisting past-discourses are different in ownership, political import, and philosophical underpinnings, what happens when they meet? How is the romance of Tupicochan sentiment and collectivity elicited from detailed records? What dialogues among discordant versions of truth make it possible at the same time to speak of a historic subject, a "we," and to leave the record open for the never-ending questioning that is civic business? How does a record which appeals to local idiosyncrasy simultaneously create the village as a part of the overarching nation and state (see figure 57)?

ECHOES OF EXTIRPATION

Peasants as members of an intellectual community have access to quite a wide range of urban-based expertise, but it is sporadic and partial access. Younger agropastoralists have a rough working acquaintance with the applied sciences, whose ambassadors are visiting "engineers" or rural technocrats. Some represent ministries; others NGOs or companies that deal in irrigation technology, surveying, or veterinary and pesticide products. From students (rarely, professors) doing fieldwork, people learn to respond to urbanites in social science lingo. Now, as in the days of the "lettered city," the most precious cultural capital is law. It is popularized by lawyers and Ministry of Agriculture administrators, and occasionally by political activists. Amid the general rejection of political party ideologies, which by 2000 were seen as interchangeable masks for a despised "political class," an amorphously political "green" ideology had caught on with younger, urban-connected peasants. Some of these regional cosmopolites have also learned macroeconomic basics, thanks to Lima-based

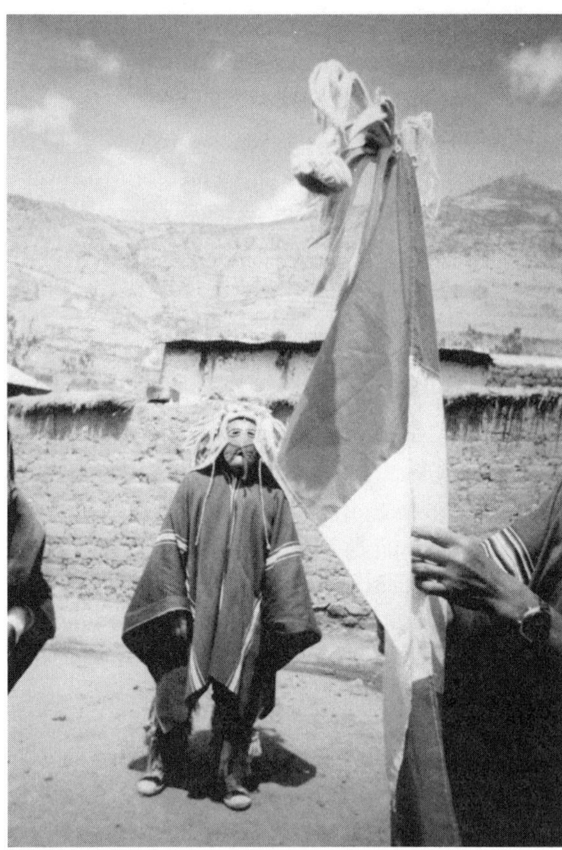

57. Local and overarching loyalties: When the Curcuches, or sacred clowns, descend from the Andean heights to Tupicocha village, they carry twin standards: the Peruvian flag and the *pullagua* flower. Pullagua is one of the plants considered regalia of Tupicocha's deified mountains. Photograph by Hilda Araujo, c. 1997.

news magazines (which cover economic matters at a higher level than is usual in the English press). Schoolteachers deliver the official understandings of citizenship and patriotism, along with spoonfuls of the natural sciences, history, and canonical literature. Public health workers provide the vigorous discourse of folk medicine with a bioscientific complement.

Missionaries and lay Catholic activists sporadically remind people of religious orthodoxies. A strikingly rich traditional Christian ritual life flourishes as common social competence, without generating much doctrinal or ideological voltage. Doctrine arrives occasionally in the form of visiting priests or villagers trained at pastoral seminars, but the bulk of Christian religious knowledge lies in the memory of elders who tend the intricate calendars and regalia of the saints and crosses. Tupicocha proper has largely been spared the Protestant assault on Andean mountain veneration, which spurs friction and even violence in some Andean areas

(Wachtel 1994:90–105). But Protestant influence emanates from an "annex" village which was formed mostly by seceding Protestant converts.

This brings us to a first key question for observing the local "community of inquiry" at its work. Given the fact that villagers have access to a range of relatively cosmopolitan people and viewpoints, to what degree are they aware of their region's important place in the academic historiography of their country, and especially its salience in the history of religious conflict? The discourse which makes Huarochirí famous beyond its own bounds is the academic historiography of its regional deities. One sociopolitical historian (Spalding 1974, 1984), one ethnohistorian (Rostworowski 1977, 1978a, 1978b) and one religious historian of "extirpation" (Duviols 1971, 1986) have raised Huarochirí to central, even canonical rank in the university-level teaching of Peruvian history. How we should interpret rural people's expressions about their past as part of a historical big picture, therefore, depends greatly on how their affirmations are related to the documentary sources these academic representations rest on.

THE BOOK POSSESSED AND THE BOOK RUMORED

The colonial sources and major academic monographs to which Huarochirí owes its "canonical" standing in scholarship were all but unseen by its rural residents until after 2000 and still lie generally outside public access. University-bred Limeños have usually heard of the renowned 1608 Quechua Manuscript of Huarochirí because it is associated with the literarily revered name of its translator, José María Arguedas, and discussed under the title he gave it: *Gods and Men of Huarochirí*. Throughout the period of this research, it has been in print and available at high-end Lima bookstores. Huarochirí agropastoralists, however, know of it as a rumored, not a possessed book. Common tradition mentions it as a text of legendary importance, which was expropriated. This subsection concerns the role that a book nobody has seen plays in answering questions about the origin of society.

Most villagers are aware that Huarochirí has a special place in Peruvian church literature. Like urbanites, they associate the name Avila with the key events. But the Father Avila whom they speak of is a grander and cloudier figure than the brilliant but vicious bilingual curate who sponsored the writing of the Quechua Manuscript of Huarochirí (Acosta Rodríguez 1979). "Hundreds of years ago," a man of Checa Community said, "Father Avila wrote 42 volumes of the History of Huarochirí but we

58. The sparsely inhabited hamlet of Llaquistambo is the "Llacsa Tampo" which serves as the orientation point for data on the Checa in the 1608 Quechua Manuscript of Huarochirí. Buildings of apparent Inka origin occupy the foreground.

Peruvians have only translated two volumes." This is echoed over and over with varying numbers. Avila has become a negative culture hero, conflated with other exemplars of the writer-expropriators (Diego Dávila Brizeño, who wrote an ethnographically solid report on the province in 1586, seems to be in the mix, as are early *encomenderos*, etc.). Avila is remembered as shaping the colonial rural society. He is a figure of cruelty but also of forcefulness as opposed to the feckless governments of our times. Remembrances of the period of *reducción* ('forced resettlement,' frequent from the 1570s onward) are associated with Avila, as, for example, in this narrative about the place once called Llacsa Tambo and today Llaquistambo (figure 58), told by a resident. Llaquistambo is an important site because it is the one which the composer of the Quechua Manuscript of Huarochirí referred to as "here," that is, the deictic anchor of his synthesis. To the eyes of visitors, it is notable for a cluster of Late Intermediate funerary buildings and a nearby group of large Inka buildings.

> Here [pointing to an outlying ridge], there's [a hamlet called] Llaquistambo [see figure 58]. A lot of Indians used to live there. "The Place of Tears,"[2] it's called. The Spanish arrived there and built a house. [The natives] wept because they didn't like this new treatment. They fled,

> they hid further away. The Spaniards needed to concentrate them. One of their missionaries who arrived there was a military man, Cortés. And there was another, a priest, I forget his name [i.e., Avila]. Those two went to find out where the town had to be built in order to teach the [Spanish] language and religion. They chose this site [San Damián]. They traced out the town.

A book-loving man who worked in Lima and later returned to San Damián as a *comunero* gave the following account of Avila as a one-man conquest. He emphasizes Avila as the local dictator who effected the oil-and-water union between the mutually unfriendly Checa and Concha "thousands."

> Since Father Avila founded the town of San Damián, only Spanish has been spoken. It was in 1556 that it was founded by Father Francisco de Avila. Before there were the *ayllus* Concha Sica and Llacsa Tambo. They used to each have their own separate gods. Concha Sica's god was a big stone Vira Cocha. Llaquistambo [which is on the Checa side] used to worship the sun and animals, the lion [i.e., puma] and others. The priest [Avila] brought the idols here, to this place. And so he forced the inhabitants to worship their idols in this place. Many of them came to worship, others out of fear of the punishments the priest dealt out. And so it [San Damián] got to be founded with a Viceroyal plan. Father Avila alone. He built the church, the cemetery, the school, the street layout.

Tupicochanos do not regard the Spanish invasion of the Inka domains as a chasm separating epochs. They lump the Inka era together with the viceroyalty because both were, in their view, eras of servitude. Based on Bolivian experience, Tristan Platt daringly calls their premodernity "the Inka-Hapsburg Age" (1987). The historic great divide in their view is that which separates modernity, the world of the free peasantry, from an earlier age of servitude. The age of servitude includes both the Inka age and the early colonial era. They tend to locate Avila on both parts of it: "The great ones of Inka times were Vilcayauri, Yauli, and Francisco de Avila." It is considered no more than common knowledge that the political preeminence of Chaucacollca Ayllu has to do with the prevalence of the surname Avila among its members; they are felt to have inherited the legendary priest's will power and adroitness.

Of course, such memories of Avila must be influenced by secondary and tertiary printed material. Once in a while sources can be tracked, as with Tuna's legend about a pagan Indian martyred for his conversion to Christianity: it echoes a civic pamphlet which picked it up from Hildegardo Sotelo's (1942) San Marcos dissertation, which in turn used Avila's *Tratado de los Evangelios* (Avila 1646–48). A "*crónica de cartón*" ('cardboard chronicle') inspired by Nilo Espinoza Haro, perhaps meaning a schoolroom poster, brought the schoolteacher Eugenio Vilcayauri Medina a version of the Avila lore seemingly filtered through back-channels of oral tradition:

> Kuniraya Wiracocha, God of Huarochirí or God of the Quechuas, lives in the zone of Huarochirí, he is the most powerful, he is commanding, he is the creator of everything and every time he meets with Huallallo Carhuincho the Huanca God who came to Lima[,][3] he turns him into water, into a snake, and into a bird even though Huallallo is also a rebel God and is the symbol of the Huancas, he forever struggles against the God of Huarochirí. But Kuniraya Wiracocha, Lord of Huarochirí, has condemned Huallallo Carhuincho to eat nothing but dogs. Some day thing will change, that is Huallallo's hope. (Vilcayauri Medina 1983–91:42)

The most influential channel of feedback recirculating old oral tradition into current conversation is the genre of provincial print discussed in chapter 7.

Perhaps it is the ayllus' distance from the Avila textual legacy that causes them to underestimate their own groups' close pre-Hispanic precedents. Or perhaps the theory of history, which puts a great rupture between the free peasantry and "*indios*" of the remote past, submerges notions of pre-Hispanic continuity. In any case, in field discussions, it was consistently the researcher and not the comuneros who raised the matter of the ayllus' pre-Hispanic origins. This was true even in the most prominent ayllus. Cacasica, the aboriginal ayllu that once held Checa's most important priesthoods, and which has an outstanding place in the 1608 Quechua texts, still exists in Tuna (not Tupicocha). When Salomon brought Gerald Taylor's Quechua-Spanish edition to a group interview, the elders of Cacasica showed astonishment—also elation—at seeing passages that showed their institution to have been eminent in the Thousand of Checa. The Thousand, an Inka administrative unit embracing roughly the same terrain mytho-historically described in the Quechua source, figured durably in early and midcolonial administration. The Thousand retains prestige in folk-historic memory as the integral regional society, whose breakup has caused unfortunate intervillage conflicts. The "Book of the Thousand" mentioned in chapter 1, a colonial survey of its boundaries, has revered standing as a charter, and the Thousand forms an intellectual framework for perceiving the Avila legacy.

The image of great but unavailable documentary wealth condenses a belief widespread through all the villages that made up the old Thousand of Checa, that in remote times Huarochirí produced intellectually great things—but those things are somewhere else today, in somebody else's hands. This belief reflects facts about the circulation of print. Actual copies of the Quechua work and its translations, or even derivative popularizations, were extremely rare to absent circa 1989–97 in most villages. We did not find a single copy of the Arguedas and Duviols 1966 edition, the one which made the source world-famous among scholars, in any village collection. Some San Damianinos remember the visits by Gerald Taylor,[4] who produced the erudite 1987 Quechua-Spanish edition. Villagers who like to read have heard of María Rostworowski, a national intellectual celebrity often mentioned on radio and television, but the books in which she set up the ethnohistoric framework for Huarochirí regional studies (1978a, 1978b) are rare in the countryside. Karen Spalding is not known even by name although she published her main findings in Spanish before English (1974, 1984). Neither did Salomon spot any copies of Ortiz Rescaniere's *Huarochirí 400 años después* (1980). Some older works (notably those of José Matos Mar's group from the 1950s) can be found in Huarochirí (provincial capital), which has, as described below, a local studious tradition. Nongovernmental organizations provide copies of their works to collaborators. (*Hijas de Kavillaca: Tradición oral de mujeres de Huarochirí*, published by Fundación Flora Tristán in 2002, is the first book specifically created with and for Huarochirí's literate women.)

The upshot is that *the* primary source par excellence—the Avila papers—hovers as a sort of legendary metabook. The corpus of alienated knowledge which Avila seized, and which he continued to build as he loosed a horde of careerist clergymen against the old gods, has remained alienated from those who best understand it. The irony is not lost on scholars. In 2001, Taylor produced a pocket edition of the 1608 Quechua Manuscript of Huarochirí designed to remedy this, and has also published a low-priced pedagogical grammar of Quechua for Huarochiranos who want to reconnect with their historic languages (2001b). Niño-Murcia donated fifty copies of Taylor's works to the village library. It seems too soon to tell whether recuperating Quechua will become a viable regional movement. Much depends on public schools, which up to 2007 remained indifferent both to the popular edition and the language revitalization idea because they lacked ministerial backing.

"PARIA CACA IS A SOUND"

What, then, is the role of oral tradition in a society that is decidedly *not* what Jack Goody, Walter Ong, or David Olson meant by "oral"? When the anonymous writer of 1608 collected Huarochirí's self-understandings, he described a society which assigned enormous performative, constitutive, and integrative force to the spoken word. It says of Cuni Raya Vira Cocha, the demiurge-trickster who gave the world both its present laws and its mysteries: "Just by speaking he made the fields, and finished the terraced fields with walls of fine masonry" (Salomon and Urioste 1991:46). For at least a century, rural Huarochirí has been reassigning more and more of that force to phonographic writing. Yet as Ortiz Rescaniere showed in his 1980 compilation of Huarochirí's modern folk narratives, the mythohistoric discourse of which the 1608 book gives a sampling still flourishes abundantly. What do these oral discourses achieve?

The questions they address are those about the bond among humanity, land, and water. Modern narratives about the sacred mountains and their waters connect the precise and convincing, but also extremely narrow and dry, script of community folk legality upward and outward to more complex and emotionally compelling experiences of using and consecrating the land. What makes these narratives compelling is ability to link the prosaic and precise to the exalted: why a particular watercourse has the shape it does, why a group has rights to it, why its waters filter in one direction and not another, and at the same time, how it is connected to superhuman greatness.

To start at the top of the mythohistoric pyramid, consider the supreme deified mountain Paria Caca (see figure 59).[5] Paria Caca, in his five simultaneous human avatars, symbolized the whole social organization of the region. The dominant ethnic group identified by Rostworowski as Yauyos (1978a:109–22) saw itself as a sib of five large descent groups. *Pichcantin* ('the five of him') form the subject of long narratives in the 1608 source.

59. The south peak of the double-peaked snowcap Paria Caca is patron of the Huarochirí region and was, until "extirpation," its chief pilgrimage sanctuary.

With the unifying apex of his religious cult destroyed (by "extirpators" in 1609), his lines of descent no longer figured as forming a coordinated regional polity.

But each village retains variant myths about how Paria Caca endowed its lands with the waters that make them green. These myths usually take the form of love stories connecting local maidens embodying earth (depth, stability, fecundity, autochthony) with invading males who embody Paria Caca's stormy, icy, watery masculine force (altitude, dynamism, insemination). Now as in 1608, the details allegorize peculiarities of the local hydrological system by connecting them to events in the courtship of water and land. All researchers on Andean agriculture notice agropastoralists' fanatically detailed interest in watercourses and catchments, filtrations, and fluctuations. This is hardly surprising, since in a zone of water-poor irrigation agriculture, small changes in water flow become life-and-death matters. When Paria Caca myths speak of water tunnels or magically opened springs, usually gifts to the mountain god's beloved or compensations for taking away an earth-girl as bride, they are explaining why a particular flow belongs to a particular ayllu or village. The hydraulic romance (Dumézil and Duviols 1974–75) makes hydrology and water rights both intimately meaningful and accurately memorable.

Even though Paria Caca has lost his unity of cult, he retains salience as a unifying motif, a symbol of the life-giving but also life-threatening situation of living at the mercy of the mountains. When Salomon asked people to sum up who Paria Caca is, he was repeatedly surprised by the answer "Pariacaca is a sound." One campesino said "Pariacaca is the sound the water makes in the stream in winter. By listening to it, you can tell whether it will be a good year for crops. We have that belief [*fe*]."[6] Throughout the central Andes the deified mountains are imagined as audible, and as a result ritualists are intensely interested in sounds such as thunder, cracking ice, bubbling water, and croaking toads (whose behavior is an index of nearby water). The implicit idea includes a sort of speech without words. Another narrator said,

> Pariacaca . . . settled in the form of a very high snowcap. There's a lake up there. Some days giant blocks of ice break off and fall into the lake. And it makes a great noise, even an earthquake; you can hear it like thunder, announcing good years or bad ones. "Paria Caca is putting us on notice," people say. It makes us nervous.

PARIA CACA'S CHILDREN GO TO COURT

One might ask why the villages' saturating interest in literacy does not make the mythohistoric genres associated with Paria Caca and his children obsolete. Joanne Rappaport (1990, 1994) has already demonstrated one reason. Colombian Pasto, Páez, and Guambianos can fight for their land claims with conviction—even, in one case, after the whole ethnic corporation had been legally dissolved—because in their view the legal titles which tie them insecurely to reservations and property, also tie them securely to irrevocable mythohistoric origin rights. The nexus consists in the fact that legalistic papers mention names, places, and events which occur as well in the lore of sacred space, genealogy, and political legend. These connections "prove" that the legalistic understanding of titles is only a penultimate interpretation of matters whose ultimate interpretation remains forever in the hands of indigenous residents.

Something similar happens all over the Andes, including Huarochirí. Because Rappaport has already explained the phenomenon so well, it is only necessary to sketch a couple of Huarochirí examples. Concha Community annually asks the mythic and divine "Owners" of Yansa or Yanascocha Lake for irrigation rights, by sending them a floating sacrifice

60. A painting tendered by Concha litigants in their lawsuit over Yansa lake (ca. 1645) shows resources (water, dam, canals) over which Concha was litigating against Sunicancha.

whose sail is a legalistic document. But how has Concha retained its access to the lake, in the face of fierce contention over its precious water? The answer is that its members have defended it in Spanish courtrooms, sometimes losing but in the long run winning. One long chapter in their struggle happens to be documented in a huge (256-folio) lawsuit that dragged on from about 1631 to 1650 (Salomon 1998).

By a splendid fluke, the 1608 Quechua Manuscript devotes its longest chapter (chap. 31) to the origin and custody of the very same Yansa Lake resources (water, dam, canals) for which Concha litigated (see figure 60). The Concha side was able to frame a unanimously voiced claim to primordial rights by translating the origin myth of the dam—in the Quechua version, a tale rich with pagan and miraculous features which could have brought down the whips of the "extirpators"—into an explanation of social investment and longstanding use rights. According to their leaders, when Paria Caca's children invaded Concha, the *yuncas*, aboriginals, fled but accidentally left behind a boy of their legitimate lineage. By marrying this boy to one of their own women, the children of Paria Caca acquired a patrilineal title to the putatively abandoned resources. This boy became the priest, and head water technician, of the deities of the lake who magically fashioned its dam.

In the Spanish courtroom, Concha witnesses retold this myth, but they stripped it to a bare-bones versions free of "pagan" traits: the lake priesthood was explained as a property right acquired by the building of the dam with local resources. Once the mythohistorical version of 1608 acquired a doublet legal version, oral-ritual and legalistic practices became symbiotic and mutually reinforcing measures for the defense of community. To understand that mountain-and-water myths are not just allegorically but generatively related to political discourse is to understand why versions are considered debatable. For example, in and out of meetings, Salomon repeatedly heard it debated whether the male or the female deity resident in Yanascocha was from Concha. The matter has a bearing on how one understands adjacent villages' respective water rights, because the inheritance of tenures has a patrilineal bias.

In the course of the lawsuit Concha village presented this landscape painting ca. 1645 (see figure 60). It demonstrates that the adversary village of Sunicancha (farthest right) has an irrigation system based on its own lake (upper right). Concha Sica, the village of pre-Hispanic design in lower center, draws water from Yanascocha or Yansa Lake (upper center) via a reservoir. The saggy cross which one can see in this village is also mentioned in the 1608 Quechua Manuscript. It is mythohistorically crucial, because it marks the spot where in mythic times the Concha won their rights over the lake by adopting a yunca boy of the primordial owning lineage, even as the other ancient owners fled. At lower left, the colonial resettlement town of San Damián faces Concha Sica across a gorge.

THE UNENDING REPATRIATION OF THE PAST

We turn now to a second stage of the inquiry into self-historiography. What happens when ex-oral material returns to its authors or their heirs via a reacquired written corpus produced in cities? The issue is not whether feedback occurs—it does, beyond dispute and beyond any chance of filtering it out—but rather, what sort of process is it? The text upon the page by itself decides little. What it means depends on what the community of inquiry asks it. As with oral lore, the questions concern the relation among people, land, and water. But when looking at printed, exogenous texts, villagers put the questions a little differently.

Salomon was witness to the local interrogation of returning printed lore on several occasions, one "natural" and the rest stimulated by himself. The natural one was the arrival of a copy of a grand two-volume compendium of scholarly works on Huarochirí archaeology and history, whose Spanish title means *Huarochirí: Eight Thousand Years of History*. A congressional candidate sponsored this work, and the archaeologist Alberto Bueno and his colleagues assembled its contents, as a prestigious civic gesture in 1992. The artificial occasions were ones on which Salomon gave away copies of Taylor's 1987 Quechua-Spanish edition of the 1608 Manuscript, asking in return to hear discussion of them.

When villagers get a book, first they go to work reinserting it into communal knowledge. They are interested above all in its chorographic value: its connections with unique reference points of local knowledge, chiefly places and persons. First they scan it for toponyms, verbally "pinning" them to known places or events. They evaluate its validity by sizing up its accuracy of geographic grounding, then estimate its relevance to current tenures and rituals of land and water. Villagers in all the Andean countries use almost incredibly detailed systems of microtoponymy, giving individual small fields, boulders, outcrops, pastures, and washes unique names. Every comunero knows hundreds of them. Ayllu books are thickly sprinkled with fine-grained geographic information unknown to the country's Instituto Geográfico Nacional. The maps which communities tender to ministries in their lawsuits, sometimes roughly drawn, beggar their official counterparts at the level of detailed coverage. Municipal and cadastral listings are the merest sketches by comparison. A book is considered as true as its connections to this knowledge.

The art of using chorographic knowledge to read papers is a much more complicated matter than simply matching toponyms. In the first place, individual names themselves tend to be durable, but their reference migrates; a name of a spring in 1670 might be the name of a nearby ruined corral today, so one must cast a wide net. Second, single places often have multiple names (often from distinguishable Jaqaru, Quechua, and Spanish or variously hybrid onomastic pools), so one must know many equations by heart. Semantically opaque names are not "moored" by meanings, and can therefore mutate over short periods, multiplying the number of equations one must learn. For example, a certain hill is called Chaymallanca, Chaumallanca, and Chaumallán; any of these could be acceptably spelled in various ways. In San Damián within the twentieth century, Quiscuyqui became known as Taraquiayqui; Anquipata became Anquipa or Arquipa; Shisquipata became Sisacorral by assimilating the opaque morpheme

Shishqui to Quechua *sisa*, ('flower'); Piedra Shunsho became Gentilcolorado, and so on (Pinaud 1957:153). A knowledgeable villager has these renamings at his fingertips. Third, certain toponyms occur over and over; for example, one can find the toponyms Allauca ('Right Bank') or Trabanda (i.e., *otra banda*, 'Other Side') in almost any village. One must not fall into false equations. An outsider's chance of guessing whether any two toponyms are synonymous is slight. Knowing the right answers is to insiders the sign of skillful reading.

Not only are microtoponyms considered important, they afford a pleasure in their own right. An effervescent old lady at her washing near Llaquistambo hamlet, just to entertain Salomon, effortlessly ticked off twenty-seven names of Checa pasture lots to the rhythm of her laundry pounding. Then she paused for a long reflective breath, looked up pleased with herself, and said, beaming, "Who could have given *so* many names? *Ancient* names!"

So the toponymic scanning of sources amounts both to a local intellectual discipline and a pleasurable art. Given its hazards, only a foolhardy researcher would try to "score" local experts on how often they correctly identify ancient or colonial terms. Most of the ancient toponyms are transparently identifiable to local people, but the referents do not always match either ancient or official records. The best exegetical essay on the Paria Caca complex, Toribio Mejía Xesspe's unjustly forgotten (1947) inquiry into "Anan Yauyo," succeeded because it was easy for him, as a man with a rural background, to follow the grain of a local knowledge system. When villagers reclaim old documents there is always a debatable residuum, but it does not always lie beyond solution. Was Maca Calla, the mythic patrimony of Allauca, the same as modern Marcajay? Or Marcayle, near San Damián? A Tupicochano well versed in old lawsuits remembered that modern Marcajay was called Marcacaya in 1711. Discussion along these lines will proceed until the story that a document attaches to its toponyms can either be plausibly placed, or has to be discarded as either confused, or relevant to some other segment of society.

This process of spatial anchoring, and not genre properties such as witnessing, imprimaturs, the prestige of author and publisher, and so forth, is the test of a text's truth value. When Salomon brought his consultant León Modesto Rojas Alberco a copy of the 1987 edition of the 1608 Quechua Manuscript of Huarochirí, Rojas spent a long while studying it, first the chapters that refer to Tupicocha and then others. Then he said:

> All those roads [mentioned in the 1608 source], I've walked where they go. Or in other words, it's not a legend but a legal course through space [*trayectoria*]. It's a *real* manuscript. It's called "Rituals and Traditions of Huarochirí."[7] But the manuscript isn't a ritual or a legend; rather it's what is *legal*. (Italic registers verbal emphasis.)

The word *trayectoria* was well chosen, for indeed most of the important deities are explained in Quechua as having an origin point, a geographic path along which they aligned the ancient kin-structured polities, and a terminus, where they congealed into sacred landmarks. In this and other consultant sessions—with Roberto Sacramento of Concha, for instance—I asked for careful exegesis of place names, and was told not only that most of them can be identified, but that their identification defines land rights.

For most villagers, reclaiming the Avila accounts is hardly front-burner business. But once set in motion, it fits in with a vigorously ongoing agenda whose other parts include, for example, the study of maps generated by lawsuits, colonial boundary surveys, and agrarian reform cadasters. In the Community hall, the bookcases contain numerous rolled maps. The unending reappropriation of material collected by cartographers, historians, lawyers, and the like forms a central armature of the village's work as "community of inquiry." Yet none of this points toward unanimity. As we will see in the next section, the resolution of material traces, written and other, into a usable self-analysis is an eminently pluralistic venture.

ANGLES OF HISTORIOGRAPHIC VISION: THE UNOFFICIAL PAST

Throughout the rural Andes discussion of the past, like so much of culture created under colonialism, is divided into a superordinate, authorized, centralized discourse and a subordinate, unofficial, locally varied discourse built around popular-historical knowledge. Schools are the fora of the former. Because state schools use a nationally uniform curriculum, and teachers are evaluated on fulfillment of it, even those teachers who care most about local culture face difficulty integrating unofficial knowledge. Outside the school, unofficial discourses of history concern a range of seemingly scattered themes, only a few of which we have mentioned so far. In addition to the "romance of the precise" built around community self-management, knowledge of the past embraces the *chullpas*, or pre-

Christian dead, legendary founders of villages and localized kindred, wars both international and civil, the lore of past trade and currency, vicissitudes of village self-defense in litigation and combat, and the emergence of a dignified citizen identity. These unofficial but repeated historic discourses have no "experts" save their own protagonists. They function as "History 2's" in Dipesh Chakrabarty's sense (2000:63–71): extraneous to the genesis of the overarching national-historical model, they nonetheless furnish the conceptual framework through which people feel themselves to be living within the bigger history.

It is not a matter of "real" versus "unreal" history. Vernacular history, though garnished with startling episodes, is neither more nor less mythological and fictional than "big," power-laden curricular history. Rather, curricular history is the voice of great but remote power, and vernacular history the voice of close but limited authority. Curricular history enjoys the privilege of publicly displacing "backward" and "Indian" ideas, or "folklorizing" them. Many teachers are aggressively ideological on this score. Rationales for erasing local narratives come and go, but they all point in the same direction. Neoliberals, nationalists, Marxists, and Protestants agree on the need to dislodge "provincial" ideas reflecting "low cultural level."

This project of erasure has genuine hegemonic status. That is, villagers are unable to imagine a school that failed to teach against their own domestic traditions. Even though Tupicochanos are champion chroniclers, if publicly asked about "history" they usually refer visitors to teachers, who in fact know nothing much about history beyond the canonical roster of generals and presidents.

Most rural Huarochiranos feel they stand in a somehow inadequate relation to their own past. As foreign researchers, we hear over and over remarks like "It's a shame that foreigners study our history more than we do ourselves." Local traditions and writings do exert some public authority, but only in subordinate contexts such as village ritual (outside the church), pilgrimages, Community and *parcialidad* meetings, or family feasts.

The "little history" is a segmentary history, the proprietary knowledge of small groups. Versions belong to ayllus or localities. The champions of curricular history can belittle and defeat them by framing them within a more universal, and therefore supposedly more important, framework. Moreover the local versions, if brought together, contradict each other and so can be called untrustworthy. Unlike curricular history, these "little" histories command no forum where they can fuse dramatically into a totalizing, "true" and chronologically continuous past. Yet the innumerable memory-holding objects, written or otherwise, which connect people to this less-recognized past, are prized as links to a history more valuable than that enshrined in churches and schools. After all, expertise on "immemorial" tenure, of titles, genealogies, and boundaries, is no hobby but the undergirding guarantee of livelihood itself.

HOW TO KNOW THE PAST

Many villages hold written but unofficial histories of themselves, drafted by amateurs who are usually full-time campesinos with a literate background. In the next few paragraphs we will explore how the oral "little history" figures in their works. We will start by itemizing some working assumptions about the villagers who construe the village's recorded life:

Every action above the circle of family intimacy should be treated as a self-recording act, that is, one which is not considered accomplished unless it has produced its constancia. This norm goes beyond the level of documentation middle-class urbanites are used to. For example, soccer matches should yield prose documents, as should the gatherings of the Curcuches (a secret society of sacred clowns) or kitchen work by the Mothers' Guild.

1. In principle, one should always maximize explicit dating because, as events acquire growing significance in retrospect, their recurrent dates create cycles of commemoration. Those who commemorate together are potential age sets or durable cohorts.
2. The treatment of social events as possessing "trajectory" through space encourages a toponymy-intensive paradigm for organizing data.
3. All groups and corporations have attributes of hierarchy or ritual precedence in relation to others of the same order. Hierarchy (unequal power) is not the same as precedence or ritual rank, but both serve as structuring paradigms. Transitions in hierarchy (e.g., elevation of Tupicocha municipality to district status) are greatly emphasized in calendar-based commemoration.
4. There is a tendency to focalize suprahousehold works and to explain changes in society in terms of their constancias, anniversaries, tra-

jectories, and rank. Outside of intimate family context, biographic or otherwise personal discourse is extremely rare.

THE TELLERS

Tupicocha and similar villages have no griot-like roles, only a certain affection for good raconteurs. Such people may be the ones called *costumbreros,* meaning experts on unwritten law. Those who enjoy talking about the local past tend to be men who have, in one way or another, experienced detours from a lifelong peasant career. To *talk* about the past is ipso facto to be talking off the record since paper is the record. Elder women tell an equally or even more profuse "little history," tending to structure it along the lines of genealogy and family history more than those of political or legal institutions. Impressionistically, it seems that female discussions about the past are more dialogical in the sense that the relation between the teller and the family of the listener forms a narrative framework: "my people" and "your people" become protagonists.

Oral history is quite different in structure from the meticulous written historiography of the corporate kindred. The grounding process has much to do with unspoken assumptions about how the social world changes. For one, episodes that have in common a theme (e.g., a rebellion, a visit by a distinguished outsider) tend to be foreshortened and conflated until they come to seem repeated instances of the "same" thing. The conflation of "similar" phenomena is at its most conspicuous in the tendency to see three successive "alien" governments—The Inka ([?]–1532), the Spanish (1532–1824), and the Chilean (1879–83)—as "the same" in salient ways. For example, the idea that alien rule outrages the order of kinship and marriage can stick equally to any of them. The alleged practice of coercively administered marriage is a colonial Spanish charge against Inkas, but to Norberto Alejandro Llata of San Damián, it could just as well stick to Spain:

> They used to make men and women stand up in lines, and they matched them. Without love or anything. For lack of love, there used to be fights. Couples used to kill each other. The [Spanish] priests forced them. If two families fought, [the priests] forced them to marry each other.

Similarly, within tales of empire, some figures shuttle across the distinction between Inka and Spanish. Chalcuchima may just as well figure as a Spanish as an Inka general.

Similarly, all those who are conquered tend to be classed as "the same," namely, as *indios*. "The Indians" are assigned to a remote past characterized by wretched servitude. The class of so-called Indians consists of one chronologically undifferentiated mass. It includes both Quechua-speaking highlanders trucked in from other provinces to work mines in the 1940s, and at the same time the pre-Hispanic makers of archaeological objects. A Checa comunero remembered that

> the Indians were the ones who talked Quechua. And they had their own bosses [*jefes*]. They used to work with the miners. The Indians came from far off. The Mantaro [Valley] or further. The didn't only talk Quechua, they also knew Aymara. It was a struggle for them to make themselves understood. If you dig you find the objects of the Indians. They used to cultivate maize, beans, they sowed some terrific beans.

The class indios does not include Inkas. If asked whether there are indios in Huarochirí today, campesinos answer unanimously, "No, not one."

Like many oral traditions, village tradition has an "event horizon" of about a century. Events more than a century in the past tend to get classed with the episode types and conflated, whereas later ones are connected with named individuals and can be situated in the web of kinship and politics. For Huarochiranos, this means that the end of Chilean occupation (1883) is more or less the beginning of chronologically structured, eventfully individuated historic thinking.

THE WRITERS

We turn now to those who create amateur village histories in writing. These works usually exist in the form of tattered notebooks which writers store in their family papers. Every Huarochirí village has a few bookish comuneros who try their hand at writing history on what counts for the large canvas, that is, whole-village syntheses. For example, the man who safeguarded Father Avila's old pulpit in San Damián was a catechist and unofficial lay "priest," the late Roberto Sacramento. In his period as a worker in a Lima noodle factory, he made friends with teachers and curates who helped him become an expert on the colonial legacy. He taught about it when he got the chance, and wrote in private. León Modesto Rojas Alberco of Tupicocha, discussed above (and in chapters 1 and 3), has immersed himself in manuscript sources. Antonio Anchelía of Ayllu Huamasica, in Sunicancha, is a grade-school educated comunero

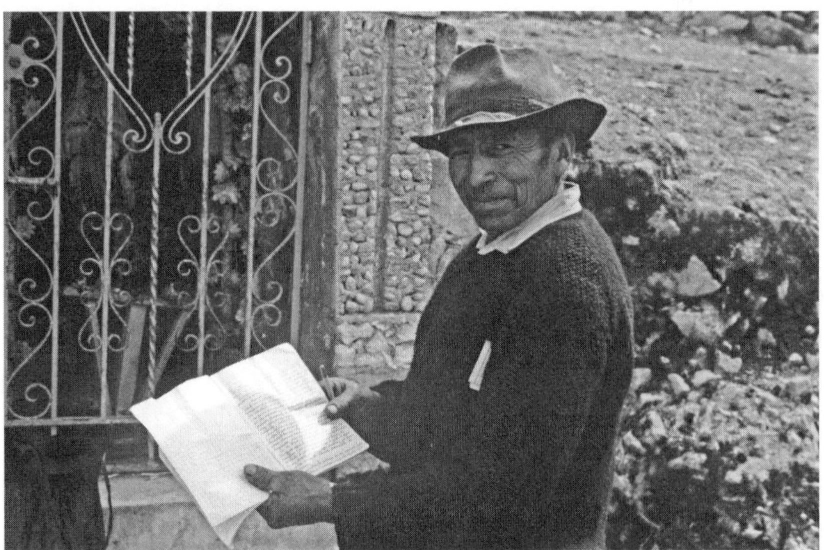

61. Don Antonio Anchelía of Sunicancha carries his manuscripts to a meeting in a neighboring village in 1995.

who writes short essays to meet the demand for a history presentable in civic festivals (see figure 61).

For example, consider Anchelía's manuscript "History of Huasca Lake." Written in ballpoint on the backs of 1992 calendar pages, it combines an orientation to sacred space at the most inclusive level with minute scrutiny of source tables and records of collaboration with a Protestant NGO. The result contains a substantial collection of precise particulars, elevated to romance by the theme of society and water in interaction. The lake in question is the one pictured on the upper right in the 1631–50 lawsuit commented above (figure 60).

> OUTLINE OF A SMALL PROFILE OF THE LAKE OF HUASCAR.
> Attention. Sunicancha. Has three small lakes called Huasca Cullco And Tres Lagunas which pour out their seasonal waters for the cultivation of subsistence crops for the Community of Sunicancha with a watercourse of 7 to 8 Km.[8] Through streams and rough-built canals. To the fields. At this point Dear Reader I will talk about the lake of Huasca.
>
> Huasca—is located at 4,020 m. over sea level—with its tasty waters coming from the snowcapped cordilleras Paria Kaka mountain and Kuni Raya according to the versions of Pedro Batán and Mama Cap-

62. A dam (this one at Yanascocha) of this type is described in Antonio Anchelía's 1994 manuscript, and also in the 1608 Quechua Manuscript of Huarochirí.

yama[.][9] Since ymperial times This Lake was Seen to be used for its waters (note: there is no suitable date)[10] by the peasants in the years 1878 its purposes remaining unprosecuted until after the war with Chile 1879[11]—in 1895 the work began again by opening a sluice for its water to be released [see figure 62]. In 1925 they emplaced the first wall to guide the waters with 4 windows in a trench with a height of 3 meters [interlineated:] the trench 4 m. 82 cm.[12]

The community year after year on each 10th of February in a general *faena* with many ancestral customary observances [i.e., dances and sacrifices] happily carried out the closing of Huasca, Cullco and Tres Lagunas with folk music bands. With this modest note I tender the warmest homage and the purest tribute to the worthy comuneros who have helped us to exist and who have left their painstaking work as our legacy.

At the same time their deeds and their faith in their children set the goal for continuing the path of our lacustrine destiny. In honor of more glory and life to our social brotherhood and sisterhood [*hermandad*].

> In the year 1990. When the President of the Community [was] Don Wilson Pumalía . . . Don Fortunato Rodríguez Abad, a son of the community through marriage, presented himself and said he had talked with relatives of a Swiss Lutheran Evangelical association [named] Diaconía. And this organization would lend economic aid and tools for the rebuilding of Huasca lake. . . . [summaries of intervening political steps follow, followed by the naming of project godparents, musicians, *ayllu* and Mothers' Club representatives] The project undertaken with a —— [not readable] sluice 4 m. of width by 120 in length and three meters deep to build a retaining wall of stone and rammed earth, to be 6 m. high and the pipes were put in place for the valve with a distance of 38 m.
>
> In 1992 the president of the Community Medardo Patrocinio Macavilca continued the project enlarging it with 35 days of work per comunero. [Further details culminate in Community President Don Felipe Pumalía's plan for a dedication ceremony in 1994.]

AN "OFFICIALIZING" PAST: PROVINCIAL ELITE HISTORIOGRAPHY

Having discussed the role of historiography at the ayllu or community level, and at the level of local educational elites, we turn now to a third voice in the historical "conversation." It is that of the provincial elites and capital-dwelling spokespersons of rural society. The difference between avocational peasant intellectuals such as Sr. Anchelía and provincial elites claiming a quasi-academic authority over the local past is clinal. The extreme cases are easily distinguishable, but the intermediate ones form a gradient.

In the provincial capital of Huarochirí, there exists a cluster of "families" (by patronymic definition) that constitute a definite and self-conscious elite. Such families are usually divided between middle-class urban branches and relatively well-off commercial-cum-agropastoral highland households which have been able to parlay up successful decades of pasture and cattle business or mining into commercial enterprises. Some have abandoned *comunidad* affiliation, and few acknowledge ayllu affiliations. They hold local power in several ways: they are creditors, local officials, links to powerful institutions and businesses, or spokespeople in dealing with bureaucracy. Some have relatives in the United States, Spain, or Italy. None accumulated giant estates of the sort whose crushing rural power in other regions provoked the 1968–75 agrarian reform, and none rank today among the national oligarchy.

The patriarchs of these families regard their peers and allies (including, e.g., some directors of local schools) as an intellectual vanguard with a mission to vindicate regional culture on the national or even international stage—and to "authenticate" and "purify" it on the local scene by offering a more schooled alternative to oral or rustically written versions like Sr. Anchelía's. Their processes of authentication and purification render the sources into literary prose, usually on the mold of Romantic "Inka" drama. The questions they bring to the villages' cultural legacy differ greatly from those of the local-minded versions we have just looked at. Regional elites are not concerned with why the locality has the peculiarities it does, but rather with how its authenticity contributes to the greatness of the national state and implicitly deserve its recognition.

THE TELLO PANAKA AND FOLKLORIC DRAMA

The plaza of Huarochirí, the capital of Huarochirí Province, is studded with icons of a commanding figure among Peruvian intellectuals who was also a child of the province: the archaeologist Julio C. Tello (1880–1947). Tello's research identified many pre-Hispanic cultures and established the nascent science of archaeology throughout the republic (Daggett 2009). Architecturally, it seems as though the whole townscape were a séance focused on recovering Tello's spirit. His squarish face, with its commanding stare fixed through perfectly round eyeglasses, is omnipresent in statuary, on classroom posters, book covers, and banners. Tupicocha in 1998 replaced the patriotic statue of Admiral Bolognesi in its plaza with one of the scientific patriarch (see figure 63), a sign that Tello's iconic stature continues to grow together with the prestige of science as a source of authority.

Tello's family, according to an admirer who published a 202-page collection of anecdotes about the great man, "were poor people, but that sort of poor people who have lands, cattle, and besides, were the ones who gave the orders in Huarochirí" (Ponce Sánchez 1957:37).[13] Tello's father, mayor of the provincial capital, sent the young "Sharuco" ('Whiz Kid') to study in Lima. Among the first Peruvians to take up the infant science of archaeology (stimulated by the German pioneer Max Uhle), Tello

63. This 1999 statue of Julio C. Tello stands in Tupicocha's plaza.

undertook private explorations of his home province's then wholly obscure pre-Hispanic remains. A 1909 scholarship took him to Harvard. Tello returned in 1911 as guide to the Harvard physical anthropologist Aleš Hrdlička, dragging mummies from the *machayes*, or pre-Hispanic funerary caverns, which overlook most Huarochirí towns.

The two men's work on pre-Hispanic surgery (Hrdlička 1914) brought Tello merited renown in Europe and North America. After 1917 Tello served two terms in Congress. His frequent visits abroad, notably to Germany, damaged his local political base, but accelerated his campaign to elevate Peru among the canonical lands of American antiquity. Tello is buried on the grounds of the National Museum of Anthropology and Archaeology, which he founded, and his Lima-dwelling successors celebrate the place as a shrine.

Panaka is an Inka word for a corporation formed by descendants of a deceased Inka king and dedicated to upholding his prestige. It would be only a slight exaggeration to say that in the city of Huarochirí Tello's descendants function as a panaka. It fosters his memory as the numen of civic and academic virtue. A handsome city park is decorated with replicas of the Chavín feline heads and stelae which Tello discovered. The technical school and library are named after him. In Tello's neighborhood, cement facsimiles of fine Inka stonework, including the Inka trapezoidal niche which became famous in Tello's time adorn once-stylish facades (see figures 64 and 65). At the Tello family's old house, some fragments of his collection form a ghostly museum (see figure 66; Carrión Cachot 1947).

To the "leading families" of the province, Tello was a culture hero who rescued the region from "the humble condition of being provincial and purely indigenous." Much is made of the triumphs of "a boy who inherited the indigenous race of his forebears the Inkas" (L. Contreras Tello 1994:13). The cult of this early twentieth-century hero of Peruvian intellectual life has become an icon of authority to the extent that the province's diverse other intellectual contributors are conflated and eclipsed.

Some elder peasants claim to have worked among Tello's peons in his 1911–13 mummy-hunting expeditions. The same Norberto Alejandro Llata mentioned above, whose identity papers say he was born in 1900, recalled:

> [Tello] came here [San Damián] with his wife, his daughter, his brother Ramón . . . he was considered a strange bird. He rented a room here; nobody thought he was important. I was a motherless boy and he asked, "Can you work for me?"
>
> We went to the countryside . . . it was the first examination of where the Covered Ones [i.e., mummies] were. 1910 or so. Tello used to ask the herders. He would ask, "Mummies? Covered Ones of the Inkas?" We used to herd up there, we knew the holes that the Inkas had dug. We still see them. And he used to be able to guess them from his own experience.
>
> In the covered places [rock shelters] there were maize grains. He used to tell us to reconnoiter those places. Following his instructions, we used to show him where the mummies were. We used to dig them out. There were twenty or thirty Covered Ones in two or three sites. Whenever Tello noticed that any skull had a thickened cranium [i.e.,

64. In the provincial capital of Huarochirí in 1994, Tello's legacy includes many buildings with neo-"Inka" facades.

65. Images of Julio C. Tello were omnipresent in Huarochirí schools and offices c. 1994, and still are.

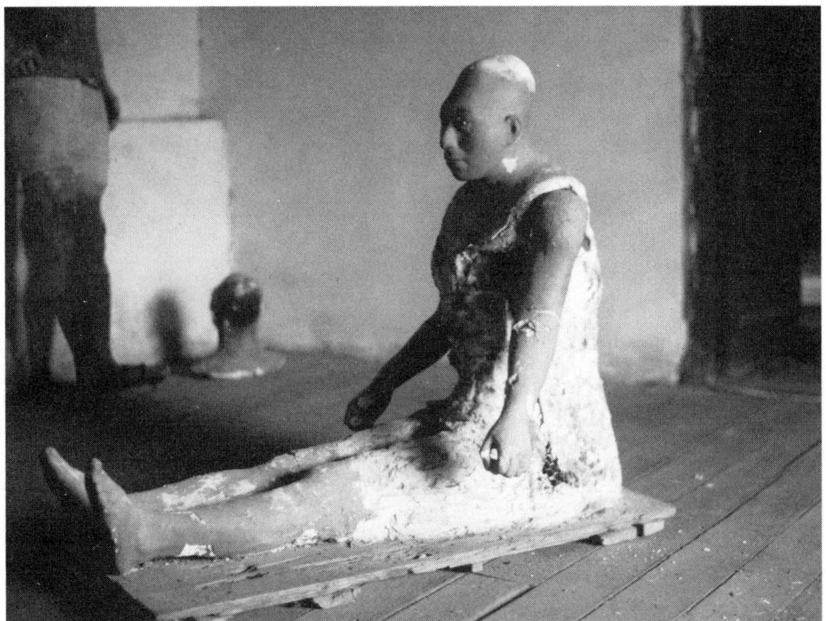

66. The former Tello home in Huarochirí housed a ghostly mannikin for a never-finished museum tableau. It was made to demonstrate Inka weaving technique.

scars of trephination] he would be elated; he would whack us on the shoulders! There was *añi* [early-ripening] maize, dried potato, sprouted grain [used for making maize beer] for the dead. He carried it all out of here on donkeys, to Lima, as cargo. In Lima he had a room near Acho and there he used to store some groups of mummies.

The mummies had tiny eyes, not much hair, most of the head naked. Like me, nowadays. We used to carry potato sacks full of human skulls.

Some of those mummies were wrapped, others already extracted. Some, intact. Yes, with clothing, something like a monk's robe, long tunics. They were crouched down with scarves to hold up their heads. Red, green yellow, rainbow-colored. The *gentiles*, people call them. They had bands or sashes on their chests like government officials do. [Tello] used to have birds; he would bring birds which could detect places where certain plants had softened up the rock. [Tello] went overseas. Then he came back, he looked me up, he and his brother invited me to [the ruins of] Cinco Cerros. There we found a beautiful golden necklace. They found coca and coca seeds. I planted the coca and it flourished.[14] Tello brought along a companion [Hrdlička?].

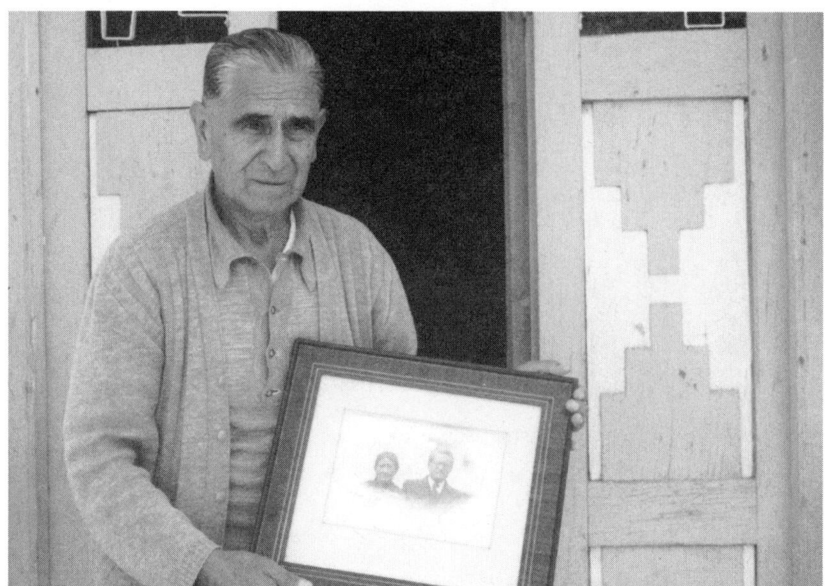

67. Abelardo Santisteban Tello, nephew of Julio C. Tello, holds a portrait with the archaeological pioneer at the door of his house.

The chief torchbearer for many years was Tello's nephew Oscar Santisteban Tello (*La Voz de San Damián* 1957:75–79), later succeeded by Oscar's brother Abelardo (see figure 67). Don Abelardo Santisteban Tello, born when Julio C. Tello was forty-four, could stand as the ideal of a traditional highland gentleman, with his sleek gray hair, tailored suit even on at-home days, and the scarf he wears against chilly fog. His home is decorated with Tello memorabilia: the digging crew at Nazca leaning on shovels, family studio portraits with "the great *amauta*,"[15] a huge Chavín-like carved condor,[16] and Inka-style step-fret designs on the house's masonry and woodwork. He was a Community member, but not a practicing campesino, in the Peasant Community of Huarochirí. Throughout his career as a teacher, he made it his avocation to dramatize the mythological legacy of the Avila papers.

ANDEAN DEITIES, STAGE CENTER

It is through such indigenism and regionalist writing that Huarochirí elites raise a voice in the conversation of history, claiming and refiguring inherited rural memory. What they ask of history is an "Inka" nexus, a bond with the greater entity above and beyond local land and water, that is, at the same time prior to and different from the Hispanic glories of Lima.

One of their most established media is the theatrical school pageant. Throughout the Andes, public schools put enormous resources into providing spectacles for their communities. These are often scripted by members of local elite families. Carried to other villages by teachers, these scripts propagate genteel versions of the regional legends. They are called *teatralizaciones folklóricas* ('folkloric stagings'), and they form a genre closely associated with indigenism (Kapsoli 1980; Tamayo Herrera 1980). School pageants, ascending up the media chain to municipal and even metropolitan spectacles, constitute the clearest example of how provincial elites gained leverage over the Avila legacy. Melding in and gussying up related oral versions, they shaped an "official" lettered version of oral narratives.

Tello and his sympathizers brought highland musicians and dancers to Lima and put on "folkloric" spectacles at museums and theaters in an effort to raise the city's then intensely "Creole" and anti-indigenous image of national identity (see figure 68).

In 1928, five Huarochirí women and eleven men in "Inka" costume, under the name of "Conjunto Pariakaka," won first place in the National Peruvian Folklore Contest. But it was Julio C. Tello's Quechua-speaking aide, Toribio Mejía Xesspe, obscured by Tello's shadow then and now, who called Santisteban Tello's attention to the existence of the Avila corpus and thereby to his home district's stellar relevance to pre-Hispanic mythology. This apparently took place during the time when Mejía was at work on his still-unpublished translation of the 1608 Quechua Manuscript of Huarochirí, which is dated 1941–43.

Abelardo Santisteban retains the theatrical scripts and photos of the performances in a scrapbook. They show Mejía Xesspe's influence in, among other things, the orthography of Quechua names. These dramas were written for local schoolchildren to perform at civic festivals. Abelardo collaborated with his brother Oscar on the first of them, namely, *Cuni Raya Pariacaca*. With patronage from the Tello group, this work was staged before what Santisteban recalls as a distinguished audience at the Teatro Segura in Lima in 1951. His later works include two from the Avila legacy *Chokesuso* (1971) and *Kapyama de Llambilla*, another Paria Caca legend, from around 1984. The latter was left unfinished.

Santisteban Tello is just as proud of his role in infusing literary indige-

68. Huarochirí's Kon Iraya troupe gives a "folkloric" performance at the National Museum of Archaeology and Anthropology in Lima (undated photo from the album of Abelardo Santisteban Tello; 1940s?).

nism into the public culture of Huarochirí, as he is of helping acquaint Lima audiences with the glory of Paria Caca. Like Cuzco's literary indigenists, he believes that "legends" contain moral truths which can regenerate the provinces, but that in order to reach them one must "deepen" their study and give them the cultivated voice of a high literary register. To refashion the indigenous legacy by a Spanish literary canon, and to recontextualize it scholastically, was seen as the way for campesino children to accredit themselves as something better than the "100% Indians" which earlier writers had described.

Through performing "Indianness," one was to extirpate one's own "indio" stigma. When children perform in Tello's dramatizations, as they still did in the 1990s, they were expected to rummage in their families' storage for old garments. They sometimes appeared on stage actually wearing their ancestors' cloaks, leggings, ponchos, or moccasins. However, the scripts they recite are like anything but their ancestors' speech.

Here is a textual comparison: first, the beginning of the story of Chuqui Suso and Paria Caca in the 1608 Quechua Manuscript; second, the corresponding part of the 1971 "Chokesuso" as staged by Abelardo Santisteban Tello. In the colonial Quechua version, the maize-planting maiden Chuqui Suso weeps watching her cornfield wither in the sun. She finds a clever remedy by flirting with the amorous mountain and water deity Paria Caca, but refusing to sleep with him until he magically replaces her meager water supply with an ample new canal.

> In those days there was a native woman of that village named Chuqui Suso, a really beautiful woman. This woman was weeping while she irrigated her maize plants because they were drying out so badly, and because her water supply was so very scarce.
>
> When Paria Caca saw this, he obstructed the mouth of her little pond with his cloak.
>
> The woman started to cry even more bitterly when she saw him do that.
>
> "Sister, why are you crying so hard?" Paria Caca asked her.
>
> "Sir, this little maize field of mine is drying up on me for lack of water!" she replied.
>
> "Don't worry about it," Paria Caca said to her. "I'll make water flow from this pond of yours, plenty of water. But first, let me sleep with you."
>
> "Get the water flowing first," she retorted. "When my field is watered, then by all means let's sleep together."
>
> "Fine!" said Paria Caca, and released an ample amount of water. (Salomon and Urioste 1991:62).

In Tello's 1971 version (see figure 69), ideas of gender, sexuality, and power are transformed to a Spanish melodramatic model. Scene 1 has Pariacaca seducing Choque Suso with his commanding masculinity. Her opening soliloquy gives way to a climax emphasizing his male majesty and romantic sentiment:

> (With tremulous voice) This celestial music says something to my heart. My hopes are drying up like the drought of my cornfields. Par-

> iacaca, the supreme god of these [my] lands, is the only one who can help me by warding off drought. . . . My poor plants! What a sad destiny awaits them! The water that comes from Yanascocha is so little, and it does not suffice for all. . . . What shall I do?
>
> Pariacaca courts her in versified recitatives:
>
> Choquesuso, my princess,
> why such melancholy?
> Are you not the one goddess
> of my tender amours?

When she coyly refuses him, Pariacaca, revealing his superhuman identity, makes his promise:

> Choquesuso of Kinti, I will place my nobility and my power at your feet. You will see clean, pure water run through your cornfields. My father Kon Iraya will increase the flow of Yanascocha, and if that should not be enough, I will have a great canal built from the Kakachi River to your domains, which will be the best testimony of love for you, and will endure in your people's memory.

The art of dressing regional lore in literate genres and high sociolinguistic registers is usually called *folclorismo*. The word's freight varies with context, reflecting the equivocal standing of the popular tradition. In campesino usage, it simply means the ritual dimension of folk legality and its celebration. Rural Huarochiranos freely use *bailes folclóricos* ('folkloric dances') as the term for functions like the salutes to the lake "Owners" without any suggestion of belittling them. These usages do not inflict the sting of the word's urban usage, which is often a catty put-down.

School personnel use the term *folclor* in a sense different from either of the above. In school *folclor* implies the edifying, institutionally sanitized version of the rough popular legacy which it claims to *rescatar* ('redeem'). Schools often celebrate patriotic days by putting on infantilized, regimented representations of the sacred or festive rituals traditional for the pupils' parents. The scholastic versions are characterized by strictly uniform garb in exaggeratedly bright colors; geometrical, military-like choreography as opposed to the swirling, stomping, lurching movements of ritual; reduction of ritual language to repeated cliché; recorded music with loudspeakers (rather than live music); and absence of those reverent gestures such as coca taking that indicate ritual sincerity. School perfor-

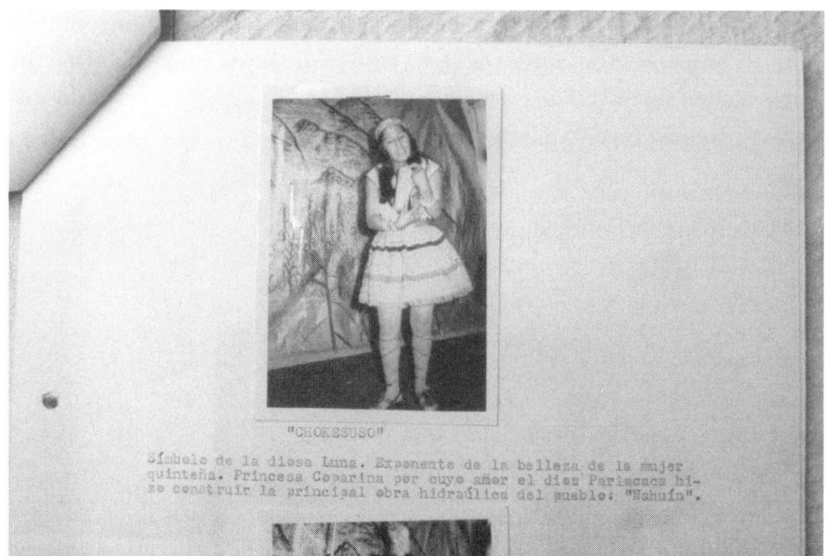

69. The heroine of the 1971 play "Chokesuso" onstage at the school in San Lorenzo de Quinti, from the album of Abelardo Santisteban Tello. The caption says: "Symbol of the moon goddess. Examplar of the beauty of Quinti womanhood. Princess of Copara for whose love the god Pariacaca had the main hydraulic infrastructure of the town constructed: Ñahuín."

mances sometimes include garbled Quechua songs as an appeal to "authenticity," using a language neither teachers nor students know. Teachers are influenced by Lima television. Some villages present infantilized folklore at nighttime spectacles which are called *teletones* ('telethons'), though they lack actual television.

The act of lifting rural traditions out of their original rugged contexts, and presenting them as cute, tenderly appealing, innocuous entertainment, neutralizes stigma at the price of rendering tradition trivial. Parents do not apparently consider the practice demeaning, because they regard children's participation in the school and its unquestioned regime as the way to fulfill a civic duty of making future generations less "cholo." (This hard-to-define but omnipresent word denotes a person of indigenous appearance but non-"Indian" lifeways; it connotes plebeian coarseness as well.) They do not comment on the possibility that this practice will diminish pupils' respect for tradition when they become old enough to take responsibility for relations with the deified mountains.

One pointed example of folklorization arises in regard to a Tupicochan ritual song called "Los Caballeros" ('The Gentlemen'; Ráez Retamozo

2005:122). Mysteriously and obsessively, this haunting air for Andean flute accompanies the Curcuches (i.e., troupe of sacred clowns) during the rainy-season festival. The ex-teacher and autoethnographer Eugenio Vilcayauri Medina invented lyrics for it:

Good morning Mr. President
Here we are in your ayllus
To constitute the Huayrona
With the flowers of our fields

Let us take positive actions
And harmonize our spirits
It can be done, victory will be ours,
Tupicocha will say,
"Tupicocha will always be"
Vilcayauri Medina. (1983–91:52)

These verses effect a folklorizing "redemption" of the tradition of the sacred clowns. To understand it, one needs to know a little about the clowns. The January festival to which "Los Caballeros" belongs expresses rejoicing when the rains at last arrive and the village's clenched anxiety about drought can relax. To meet the occasion, Tupicocha has two dancing societies, each composed of alliances between villagers and their diaspora relatives in Lima and beyond. The societies sponsor the rainy-season festival (January 5–8) in alternate years. The sacred clowns form secret brotherhoods within each society.

Just before the festival, the Curcuches retire to hideouts on the high puna, where they commune with the mountain deities, and temporarily renounce their baptismal names in favor of ritual ones (as do the Huaris noted in chapter 2). They costume themselves as human mountains, with puna herbs growing out of their heads. They thus become the beloved protégés of the divine peaks. The Curcuches are the heralds of rain, the longed-for gift of the deities. When they descend to meet the villagers waiting for them in the dusk, they get an adoring welcome. For three days, the village pampers and indulges these sublime buffoons. The Curcuches douse people with water, drink rain from downspouts, and dance their crouching, pouncing *mudanzas* ('moves') in patio puddles. Every gob of mud they splash on onlookers is a blessing. The Curcuches mercilessly ridicule every institution, from the Community to the schoolhouse, in bawdy, unscripted skits (see figures 70–71). The Curcuches lampoon writing along with all the rest. Seeing writing as the mountains see it, they "write" illegible scribbles when they parody engineers or functionaries. These "written" plans always give rise to ludicrous brouhahas. Acting the teacher, one becomes a moron who can't explain what a shoe is, but excels in lechery. In short, the divine clowns play the human comedy as the mountain gods see it. They afford everyone the huge relief of laughing at their own life, secure in the knowledge that after all and in spite of all, the love of the mountain deities will sustain it for another year. Nothing could be a stronger tribute to the centrality of writing than the fact that secret societies of the Curcuches themselves practice the *acta*-writing regime they themselves mercilessly spoof (see figure 71).

The autoethnographer and ex-schoolteacher Vilcayauri Medina knows all this intimately. The words he proposed for the flute anthem of the clowns thoroughly subvert the meaning of the festival. Adding words he has the villagers responding to their heralds of creative chaos by promising a mild civic piety and "positive resolutions." The autoethnographer, in taking it upon himself to write lyrics, assumed that the role of writing is *always* the service of piety and order.

SHIFTING CONVERSATIONS

At the start of this chapter we asked what difference it makes that Tupicocha has become a community of writers. If the first champions of written authority—the priests and lawyers of the sixteenth century—could return, they might be surprised at the results of their interventions. They meant to shift the conversation about divine mountains, land, water, and people off the ground of entitlement and heredity, and onto the ground of diabolism versus Christianity. But writing did not turn out to be the controlled "technology of intellect" which the lettered elite proposed. Writers multiplied and so did contexts for writing. As literate peasants have taken up writing, the conversation has instead shifted in various directions far from the colonial program of conversion and colonization—and far as well from the modernist program of education. Today's conversation takes place in several different, overlapping sets formed by different "literate event" contexts: internal business of the ayllu, community-level commemoration and self-presentation, and interaction with the official custodians of literacy. Each set has a characteristic way of making text out of memory. And each context generates a characteristic way of reading text.

70. The Curcuches, or sacred clowns, never fail to spoof officials who try to command society through writing (Tupicocha in 1997).

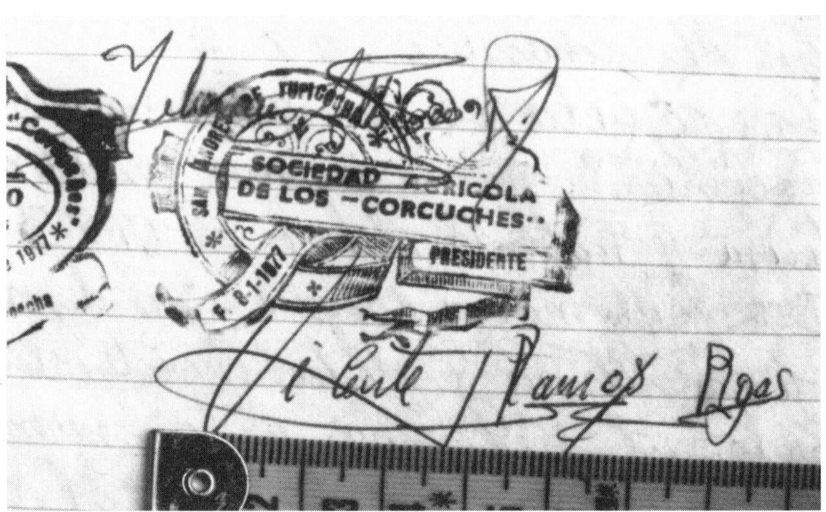

71. Nonetheless, the secret society of Curcuches Agrícola itself writes its own records and since 1977 has used this stamp to ratify them.

One context arises when members of the smaller and more-inward looking sets—ayllus, communities in session—inquire toward a synoptic overview of the accumulated "precise" record built up in the course of maintaining relations with land and water. This occurs when there is need of ritual commemoration (on building a structure or completing an anniversary, etc.). The credential for such writing is strong knowledge and participation in the "atomic" level of self-documenting acts which make up the group's prosaic practice. The accumulation of constancias, summarized in overview, is typically a fact-packed historic summation in a reportlike format but ornamented with some rhetorical garlands. Such products often have prosaic titles such as "Historic Memorandum" or "Historical Keepsake," and they are sometimes copied into books of acts. The genre usually does not overtly address the sacred, yet it is implicitly structured upon very deep-rooted relations to revered places and waters, and to ancestors to whom the accumulated merit of deeds is dedicated. The emotional satisfaction afforded by a synthesis consolidating innumerable meritorious constancias is a species of romance, anchoring loyalty and solidarity. The word *love* is often used in these otherwise pedestrian documents. The reading of such documents becomes more important with the passage of time, as some of those mentioned themselves become ancestors and their participation becomes a touching thing to remember. The value of these papers inheres in their intimacy with the vernacular context. They are marked by all the peculiarities of vernacular prose noted in chapters 4 and 5.

A second context arises when local literate elites (regionally eminent families, educational leaders, returned emigrants) seek to dramatize the local society as a part of some larger transcendent subject such as the Peruvian nation, the working class, and so on. In these cases, the mythic knowledge which is left implicit in historical keepsakes becomes foregrounded, but the whole range of "the precise," which is foregrounded in prosaic genres, is relegated to invisibility. From mythology and ritual, writers extract motifs that are easily recast within the ideologies of national institutions and ideologies. The usual ones are eros—recast from the embrace of earth and water to become romantic marriage—and conflict—recast from legends of the "gentile" mummies into the pomp of "Inka" statecraft. The emotion evoked in such products as texts for school pageants and programs for infantile mimicry of traditional rituals is romantic pathos in the conventional sense of the word. The context for reading such products is the programming of institutional events, usually patriotic festivals. To alter or innovate in these arenas is to bid for revision of political ideology. It is usually holders of state-sponsored jobs and offices who do so. Because such products are predicated on the idea of the village as a worthy part of overarching transcendent bodies, these products are to an extreme degree beholden to the graphic standards of academies and the "cultured norm." They are carefully filtered for stigmatizing vernacularism in script, and pitched toward an archaistic, high register of literary prose.

Up to this point we have been summarizing writing done for use within villages. But in becoming literate, villages became part of a vastly wider graphic universe. For Tupicochanos, the supremacy of that nearby Goliath, the capital city, marks a wider context for the uses of the written word. The village's relations with its commuter emissaries, its city-dwelling "children," and its far-flung diaspora, have become heavily enmeshed in literacy. In the next chapter we will examine products of these relationships.

SEVEN

Village and Diaspora as Deterritorialized Library

In the dusty flea markets of central Lima, some low-end book dealers offer stacks of obscure publications from the country's provinces, towns, and villages. These catchall volumes of local lore come from job printers in central Lima. They are contracted by villagers or townspeople who promote them as festival souvenirs, civic publicity, or political campaign favors. Such print productions exist at the farthest edges of the global print sphere. They rarely show copyright information. They usually have no ISBN numbers, no recognized publishers, and no entries in union catalogues. Most never appear in "proper" bookstores. Libraries—even the greatest Latin Americanist collections—have only samplings of such literature. Scholars cite them sparingly if at all. Librarians refer to them as "gray imprints."

But they are treasures in the communities whose lives they depict. In this chapter, we will consider a range of print works which reflect the orbit of vernacular and provincial writing so closely that many of its contents are hard for outsiders to understand. Just about all Andean provinces generate such print[1]—with Huarochirí perhaps slightly more productive than most because proximity to Lima makes presses accessible—and all set high value on them.

Rural villages, of course, do not have printing facilities of their own. But since migration of villagers into the city of Lima began after the Second World War, and especially since city-bound migration surged from the 1960s onward, villages have ceased to live as remote, self-sufficient territorial enclaves in the mountains. Every highland village, Tupicocha being quite typical in this regard, now consists of its resident peasantry plus an elastic web of its "children" who have worked their way into the city of Lima and then cities abroad. Indeed, villages might not even be able to sustain themselves were it not for the fact that virtually every family has members in the capital able to help sell products, remit cash, speak for kinspeople in the orbits of business and officialdom, and guide children toward opportunities better than the economically retreating agropastoral economy can provide. And ex-peasant families in the city in turn depend upon their home villages to supplement what may actually be less than living wages, by furnishing shipments of food. They also depend on their at-home relatives to keep using and thereby defend their inherited land rights. Since the 1980s ex-villagers and children of villagers have increasingly taken off for richer countries in the Southern Cone, North America, and Europe. Today, the web stretching from any high-altitude herding village is likely to reach Buenos Aires, Madrid, Milan, Dallas, or Sydney.

This partnership between a core Andean territory and a durable web of diaspora "children" established in urban space gives birth, village by village, to "provincial societies." These clubs provide structures of leadership and fiduciary channels linking country and city. Their number is unknown but probably in the thousands. Certainly they rank among the main civil-society achievements of modern Peru. They range in scope from small societies which band together the "children" of a single village (like the above-mentioned Tupicochan society, currently called the Association of Tupicochanos Resident in Lima), through provincial societies proper, to large bodies named after whole departments. They are formal corporations which write internal statutes, elect officers, and hold treasuries. Their festive fundraising gatherings include bullfights, "folkloric" dances, and soccer matches and chicken barbecues in the outer boroughs. The larger the scale of the society, the more its leadership tends to embrace and reproduce the homeland's elite stratum of wealthy landholders, merchants, and professionals. To some degree (for example in sporting tourneys), smaller-scope societies federate within larger-scope ones to produce segmented pyramidal organizations. But in a society riven by bitter class differences, as well as horizontal rivalries among villages, many village-level societies keep a distance from the palatial clubs of those who were seen as oppressors in the times before Agrarian reform (that is, up to the early 1970s). The provincial societies are not exempt from exploitation, of course; some villagers suspect that the traders who sponsor village events profit more by them than the village does. Yet no village thinks it can do without them.

For innumerable ex-peasant families, the small homeland is precious in several ways. To return "home" for patron saint festivals, together with the other members of one's hometown society, is a chance to embrace far-flung kin and rekindle old friendships, or to wrangle promising patronage. It is to enjoy, in the landscape of sacred mountains and ancestral pathways, a wealth of richly meaningful dances and rites. It is to relax among trusted peers, far from the besetting cultural anxiety, the physical stress, and the dangers of Lima life. It is a chance to show off successes, court a fiancée, or look for a business partner. And it is to be reassured of a "safety net" where one can retreat should poverty, conflict, or old age make it necessary. In festival time, Andean villages become the resort spas of urbanites climbing out of poverty. Older emigrants are wined and dined with respectful homage. Young ones have license to strut and flirt and dance all night (high heels wobbling on cobblestones, white peasant hats tilted rakishly over made-up faces). Marriages that germinate in this setting are likely to be endogamous to the village, and therefore desirable, so elders feel all right about allowing a margin of partying license.

In return for what it gives its "children," the village expects and usually gets substantial support in the form of funding for public works. The iron letters decorating Tupicocha's bullring, remodeled cemetery, and schoolyard gates commemorate donations that urban "children of the village" made. So important is it for urbanites to be strong actors in this web that they spend hard-won discretionary income attending "folklore academies," private schools which have sprung up in all the self-built boroughs to teach (and, of course, modify) the dances and songs rural home districts cherish. Tailoring and costume rental shops specialized in providing urban versions of Andean ritual garb have become substantial businesses. Commercial television stations win high ratings with shows spotlighting the most artful or gaudy "folkloric" productions.

Campesinos address the diaspora and vice versa via both ephemeral and durable print media (and sometimes on the radio via call-ins and public service announcements). One important kind of ephemera is the festival program. These brochures (e.g., the one whose banquet menu is translated in chapter 1) are composed by the organizers of patron saint days and other rituals, printed in large batches, and hand-distributed through urban neighborhoods where the "children of the village" dwell.

The connection through print does more than reinforce villages' ability to tap their diasporas for fundraising purposes. Its publications go far beyond fliers and menus. Villagers or "children" of a village often sponsor substantial volumes, usually for distribution on a festival day. In settlements that have marked elites (such as the provincial capital), these volumes serve elites as gatekeeping mechanisms that confer various levels of "distinction." By accepting some written contributions, and by editing them in an "elevating" way, the creators of provincial print canonize individuals as notables and canonize parts of regional verbal culture as traditional folklore. Local-interest publications bear some resemblance to *yizker-bukher*, or memorial books, compilations of lore remembered by Yiddish-speaking immigrants to America about their longed-for and often completely destroyed home communities (Kugelmass 1998). But they differ in a crucial respect: they are not so much memorials to the past, as current "correspondence" between a center and its diaspora. Some are fairly broad-based civic efforts, while others represent bids for leadership by particular political-cum-kinship networks. Both in the village and among the urban "children of the village," those left out speak of them with a sour-grapes attitude as *huachafo* ('pretentious, fake-bourgeois'). One finds well-thumbed copies in the homes of civic activists, peasants who like to read, and some teachers; other copies probably lie hidden in trunks and the lumber rooms of private homes, village halls, and schools.

ON PERUVIAN IDEOLOGIES OF CULTURAL DIFFERENCE

Before trying to interpret the genres of rural print, a non-Peruvian reader may want to ponder the role of print in Peru's peculiar economy of identities. Peruvian and North Atlantic viewpoints on "ethnicity" and "the indigenous" differ fundamentally. Many ethnographic writings by foreigners, and virtually all travel-and-tourism writings, impart a mistaken notion of Andean villagers' feelings of identity. Foreign visitors are puzzled by the fact that Huarochiranos, especially in smaller and poorer villages such as Tupicocha, practice a great deal of what ethnology classifies as indigenous Andean culture, yet reject with bitterly hurt feelings to any suggestion that they are an indigenous or Native American people. Equally puzzling to foreigners is that elites in smaller cities such as Huarochirí rhetorically and ritually identify with Inkas, yet in their way of life flee Andean habits and energetically copy the "whiter" Creole and cosmopolitan styles of Lima. Visitors who are used to the North American ideology of diversity sometimes suppose that as intimidated victims of a racist system, people are hiding their real "ethnic" sentiments. The actual situation is quite different.

The ideology of race in rural highland and coastal (but not Amazonian) Peru still has almost unquestioned status, although it is rarely made explicit. It could be summed up as follows. Peru was formed of three races: Inka, Spanish, and Black. All had attributes of nobility to the degree that they had kings and "cultures." But because it was Creole children of the Spanish race who created the Peruvian nation-state, the "national" identity requires competence in a modern variant of Creole culture. This metropolitan Creolism is today associated with a vague ideology of *mestizaje* and a "civil religion" focusing on state insignia. Competence in this hegemonic culture alleviates still-strong racial stigmas on markedly African or markedly American skins and faces. It confers "national" identity. The term "Indian" (a weak translation for the odious word *indio*) and its euphemisms imply incompetence in this culture. To accept identity within the indigenous category is to accept less than citizen dignity. Terms such as *indigenous* and *ethnic* are understood by most campesinos as synonyms for *race*—that is, "Indian"—and are therefore rejected as self-identifiers.

This attitude is under challenge; ideologies which affirm "diversity" on the North Atlantic model grew among intellectuals, cosmopolitans, and NGO personnel, and are greatly amplified in Peru's fast-growing university forums. In the 2000s programs for multiculturalism have been spreading also through urban print media and schools, as well as the Internet and broadcasting. The indigenist example of Evo Morales' Bolivian presidency, and of Ollanta Humala's ethno-nationalist 2006 presidential campaign, emboldened many to assert indigeneity as an idiom of defiance toward Lima elites. In quieter approaches to inclusiveness, most state institutions have become open and respectiful to formerly excluded sectors. Carlos Iván Degregori and Pablo Sandoval, longtime critics of Peru's exclusivist legacy, now sum up recent cultural trends as irreversible movement toward "a 'diverse We' " (2008:163).

And yet in Tupicocha, for example, multiculturalism hardly sets the tone. Rural people of central Peru solve their "identity issues" by a different route. The route involves the option of retaining what seem to

TABLE 8

Economy of Identity Formation: Peruvian vs. North Atlantic

	Retain practice	Change practice
Retain label	"Indian ethnicity"	"neo-Indianism"
Change label	"de-Indianization"	Assimilation

foreigners indigenous cultural traits, while recategorizing them as "regional" or "Inka" rather than as indigenous. This is the case with all the Huarochirí customs discussed in the present and preceding (Salomon 2004a) studies. The reign of the sacred clowns called Curcuches, for example, partakes of strikingly Andean ideas. But it is counted as a regional rather than an indigenous custom. The retention of *khipus*, once a stigma of "Indian illiteracy," has a different meaning when one calls it Inka.

One might think of a four-box grid, as in table 8. In the North American context, the upper-left and lower-right internal cells are thought of as the normative options. To be a "real Indian," one is expected to retain both the ethnic label and with it the inherited practice. To abandon both and join the unmarked "majority" is also normative. In North America one may or may not like the assimilationist option, but it is not a deceit. The North American ideology of diversity envisions a bundle of minority peoples who carry on practices seen as authenticating their labels, and a large matrix of assimilated, nonethnic Americans around them. By contrast the options on the upper right and lower left are felt as a kind of cheating, namely, untruth in self-labeling. If an "ethnic" population changes lifestyle while continuing to claim its ethnic label (upper-right option), outsiders will question its "real" identity and the legitimacy of its demands. "Casino Indians" is a slur of this sort. If, on the other hand, an "ethnic group" retains old modes while refusing the corresponding ethnic label, its members may be open to charges of self-hatred or neglect of tradition.

By contrast, in Peru and perhaps much of modern Latin America, the upper-right and lower-left options are normative and overt. On the upper right, "neo-Indianist" movements such as the Bolivian Aymara nationalists, or the 2006 Peruvian presidential campaign of Ollanta Humala, or the Ecuadorian Pachacuti Party invent an onslaught of new, assertively "Andean" usages only tenuously linked to the Quechua and Aymara past.

(The *wiphala*, a banner often called the "Inka flag," or the "ecological Indian" with his New-Age imagery are examples; Galinier and Molinié 2006.) María Elena García, an ethnographer of Peru's newly assertive pro-Quechua educators and of neo-Indianist movements, emphasizes that southern highlanders newly willing to self-identify as indigenous simultaneously insist on "a redefinition of what being *indígena* meant" (2005:140–41). It can, for them, include Spanish speech and an ethnically accented modernism.

As for the lower-left cell, the option of retaining deep-rooted Andean practices while stripping them of the indigenous label is also quite acceptable. De la Cadena (2000:6–7) gave it the name "de-Indianization" and explored in depth its potency in reconfiguring the culture of Cuzco. Substitute labels—regional tradition, Inka commemoration, "typical" spectacle of a province—are never taken by outsiders as fraudulent but, on the contrary, commendable and patriotic. Peasant Huarochiranos as a population have opted decisively and consistently for the lower-left option, "de-Indianization."

PROVINCIAL PRINT

In these pages we will suggest that the process of putting cultural peculiarities into print (as contrasted with manuscript) has been, among Huarochiranos, very much a vehicle of de-Indianization. For perhaps sixty years, writers of print have been seeking to give inherited culture a niche within the lettered and respectable order of things, while at the same time washing from it the stain of the indigenous.

Aside from the festival programs mentioned above, campesinos get into print via three genres. First in importance are provincial monographs, for instance, *Añoranza huarochirana: Trabajo monográfico dedicado a la gran familia huarochirana que quiere y añora a la tierra natal* ('Huarochirí Longings: A Monographic Work Dedicated to the Great Huarochirano Family Which Loves and Longs for the Land of its Birth'), by Juan Contreras Tello (1994). A second genre consists of collective commemorative books to which local notables, teachers, and prominent diaspora members are asked to contribute. One example, *La Voz de San Damián* (1957), was a commemorative project of locally prominent families celebrating the 100th anniversary of the town's promotion to district status. *La Voz* has become very rare and locally famous. It is considered an authoritative or at least a privileged source on matters that village manuscripts do not treat. Third, one finds irregularly published provincial journals: *Huarochirí, Revista de unidad cultural* (HRUC 1991) is an example. Regardless of these packaging systems, all are essentially scrapbooks of work by multiple contributors. All have similar content. The authors usually include schoolteachers and principals, politically ambitious local individuals, Lima-dwelling leaders of immigrant associations, factional or party activists (but not writing under party banners), subprefects or other bureaucrats showing formal sympathy, lettered relatives of *costumbreros*, and Community members eager to promote development or modernization programs.

Businesses owned by countrymen in Lima, and occasionally Lima firms that sell to rural Huarochiranos, subsidize editions by buying advertising space. Among these businesses are trucking companies, grocers, radio stations, and tent restaurants or bars that serve *provincianos.* "Informal" industries (i.e., unlicensed small factories which grow in the self-built boroughs of the urban immigrant poor), clothing shops, taxi owners, laundries, furniture shops, pesticide suppliers, photographers, liquor dealers, hardware stores, bakeries, garages, barbers, and wholesalers of Huarochirí-grown foodstuffs also buy ads. Publications are sold by the editor, sometimes even hand to hand, or by an urban "cultural society" or, in the home village, sometimes by the municipality. Some books are never printed at all but circulate in photocopies of typescripts.

THE INVERSE OF SCHOOLBOOKS

It would be an exaggeration to call such rural-urban and diaspora publications documents of resistance, but not so to call them "alternative media." One indication of wide social distance between metropolitan and provincial print is that academic social science has generally taken no notice of the latter.

In 1957, when *La Voz de San Damián* came out, a team of San Marcos University researchers were finishing an intensive study of Huarochirí Province. Its compendium would become a cornerstone of Peruvian social science: *Las actuales comunidades indígenas* ('Indigenous Communities of Today'; Matos Mar et al. 1958). The book has nothing to say about provincial print. Neither did the writers of *La Voz* choose to mention the San Marcos University project. This suggests that small-town intellectual elites did not welcome, or maybe were not even contacted by, metropolitan ones. Between *La Voz* and the contemporaneous, widely read book published by José Matos Mar and his students, one sharp and even painful contrast stands out. The title of Matos's social science classic and all its text flatly attribute Indianness to Huarochiranos. To that decade's social science field researchers, Huarochiranos appeared a generically, colorlessly "peasant" population, unlettered, destined for a modernization sure to leach out what few cultural idiosyncrasies they thought worth noting. But, to the authors of the provincial monograph, the village is a society rich in "history" and idiosyncrasy. The imputation of Indianness was to the authors of *La Voz* an unjust challenge. In more recent times, provincial writers have become more welcoming to academic writing, and usually are pleased to see their villages' fame spread through research.

Today international NGOs, visiting researchers (often students at Andean universities), and local government entities themselves sponsor local-oriented publications. One result is the modification of old styles of provincial print. Newer formats typically owe something to the vogue of testimonial literature and ideologies of multiculturalism. Diasporic Andeans with academic connections are often the compilers or translators. The latest print reincarnation of Huarochirí's classic mythology is a book of this kind (Fundación Flora Tristán 2002).

Most Huarochirí villages have produced at least one "local monograph." Books of this genre often lay claim to authenticity via various essentialisms; in Huarochirí a common one is emphasis on *rebeldía* ('rebelliousness,' understood to mean defiance of tyranny or insult), which is treated as Huarochiranos' characteristic virtue. Its canonical text is Sotelo's often-extracted San Marcos dissertation. This book constructs as master narrative a story of the Huarochiranos as Andean Cincinnati: men and women of the soil rising in arms whenever the Peruvian nation is threatened or oppressed. In every century they gather from pastures and fields to battle the enemies of the authentic Peru, whether the enemies be the viceroyal bureaucrats of 1750, the Spanish *gachupines* of 1820, or the Chileans of 1879. (Today, one hears some nostalgic talk about members of the Shining Path as righteous rebels, but most adults remember their disrespectful and violent conduct and assign the glory, rather, to the anti–Shining Path peasant militias called *rondas*.) Typical epithets for the archetypal highlander are "Descendents of a fierce race like the Yauyos . . . fighting chieftains [*caudillos*] who shook the Metropolis . . . symbols of the Peruvian patriotic guerrilla [*montonera*]" (*La Voz de San Damián*

1957:20). Invaders challenge national honor, while inauthentic Peruvians hold back progress by ignoring the just claims of the countryside. History is narrated as a struggle to rise from the futility of muddy labor through combat against such foes, and through the acquisition of technology. Provincial publications avoid politically radioactive matters, such as certain local details of Shining Path warfare, the discredited performance of the major parties, or abuses and corruption by state personnel in the countryside (though pungent subtexts are not lacking).

Like school drama, provincial print is imagined as the vector of an improved and enlightened culture. Editors usually fill blank spaces with aphorisms from classical authors, eighteenth-century savants, or prestigious modern ideologues. Cultivated poetry—of Santa Teresa de Jesús, César Vallejo, Longfellow in translation—enlivens pictures of trucks and maps of projected sewerage lines.

Accordingly, provincial print glorifies innovations and anniversaries of "progress": the arrival of the first motor vehicle in 1944, after years of grueling and dangerous *faena* work on the new road; the anniversary of building the railroad through the Rímac Gorge; the elevation of villages to district status; the installation of Huarochirí's first TV antenna (1989). Related state documents, which in the English-speaking countries would be taken as "purely legal" in interest (and as distant from popular prose registers as one could imagine), get reproduced in full and carefully reread—even read out loud—as *constancias*, consubstantial proofs. The provincial book is in this regard an extension of *ayllu* writing in an old Lettered City style.

When profiled as individuals, villagers invariably choose to be portrayed in urban and formal style dress (neckties, suits, gowns). Likewise articles celebrate people from the province who have become notable in urban settings or are trying to do so. The painter Milner Cajahuaringa García, who went to study in Argentina (*HRUC* I, 1991:124–25) and has enjoyed some success on the gallery and embassy circuits, gets much self-generated attention, as do numerous members of the Tello *panaka*, the Contreras family (see later in this chapter) and the Cajahuaringa family with their extensive emigrant networks. Others with high profiles in provincial print include publicity-dependent personalities such as disk jockeys on provincial radio, singers, and band leaders.

In the conquest of social dignity, the provincial societies and village-based social clubs in Lima have a very special leadership role. Extremely detailed reports from the emigrant colony to the parent society, with honors to Lima patrons, are always in demand. Provincial publications carry verbatim texts of ceremonial speeches at urban social functions, themselves laden with exact dates, rosters of office, and lists of donated amounts. All this partakes of the "romance of the precise." Provincial organizations in the city's self-built boroughs, such as the San Damián Social Center, sometimes supply the longest articles.

Photographs illustrate urban provincial society in the making. A modern variant of the "historical memorandum" genre used in villages commemorates the "invasions" through which migrants to the city pioneer new neighborhoods: a photo shows a crowd in Sunday clothes, massed around a pole bearing a megaphone horn and a Peruvian flag, in the midst of a patch of desert that contains nothing else. When these people take over underused lands, first building shacks and later houses, they become the founders of self-built boroughs which will in a short time become the homes of the village's proudest "children." Such new urban "colonies" have become a spectacularly growing edge of ex-peasant society. Some are already forty or more years old. Most have transformed themselves by "sweat equity" from shantytowns to solidly built formal neighborhoods, and some have achieved enough economic success to attract "big box" shopping centers. It is no wonder that successful pioneers on the urban frontier are influential in, and courted by, provincial media.

Provincial print publications reinforce the loyalty that brings crowded busloads of Limeños back to their natal villages for annual rituals and festivals. Eugenio Vilcayauri Medina, who belongs to the Tupicochan colony in Chosica (one of Lima's "edge cities," a couple of hours up the Carretera Central [Central Highway]), included in his monograph a directory of seventy heads of emigrant households "who have houses of their own in Lima" and sorted them by their urban neighborhoods (Lobo 1982). Such lists evoke feelings of pride that the "children of the village" have succeeded in the brutal scramble to advance from squatting in the sand to home building and ownership (Degregori, Blondet, and Lynch 1986; Golte and Adams 1987). At the same time they underline the conviction that such people owe a debt to the village, which supports urban pioneers by sending bags of food to sustain them during the grueling early phases of settlement.

Provincial publications sometimes partake of aggressive cultural hegemony. A female schoolteacher contributed to the 1957 volume *La Voz de*

San Damián an article called "Negative Factors of Education" in which she damns the "complete promiscuity" of "indigenous homes" as an obstacle to learning. Those who "sleep on the floor on rawhides and rough blankets," those who wear "the cloak, scarf, and sandals" are guilty of "immorality" because they practice "vices" (meaning boozy sex) in front of children. Similarly Tupicocha's semipublished self-ethnographer Eugenio Vilcayauri Medina set out to glorify "tradition," but also felt free to rebuke the "degenerative love of custom [*costumbrismo*] and of the ill-interpreted folklore for which the traditional festivals are always a pretext" (1983:17). What he objects to most is the ritual expense. He offered a tally to prove that in 1984 Tupicocha and its satellites were annually "wasting" the equivalent of approximately $368,620 U.S. dollars per year on six "incoherent, vain and useless" festivals—more than enough to pay for every young villager's modern education (1983:31–32). "We have a rich folklore, but an uncultivated one." In a more polished second edition (2009), Vilcayauri softened the language but insisted on his point.

As villages' productive importance shrinks, their symbolic roles grow. Increasingly, places such as Tupicocha must succeed as ceremonial centers or else depopulate. It is therefore hard to overestimate the priority that sheer emotion receives in composing provincial publications. Every sentimental button is pressed, sometimes most ingeniously. Panoramic photos of the home village—the welcoming view one sees when climbing down from a day on the high fields, or the hometown landscape that opens to a road-weary returnee as the bus rounds the last curve—are a must. Many a page is dedicated to the words of songs, especially *huaynos*, on themes of homeland and wistful love. Villagers enjoy seeing familiar food (for example, the *huatia*, or earth-baked potato, mentioned in chap. 5 of the 1608 Quechua Manuscript of Huarochirí) dignified in culinary lexicons or recipes. Poetry in an elevated pseudo-nineteenth-century diction endows the *patria chica*, or local homeland, with anthems similar in genre to those of the nation.

Although children as individuals get little attention some authors play on nostalgic feelings by writing in detail about childhood games (Juan Contreras Tello 1994:95–111). Soccer articles are more than just sports news, because soccer teams formed in youth tend to function as cohesive age sets that go on to become political alliances. Soccer news and team portraits from city and country abound, projecting glowing vigor and promise. Women are underrepresented—at least they were through the mid-1990s; a section glorifying motherhood and female patriotism is never lacking, but only a few teachers and hardly any *campesinas* or even female entrepreneurs emerge as profiled personalities. On the other hand, men whom the metropolis slights as transients or actors on the periphery receive in these pages a recognition that would hardly come their way in urban media. Provincial publications provide lavish obituaries which include fine-grained biographies. Photographs of the deceased are one reason such books become carefully guarded keepsakes, eventually verging on heirloom status.

Articles include a fair amount of narrative meant to evoke poignant memories of rural life:

> [In the rainy season in Tupicocha,] when the tillers go home after their day's work, and rain catches up with them, flash floods sometimes leave them cut off across inundated canyons . . . children go along trembling from the cold . . . torrents roar fiercely in the canyons, thunder and lightning crashes strike ever harder on the mountains.
> . . . the herdsmen suffer a lot in those time. Water leaks into their rickety huts. Their soaked firewood won't burn and clean water is hard to get.[2] The herdsman sometimes loses his cattle in fields smothered by cloud cover so thick it makes one feel deaf . . . when the cattle get too skinny they refuse to walk or sometimes they get lost or die. (Vilcayauri Medina 1983–91:8)

Other prose contributions can fairly be called self-ethnography, including an account of the launching of the sacrificial boat to the Owners of Yansa Lake as described in chapter 2 (*La Voz de San Damián* 1957:187). However, the "writing of culture" here stands poles apart from academic ethnography. In the first place, it assumes native familiarity with concepts and places. For example, one would have to know the plants and animals serving as totemic emblems of particular settlements to understand a clever satire of Huarochirí's various towns in dialogue with each other around a campfire. In this dialogue herbs stand in allegorically for moral qualities (*HRUC* I, 1991:164) according to a code that only countrymen would know. Since self-ethnography already assumes the reader knows the rites and customs, it does not bother to descriptively restate them in plain prose. Rather, "good" writing in this context involves clever transposition of the vernacular practice from vernacular to literary registers. When the Andean gods appear, as they often do, their loves and rivalries are told in courtly or "elevated" language perhaps derived from Spanish imitators of Jean Racine. (The excerpt in chapter 6 from the Chokesuso play will do for an example.) A person unfamiliar with the terrain might even fail to recognize some "traditions" as referring to the same narratives and rites which seem so intensely "Andean" when described by Arguedas, the indigenists, or by modern cultural anthropologists.

Among all the "customs," bullfighting gets supremely emphasized by publications. Rural bullfights do not involve killing bulls. Professional *toreros* star, but crowds love to see their young friends leap into the arena. Bullfighting is not so much about bulls as such, as about their standing as symbolic distillates of local virtues: "Fighting bulls, whose fierceness has endured through time. . . . The cattleman's commitment spares no effort to conserve the purity of fierce blood . . . the spilling of blood with renewed frequency in bullfights, [is] a happy augury of earthly fertility and a good year" (*La Voz de San Damián* 1957:16–17). The belief that bloodshed during ritual is an offering to Earth and will redound to the celebrants' benefit is a very widespread and deep-rooted Andean one. Village bullfights boomed in the 1980s and became a prime engine of village fundraising, so much so that many villages have devoted endless faenas and major expenses to their bullrings.

PROVINCIAL WRITING AND THE IDEOLOGY OF WRITTEN NAMES

Provincial publications take a double stand in the ideology of language and writing. On the one hand, in their gatekeeping role, they uphold the acquisition of standard orthography and high registers of speech. Sometimes they contain articles advising locals how to avoid expressions that urbanites regard as solecisms. But on the other, unlike schoolbooks they glorify the rural sociolect's linguistic peculiarity in specific contexts. They invite highlanders to revel in their distinctive lexicon, and include long, loving glossaries of regional words (e.g., Contreras Tello 1994:153–57; Vilcayauri Medina 1983–91:43–45). The implicit notion seems to be that standard oral Spanish and literate competence license one's command of regionalisms by enabling one to pigeonhole them "where they belong": namely, in the heart and in the circle of hometown friendship. An enlightened countryman loves them, but as conscious identity-signs rather than unselfconscious colloquialisms. They are lexically folklorized.

Another way provincial authors line up with metropolitan scribal elites in conserving Creole academic authority at the "high end" of the written stylistic spectrum, is their huffiness over popular liking for names from "foreign" languages. One periodically finds protests that the law should stop civil registrars from writing into the official record such names as Elizabeth, Fritz, Harris, Milner, Piter (Peter), Douglas, Jhony, Ledy (Lady), Mery (Mary), Walter, Wilmer, Yanet, Yimi (Jimmy)—all favorites of the current soap-opera-influenced parental generation.[3]

But provincial literati are ready and eager to defend personal names at the "low," "peasantish," regional, and intimate end of multiregister name usage. A Huarochirano's name is a layered linguistic construct whose different forms mark levels of contextual formality and social distance.[4] Its innermost shell is one's *querer* ('love,' that is, the name used affectionately by the inner circle of kin and generation mates), for example, Cashimoyo for Cuasimodo, Fuyensho for Florencio, Shindo for Gumercindo, Mashaco for Marcial, Shufa for Sofía, Lensha for Florencia, Quilish for Eráclides, Pesh for Perseveranda, Shico for Francisco, Shufeo for Saturno, Yengo for José. The prominent /sh/, which is not a phoneme of Royal Academy Spanish, may relate to Quechua I, but it is also common in adult versions of "baby talk." The querer of a deceased person is almost unbearably evocative; it is likely to call forth tears of renewed grief, and for this reason one should not mention it during mourning.

Since it is usually one's age mates and ayllu mates who know quereres and satirical nicknames, these constitute richly rewarding emotional triggers. One provincial monograph feature (Contreras 1994:160–62) is a trivia quiz challenging the "children" of Huarochirí to remember the quereres of specific local hometown figures. Vilcayauri Medina thought them worthy of a three-page list (1983–91:[no page number]).

Baptismal names are a less intimate layer of the name, but they are also a hotspot in language-and-writing ideology. A person's name in the civil register is what anchors her or him to the whole edifice of law and national power (via identity numbers repeated on documents). The unmarked default of "correct" naming is the onomasticon of biblical persons and saints, augmented by Greco-Roman and Gothic names. Sophisticated urbanites regard "fancy" baptismal names such as Melquíades, Gumercindo, Macario, Ninidio, Florentino, Horlinda, Perseveranda, Sócrates, and so forth, as "peasant" or even "folkloric" in the put-down sense, but self-consciousness about this had not as of 1998 invaded the rural press. These names are typical of the pretelevision generation, and their "vibe" is parental. Baptismal names do, however, provoke anxious self-consciousness in another regard. This is acute orthographic anxiety and scolding about spelling. Peasants run into trouble when they find out that agents of the civil registry and bureaucrats regard their habitual onomasticon as "wrong": A man who signs as "Froibel" instead of "Floribel" may find himself condemned to wasted days lingering at a registry office to prove that he is who he says he is (Lund 2001). The provincial press favors the canonical forms, while ayllu books favor the colloquial ones. Individuals themselves are sometimes left in chronic doubt which is "correct."

Toponyms also play starring roles in the lexicography of local sentiment. No medium is more toponym intensive, more dedicated to "trajectory" or the touring of space in imagination than provincial monographs. Landscape panegyrics occur every few pages. The writer remembers landscape features, fauna, and flora as richly evocative. The faithful pair-bonding of the *huáchihua*, or Andean goose (*Chloephaga melanoptera*) suggests faithful peasant marriage. The Arcadian vegetation of the upper Mala riverbanks—whose locations, herbs, and views are named and praised one by one—speaks of the healthful rural life. Toponymy is also memorable, but not unchanging: a spot along a pasturing trail called Piter, "named after an engineer who got sick there," commemorates an evidently recent event. Even pure trajectory, without prose cues to any exterior connotation, is a sought-for effect. For example, one article consists of nothing but a list of the 50 named landmarks one passed on the old route from Huarochirí to Lima (*HRUC* I, 1991:153).

A rich crust of toponymy covers many pages, like embroidery on a ceremonial garment:

> When we talk of "Gurmanchi," swiftly we remember "Chilcanchi," "Ollucanchi," "Matahuanchi," "Canchanchi," "Shiquircanchi." Likewise, when we think of "Macachaya," by association we think of "Huahuilcaya," "Sincocaya," "Matiacaya," "Cornaya"; likewise of "Culcushica," "Cushashica," of "Huayqui," "Calmayqui," "Chacuayqui." (*HRUC* I, 1991:8)

Not a single one of these toponyms is lexically transparent. The terms derive from the extinct ethnic language of the region. The enjoyment they give is that of mentally ranging through one's homeland. The apparently boundless appreciation for proper names gives a clue to the intellectual inclinations behind this literature. Proper nouns, unlike all other kinds of words, are commonly taken as denoting not a class of entities grouped under a cultural criterion but unique referents (only one entity corresponding to any given proper name). To be a learned person in this lore of uniqueness is to be headed upstream against the trend of organized intellectual life in general, with its nomothetic and generalizing aspirations. Nobody gives this mentality a clearer voice than the pseudonymous "Eveme" of Tupicocha, who typed a whole lexicon to express his aspirations for a form of learning that flees the nomothetic to ground itself in the unique:

> TUPICOCHANIZARSE: To affiliate oneself with one's environment; to identify oneself with Tupicocha.
> TUPICOCHOLOGÍA: Science which deals with the subjects that constitute and integrate Tupicocha.
> TUPICOCHOGRAFIA: Science that deals with the description of Tupicocha in its various aspects.
> TUPICOCHOLOGO: One who professes Tupicochography. (Etc. Vilcayauri Medina 1983–91:42)

This passage might seem satirical, but it was not meant so. What, in seriousness, did the author have in mind? The motion toward a "science" whose subject matter resolves itself into an indefinitely large universe of the unique—a strictly chorographic study diametrically opposed to the usual philosophy of scholarship—is offered as a path to certainty of selfhood: a firm existential grip which enables people to be strong and authentic.

"COMMANDER TUTAYQUIRI" AND THE USES OF TOURISM

Do village writers address readers beyond their own social networks? Villagers have begun exchanging texts with travelers who have no village kinship.

Although up to the late 1990s the traffic of visitors through San Damián's Spartan hostelries was an insignificant trickle by the standards of the "Inka Trail," villagers say "a lot of foreigners" pass through. The guest register at one of two hotels in the provincial capital of Huarochirí shows that in 1992 there were eighty-four guests, of whom twelve gave *paseo* ('excursion') as their purpose. Only one was a foreigner. In 1993, of fifty-two guests, twelve were possible tourists, none foreign. In 1994, of ninety-nine guests, twenty-three were possible tourists, none foreign. By the

2000s vogues for "ecological" tourism and new-agey mountain quests increased traffic. Visitors include "edge" tourists, such as Lima's mountain-bicycling clubs, university students in search of a taste of the highlands or a term paper to write, wealthy Limeños giving their Land Cruisers a workout, rural ministerial technocrats and teachers, mine personnel, and a few foreigners interested in artisan crafts or mountain biota. When villagers explain their region to outsiders, they rely heavily on provincial publications and can expound their contents with startling fluency. Señor Héctor Chumbimuni, proprietor of a hotel in Huarochirí town (the provincial capital), is also a *comunero* of a nearby village and a prominent cattleman. His speech for the edification of tourists makes a good example of the genre of recycled Avila lore, illustrating how references to detailed toponyms make it easy for local people to memorize Avila-derived versions. It also shows the sheer enjoyment people get from these stories.

> [Greeting in English :] Hoo—oola my dear Mister Franklin, good afternoons! [switches to Spanish]. . . . You should visit us at the Community [of Llambilla]. We are the heirs of what God gave us through Paria Caca. Pariacaca came and gave Llambilla the springs of Capiama.[5] And he came through here [Huarochirí, provincial capital] too! He came when they were having a festival half dead from thirst. The people didn't even give him a glass of water. They were scared of him. He was gigantic, glittering! They ran and hid in their crannies [*covachas*]. Except one lady. He told her she could escape. He came in the form of a giant rainstorm. He washed Wayquiula away,[6] everybody. Except that old lady! And she's gone too, an old granny, whew, she's already dead from old age.

A few Huarochiranos who have been to Cuzco hope to increase tourism upon the model of the celebrated "Inka city." Alcides Granados, the mayor of Avila's old parish of San Damián in the early 1990s, wanted his village to at least enjoy more of the commerce that reaches the provincial capital. In 1994 he wrote a petition to ENTUR, a government-sponsored nonprofit corporation promoting tourism, asking to have his district included in a listing of tourist zones and also asking a subsidy to build a Municipal Tourist Lodge. The document contains a fascinating summary of the official history (stamped and signed) which well-read and tourism-conscious villagers have fashioned from the Avila legacy. The following paragraphs retell the pre-Hispanic origins of the district:

> [The campesinos of Concha and Checa] are especially dedicated to the raising of brave bulls and other customs inherited from their ancestors, families of Spanish speech and Catholic faith.
>
> Their first Community leader was the Cacique Juan Tutayquiri, a warrior by heritage, who organized them under his command and prepared his army by widening his domains toward the neighboring villages of Tupicocha Santiago de Tuna, Chaute; forming in this way the region of San Damián [statement of boundaries follows]. Anxious to expand its territory, he asked his subordinate peoples for recruits; an army with which he headed toward the coast, along the existing Inka roads, passing through the towns of Cocachacra, Chosica, and arriving at Chaclacayo, where he installed a garrison for an advance toward Lima, but it so happened that the lord who was the seigneur [*hacendado*] of that domain [*feudo*] and his daughter worked out a treaty, offering to let Commander Tutayquiri made himself the owner [*se adueñó*] of all the lands of Chaclacayo, and among other things, court the daughter as his wife; but after they had made the agreement, the troops became torpid from excessive heat, the mosquitoes and malaria and the lack of food, and they opted to go home to their place of origin, so the commander, understanding this situation to be critical, gave the order to return before handing over to each participant the stretch [*topo*] of land due for his participation in the conquest of Chaclacayo.

This short narrative is interesting not so much for its style, which echoes durable conventions of military historiography, but for its implied vision of who the actors were. Concha and Checa are specifically labeled as Spanish speaking and Catholic—that is, not Indian—from the immemorial start. Both the trajectory of action through space and the argument are almost exactly those of the Quechua oral authors of 1608.[7] Yet the context and other cultural assumptions are those of Christendom and of the Spanish cultural framework, perhaps being modeled on chronicles of medieval Spain and the *reconquista*. Like the "Lake Owners" Pedro Batán and María Capyama, Tutayquiri—the apical hero of the Checa—is a pre-Columbian personage equipped with a baptismal name and a Spanish title.

In the 2000s tourism grew slowly but steadily. The semigovernmental organization in charge of fomenting tourism (PROMPERU) has promoted "circuits" for weekend tourism out of Lima. A Tupicochan entrepreneur built a comfortable hostelry. As of 2010, a fast-moving government program to pave secondary roads promises to make the arduous journey easier. The slopes of Paria Caca have been publicized as a majestic nature zone by the National Institute of Culture's media-savvy project on Inka roads (*Proyecto Qhapaq Ñan*). And journalism about Tupicocha's unusual cultural patrimony, the khipus and the customs around them, have made Tupicocha better known than most villages of its size. In this same interval, the Internet became substantially available to Huarochiranos (at least those who can travel down the mountain to Chosica), and they have used it for two advantages: strengthening diasporic communication, and projecting an image to the world for potential visitors.

THE CHILDREN OF PARIA CACA TAKE TO THE WEB

As the Huarochirí diaspora has become international, its media system is quickly shifting from letters to telephones or Skype, and from paper to electronic media. The current transition from provincial print to the Internet, no less than the earlier transition from handwriting to print, is the work of civil society organizations. In the early 2000s Huarochirí's diaspora included colonies in various parts of the United States, Australia, Italy, and Spain, and to some degree Germany, the United Kingdom, and Canada. Sophisticated national-level websites in the 1990s (e.g., Club de Peruanos en el Mundo: www.clubdeperuanos.com) or Peru.com (www.peru.com). One, Peruanos en USA, (www.peruanosenusa.net) includes an impressive directory of emigrant societies on the Internet. Interestingly, religious confraternities are frequent initiators of international websites. Other sites represent departments, provinces such as Huarochirí, and a few villages. The sites are grouped according to important Peruvian colonies: Paterson (New Jersey), Miami, and New York spawn sites that claim Huarochirí as their anchor.

The Internet also attracts a massive public closer to home, in the outlying boroughs of Lima, where even poor neighborhoods host innumerable cybercafés. As of the early 2000s, however, the Internet was only beginning to function in the Huarochirí highlands, because most of the villages had the barest of bare-bones telecommunications connections. In most villages as of 2008, a few young technically minded people are poised to mount cybercafés as soon as telephone companies become willing to improve the presently minimal and unreliable system of connections. For the time being, however, hometowns are passive and urban diasporas active agents in the Peruvian "cybersphere."

Huarochirí's diaspora presence on the web directly carries on the genre and the hierarchy of provincial print. One important web presence is a social network derived from a football club with century-deep roots, Club Héroes de la Breña. Club Héroes was formed in Huarochirí's "high neighborhood" (in Andean terms, upper moiety) in 1911. Since 1963 it has sponsored a "Folklore Group," meaning a society for performing such roles as the pre-Hispanic "Chief of Ayllu Cushpata in Llambilla, Warirumo." Like many emigrant sites, theirs puts a high priority on internationalizing costume drama and song of the sort discussed in chapter 6. Its website (www.huarochiri.net) is also dedicated to soccer history and personality profiles.

The same network also runs an accomplished website, "Huarochirí USA" (www.huarochiriusa.com) serving the Huarochirí diaspora colony in North America. It is sponsored by the Asociación de Residentes Huarochiranos en Texas USA (ARHTUSA), a well-established provincial society based in Dallas and Houston, through a committee called Contigo Huarochirí ('With You, Huarochirí'). The Texas-based association was founded in 1965. The Contreras family, which in the past was active in producing provincial print, led the society in the 1990s; its patriarch is a retired chemical engineer, Carlos Contreras Chucle. The editor of the website, Pedro P. Inga Huaringa, made his career as a systems engineer for Baylor and other Dallas hospitals. In 2003 he privately printed in Lima his autobiography *Soy peruano americano* ('I Am a Peruvian-American'). He gives as the website's first objective that of helping members stay mutually up to date, and as second, that of fostering tourism in the province. Inga Huaringa says Internet "lets us share our Peruvianness and exalt the name of Huarochirí beyond its borders, carrying forward the purposes, hopes, and aspirations that from this country the United States we will be able to diffuse the high cultural and social values of our land of birth."[8] The website is edited entirely within the *norma culta* of Peruvian Spanish, conforming in prose style to the rhetoric of Peruvian civil society groups. A 1995 group portrait of society members shows prosperous-looking people of three generations, in conservative urban garb, banqueting in a Texan home.

The web page is in many ways an extension of provincial print. It is the

72. The Huarochirí colony resident in Texas performs "Danza de las Ingas" (Dance of the Inka Women) and photographed the performance c. 2005 for its website. Photo by permission of Pedro Inga Huaringa.

organ of a provincial society like those of Lima in its federated structure, its centralization in a few family lineages, and its program of "elevating" regional culture to the status of dignified "Inka" heritage. The costume dances represented in figure 72 are Texan in background but exactly fit the genre styles developed in the school pageants and town-centered festivals described in chapter 6. The "Inka" costumes are rich and elaborate by comparison to those seen in the Sierra de Lima, but of identical workmanship. As with Lima's provincial society, the objective of so-called Inka fetes is to raise funds for bringing electricity, telephones, Internet, medical improvements, and better schooling to the highland home.

Although the makers of these pages have become familiar with many printed reworkings of the legacy of the 1608 Quechua Manuscript of Huarochirí, they do not quote the original. They apparently regard Quechua as a closed chapter of their history and English as an opening one. The legends of Paria Caca Mountain as regional divinity remain prominent. One page lists several works about Paria Caca, including scholarly ones. As of 2007, YouTube hosted footage of an endearing hometown dramatization of the second chapter of the mythology of the 1608 Quechua Manuscript. In it a mysterious orphan baby identifies the god Kuni Raya, disguised in rags, as his father (Martí 2007). The authors of such web pages are familiar with the provincial monographs and compendia discussed above, sometimes citing and imitating them.

Changes do occur. The Inka motif is heightened and defined more sharply than in older print expressions. The page on regional history explains that the Inkas expelled an unruly pre-Inka people (whom ethnohistorians see as ancestors of modern Huarochiranos) into neighboring Yauyos Province. By this device the four founding ayllus of the modern provincial city can be construed as purely Inka. At its social functions the ARHTUSA now raises the rainbow-checkered "Inka flag" or "flag of Tawantinsuyu," an international invented tradition symbolizing "neo-Indian" identity.

Despite such curtsies to nationally dominant Inka lore, diasporic Internet, like the older print media, plays on the pleasures of remembering the unique in all its obscure peculiarity. A slight rewrite of older lore explains the transition from ayllu names to names of the Peasant Communities and to their hometown nicknames: "The Spaniard gave each ayllu a nickname depending on how they worked: to Cajahuaman, now called Suni, 'dogs'; to Cushpampa, now Llambilla, 'worms'; to Hualashcoto, now Lupo, 'llamas'; and to Chuycoto, now Huarochirí, 'pigs.' "[9] Like older print media, the website features a profuse section about the surnames associated with local authenticity, albeit commenting that in the second generation of North American Huarochiranos, new surnames (and "gringo" physical features) are appearing. Also like the older literature, the website makes "rebellion" against tyranny (the Spanish Empire, the Chilean occupation) a durable essence of the homeland. Even more than the old print media, it describes in detail the cults and the religious sodalities of Saint Rose of Lima as well as of the Lord of Miracles, a much-loved Christ image resident in Lima. And finally, ARHTUSA's website, no less than the older media, features didactic essays on the art of becoming an educated person.

Huarochirí USA shares with the print tradition an intensely localistic tacit philosophy. Its writers take no interest whatever in other parts of the province other than the eponymous capital, make no mention of overseas Huarochiranos from other settlements, and take no notice of other villages' presence in the historic sources. The lettered tradition of the village leaped into the World Wide Web with little or no alteration of its sociological habit and function. The provincial cybersphere is not, to date, an example of globalization in the sense of emergent cosmopolitan culture, so much as a new way of reinforcing exclusivistic locally rooted social networks over immense distances, amid rapid change.

CONCLUSIONS

Unheralded and uninvited, Native South Americans became a part of the worldwide literate sphere nearly half a millennium ago. Strangely, this bothers many intellectuals. Far from welcoming Amerindians as peers in the republic of letters, they like to pose Native South Americans as lamentable exemplars of humanity denatured or defrauded by letters. Three well-known examples illustrate the tendency.

The first is the most famous single passage in the ethnography of writing: the "Writing Lesson" chapter of Claude Lévi-Strauss's *Tristes Tropiques*. In a clearing of the Brazilian forest, where the ethnographer sat to write his notes, an ambitious Nambikwara chief began to imitate script with squiggles of his own. Soon he set about trying to intimidate his peers with feigned mastery of the graphic art. Lévi-Strauss reflected that this only vindicated Rousseau's conviction about the link between writing and slavery:

> [Writing] had been borrowed [by the Nambikwara] as a symbol, and for a sociological rather than an intellectual purpose, while its reality remained unknown. It had not been a question of acquiring knowledge, of remembering or understanding, but rather of increasing the authority and prestige of one individual —or function—at the expense of others. . . . The scribe is rarely a functionary or employee of the group: his knowledge is accompanied by power, with the result that the same individual is both scribe and money-lender; not just because he needs to be able to read and write to carry on his business, but because he

thus happens to be, on two different counts, someone who *has a hold* over others.

> The only phenomenon with which writing has always been concomitant is the creation of cities and empires . . . and their grading into castes or classes . . . [writing] seems to have favoured the exploitation of human beings rather than their enlightenment. . . . The primary function of written communication is to facilitate slavery. The use of writing for disinterested purposes, and as a source of intellectual and aesthetic pleasure, is a secondary result, and more often than not it may even be turned into a means of strengthening, justifying, or concealing the other. (1992 [1955]:298–99; emphasis in original)

Lévi-Strauss's disquiet is moral. It concerns writing's inherent potential to "hold" people under control by fixing knowledge about them as a property, an instrumental thing that can trump their personal agency. In the Rousseauian view literacy becomes an original sin of civilization. This view merely inverts the equally ideological notion of literacy as a "state of grace," which Sylvia Scribner (1984) exposed to ethnographic critique, and it is of no greater analytical use. It has played its part in the unfortunate stereotyping of South American ethnology and history as *triste histoire.*

This mindset was unfortunately influential. Until the 1990s, the very fact that an "Indian" was a writer would disqualify her or him as a "real Indian" in the eyes of most South Americanist ethnographers. The interesting question of what the Nambikwara and other peoples did with writing once they learned it was not broached by the author of *Tristes Tropiques.* (As of 2008, *Ethnologue* reported that about 10 percent of Nambikwara were literate in their own language.) It may be that anthropologists' reluctance to engage with the role of writing in lowland societies has to do with repugnance toward missionaries. In much of South America, after 1767 and the expulsion of the Jesuits, the groups that promoted alphabetic text among "tribes" were Protestant Evangelicals, and the convert enclaves they organized were long seen as beneath ethnographic notice.

In the cases of highland peoples, and others closer to the viceregal foci of alphabetic literacy than Amazonians were, this ethnological blind spot substantially deformed the image of native South American cultures. For the pre-Hispanic peoples were not without graphic resources. After 1532, the process of becoming "the people called Indians" was itself conducted through writing, and not unilaterally. The sixteenth-century insertion of post-Inka societies into mercantilism, tribute administration, property law, and Christendom largely took the form of written transactions. As recent historiography shows, Andean parties learned early on to assert themselves in them. In some respects one can even say that post-1532 Andean society constituted itself through writing. Yet the stereotype of highlanders as an unlettered residue of ancient Amerindia lingers on in educational ideology and tourist mirages.

Second and more recently, some have written against Amerindian writing on the grounds that it destroyed a form of human integrity inherent in the "oral" order. The "violence of writing" becomes a leitmotif (No 1999). An example is Constance Classen's article "Literacy As Anticulture: The Andean Experience of the Written Word" (1991). Like many readers, Classen is struck by the "School Myth" collected around 1970 by Alejandro Ortiz Rescaniere. According to the Ayacuchan ex-campesino Isidro Huamaní, evil beings who hate the Inka and Mother Earth have trapped generations of native children inside a "mountain called School":

> Ñaupa Machu [the Old One from before the age of the Incas, before civilization] was happy the Inca was dead, because while he was alive, he had had to hide himself. He lived in a mountain called School. The two sons of the Inca passed by and he said to them, "Come I'm going to show you where the Inca and Mother Earth are." The children happily went to the school. Ñaupa Machu wanted to eat them. He said, "Mother Earth doesn't love the Inca any more. The Inca has made friends with Jesus Christ and now they live together like two little brothers. Look at the writing, it says so here." The children escaped, afraid. Since that time, all children have to go to school, and like the two sons of Mother Earth, almost all of them don't like it and escape. (Classen 1991:418; translated by Classen from Ortiz Rescaniere 1973:238–43)

Classen claims to believe that "up until the time of the Conquest, Andean culture was exclusively oral . . . in the sixteenth century, the continuity of the oral traditions . . . was broken and the world was reordered, not by sound, but by a realm of written documents" (404–5). Since then, she thinks, Andean people have consistently repudiated writing as the very opposite of valid knowledge. "If their experience of writing had not been so traumatic, perhaps the Andeans . . . with their emphasis on the visual would have been able to make a voluntary transition" (420). But it is just as well they did not, for then they would "have to learn to deal with the silence that comes with literacy, the experience of alienation and individualism." Classen's disquiet comes from the still-Rousseauian direction of "anthropology as cultural critique"; she fears that literacy dissolves a more authentic social contract by dissociating knowledge from personal bonds.

Classen, like most writers about "oral" cultures, establishes "orality" by simply choosing not to know about its alternatives (Pavez 2008:27). There is never a trace of research about what Andean peoples have actually done with inscription. Yet every Andean archive is stuffed with evidence that Andeans of all social classes over several centuries have acquired writing as fast as they could. Even unlettered "Indians" embraced the "truthfulness" of villages' writs with a dogged faith that wore out the patience of bookish jurists. The campesino Isidro Huamaní, who told the myth of the "mountain called school" to Ortiz Rescaniere, expresses bitterness not about writing as such, but about the injustices that occurred during centuries of engagement with it, and notably the hostile cultural climate of schools. In the first chapter, we surveyed the presences of script in one modern Andean village, noting that writing is present in great volume, but not in the places where an urbanite might expect to find it. We also observed that far from the aversion the "oralists" posit, villagers are avidly attached to writing and carry "alphabetization" to extremes unseen in cities.

Very different, and much more estimable, is a third critique of the lettered order in Spanish America. In his monograph *The Lettered City*, Angel Rama argues that colonial *letrados* quickly built an American regime of authoritative language founded upon the notion of script as the performance of divine Logos. Writing formed a seamless chain of authority from revelation down to legalistic regulation. In total it constituted the source—not the reflection—of human order. It was a version of this dogma with which "Indians" had to engage through translators, scribes, and notaries. Rama sympathizes with Bolívar's intellectual ally Simón Rodríguez, one of the few intellectually revolutionary champions of independence, who argued in the 1849 *Neo-Granadino* that republican education should supplant the scribal arts with "an art of thinking," namely logic (Rama 1996:47–49). Rama's objection is not to literacy but to a singularly obstinate politics of literacy. He argues that writing came to Americans (not just indigenous Americans) as a power-driven constraint upon public discourse, making it impossible to generate effective (legal, ecclesiastical) language without having one's own testimony transmuted by the lettered caste into an opaque, homogeneous, and conservative idiom. As Tamar Herzog put it in her rich monograph on the lettered establishment of colonial Quito, "the scribes made their truth into 'the Truth' " (1996:113).

Without disparaging Rama's impressive analysis of colonial literate ideology, one has to add something to it to make it anthropologically lifelike. Rama is right that the peculiar ethos of the "lettered city" left a powerful imprint on Andean *grafismos*. But he failed to observe that the lettered City of the Kings was not built in a semiotic void. In the second chapter, we demonstrated that it was built in an Andean world already richly supplied with systems of inscription. To the degree that they are understood, they seem to be systems radically different from "writing proper" (i.e., phonographic writing). The most important was that of the *khipu*, or Andean cord record. The lettered city therefore did not simply enter and dominate a Peruvian countryside otherwise empty of records. Rather, it entered into a cycle of interactions that produced a "cord plus paper" solution, at first within the scope of colonial administration and later (after 1600) outside it at the level of unofficial rural recordkeeping.

The dual order added up to a distinctive rural grafismo. It functioned as a semipermeable membrane, regulating flows of information. There are resemblances to Gruzinski's "conquest of the imaginary" in Mexico, whereby an indigenous graphic order (glyphs) acquired signs for such Iberian cultural entities as saints and kings: toward 1600, khipus carried Catholic content and thereby contributed to the intra-"Indian" building of a popular Andean Christendom. On the civil side one might point analogously to tribute khipus. But, perhaps because of their opacity to Spanish eyes, khipus persisted in Tupicocha as an independent registry which served as a check on claims of the lettered city and a resource for endogenous organization. Tupicocha possesses to this day the khipus of its *ayllus* (kinship corporations, also called *parcialidades*). Khipus served as the means of holding members accountable in the intricate cycles of reciprocity which underpinned the commons, and today still symbolize that function.

The lettered city was built *in* something: in what might fancifully be called *khipusqa llahta*, a "knotted country." The introduction of alphabetic writing therefore was a matter of interaction rather than replacement. While Rama's urban-oriented chronicle of colonial literacy as an exploitative constraint on public discourse tells a crucial part of the story, it fails to tell how rural groups endowed with their own graphic inclinations and internal graphic needs responded to the scribal order and reworked it. For this reason we have tried to complement his account with a detailed historical ethnography about the lettered, and knotted, countryside.

One might sum up the history as a narrative of three instantiations of writing as a part of political order. Three times since 1532 and the Spanish invasion, Peru has reconfigured relations among polity, discourse, and script: during the early colonial period, during the late colonial period, and after independence. In each case the play of power gave birth to a particular regimen of graphic practices, and a distinctive view of how writing underpins res publica: the domain of public affairs and the common good.

Legal theorists of the colonial legal order engendered a doctrine of "two republics": a "Republic of Indians" and a "Republic of Spaniards" (Gareis 1993; Levaggi 2001). Two subsocieties were to interdepend as endogamous and ethnically exclusive wholes, each with its internal hierarchy, but both yoked (with unequal powers) under a single, imperial political economy. For each hierarchy, the letter of the law was to form a chain of ascending connections to imperial and ultimately divine authority. One way to see sixteenth-century campaigns reorganizing Inka-era *curacazgos* (domains of ethnic nobles) as "reduction" towns is to think of these as attempts to restructure native collectivities as parts of a letter-linked "Republic of Indians." Spanish-style councils with scribes and treasuries were to guarantee political *razón* (reason, civilization), while continuing Andean dynasties were to demarcate separateness from the Spanish "republic" and warrant legitimate forms of indigenous tributary rule.

Both within "Indian" governance and between the two republics, the model—the first of three relationships centering on literacy mentioned above—entailed channeling flows of information so as to move data yet simultaneously reinforce boundaries. In this regard, Peru had its singularities. For Peru (but not all the other viceroyalties), the mechanism was often one of transmediation. Data had to pass not just from one language to another but from one medium to another. The early viceroyalty evolved protocols to transfer information from the indigenous code, the khipu, into the letter-linked Republic of Indians. But in the very act of co-opting the khipu, the colony caused it to endure not just as a "native" language might, but as an opaque medium providing segregated spaces for cultural privacy and ethnically restricted data. Native nobles as well as village councils were privy to it, and used it as a way to independently control tribute information which, once transmediated to Spanish numeracy and literacy, became subject to manipulation by outsiders. Naturally, both sides found fault with the khipu-paper interface: Indians protested administrative tergiversations, while Spaniards became uneasy at not being able to audit the data tendered by transmediation. Yet duality of graphic regimen rather than being taken as a defect within the system was, for the first colonial lifetime, a part of its integrity.

The khipu–paper interface gradually lost viceregal currency in the first few decades of post-Toledan times. The scribal ascendancy in this period left the "lettered city" without rivals as the supremely authoritative form of language. The second refiguring of relations centers on literary after 1600; for about 270 years, the alphabet as Andean writers and readers knew it was the high end of an ever more steeply diglossic graphic regimen, while the sphere of khipus sank to that of intravillage intimacy, of use by range bosses in the command of peons, or withered altogether. "Indian chroniclers," and incomparably more numerous Indian petitioners, entered as subalterns into the empire of letters—but they entered irrepressibly. In the mid-colonial era, archives were filled to overflowing with correspondence from the lettered city's unwanted interlocutors.

By the eighteenth century, the same forces which undercut Habsburgian viceregal institutions also disturbed the hegemony of its graphic order. The nascent Creole aristocracy of learning, like civil elites in Europe, embraced as an alternative to the "lettered city" a utopian graphic regime, the "republic of letters" (Goodman 1996:10). The project of a universal res publica in print, a common ground for scientific and humanist discourse in multiple languages sharing a common alphabetic code, is considered by many no less seminal to Enlightenment than the old lettered city had been to absolutism. Certainly, it appealed greatly to scientific and political New World patriots. Script now became idealized as the herald of discovery and human agency, rather than the channel of eternally fixed authority emanating downward from the Logos of Creation.

But, considered as an earthly user community, the republic of letters was as sociologically exclusive as it was conceptually inclusive. To be a man or woman of letters entailed certain registers of erudition and courtesy worlds apart from the grubby interethnic pen-pushing of Habsburgian rural administration. In literary and courtly circles, as in the emerging network of scientists, postures of retirement from more vernacular and "vulgar" arenas were the mark of the cosmopolitan. The Creole salons and academies where New World adherents of the republic of letters gathered were scarcely more likely to include recognized "Indians" in Mexico or Lima than they were in Philadelphia or Boston. Media proper to the republic of letters—pamphlets and a particular style of correspondence, but most characteristically the new genre of the magazine—linked together people who cultivated social or mental distance from the hierarchies of the marketplace, the hacienda, and the plantation. It is more than an accident that the literature of Enlightenment in Peru contains lots of good advice projected toward the benighted countryside, but absorbed hardly any incoming information from the far side of the ethnic divide. At least in Peru, late-colonial writing proved more impervious to interethnic discourse than had early-colonial literacy. It is not surprising, then, that as the era of Creole independence dawned, rural graphic practices clung to scribal habits of the older, plural order.

When Creole patriot intellectuals such as Bolívar's friend Simón Rodríguez, or Andrés Bello, set out to create American academies, their intent therefore was to accommodate America in the republic of letters within an existing notion of cosmopolitanism. The upshot was that early "national" lexicographers and teachers saw the multitude of habits through which rural people had accommodated to the older empire of letters as mere deficiencies: archaic legalism, formulaic pedantry, and rustic grammar. Ministries of education and normal schools in the emerging independent republics enshrined the assumption of illiteracy and the graphic *mission civilisatrice.*

With independence (various dates of the 1820s for different countries), the cosmopolitan republic of letters ceded discursive ground to a third notion of literacy in the public forum, namely, literacy as a "national" project leading toward the transformation of Indians into citizens. A historical bond to the national territory did not suffice to make a citizen. The desired information regimen was to be monolingual, undivided by ethnic discontinuities, and evenly documented throughout. The new regime would create for any citizen and his or her relations with the state a uniform type of dossier, universal within Peru and recognized to the exclusion of all others. Alleged illiteracy and ignorance of the language in which official literacy had been vested made "Indians" seem poor prospects for this sort of citizenship. These were taken as reasons to push the

Andean majorities (of Bolivia, Peru, and Ecuador) toward either of two statuses: on the one hand "incapable" wards of the state, to be sheltered by group rights and tutelage pending "civilization"; and on the other, citizen standing entailing purely individual, literate relations with the state. Neither relation, however, reflected reality. Quechua-speaking communities during the early independent republics did tend to consider themselves as having "native" (natural) group rights legitimized by tributary vassalage to the Spanish crown. But in practice this status had long been articulated with many institutions by writing. Indeed, we have argued, by this era a lot of the culture usually styled Andean or traditional or indigenous was already being mediated and reproduced by writing.

The hereditary *kurakas* with their "native scribes" lost their grip on power after the defeated rebellions of the 1780s. A century later, for better or worse, peasants were becoming their own letrados. In other words, the conquest of literacy in the countryside was not taking the form that advanced nineteenth-century republicans such as Simón Rodríguez hoped for, namely, the diffusion of Enlightenment. It had become something unforeseen: the democratization of the lettered city. So deeply have the villagers of Huarochirí internalized it that today they use scribal forms in writing petitions to the same pre-Christian deities Catholicism tried to extirpate in the seventeenth century.

Not unlike the scribes of the colonial lettered city, modern Tupicochans perceive a break between the domain of the oral—useful for the pragmatic, transient, changing, or ludic play of expression—and the domain of the written—proper to durable, consequential, serious, and compelling expression. The "high" and archaic legalistic idiom which villagers prefer to write has to their eyes the advantage of being maximally different from speech. Speech and writing in the village are not two media for the same utterances, but rather a diglossic system in complementary use. This still-firm norm and the internal needs these usages serve militate stubbornly against the centripetal force of centralized linguistic authority.

The lettered cycles of village reproduction have deposited in village archives a stratum of "little history," that is, alphabetic discourse with roots separate from the "national" republican project though increasingly embedded in it. This embedding process was hardly unconscious or accidental. From independence onward, Andean communities' ways with writing have to be understood as attempts to construct citizenship endogenously. The autonomous constitutions of ayllus speak volumes about the will to refashion local inheritances of group rights in articulation with the institutions of free and individual citizenship.

Yet this endeavor has at every step been an uphill fight. Like Christianity before it (Estenssoro Fuchs 2003), Literacy—deserving the uppercase initial peculiar to institutional creeds—advances by discrediting and attacking its own former instantiations. State schooling entered village life as a late intervention into an already well-developed graphic order. The schools have successfully implanted the hegemonic ideology of "standard" literacy as the threshold of progress. They have become central institutions of villages, albeit not quite in the way that ministries of education intend. The more Andean society has drawn the republic of citizens to its bosom, the more it has subjected its own self-reproduction to the attention of linguistic authorities disdainful of its graphic habits and zealous for urban hegemony over letters. For small idiosyncrasies, Andean vernacular writing pays a high price in terms of "cultural capital" value.

Modern ethnography is witness to abiding tension between vernacular writing's two functions and their consequences. On the one hand, writers have striven to make the community present within the state, emulating and even enforcing characteristics of state-sanctioned writing. At every scale, from the fine filigree of word choice and spelling, to intravillage tensions between school and peasantry, to national or international relations with ministries and NGOs, vernacular textual constructions of local self-knowledge and memory contend on an unequal footing with language-standardizing literacy regimes and with state-regulated cultural capital.

On the other hand, vernacular writers have taken up the quill to articulate internal relations of the community. This implies maintaining difference and autonomy vis-à-vis rival polities or overarching ones. The former function, articulation with the state, impels writing toward mimicry of state forms, albeit with discrepancies that result in part from disadvantage within the scribal and (later) bureaucratic orders. The latter, the demand for distinctiveness, fuels idiosyncrasy in lexicon and content.

Today, the main village-level use of writing is to enact and enforce the web of labor reciprocities which underpins the collectively held infrastructure (*comunidad*). It is, as Lévi-Strauss saw, a matter of social control but one of mutual rather than stratified command. The ritual surround peculiar to coca-leaf sharing and collective labor, a symbolic artifice of pre-Hispanic origin, now also encloses the art of communal writing. Indeed, one can speak of ayllu or community action only as the union of three things: rite, work, and script. The resulting ethos promotes exactitude as the guarantee of solidarity: a "romance of the precise." The perfection of a cycle of *constancias*, celebrated at the Huayrona (the new year's civic plenum), manifests the overarching social enterprise as a trustworthy and beloved virtual entity. The word *romance* implies idealism to the point of illusion. And indeed there is no denying that the "precise" audit leaves untouched sources of conflict and insufficiency. To this degree Tupicocha's way with writing does express an aspiration that can never be fully realized. But romance also implies strong feeling, commitment, and delight. These things, too, arise within the spirit of the same customary law whose letter seems so dry and strict. And they give life and color to the ethos of the Tupicochan commons, which, after all, has endured so many trials and challenges with quiet but proud success.

APPENDIX

Examples of Document Genres

Note: Chapter 4 emphasizes the role of genre in the making of authoritative script. The examples below flesh out its argument by demonstrating some common genre templates used in Tupicocha and similar communities.

RELACIONES, LISTAS ('LISTS')

The following example is a full attendance check from a faena of Mujica ayllu. Some comparable lists name participants or absentees but not both.

> Asistencia de los socios de la parcialidad de Mojica al trabajo Fecha 15 de febrero 93 de la serrada de Moya de Huaychuri. 1993. (APM/SAT 04 [1993]:160)
>
> [Attendance of the partners of Mujica parcialidad of the closing of Huaychuri pasture lot 1993.]
>
> C = cumplió / F = faltó ['C=fulfilled / F=was absent']

Zenon Días Romero	C
Hilario Urvano Avila	C
Ceviriano Antiporta C.	C
Avel Urvano Pérez	C
Epifania Aquino R.	C
Edilberto Advincula C.	F
Zenon Antiporta A.	F
Alejandro Advincula C	C
Donato Romero A.	F
Felix Romero M.	F
Ermindo Antiporta	C
Margarito Romero	C
Arturo Miranda R.	C

PLANIFICACIÓN DE FAENAS ('PLANS FOR FUTURE WORK DAYS')

Cecion de la parcialidad de Cacarima allandonos reonidos los de la Parcialidad de Cacarima en casa del Señor precedente de esta Don Cornelio Florencio y siendo a h 1 pm. *se acordo* lo siguente.

1. Andar faenas entre todos nos otros una buelta y esto se andara en los dias viernes de cada semana ciendo la ganancia por cada fayna dos soles, sea el numero de personas que concurran al travajo y tambien la multa de los que no concurren a la fayna pagaran la multa de un sol y esto sera habien del fondo y las multas cobrara el tesorero se acordo tambien por el cumplimiento como es coca una libra sigarro a los que alcanse las tres rrueda ron media botella de escretura
2. Tambien se acordo que esta parcialidad selebrara sicion en cada primer Domingo de cada mes de h 7 a.m. la persona que no llege a la secion pagara la multa de cuarenta centabos y si el Señor precidente no isiera secion pagara la multa de un sol y los mismos que los nombrados y no abiendo otra cosa que acordar se serro la secion a h 3 p.m. y lo firmamos en esta Tupicocha Febrero cuatro de mil nobecientos veinte y tres. (APC/SAT 01 1923b:84)

Meeting of the Parcialidad of Cacarima, we of the Parcialidad de Cacarima, finding ourselves gathered in the house of the honorable president of this [group] Don Cornelio Florencio and it being at 1:00 PM, the following *was agreed.*

1. To walk faenas among all of ourselves one cycle and this will be walked on the Friday days of each week the earning for each faena being two soles, [whatever] be the number of persons who attend at the work and also the fine of those who do not attend at the faena will pay the fine of one sol and this will be in benefit of the [common] fund and the treasurer will charge the fines Also it was agreed that the cumplimiento [ceremonial gift distributed by the faena's beneficiary] as is one pound coca cigarettes enough to make three rounds rum half a bottle as writ [confirmation]
2. Also it was agreed that this parcialidad will hold a meeting on each first Sunday of each month at 7:00 A.M. the person who does not get to the meeting will pay the fine of forty cents and if the Honorable president does not convene a meeting he will pay the fine of one sol and the same as those named and there not being anything else to agree on the meeting was adjourned at 3:00 P.M. and we sign it in this Tupicocha February fourth of nineteen twenty three

Comment: One telling feature of this act is the phrase "rum half a bottle as writ [escretura]." It remained fairly common as of 2007 to give a bottle of liquor called a "writ" as a gesture sealing an agreement. For example, when Tupicocha annually rents pasturage from a neighboring Community, it gives its counterpart an *escritura* bottle. Why should a bottle be called escritura ('writing')? The implication through metaphor is that writing is less like a referential code than like a performative gesture (APC/SAT 01 1934:166).

INVENTARIOS DE ENSERES ('INVENTORIES OF BELONGINGS')

En el pueblo de San Andres de Tupicocha comprension de la Provincia de Huarohiri. Reunidos los hermanos de la parcialidad de Cacarima en casa del Presidente o Camachico cesante don Manuel Perales se procedio hacer *el inventario de los vienes de ésta parcialidad* para entregar al nuevo nombrado Don Cornelio Florencio para el desempeño del presente año.

Primeramente:

Dos frontales amarillos con ocho ajares nueve gusanillo y cuatro borlas, dos manteles usados uno con blonda, una adobera, un combo, una cuchara, un barreno, un retasito mas queda en su poder de Perales obligandose a debolver reformado en una cruz

Se hace presente durante en esta venio que por haberse arrendado y preferido el arriendo a uno de los hijos de esta parcialidad la moya comunal "Chanchana" resulta su producción de preferencia al *aumento de inceres que conciste en los cellos de jebe* De "Presidencia y Tesoreria y para que conste se sienta el presente.

Tupicocha Enero 8 de 1923
Siguen tres firmas y tres sellos
(APC/SAT 01 1923a:82)

* * *

In the town of San Andres de Tupicocha jurisdiction of the Province of Huarochiri. The brothers of the parcialidad of Cacarima gathered in the house of the President or outgoing Camachico don Manuel Perales proceeded to do *the inventory of the parcialidad's* belongings in order to hand them over to the new designate Don Cornelio Florencio for the execution of this present year.

Firstly:

Two yellow altar cloths with eight [pleats?] nine spiral fringes and four tassels, two used mantles one with gold embroidery, a mold for adobes, a pick, a pointed shovel, a crowbar, and one more little scrap which is in Perales' power which he is obliged to return made over in a cross.

Let it be on record that during this biennium because a pasture lot was rented preferentially to one of the sons of this parcialidad the common pasture lot [called] Chanchana its yield by preference [was] *an increase of the belongings which consists of the rubber stamps* Of "Presidency and Treasury" and so that it will be on record the present [act] is instated.

Tupicocha January 8 of 1923
Three signatures and three stamps follow.

ACOMODAS ('WRITS OF RELIGIOUS VOWS')

Conste que yo al final suscribo Pedro Alberco en presencia de mi espoza Antonina de Alberco mi ofrezco con la Santisima Crus dando su lemosna la sumade tres soles S/3 plata para cumplir en su dia del 3 deMayo del año 1936 y para la mayor costacia lo firmo en Tupicocha de 1935 [anotación posterior: *Cumplido dos soles*]. (APC/SAT 01 1935b:176)

⁂

Be it known that I [who] sign at the end Pedro Alberco in the presence of my wife Antonina de Alberco offer myself before the Most Holy Cross giving its alms-gift in the amount of three soles s./3 cash to fulfill on its day the 3 of May of the year 1936 and for the greatest constancia I sign in Tupicocha of 1935 [added later note: Fulfilled two soles].

NOTES

INTRODUCTION

1. Peru's Instituto Nacional de Estadística e Informática maintains a website, www.inei.gob.pe, which furnishes current census information.
2. It is possible that by 1839 knowledge of the aboriginal language was already scarce, because Córdova, trying to explain the probably non-Quechua toponym Huarochirí, fell for a cute but implausible local folk-etymology: When visiting this famously chilly area, the Inka Pachacuti felt a breeze where he didn't want additional ventilation and said, "*huarachirini*, 'I'm putting on a breechclout'" (Córdova y Urrutia 1992 [1839]:61). There is a pun on *huarachiri*—"put on a breechclout"—and *chiri*—"cold."
3. The apparently greater Hispanicization of women is a mirage due to the fact that more men than women were listed in the category of knowing "Castilian" plus another Old World language. Such men were not counted in the "knows Castilian" category.

1. AN ANDEAN COMMUNITY WRITES ITSELF

1. The contents include social science monographs of the 1970s and '80s, compilations of primary sources for Peruvian history, old and new titles on colonial history, Quechua grammars, primary school texts, several uniformly bound series of classic authors in Spanish, encyclopedias, documents of state (e.g., budgets), philosophical classics, technical books on mining and on administration, and best-selling novels translated from various languages.
2. *Fundador* means "Founder," that is, overall chief sponsor.
3. San Damián is reputedly the home of the fiercest bulls. When rebuilding its plaza in 1993, it erected a polychrome statue of a bull as the centerpiece, much to the annoyance of a faction which preferred the less mercenary and more traditional imagery of patriotic heroism.
4. Religious brotherhoods are sponsors of certain rituals, including some of pre-Hispanic origin; they are also civic improvement organizations.

5. An invented "neo-Indianist" tradition, popularized by Bolivian Katarista parties and the Catholic Left of Ecuador and Peru from the 1970s onward. In Peru it is often called the "Tawantinsuyu flag," alluding to the Inka state.
6. The Suni motto "AMA SUA" is quoted from Garcilaso's supported summation of pre-Hispanic moralism.
7. José Carlos Mariátegui, founder of the Peruvian Socialist Party in 1928, was also claimed as an ancestor by the Communist Party (i.e., the Third International affiliate), Shining Path, and most other factions of the Peruvian Left.
8. This observation is based upon a complete inventory of public inscriptions, San Damián village, 1994.
9. Marta Hildebrandt (1969: 40–41) points out that this usage is attested as early as 1753 and has an Andean distribution extending to Bolivia and inland Argentina. Her 1753 instance concerns installment payments on tobacco sold by the royal monopoly, a product required by peasant ritual. Hildebrandt cites a still earlier (sixteenth-century) New World usage of armada as a gambler's advance to another gambler, to be played in the name of the donor.
10. The puzzling word *piónjar*, locally meaning "power drill," is a Hispanicized version of the manufacturer's name.
11. For this reading, thanks to Professor Yongming Zhou.
12. "Chicha music" is a style derived from the highland *waynu* but played on electrical instruments.
13. Hence the common belief that during Holy Week one may loot pre-Hispanic tombs with impunity. The Peruvian film *Madeinusa* envisions a village that extends such permission to much worse sins.
14. Chapulín Ponguino Bueno is another and more Hispanicized name for the Muqui, a sort of pre-Hispanic gremlin or dwarf semihuman, "the naughty child of the Mountains," who teases or enchants herders. His name evokes Chapulín Colorado, the inept antisuperhero of a Mexican comic book popular since the 1950s.
15. *Allauca* is a far-flung term in the west central Andes, referring in Inka and early colonial times to the right bank side of a valley, which also tended to be the upper moiety in villages that have moieties. The uppermost standing of Allauca in Checa's order of precedence may be related to its upper-moiety associations.

2. FROM KHIPU TO NARRATIVE

1. One argument about why Europeans failed to learn it concerns "incommensurability": allegedly Europeans working with the presumption that signs exist *upon* things were baffled by textile meaningfulness, which saturates material in three dimensions (Cummins 1998:192–98).
2. *Wallkis* are decorated coca bags.
3. *Shukank'as* are decorated gourds for lime or vegetable ash to accompany coca.

4. *Ishkupurus* are bone sticks for dipping lime.
5. *Wari* is Quechua for "ancient," "primordial"; *runa* is Quechua for "person, people."
6. "Un caxoncito de papeles . . . y un libro del aillo Anan Cancha" (AAL/L IyH Idolatríás y Hechiceríás Leg. 13 exp. 5 f. 11r).
7. Registry of University of Arizona Radiocarbon Laboratory dates numbers WG451–53 and 523–30.
8. The ayllu *fundo* ('fund') was used as a credit union and was therefore expected to earn interest. This fundo was audited apart from running expenses, which were to be collected and spent within the year.
9. The emergence of concern for more equitable relations between rural men and women is a minor but fascinating leitmotif of 1920s reformism and would reward research.
10. Orison Swett Marden (1848–1924) was a widely translated North American pop philosopher of the Dale Carnegie school, two of whose works appeared in Spanish. The likely source of Allauca's inspiration is a work whose title means 'Opening the Way' (1913).
11. Perhaps out of piety, the 1994 Mujica scribe refrained from specifying the names of the Huaris. Other ayllus do make these divine names a matter of constancia.
12. The ellipsis probably signified that the Mujica secretary could not hear the name pronounced and meant to fill it in but forgot to.
13. The music, as well as much of the ceremonial order, virtually duplicates the pre-Spanish regimen which the "Extirpators" of the seventeenth century imagined they had erased.
14. The abbreviation J.N.R. follows; it may signify the name of the treasurer.
15. The point is that the governor reminded villagers not to damage their health during their consecrated labor. This is a very real danger, because the work that older members do requires extreme effort in the oxygen-poor heights, with only minimal protection from icy nights. If members got ill, he suggests, the damage might reflect on the collectivity's own prudence.
16. That is, the treasurer's son, Cipriano Rojas, stood in for the treasurer, Cilvano Rojas.
17. The second break was for rest, ritual, and recording.
18. That is, at the midday break, the Huaris with their musicians and political companions returned from their ascent to the secret place where the water-owning deities live. They brought along a written reply from the divinities.
19. That is, the civic authorities said farewell to the Huaris so they could carry the skulls of the water-owning deities back to their resting place.
20. Biscacheros, one of the numerous microtoponyms used in marking canal "stretches," alludes to the Viscacha (*Lagidium* spp., or long-eared, long-tailed, luxuriantly furry rodent who inhabits crevices in the high cliffs).

21. The overall program, including its closing festivities, has a strong resemblance to the one which José María Arguedas so memorably recorded in his home district of Puquio, Ayacucho (1956).
22. This nonstandard coinage may be formed by analogy with *lealtad*, 'loyalty.'

3. SCHOOLING FROM AYLLU TO STATE

1. "Hacer un local del colegio en la plaza publico [*sic*]."
2. This fact may call to mind the famous "Ayllu-School" of Warisata, Bolivia (1930–41), which also grew around a social-structure armature of pre-Hispanic origin. But there is an important difference: In Bolivia, segmentary ayllu organization is territorial, and extends up to regional scale. Huarochirí's ayllus are small kinship corporations, generally nonterritorial, federated to form the traditional governance of small communities.
3. "Años más tarde, si el crudo invierno ocasionaba guaycos (torrenteras) y la carretera se obstruía, llegaban caminando 'desde Chilca (antes de Tuna) y caminan 10 horas para llegar a Tupicocha y realizar los turnos de la matrícula.'"
4. *Arte subtilissima, por la qual se enseña a escreuir perfectamente: hecho y experimentado, y agora de nueuo añadido, por Juan de Ycar, vizcayno.*
5. "Sobre las tiradas conocemos, por suerte, el número de cartillas vendidas por la catedral de Valladolid desde 1588 a 1781. El total—54.250.600—es abrumador. Dado que buen número de ellas, quizás la mayor parte, fueron llevadas a América, resulta imposible saber las que se quedaron en la península. No obstante, dos cosas son ciertas. Una es su poca duración ya fuera por pérdida, ya por rotura, desgaste o despedazamiento. Otra, que la cifra media de 281.091 cartillas vendidas anualmente desde 1588 a 1781 esconde diferencias importantes entre períodos de incremento de las ventas en relación con el precedente (1624 a 1659, 1660 a 1696 y 1724 a 1781) y años de estancamiento o retroceso (1600 a 1623 y 1697 a 1723), es decir, las dos primeras décadas del siglo XVII y los años finales de este siglo y primeros del XVIII" (Viñao Frago 1999:65–66).
6. "Redonda escrita algo caprichosamente, con notable desaliño y en extremo ligada."
7. The original title was *Tratado / llamado / Manual / de Escribientes Di / rigido Al Ill[ustrísi]mo y muy / Excelente Señor / don Antonio Alfon / so Pimentel y de He /rrera, Conde de Be [nave] nte / etc. % Ua diuidido / En quatro partes* (Torquemada 1970 [1552]:59).
8. "Literario Epistolar para ejercitarse los niños en la lectura de manuscritos compilado por A.J. Bastinos y L. Puig Sevall . . . colección de textos autógrafos de algunos hombres célebres contemporáneos y de distinguidos literatos, profesores, comerciantes, industriales, etc. . . . Obra declarada de texto en la Península, Cuba y Puerto Rico y en las Repúblicas Argentina Oriental, Perú y Guatemala."

9. "Cuando la escuela no era oficial (con maestros mandados desde Lima), alguien que supiera leer *Mosaico* les enseñaba a los otros a leer y a escribir. Incluso quienes ya sabía les enseñaron a los otros cómo descifrar y reproducir documentos muy antiguos (coloniales)."
10. 'It suffices to mention some of the titles of these excerpts: "God"; "the commandments of God's Law"; "The Peruvian coat of arms"; "Right Conduct"; and various themes about animals.'
11. A well-read man, he may have been drawing on an Iberian counterreformation tradition of devotional books to help the readers take their own measure. The mirror metaphor had a seventeenth-century vogue. Cajahuaringa's title may be homage to a once-famous seventeenth-century title, *Espejo de christal fino* (Mirror of Fine Crystal, 1625) by Pedro Espinoza. This hugely successful primer, as was normal, imparted Catholic tenets along with reading skills. The 1625 *Espejo* was the most highly reputed of primers, "the best and most effective." *Espejo* was printed four times in the seventeenth century, ten in the eighteenth, and four in the nineteenth (Viñao Frago 1999:69). Modern Tupicochans routinely curate books well over a century old. So it is not far-fetched to suppose Sixto Cajahuaringa could have laid eyes on the *Espejo de christal fino* in his youth in Huarochirí in the 1920s, and imagined his *Espejito* as a child-scale homage to the *Espejo*.
12. In 1991 Editorial Escuela Nueva printed 8,740 copies. Sales must have been good, because the annual production was not reduced until 1999, when it fell to 1,200.
13. "Generaciones más jóvenes, uno de los entrevistados (23 años en el momento de la entrevista, 2001), secretario de la Municipalidad de San Andrés de Tupicocha recuerda sus memorias de la escuela un texto más, *Panchito, Panchito* el cual no ha sido localizado:"

    "Bueno: los primeros estudios ha sido este con los libros que nosotros estudiamos que llamamos el *Coquito* y . . . *Espejito* también. . . . Cuando yo me sentía aprender más: era en el segundo grado de primaria. Segundo, tercero, tercero era más por lo que allí había un libro que el profesor nos ubicó . . . un libro de llamado: *Panchito, Panchito*. Ese libro me gustaba leer cuando ya comencé leer y me gustaba un poco más el estudio." (Eliser Ramos Llaullipoma, secretary of the Municipality of San Andrés de Tupicocha, tape 4, lines 47–48, 58–61).

    [Well: The first studies were with the books we studied which we call the *Coquito* . . . *Espejito* also . . . When I felt I was learning more, was in second grade. Second, third; third was more [important] because there was a book which the teacher located for us . . . a book called *Panchito, Panchito*. I liked reading that book when I did begin to read, and I like studying a little more.]
14. Anchilía is a surname typical of nearby Sunicancha. Rosa Tello probably came from among Julio C. Tello's relatives, who were attracted to cultural work.

15. “Los recortes de prensa resaltan el ‘verdadero entusiasmo . . . exteriorizando el pueblo sus agradecimientos al Gobierno y al representante de la Provincia por esta obra de beneficio local.’ ”
16. “El local comunal, donde actualmente funciona las Escuelas de Varones y de Niñas, de segundo grado 457 y 464. Este local no se ha terminado por que nuestras rentas comunales y municipales es deficiente solamente es para otros gastos, que se necesita de menor countia [*sic*].”
17. “Las letras tienen amargas las raíces, si bien son dulces los frutos. Nuestra naturaleza los aborrece, y ningún trabajo siente más que el de sus primeros rudimentos” (cited in Cortés Alonso 1986:6).
18. “En ese tiempo ¡eran tan estrictos en la escuela! Nos castigaban si no sabíamos, a la mujercitas nos pegaban con ortiga, la que llamamos localmente *chinga*. Dolía, mucho dolía! Pero era peor para los niños pues a ellos les hacían el “callejón oscuro,” niños y maestro formaban una fila doble, como un túnel por donde el castigado tenía que pasar y le daban con la correa. Le daban duro. Mucho dolía hasta que todos le pegaban con la correa. ¡Pero se aprendía! [con un dejo de nostalgia]. A nosotros nos pegaban pues ‘la letra con sangre entra’ y aunque fuera por miedo, aprendimos.”
19. “Tranquilo vivíamos sin saber leer ni escribir” (Zavala 2002a:105).
20. “Leer quiero saber y también / Escribir para que nuestro / Pueblo deje ya de sufrir.”
21. “De Acuerdo general en bien del derecho de nuestra comonidad y que emos visto, al suidadano, D. Antonio Avila sosio de esta Parcialidad como *conocidor de los Titulos que ampara nuestro derechos y es capas de defendernos* por lo que le nombramos Delegado ante la Personería.”

4. POWER OF WRITING

1. Philologists have found, from Roman times to the present, examples of popular belief in writings as actual independent agents. In the Roman Empire *defixionum tabellae*, “execration tablets” or “curse tablets,” were considered effective in bringing misfortune to enemies or rivals if they were carved on lead tablets and thrown into wells where they would attract the attention of gods and demons. Writing would be magical or sacred. They needed to be explicit as in the curse “may he flow away like water, Gods of the nether world, if I will have seen her wasting away, . . . ; whatever she may do, may everything turn out badly.” Some such tablets were almost identical among themselves, suggesting magical boilerplate to which only names had to be added. Votive inscriptions found in a temple of Reitia, goddess of healing, suggest that it was a sanctuary-scriptorium (Pulgram 1978:8, 236n221). The Portuguese inquisition sometimes confiscated writings because people construed them in an unorthodox way: the text was popularly understood as a sort of praying machine, which was constantly “saying” the owner’s devotions. People even ate

scripts to cure illnesses (Marquilhas 1997). See Judy Kalman (2009) for a related modern instance in Mexico.

2. Rarely, fingerprints with labels have been used. In all cases, it is close kin who acted as proxies: parents, uncles, siblings, children, or grandchildren, who are all consanguines, as one would expect. Men often signed for unlettered women, but sometimes the reverse happened: "I sign it for my father—Eulalia Laymito" (Lo firmo por mi papá Eulalia Laymito) (APC/SAT 01 1934:165).
3. In the past a bias against female signature reflected doubts about female agency: when one woman became a full member in her own right, she did not sign for her own induction (Niño-Murcia 2004). But today women do sign, and only the very oldest have trouble doing so. Since 1952 at least one ayllu (Chaucacolca) uses terms of both grammatical genders to head membership lists. In 1982 Mujica chose a female secretary, Epifania Aquino Rojas, who later advanced to its presidency.
4. The sign ">" in the next pages is used in its linguistic sense, meaning "changes into" or "is replaced by."

5. POWER OVER WRITING

1. "En el contexto andino la variabilidad de acceso a los códigos lingüísticos afecta la posibilidad comunicativa y la capacidad de ejercer influencia dentro de las redes de poder."
2. The text in Spanish is: "Yo no creo que haiga duendes en las minas"; "Es que tu no vinistes con nosotros al encuentro que tuvimos con los mineros. Ellos dicen que sí existen"; "¡Ni los escuches, porque ésos no saben hablar!"
3. We thank Susana De los Heros for her comments on this chapter and for sharing these materials with us.
4. "El pasado de 'ando' es 'anduve' y no 'andé.'"
5. "Escrivo las letras ami amigo."
6. "Mas digo que el día de oi ninguno puramente escriue nra lẽgua por falta de algunas letras: que pronunciamos y no escreuimos; y otras, por el contrario, que escreuimos y no pronunciamos."
7. "Nebrija, con sus Artes y Diccionarios, fue el autor español más difundido en las Indias. En todas las colonias se siguieron las doctrinas del maestro español."
8. The cited volume, belonging to Ayllu Primera Satafasca, is a 1928 transcription of the collection of boundary inspections that villagers call the *Libro de la Guaranga*, or 'Book of the Thousand.' The term refers to the Inka-era polity, which included Tupicocha and adjoining villages. The transcription embeds older documents of the eighteenth and nineteenth centuries.
9. Italics are used for words given as examples (such as *voltiado*). Square brackets are used for phonetic transcription: [e]. Slashes (parallel diagonal lines) are used for phonemic representation: /*irmanu*/. Angle brackets are used to enclose a grapheme such as <*c*> and thereby differentiate it from a phonetic

symbol [k] or an allophone /k/. The right angle bracket means "becomes" or "goes to": *hermano* > /*irmanu*/. The left angle bracket means "comes from" or "is derived from": irmanu < hermano. The tilde indicates that either of two forms are possible or coexistent in a dialect: *agua* ~ *awa*. And, finally, single quotes identify glosses: 'glosa.'

10. The solutions rural writers improvise address difficulties that metropolitan intellectuals from Nebrija on have recognized (Quilis 1977:25–26). In the seventeenth century Gonzalo Korreas published a linguistically solid reform "para ke la ortografía salga de la esklavitud en ke la tienen los ke estudiaron latín" (1971 [1630]:51–52; in Axel Wijk's 1959 "Regularized Inglish," another project for "rational" spelling; this equates to "foar speling to emerj from the slaeveri in which thoze hoo noe Latin hoeld it."). South American patriot-intellectuals Andrés Bello (1823, 1842) and Domingo Faustino Sarmiento (1843–44) (Niño-Murcia 1997) wanted America to outpace the Royal Academy's reforms. Orthographic reform has been resuscitated by the Academia Cubana de la Lengua (1961), Lidia Contreras (1994, Chile), Jesús Mosterín (1993, Spain), and Gabriel García Márquez (1997, Colombia). All these propose to resolve the multiple-grapheme issues reviewed above, abolish the digraph *<gu>* in favor of a uniform <g> rendering phoneme /g/, and suppress <h> altogether. Some propose <s> as the single sibilant grapheme. Their main disagreement is about a grapheme for /*k*/, which is now rendered *<c>* (before *<a>*, *<o>*, and *<u>*), *<qu>* (before *<e>* and *<i>*), or *<k>* in words of foreign derivation (Mosterín 1993).
11. The history of orthographic *<h>* is tortuous. *H* was not used in medieval written Spanish. At the beginning of the fifteenth century, *<h>* was used to represent the aspirate that had commonly replaced Latin */f/*. But the aspirate itself had already become variable and eventually disappeared, leaving a uniformly mute character.

6. WRITING AND REHEARSAL OF THE PAST

1. Taking the most conservative assumption, namely, that the 1608 Quechua Manuscript is among the earliest fruits of rural literacy in the region.
2. The folk etymology, like most, is hispano-Quechua. *Tambo* means way station. An Inka ruin at the site might indeed be a way station. *Llaquis* is taken in folk etymology as the verb root *llaki-*, 'weep.'
3. The term Huanca refers to the ancient inhabitants of the inter-Andean valley east of Huarochirí, in ancient times adversaries of the Huarochiranos.
4. It is hard to tell for sure, since villagers find non-Spanish names hard to remember. Descriptions match.
5. The once tightly interrelated mythological complex about Paria Caca's female counterpart, the great valley goddess Chaupi Ñamca, has almost been forgot-

ten in Tupicocha, perhaps because Tupicochanos lost their political grip on their enclaves in Chaupi Ñamca's down-valley domains a long time ago.

6. The use of *fe*, 'faith,' to mean a highly specific belief, rather than a religious outlook more broadly, is common in Huarochirí.
7. The title of the 1987 Taylor edition. Since the original is untitled, each edition bears a different name.
8. Tres Lagunas refers to three lakes; that is, in addition to Lakes Huasca and Cullco, the village owns three ponds which together count as a single third lake.
9. These deities are the same male and female lake deities honored in the Concha Community ceremonies discussed in this chapter, but Sunicancha considers them to live in a different lake.
10. That is, the author takes note that he has not found a date in the archives indicating when the idea of damming the lake was first considered.
11. The word *unprosecuted* is an attempt to render a nonstandard usage. *Ynpune*, in the original, generally means "unpunished," but in context it means "unrealized."
12. That is, they built a dam within the outlet sluice so as to regulate flow. The four "windows" are apertures at varying altitudes, which can be successively opened as the lake level falls through the dry season. The design as described not only resembles an extant dam at Yansa Lake but also one described in chap. 31 of the 1608 Quechua Manuscript.
13. This memory is very much alive in oral tradition: "In those days [ca. 1920] there was a landlord who made and unmade everything. A Tello. . . . This person sent a boss with 25 soldiers, the chief on a mule, with rifles" to enforce what he claimed as a property right. In this story Tello's men jailed the protesting peasants in a room adjacent to the one where they were drinking victory toasts, but a peasant picked the lock, stole down a hidden path to Lima, and began a lawsuit which eventually dislodged the Tello claim.
14. The discovery of coca in settings which seem patently too high for it to grow is a commonly mentioned attribute of places which contain the vital force of pre-Hispanic beings. Other examples: in Canlli, near Lahuaytambo, the proof that a spring was created by divinity is that ecologically out-of-place banana trees grow there. Mosquitoes are said to fly on the high puna beaches of Mullucocha, Paria Caca's lake. In 1608, the tellers of the Quechua legends already considered that the vital force of ancient times was such as to make tropical life flourish on what they knew as barren heights.
15. This famous Inka term, meaning a person of high discernment and also a court intellectual, has become an honorific for patriot-scholars.
16. Made in honor of a visit by Víctor Raúl Haya de la Torre, founder of the American Popular Revolutionary Alliance (or APRA party) and an important ideological influence on Peruvian nationalism.

7. VILLAGE AND DIASPORA AS LIBRARY

1. To complement Huarochirí literature, here are a few examples from other parts of Peru: Vladimiro Bermejo, *Puno: Historia y paisaje* (1947); Mercedes Bueno Morales, *Síntesis monográfica de la provincia de Melgar* (1972); Antonio Viza Yucra, *Monografía sintética del distrito de Achaya* (1977); Pedro Antonio Paredes Ochoa, *Ensayo monográfico del distrito de Chupa provincia de Azángaro* (1998); Félix Paniagua Loza, *El Jaq'e Arjatiri Maestro Telésforo Catacora Defensor del Indio* (1991); Roberto Ramos Núñez, *Monografía de la provincia de Lampa* (1967); H. Sanabria et al., *Apurimac* (1989); Andrés Avelino Serruto Loayza, *Monografía del distrito de Pichacani* (1953); Juan Manuel Talavera Cervantes, *Monografía de Azángaro* (1985?); Alberto Urquiaga Vásquez, "Huella histórica de Putina" (1981?).
2. When rain is falling, water is still hard to gather because it takes the form of muddy, dangerous torrents on the slopes.
3. In Peru of the 1990s, unlike in Ecuador and Bolivia, one rarely found parents eager to revive "Inka" names such as Sayri, Inti, Sisa, or Katari, but in the late twentieth century and early twenty-first some Peruvians have started to use them. Some bureaucrats resist the registration of non-"Spanish" names, a sociolinguistic shibboleth for norma culta hardliners. But the onomastic meaning of "Spanish" has for many decades if not centuries been flexible. For example, in the later twentieth century some names derived from Russian (e.g., Lenín, Iván) seem to have become naturalized as Spanish. Hostility to Quechua naming has to do with hostility toward ethnonationalism and regionalism.
4. For example, a man named Gregorio Llaullipoma Capistrano would give his name, in contexts of decreasing formality, as "Lllaullipoma Capistrano, Gregorio"; "Gregorio Llaullipoma"; "Gregorio," or "Goyo."
5. Corresponds to chap. 31 of the 1608 Quechua Manuscript (Salomon and Urioste 1991:137–44).
6. Wayquiula corresponds to chap. 6 of the 1608 Quechua Manuscript (ibid.:76).
7. Corresponds to chaps. 11–12 of the 1608 Quechua Manuscript (ibid.:79–83).
8. "[La Red] nos permite compartir nuestra peruanidad y para elevar el nombre de Huarochirí más allá de las fronteras, llevando adelante los propósitos, esperanzas y aspiraciones que desde este país de Estados Unidos podremos difundir los altos valores culturales y sociales de la tierra natal."
9. "De acuerdo al modo o forma de trabajar, los españoles les dieron un sobrenombre a cada ayllu. A Cajahuaman hoy Suni Perros, a Cushpampa hoy Llambilla gusanos, a Hualashcoto hoy Lupo Llamas y a Chuycoto hoy Huarochirí Puercos."

REFERENCES

Notes: These references are divided into two parts: archival references and other references. Square brackets [ ] indicate titles supplied by the present authors for documents not bearing original titles. Ayllu/parcialidad documents are frequently written in nonstandard Spanish. Original spelling is preserved.

ARCHIVE ABBREVIATIONS (NAME/LOCATION)

AAL/L	Archivivo Arzobispal de Lima/Lima
ACCSAT/SAT	Archivo de la Comunidad Campesina de San Andrés de Tupicocha/San Andrés de Tupicocha
ACCV/SAT	Archivo del Colegio César Vallejo/San Andrés de Tupicocha
AMSAT/SAT	Archivo de la Municipalidad de San Andrés de Tupicocha/Tupicocha
AP1A/SAT	Archivo de la Parcialidad Primera Allauca/San Andrés de Tupicocha
AP1G/SAT	Archivo de la Parcialidad Primer Guangre/San Andrés de Tupicocha
AP2A/SAT	Archivo de la Parcialidad Segunda Allauca/San Andrés de Tupicocha
AP1SF/SAT	Archivo de la Parcialidad Primera Satafasca/San Andrés de Tupicocha
AP2SF/SAT	Archivo de la Parcialidad Segunda Satafasca/San Andrés de Tupicocha
APC/SAT	Archivo de la Parcialidad Cacarima/San Andrés de Tupicocha
APC/Santiago de Tuna	Archivo de la Parcialidad de Cacarima/Santiago de Tuna
APM/SAT	Archivo de la Parcialidad Mujica/San Andrés de Tupicocha

APUCh/SAT — Archivo de la Parcialidad Unión Chaucacolca/San Andrés de Tupicocha

LCSI/SAT — Libro de la Cofradía de Santa Isabel/San Andrés de Tupicocha

ARCHIVAL REFERENCES

AAL/L

Idolatrías y hechicerías Legajo 13 Expediente 5. Criminal contra Juan de Roxas su muger y otros Indios Carampoma. 1723. 73 fos.

ACCSAT/SAT, FOLDER 7

1748 Folder 7 Testemonio de la Huaranga de Checa San Damian.

ACCSAT/SAT, FOLDER 26

1670 [Provisión real de] Don Pedro Fernández de Castro y Andrade Conde de Lemos Castro, Andrade y Billalba . . . birrey . . . [sobre tributos de Huarochirí; 14 julio 1670].

ACCSAT/SAT 01

1904 Libro de actas terminados Desojado del año 1904.

ACCSAT/SAT 05

1893 Razon de las entradas que se ha tenido la sindicatura, 2 abril 1893. Libro de Comunidad de este pueblo de "Tupicocha" Comensado ciendo Sindico personero Don Ancelmo Medina Mayo 16 de 1892 de Entradas. [1892–1917]: 4–5.

1909 [Acta para inspección de linderos, 21 febrero 1909]. Libro de Comunidad de este pueblo de "Tupicocha" Comensado ciendo Sindico personero Don Ancelmo Medina Mayo 16 de 1892 de Entradas. [1892–1917]: 135.

ACCSAT/SAT 06.

Libro de actas Terminado 1858.

ACCV/SAT

1942 Instalación del patronato escolar de la Escuela de Varones número 44032. Libro de Actas Patronato Escolar Escuela No. 4432. Año 1942–59: 5.

1972 Acta Lima de los profesores de ambas escuelas, 28 febrero 1972. Libro de acta de los padres de familia de varones número 457 1969.

1983 Reunión de padres de familia con la finalidad de asignar un nombre al colegio secundario de la localidad, 28 de junio de 1983. Patronato Escolar.

AMSAT / SAT 06

1903–44 Libro de actas de los acuerdo de la agencia de Tupicocha [1903–44].

1907a [Acta de sesión en la Agencia Municipal sobre colegio. 10 mayo 1907.] Libro de actas de los acuerdo de la agencia de Tupicocha [1903–44]: 14.

1907b [Acta de sesión en la Agencia Municipal, sobre colegio. 2 noviembre 1907.] Libro de actas de los acuerdo de la agencia de Tupicocha [1903–44]: 17–18.

1907c [Acta de sesión en la Agencia Municipal sobre maderos para el colegio, 10 noviembre 1907.] Libro de actas de los acuerdo de la agencia de Tupicocha [1903–44]: 22.

1923 [Acta de sesión en la Agencia Municipal sobre contratación del maestro para el colegio, 8 abril 1923.] Libro de actas de los acuerdo de la agencia de Tupicocha [1903–44]: 87.

1927 [Acta de sesión en la Agencia Municipal creación de una biblioteca escolar, 10 de noviembre 1927.] Libro de actas de los acuerdo de la agencia de Tupicocha [1903–44]: 113.

1940 Libro de actas de los acuerdo de la agencia de Tupicocha 1940 [Acta de sesión en la Agencia Municipal sobre terreno para el colegio, 20 noviembre 1940.] Libro de actas de los acuerdo de la agencia de Tupicocha [1903–44]: 190.

1941 [Acta de sesión en la Agencia Municipal sobre nombramiento de personales de la escuela, 2 mayo 1941.] Libro de actas de los acuerdo de la agencia de Tupicocha [1903–44]: 194.

AMSAT / SAT 07

1944 Acta para dar apoyo monetario al colegio, *setiembre [*sic*] 24 1944. Libro de Actas y Acuerdos de la Municipalidad de Tupicocha, 1944–58. f. 25.

1946 [Acta para completar construcción de las aulas de los colegios masculino y femenino.] 23 setiembre [*sic*] 1946. Libro de Actas y Acuerdos de la Municipalidad de Tupicocha 1944–58: f. 70.

AP1A / SAT 01

1948 Acta de Organización de la Nueva Reforma de la Primera Parcialidad de Allauca, 15 julio 1948. Ingresos Anterior Del año 1960 [1948–60]: 1–18.

1948–60 Ingresos Anterior Del Ano [*sic*] 1960 [1948–60].

AP1A / SAT 02

1964–96 [Libro de actas de la construcción del canal de] Wuillkapampa [1964–96].

1991 [Acta de trabajo en la champería en Chupaya, 15 abril 1991.] [Libro de actas de la construcción del canal de] Wuillkapampa [1964–96]: 27–30.

1993 [Acta para nombrar los Huaris, 11 mayo 1993.] [Libro de actas de la construcción del canal de] Wuillkapampa [1964–96]: 40.

AP1G/SAT 01

1939 [Acta sobre un poder otorgado por la Municipalidad 8 febrero 1939.] [Libro sin título, no.1, de actas y otros documentos de la Parcialidad Guangre, posteriormente Primer Guangre, 1913–73]: 76.

1945 [Acta para nombrar nuevas autoridades, 2 enero 1945.] [Libro sin título, no. 1, de actas y otros documentos de la Parcialidad Guangre, posteriormente Primer Guangre, 1913–73]: 119.

AP1SF/SAT 01

1918 [Acta para fijar "porratas" de paja, 13 enero 1918.] [Libro sin título: Actas de Primera Satafasca, 1913–45]: 19.

1928 Este Libro Pertenece al auto de la redonda de la guaranga de Checa: 76, 78.

AP1SF/SAT 02

1919 [Acta para nombrar nuevas autoridades, 2 enero 1919.] [Libro sin título: Actas de Primera Satafasca, 1913–45]: 23.

AP2A/SAT 02

1923–32 [Libro sin título, no. 2, de multas y listas de Segunda Allauca 1923–32].

AP2SF/SAT 01

1921 Constitución Reglamento de la Sociedad de "Satafasca." Libro [no. 1] y Reglamento de la Parcialidad de Satafasca hecho en el año de 1921 [–1946]: fos. 10–13.

1935 [Acta sobre utilización de un terreno para sembrar cebada en pro del ayllu, 11 febrero 1935.]. Libro [no. 1] y Reglamento de la Parcialidad de Satafasca hecho en el año de 1921 [–1946]: 81–82.

AP2SF/SAT 08

1965 [Acta de trabajo en la construcción del nuevo canal de Willcapampa, 20 julio 1965.] Libro de la Parcialidad Segunda Satafasca Wullkapanpa [*sic*] 1965–84: 6–7.

APC/SAT 01

1905a [Estatuto orgánico. 6 mayo 1905.] *Libro No. 1 del año 1905 Perteneciente A la Parcialidad de Cacarima* del año 1905 Al 1989: 1–4.

1905b [Recibo de entrega de enseres del ayllu, 6 mayo 1905.] Libro No 1 del año 1905 Perteneciente A la Parcialidad de Cacarima del año 1905 Al 1989: 5.

1906 [Acta para cobrar multasa ausentes, 4 mayo 1906.] Libro No 1 del año 1905 Perteneciente A la Parcialidad de Cacarima del año 1905 Al 1989: 9.

1910 [Recibo de entrega de enseres del ayllu, 2 enero 1910.] Libro No 1 del año 1905 Perteneciente A la Parcialidad de Cacarima del año 1905 Al 1989: 19–20.

1911 [Recibo de entrega de enseres del ayllu, 4 enero 1911.] Libro No 1 del año 1905 Perteneciente A la Parcialidad de Cacarima del año 1905 Al 1989: 24.

1913 [Acta para nombrar nuevo Camachico, 2 enero 1913.] Libro No 1 del año 1905 Perteneciente A la Parcialidad de Cacarima del año 1905 Al 1989: 31.

1916 [Acta para nombrar nuevo Camachico, 2 enero 1916.] Libro No 1 del año 1905 Perteneciente A la Parcialidad de Cacarima del año 1905 Al 1989: 46.

1921 [Acta para nombrar oficiales, 2 enero 1921.] Libro No 1 del año 1905 Perteneciente A la Parcialidad de Cacarima del año 1905 Al 1989: 68.

1922a [Acta para nombrar nuevos oficiales, 2 enero 1922.] Libro No 1 del año 1905 Perteneciente A la Parcialidad de Cacarima del año 1905 Al 1989: 72–75.

1922b [Recibo de un préstamo, 3 enero 1922.] Libro No 1 del año 1905 Perteneciente A la Parcialidad de Cacarima del año 1905 Al 1989: 75.

1923a [Inventario de enseres, 2 enero 1923.] Libro No 1 del año 1905 Perteneciente A la Parcialidad de Cacarima del año 1905 Al 1989: 82.

1923b [Acta para fijar la agenda del año en curso, 4 febrero 1923.] Libro No 1 del año 1905 Perteneciente A la Parcialidad de Cacarima del año 1905 Al 1989: 84.

1929a [Acta para asentar un voto religioso, 3 mayo 1929.] Libro No 1 del año 1905 Perteneciente A la Parcialidad de Cacarima del año 1905 Al 1989: 131.

1929b [Acta para asentar un voto religioso, 3 mayo 1929.] Libro No 1 del año 1905 Perteneciente A la Parcialidad de Cacarima del año 1905 Al 1989: 132.

1930a [Acta para formar agenda de obras para el año en curso, 12 enero 1930.] Libro No 1 del año 1905 Perteneciente A la Parcialidad de Cacarima del año 1905 Al 1989: 136.

1930b [Acta de trabajo en el cerco de una moya, 20 enero 1930.] Libro No 1 del año 1905 Perteneciente A la Parcialidad de Cacarima del año 1905 Al 1989: 137.

1934 Escritura de Arriendo, 16 abril 1934. Libro No 1 del año 1905 Perteneciente A la Parcialidad de Cacarima del año 1905 Al 1989: 166.

1935a Primera Sesión de 1934 [11 marzo 1934]. Libro No 1 del año 1905 Perteneciente A la Parcialidad de Cacarima del año 1905 Al 1989: 164–65.
1935b [Promesa sobre una limanda, 3 mayo 1935.] Libro No 1 del año 1905 Perteneciente A la Parcialidad de Cacarima del año 1905 Al 1989: 176.
1939 [Acta para nombrar nuevas autoridades, 2 enero 1939.] Libro No 1 del año 1905 Perteneciente A la Parcialidad de Cacarima del año 1905 Al 1989: 199.

APC/SAT 02

1949 Libro No. 2 del año 1940 de Actas y Otras Actuaciones de la Parcialidad de Cacarima 1940 al 1955: 106–12.

APC/SANTIAGO DE TUNA 01

1905 [Libro de Actas de la Parcialidad Cacarima de Santiago de Tuna 1905.]

APM/SAT 01

1875(?)–1918 [Libro sin título de actas de la parcialidad de Mujica 1875(?)–1918.]
1875 [Acta de acomodo, 3 enero 1875.] [Libro sin título de actas de la parcialidad de Mujica 1875(?)–1918.]: 1r.
1890 [Recibo, sin fecha, enero 1890.] [Libro sin título de actas de la parcialidad de Mujica 1875(?)–1918.]: 4r sin número.
1893 Acta de traspaso de tesorería, 3 enero 1893.] [Libro sin título de actas de la parcialidad de Mujica 1875(?)–1918.]: 8v.
1911 Acuerdo de los que deven la faena [sin fecha]. [Libro sin título de actas de la parcialidad de Mujica 1875(?)–1918.]: 53r.
1912 Lista de la errogacion de ganado [sin fecha]. [Libro sin título de actas de la parcialidad de Mujica 1875(?)—1918.]: 55r.

APM/SAT 02

1926 [Acta para asumir gastos de la fiesta patria, 3 enero 1926.] Libro de la parcialidad de mojica Reformado un reglamento en el año 1913 [1913–35]: 126.

APM/SAT 03

1960 [Acta para distribuir trechos para inspección de linderos, 6 enero 1960.] [Libro de Actas de la Parcialidad Mujica 1947–63]: 92–93.

APM/SAT 04

1974a [Acta para instalar nuevo tomo de actas, 22 febrero 1974.] Libro de Actas Perteneciente a la Parcialidad e Mojica Año 1974 [contents to 1997]: unnumbered front page.

1974b Constancia de sesion sobre trabajos del campanario, 10 abril 1974. Libro de Actas Perteneciente a la Parcialidad e Mojica Año 1974 [contents to 1997]: 2–3.

1974c Challachalla el Diposito de esta comonidad, 23 abril 1974. Libro de Actas Perteneciente a la Parcialidad e Mojica Año 1974 [contents to 1997]: 5.

1974d Constancia del trabajo para las torres, 22 mayo 1974. Libro de Actas Perteneciente a la Parcialidad e Mojica Año 1974 [contents to 1997]: 8.

1975a Constancia de Trabajo, 27 enero 1975. Libro de Actas Perteneciente a la Parcialidad e Mojica Año 1974 [contents to 1997]: 15.

1975b Constancia de trabajo de la parcialidad, 18 agosto 1975. Libro de Actas Perteneciente a la Parcialidad e Mojica Año 1974 [contents to 1997]: 28–29.

1975c Constancia de Trabajo, 10 noviembre 1975. Libro de Actas Perteneciente a la Parcialidad e Mojica Año 1974 [contents to 1997]: 35.

1975d Constancia de Trabajo, 10 noviembre 1975. Libro de Actas Perteneciente a la Parcialidad e Mojica Año 1974 [contents to 1997]: 37.

1975e Constancia del trabajo de la parcialidad, 12 noviembre 1975. Libro de Actas Perteneciente a la Parcialidad e Mojica Año 1974 [contents to 1997]: 38.

1975f Constancia del Trabajo de la Parcialidad 17 noviembre 1975. Libro de Actas Perteneciente a la Parcialidad e Mojica Año 1974 [contents to 1997]: 39.

1976 Constancia del trabajo de la cierra moya, 2 febrero 1976. Libro de Actas Perteneciente a la Parcialidad e Mojica Año 1974 [contents to 1997]: 44.

1977a Constancia de trabajo de la parcialidad, 11 abril 1977. Libro de Actas Perteneciente a la Parcialidad e Mojica Año 1974 [contents to 1997]: 49–50.

1977b Constancia del Trabajo, 30 mayo 1977. Libro de Actas Perteneciente a la Parcialidad e Mojica Año 1974. [Acta para asignar trecho de construcción en el centro educativo al ayllu.] [–1978 y sueltos hasta 1997.] En la que se consta las constancias de Trabajo y Acuerdos [contents to 1997]: 51.

1977c [Acta de trabajo, 14 setiembre 1977.] Libro de Actas Perteneciente a la Parcialidad e Mojica Año 1974 [contents to 1997]: 52.

1978 Constancia de Trabajo 1 marzo 1978. Libro de Actas Perteneciente a la Parcialidad e Mojica Año 1974 [contents to 1997]: 55.

1979a Constancia de Trabajo de la Parcialidad . . . Carretera, 25 abril 1979. Libro de Actas Perteneciente a la Parcialidad e Mojica Año 1974 [contents to 1997]: 7.

1979b Constancia de trabajo, 26 febrero 1979. Libro de Actas Perteneciente a la Parcialidad e Mojica Año 1974 [contents to 1997]: 60.

1983 Constancia de Travajo . . . Willcapampa, 8 junio 1983. Libro de Actas Perteneciente a la Parcialidad e Mojica Año 1974 [contents to 1997]: 80.
1986 Constancia de trabajo de Mejora del lugar de la Toma Ausurí, 3 febrero 1986. Libro de Actas Perteneciente a la Parcialidad e Mojica Año 1974 [contents to 1997]: 119.
1993 Asistencia de los socios . . . serrada de Moya de Huaychuri, 15 febrero 1993. Libro de Actas Perteneciente a la Parcialidad e Mojica Año 1974 [contents to 1997]: 160.

APM/SAT 05

1965 [Acta de trabajo en la champería, Pampa Chancha, 20 julio 1965.] Libro [de actas] de la parcialidad de mojica del año 1980 [sic; contiene 1963–70]: 81.

APM/SAT 07

1982 [Acta para asignar trechos en la obra del canal a los socios, 8 setiembre 1982.] [Libro de actas del canal de] Willcapampa [1973–94]: 65.
1994 Acta de Trabajo de champeria de Willcapanpa. [Libro de actas del canal de] Willcapampa [1973–94]: 89–91.

APM/SAT 08

1993 Acta de trabajo de la champería de Chupaya 3r día, 12 marzo 1993. Libro de Actas Perteneciente a La Toma de Willcapama [*sic*] Año 1,988 2-do Libro: 41.

APUCH/SAT 03

1936 [Acta estableciendo cambios en el reglamento del ayllu, 19 enero 1936 Libro de Actas de Instalación de la Parcialidad de Chaucacolca [1936–52]: 1.
1940a [Acta para nombrar un delegado que acompañe al Presidente de la Comunidad en dos litigios, 3 enero 1940.] Libro de Actas de Instalación de la Parcialidad de Chaucacolca [1936–52]: 107–8.
1940b [Acta sobre reparación de daños por terremoto, 24 mayo 1940.] Libro de Actas de Instalación de la Parcialidad de Chaucacolca [1936–52]: 126.
1941 Recuerdo para los futuros hijos de la Parcialidad de "Chaucacollca" de aquellas faenas . . . 23 julio 1941. Libro de Actas de Instalación de la Parcialidad de Chaucacolca [1936–52]: 162–63.
1943 [Acta para repartir trechos en la construcción de la escuela.] 13 diciembre 1943. Libro de Actas de Instalación de la Parcialidad de Chaucacolca, [1936–52]: 199.
1950a [Actas referentes a cobros de multas por faenas.] Libro de Actas de Instalación de la Parcialidad de Chaucacolca [1936–52]: 330–37.

1950b [Inventario de limandas, 3 enero 1950.] Libro de Actas de Instalación de la Parcialidad de Chaucacolca [1936–52]: 368.

1951 [Acta para instalar nuevos oficiales, 3 enero 1951.] Libro de Actas de Instalación de la Parcialidad de Chaucacolca [1936–52]: 388.

LCSI/SAT

1905 Libro de la Cofradía de Santa Isabel: 7.

BOOK AND ARTICLE REFERENCES

Abercrombie, Thomas Alan. 1998. *Pathways of Memory and Power: Ethnography and History among an Andean People.* Madison: University of Wisconsin Press.

Academia Cubana de la Lengua. 1961. "Proyecto de reforma de la Ortografía." In *III Congreso de Academias de la Lengua Española: Actas y labores.* Bogotá: Academia Colombiana, Editorial Iqueima.

Acosta Rodríguez, A. 1979. "El pleito de los indios de San Damián, Huarochirí, contra Francisco de Avila, 1607." *Historiografía y Bibliografía Americanistas* (23): 3–33.

——. 1987. "Francisco de Avila Cusco 1573(?)–Lima 1647." In *Ritos y tradiciones de Huarochirí del siglo XVII,* Gerald Taylor, ed. and trans., 551–616. Historia Andina, no. 12. Lima: Instituto de Estudios Peruanos.

Adelaar, W. F. H. 1994. "La procedencia dialectal del manuscrito de Huarochirí en base a sus características lingüísticas." *Revista Andina* 12(1): 137–54.

——. 1997. "Spatial Reference and Speaker Orientation in Early Colonial Quechua." In *Creating Context in Andean Cultures,* R. Howard-Malverde, ed., 135–48. New York: Oxford University Press.

Ahearn, Laura M. 2001. *Invitations to Love: Literacy, Love letters, and Social Change in Nepal.* Ann Arbor: University of Michigan Press.

Aho, James. 2005. *Confession and Bookkeeping: The Religious, Moral, and Rhetorical Roots of Modern Accounting.* Albany: State University of New York Press.

Aikman, Sheyla. 1999. *Intercultural Education and Literacy: An Ethnographic Study of Indigenous Knowledge and Learning,* Amsterdam: John Benjamins.

——. 2004. "¿Es la educación bilingüe un medio para mantener la lengua? Un estudio en la Amazonía peruana." In *Escritura y sociedad: Nuevas perspectivas teóricas y etnográficas,* Virginia Zavala, Mercedes Niño-Murcia, and Patricia Ames, eds., 411–36. Lima: Red para el Desarrollo de las Ciencias Sociales en el Perú.

Alaperrine-Bouyer, Monique. 2002. "Saber y poder: La cuestión de la educación de las élites indígenas." In *Incas e indios cristianos: Elites indígenas e identidades cristianas en los Andes coloniales,* Jean-Jacques Decoster, ed., 145–67. Travaux de l'Institut Français d'Études Andines, 149/Archivos de Historia Andina, 38. Lima: Institut français d'études andines (IFEA) and Centro Bartolomé de las Casas (CBC).

Amelang, James S. 1999. "Formas de escritura popular: Las autobiografías de artesanos." In *Escribir y leer en el siglo de Cervantes*, Antonio Castillo, ed., 129–42. Barcelona: Gedisa.
Ames, Patricia. 2002. *Para ser iguales, para ser distintos: Educación, escritura y poder en el Perú*. Lima: IEP.
——. 2004. "La literacidad en un caserío mestizo de la Amazonía: Organización local, identidad y estatus." In *Escritura y sociedad: Nuevas perspectivas teóricas y etnográficas*, Virginia Zavala, Mercedes Niño-Murcia, and Patricia Ames, eds., 389–409. Lima: Red para el Desarrollo de las Ciencias Sociales en el Perú.
Anderson, Benedict. 1983. *Imagined Communities*. London: Verso.
Andrien, Kenneth J. 2001. *Andean Worlds: Indigenous History, Culture, and Consciousness under Spanish Rule, 1532–1825*. 1st ed. Albuquerque: University of New Mexico Press.
Animato, C., P. A. Rossi, and C. Miccinelli. 1989. *Quipu: Il nodo parlante dei misteriosi incas*. Genova: Edizioni Culturali Internazionali.
Anonymous. 1991. *The Huarochirí Manuscript: A Testament of Ancient and Colonial Andean Religion*. Austin: University of Texas Press.
Ansión, Juan. 1989. *La escuela en la comunidad campesina*. Lima: Proyecto Escuela, Ecología y Comunidad Campesina.
Ansión, Juan, Daniel del Castillo, Manuel Piqueras, and Isaura Zegarra. 1992. *La escuela en tiempos de guerra: Una mirada a la educación desde la crisis y la violencia*. Lima: Grafimace.
Apaza, T. P. 1948. "Los adventistas y la educación del indio de Puno." Ph.D. diss., university and department not listed.
Arellano, Carmen. 1999. "Quipu y tocapu: Sistemas de comunicación inca." In *Los Incas: Arte y símbolos*, Franklin Pease et al., eds., 214–61. Lima: Banco de Crédito del Perú, Colección Arte y Tesoros del Perú.
Arguedas, José María. 1956. "Puquio: Una cultura en proceso de cambio." *Revista del Museo Nacional* (Lima) 25: 184–232.
——. 1987. *Formación de una cultura nacional indoamericana*. 4th ed. Mexico City: Siglo XXI.
——. 1941. *Yawar Fiesta*. Lima: CIP.
Arguedas, José Maria, trans., and Pierre Duviols, ed. 1966. *Dioses y hombres de Huarochirí*. Lima: Instituto de Estudios Peruanos.
Arias, L. A. 1999. "Propuesta de educación en el altiplano." *Allpanchis* 31(53): 151–61.
Arnold, Denise Y., and Juan de Dios Yapita. 2000. *El rincón de las cabezas: Luchas textuales, educación, y tierras en los Andes*. Colección Academia, 9. La Paz: Universidad Nacional Mayor de San Andrés e ILCA.
Aronoff, Mark. 1992. "Segmentalism in Linguistics: The Alphabetic Basis of Phonological Theory." In *The Linguistics of Literacy*, Pamela Downing, Susan Lima and Michael Noonan, eds., 71–82. Amsterdam: John Benjamins.

Ascher, Marcia, and Robert Ascher. 1997. *Code of the Quipu: A Study of Media, Mathematics, and Culture.* New York: Dover. 1st ed. Ann Arbor: University of Michigan Press, 1981.

Astuhuaman, César. 1998. "La ruta de los dioses y el adoratorio de Pariacaca." *Sequilao: Revista de Historia de Arte y Sociedad* 12: 23–42.

Austin, J. L. 1962. *How to Do Things with Words.* 2nd ed. J. O. Urmson and Marina Sbisà, eds. Cambridge: Harvard University Press.

Avila, Francisco de. 1646. *Tratado de los evangelios, que nuestra madre la iglesia propone en todo el año. . . .* Lima: n.p.

——. 1646–48. *Segundo tomo de los sermones de todo el año, en lengva indica, y Castellana, para la enseñanza de los Indios, y extirpación de sus Idolatrias.* Lima: n.p.

Bakhtin, Mikhail M. 1981. "Discourse in the Novel." In *The Dialogic Imagination: Four Essays by M. M. Bakhtin,* M. Holquist, ed., 259–422. Austin: University of Texas Press.

Barton, David. 1991. "The Social Nature of Writing." In *Writing in the Community,* D. Barton and R. Ivanič, eds., 1–13. London: Sage.

——. 1994. *Literacy: An Introduction to the Ecology of Written Language.* Oxford: Blackwell Limited.

Barton, David, and Mary Hamilton. 1998. *Local Literacies: Reading and Writing in One Community.* London: Routledge.

——. "Literacy practices." 2000. In *Situated Literacies: Reading and Writing in Context,* D. Barton, M. Hamilton and R. Ivanič, eds., 7–15. London: Routledge.

Barton, David, Mary Hamilton, and Roz Ivanič, eds. 2000. *Situated Literacies: Reading and Writing in Context.* London: Routledge.

Barton, David, and Roz Ivanič, eds. 1991. *Writing in the Community.* London: Sage.

Basadre, Jorge. 1931. *Perú: Problemas y posibilidad.* Lima: F and E. Rosay.

Basso, Keith. 1974. "The Ethnography of Writing." In *Explorations in the Ethnography of Speaking.* R. Bauman and J. Sherzer, eds., 425–32. Cambridge: Cambridge University Press.

Bastinos, A. J., and L. Puig Sevall, eds. 1927 [1866]. *El Mosaico literario epistolary.* 54th ed. Barcelona: Imprenta Elzeviriana.

Bauman, Richard, and Charles L. Briggs. 1990. "Poetics and Performance as Critical Perspectives on Language and Social Life." *Annual Review of Anthropology* 19: 59–88.

——. 2000. "Language Philosophy as Language Ideology: John Locke and Johann Gottfried Herder." In *Regimes of Language: Ideologies, Polities, and Identities,* Paul V. Kroskrity, ed., 139–204. Santa Fe: School of American Research Press.

Baynham, Mike. 1995. *Literacy Practices: Investigating Literacy in Social Contexts.* London: Longman.

Bello, Andrés. 1884 [1844]. *Obras completas de Don Andrés Bello. Opúsculos gramaticales*. Volumen V. 381–415. Santiago de Chile: Impreso por Pedro G. Ramírez.

——. 1850 [1847]. *Gramática de la lengua castellana, destinada al uso de los americanos*. Caracas: V. Espinal.

Bender, John, and David E. Welberry. 1991. *Chronotypes: The Construction of Time*. Stanford: Stanford University Press.

Bermejo, Vladimiro. 1947. *Puno: Historia y paisaje*. Puno, Peru: n.p.

Bernstein, Basil. 1971. *Class, Codes and Control*. Vol. 1: *Theoretical Studies towards a Sociology of Language*. London: Routledge.

Bertonio, Ludovico. 1984 [1612]. *Vocabulario de la lengua aymara*. Cochabamba, Bolivia: Centro de Estudios de la Realidad Económica y Social.

Besner, Derek, and Mary Chapnik Smith. 1992. "Basic Processes in Reading: Is the Orthographic Depth Hypothesis Sinking?" In *Orthography, Phonology, Morphology and Meaning*, Ram Frost and Leonard Katz, eds., 45–66. Amsterdam: Elsevier Science Publishers B.V.

Besnier, Niko. 1988. "The Linguistic Relationship of Spoken and Written Nukulaelae Registers." *Language* 64 (1988.): 707–36.

——. 1993. "Literacy and Feelings: The Encoding of Affect in Nukulaelae Letters." In *Cross-Cultural Approaches to Literacy*, B. Street, ed., 62–86. New York: Cambridge University Press.

——. 1995. *Literacy, Emotion, and Authority: Reading and Writing on a Polynesian Atoll*. Cambridge: Cambridge University Press.

Biber, Douglas. 1988. *Variation across Speech and Writing*. Cambridge: Cambridge University Press.

Bledsoe, C., and K. M. Robey. 1993. "Arabic Literacy and Secrecy among the Mende of Sierra Leone." In *Cross-Cultural Approaches to Literacy*, B. Street, ed., 110–34. New York: Cambridge University Press.

Bloch, Maurice. 1989. "The Past and Present in the Present." In *Ritual, History, and Power*, 1–18. London: Athlone Press.

——. 1993. "The Uses of Schooling and Literacy in a Zafimaniry Village." In *Cross-Cultural Approaches to Literacy*, B. Street, ed., 87–109. New York: Cambridge University Press.

Blommaert, Jan. 2004. "Writing as a Problem: African Grassroots Writing, Economies of Literacy, and Globalization." *Language in Society* 33(5): 643–71.

——. 2008. *Grassroots Literacy: Writing, Identity and Voice in Central Africa*. New York: Routledge.

Bloomfield, Leopold. 1958. *Language*. London: George Allen.

Boltz, William G. 1994. *The Origin and Early Development of the Chinese Writing System*. American Oriental Series, vol. 78. New Haven: American Oriental Society.

Boone, Elizabeth Hill. 1994. "Introduction." In *Writing without Words: Alterna-

tive Literacies in Mesoamerica and the Andes, Elizabeth Hill Boone and Walter D. Mignolo, eds., 3–26. Durham: Duke University Press.

Boone, Elizabeth Hill, and Walter D. Mignolo, eds. 1994. *Writing without Words: Alternative Literacies in Mesoamerica and the Andes*. Elizabeth Hill Boone and Walter D. Mignolo, eds. Durham: Duke University Press.

Bortoni-Ricardo, S. M. 1985. *The Urbanization of Rural Dialect Speakers: A Sociolinguistic Study in Brazil*. Cambridge: Cambridge University Press.

Bourdieu, Pierre. 1984. *Distinction: A Social Critique of the Judgement of Taste*. Cambridge: Harvard University Press.

——. 1991. *Language and Symbolic Power*. Cambridge: Harvard University Press.

Boyarin, Jonathan, ed. 1993. *The Ethnography of Reading*. Berkeley: University of California Press.

Brokaw, Galen. 2003. "The Poetics of Khipu Historiography." *Latin American Research Review* 38(3): 112–47.

——. 2010. *A History of the Khipu*. New York: Cambridge University Press.

Buckland, Michael K. 1998. "What Is a 'Document'?" In *Historical Studies in Information Science*, T. B. Hahn and M. Buckland, eds., 215–20. Medford, N.J.: Information Today.

Bueno, Alberto, et al. 1992. "Huarochirí: Ocho mil años de historia." In *Santa Eulalia de Acopaya, Provincia Huarochirí, Huarochirí-Lima*, V. Thatar Alvarez, ed., 115–94. Peru: Municipalidad de Santa Eulalia de Acopaya.

Bueno Morales, Mercedes. 1972. *Síntesis monográfica de la provincia de Melgar*. Puno, Peru: Editorial "Los Andes," 1972.

Buigues, Jean-Marc. 1995. "Bibliotecas de las élites leonesas en el siglo XVIII." *Bulletin Hispanique* 97(1): 397–413.

Burns, Kathryn. 2004. "Making Indigenous Archives: The Quilcay Camayoc of Colonial Cuzco." Paper presented at conference "Archives and Empires," University of Notre Dame, April 3–5.

——. 2007. "Notaries, Truth, and Consequences." *The American Historical Review* 110(2) (22 Mar): 48 pars. Web pages of History Cooperative, www.historycooperative.org, printouts on file with authors.

——. 2010. *Into the Archive. Writing and Power in Colonial Peru*. Durham: Duke University Press.

Cajahuaringa Inga, Sixto. n.d. *Mi tierra y mi escuela: Pasajes y vivencias*. 2nd ed. La Cantuta, Chosica: Editorial Universo.

——. n.d. [ca. 1940–50]. *Espejito: Libro de lectura, segundo grado*. 1st ed. Lima: Editorial Escuela Nueva S.A.

Cajahuaringa Inga, Sixto, and Teresa de Cajahuaringa, n.d. *Espejito: Libro de lectura inicial, primer grado*. 4th ed. Lima: Editorial Escuela Nueva S.A..

Calvet, Louis-Jean. 1998. *Language Wars and Linguistic Politics*. M. Petheram, trans. Oxford: Oxford University Press.

Calvo, Julio. 1995. "El Castellano Andino y la Crónica de Guaman Poma." In *Actas*

del Primer Congreso Historia de la Lengua Española en América y España, M. T. Echenique Elizondo et al., eds., 31–39. Valencia: Universitat de València.
Cameron, Deborah. 1995. *Verbal Hygiene.* London: Routledge.
Camitta, Miriam. 1993. "Vernacular Writing: Varieties of Literacy among Philadelphia High-School Students." In *Cross-Cultural Approaches to Literacy,* B. Street, ed., 228–46. New York: Cambridge University Press.
Caravedo, Rocio. 1990. *Sociolingüística del español de Lima.* Lima: Pontificia Universidad Católica del Perú.
Carbajal Solís, Vidal, Mahia Maurial, and Elizabeth Uscamayta. 2006. "Los khipu q'irus: Construyendo una propuesta de currículo intercultural." Paper presented at the 7th Congreso Latinoamericano de Educación Intercultural Bilingüe, October 1–4, Cochabamba, Bolivia.
Cárdenas Ayaipoma, Mario. 1977. "El colegio de caciques y el sometimiento ideológico de los residuos de la nobleza aborigen." *Revista del Archivo General de la Nación* (Lima) 4–5: 5–24.
Carranza, Isolda E. 1997. *Conversación y deixis de discurso.* Córdoba, Argentina: Universidad Nacional.
Carrión Cachot, Rebeca. 1947. "La obra universitaria de Julio C. Tello." *San Marcos* (Lima) 1(1): 35–43.
Cassany, Daniel. 1999. *Construir la escritura.* Barcelona: Paidós.
——. 2006. *Tras las líneas: Sobre la lectura contemporánea.* Barcelona: Editorial Anagrama.
Castillo Gómez, Antonio. 1999a. "Introducción." In *Escribir y leer en el siglo de Cervantes,* Antonio Castillo Gómez, ed., 19–37. Barcelona: Gedisa.
——, ed. 1999b. *Escribir y leer en el siglo de Cervantes.* Barcelona: Gedisa.
Castillo Morales, Juan. n.d. *Historia del Perú en el proceso americano y mundial. 3r grado de secundaria, edición conforme al programa oficial.* Lima: Editorial el Bruño.
Cerrón-Palomino, Rodolfo. 1992. "Diversidad y unificación léxica en el mundo andino." In *El quechua en debate,* Juan Carlos Godenzzi, ed., 205–35. Cuzco: C.E.R.A. Bartolomé de Las Casas.
——. 2003. *Castellano andino: Aspectos sociolingüísticos, pedagógicos y gramaticales.* Lima: Pontificia Universidad Católica del Perú.
Chafe, Wallace, and Deborah Tannen. 1987. "The Relation Between Written and Spoken Language." *Annual Review of Anthropology* 16: 383–407.
Chakrabarty, Dipesh. 2000. *Provincializing Europe: Postcolonial Thought and Historical Difference.* Princeton: Princeton University Press.
Chartier, Roger. 1999. *Cultura escrita, literatura e historia.* Mexico City: Fondo de Cultura Económica.
Clark, Romy, and Roz Ivanič. 1997. *The Politics of Writing.* London: Routledge.
Classen, Constance. 1991. "Literacy as Anticulture: The Andean Experience of the Written Word." *History of Religions* 30(4): 404–21.

Cohn, Bernard S. 1961. "The Pasts of an Indian Village." *Comparative Studies in Society and History* 3(3) (April): 241–49.
Collins, James, and Richard K. Blot. 2003. *Literacy and Literacies: Texts, Power, and Identity.* Cambridge: Cambridge University Press.
Combès, Isabelle, and Thierry Saignes. 1991. "Alter ego: Naissance de l'identité chiriguano." *Cahiers de l'homme: Ethnologie, géographie, linguistique.* EHESS, Nouvelle série, 30: 143–52. Paris: École des hautes études en sciences sociales.
Condori Chura, L. 1992. *El escribano de los caciques apoderados/Kasikinakan Purirarunakan Qillqiripa.* E. Ticona Alejo, ed. La Paz: THOA.
Condori Mamani, Gregorio, and Asunta Quispe. 1996. *Andean Lives: Gregorio Condori Mamani and Asunta Quispe Huamán.* R R. Valderrama Fernández and C. Escalante Gutiérrez, eds.; P. H. Gelles and G. Martínez Escobar, trans. Austin: University of Texas Press.
Connerton, Paul. 1989. *How Societies Remember.* New York: Cambridge University Press.
Contreras, Carlos. 1996. "Maestros, mistis y campesinos en el Perú rural del siglo XX." Documento de Trabajo No. 80. Lima: Instituto de Estudios Peruanos.
Contreras, Carlos y Marcos Cueto. 2004. *Historia del Perú contemporáneo.* 3rd. ed. Lima: Instituto de Estudios Peruanos.
Contreras, Lidia. 1994. *Ortografía y Grafémica.* Madrid: Visor Libros.
Contreras Tello, Juan. 1994. *Añoranza huarochirana: Trabajo monográfico dedicado a la gran familia huarochirana que quiere y añora a la tierra natal.* Lima: IMPOFOT.
Córdova y Urrutia, José María. 1992 [1839]. "Estadística histórica, geográfica, industrial y comercial de los pueblos que componen las provincias del Departamento de Lima." César Coloma Porcari, ed. Lima: Sociedad "Entre Nous."
Corominas, Joan. 1976. *Breve diccionario etimológico de la lengua castellana.* 3rd ed. Madrid: Gredos.
Coronel-Molina, Serafín M. 2007. "Language Policy and Planning, and Language Ideologies in Peru: The Case of Cuzco's High Academy of the Quechua Language (Qheswa simi hamut' ana kuraq suntur)." Web pages of *Scholarly Commons@penn,* repository.upenn.edu/dissertations/AAI3271734/, visited November 27, 2010, printouts on file with author.
Cortés Alonso, Vicenta. 1986. *La escritura y lo escrito: Paleografía y diplomática de España y América en los siglos XVI y XVII.* Madrid: Ediciones Cultura Hispánica, Instituto de Cooperación Iberoamericana.
Coseriu, Eugenio. 1982. "Sistema, norma, habla." In *Teoría del lenguaje y lingüística general,* 11–113. Madrid: Gredos.
Costales de Oviedo, Ximena. 1983. *Etnohistoria del corregimiento de Chimbo 1557–1820.* Quito: Mundo Andino.
Cotacachi, Mercedes. 1994. *Ñucanchic quichua rimai yachai.* Cuenca (Ecuador):

Licenciatura en Lingüística Andina y Educación Bilingüe, Universidad de Cuenca.

Crowley, Tony. 1989. *Standard English and the Politics of Language*. Urbana: University of Illinois Press.

——. 1991. *Proper English? Readings in Language, History and Cultural Identity*. London: Routledge.

Cueto, Marcos. 1991. "Indigenismo and Rural Medicine in Peru: The Indian Sanitary Brigade and Manuel Núñez Butrón." *Bulletin of the History of Medicine* 65: 22–41.

Cummins, Thomas B. F. 1998. "Signs and Their Transmission: The Question of the Book in the New World." In *Writing without Words: Alternative Literacies in Mesoamerica and the Andes*, Elizabeth Hill Boone and Walter D. Mignolo, eds., 188–219. Durham: Duke University Press.

Dagget, Richard. 2009. "Julio C. Tello: An Account of His Rise to Prominence in Peruvian Archaeology." In *The Life and Writings of Julio C. Tello: America's First Indigenous Archaeologist*, Richard Burger, ed., 7–54. Iowa City: University of Iowa Press.

Das, Veena, and Deborah Poole. 2004. "Introduction." In *Anthropology in the Margins of the State*, Veena Das and Deborah Poole, eds., 3–34. Santa Fe: School of American Research Press.

Dedenbach-Salazar Sáenz, S. 1997. "Point of View and Evidentiality in the Huarochirí Texts (Peru, 17th Century)." In *Creating Context in Andean Cultures*, R. Howard-Malverde, ed., 149–67. New York: Oxford University Press.

Degregori, Carlos Iván. 1986. "Del mito de Inkarri al mito del progreso: Poblaciones andinas, cultura e identidad nacional." *Socialismo y Participación* (36) (Lima).

——. 1991. "Educación y mundo andino." In *Educación Bilingüe Intercultural: Reflexiones y desafíos*, Inés Pozzi-Escott, Madeleine Zúñiga, and Luis Enrique López, eds., 13–26. Lima: FOMCIENCIAS.

——. 1994. "Educación y sociedad en el Perú contemporáneo." In *Crisis Educativa: ¿Modernismo o la escuela que el Perú necesita?* Segundo Forum Educativo 94: 28–30. Lima: SUTEP (Sindicato Unitario de Trabajadores en la Educación del Perú).

——. 2008. "Educación: La soga se rompe por el hilo más débil." *LASA Forum* 39(3): 26–29.

Degregori, Carlos Iván, Cecilia Blondet, and Nicolás Lynch. 1986. *Conquistadores de un nuevo mundo: De invasores a ciudadanos en San Martín de Porres*. Lima: Instituto de Estudios Peruanos.

Degregori, Carlos Iván, and Pablo Sandoval. 2008. "Peru: From Otherness to a Shared Diversity." In *A Companion to Latin American Anthropology*. Deborah Poole, ed., 150-173. New York: Blackwell.

de la Cadena, Marisol. 2000. *Indigenous Mestizos: The Politics of Race and Culture in Cuzco, Peru, 1919–91*. Durham: Duke University Press.
De los Heros, Susana. 1999. "Prestigio abierto y encubierto: Las actitudes hacia las variantes del castellano hablado en el Perú." *Revista de Humanidades de la Universidad Tecnológica de Monterrey* 6: 13–14.
——. 2008. "'Peruvian Teachers' Ideologies about Standard Spanish: Preliminary Results." Paper presented at the International Sociolinguistics Symposium 17, Amsterdam, April 5.
——. 2009. "Linguistic Pluralism or Prescriptivism? A CDA of Language Ideologies in *Talento*, Peru's Official Textbook for the First-Year of High School." *Linguistics and Education* 20(2): 172–199.
Derrida, Jacques. 1972. "Signature, Event, Context." *Glyph* 1: 172–97.
——. 1976. *Of Grammatology*. G. C. Spivak, trans. Baltimore: Johns Hopkins University Press.
——. 1996. *Archive Fever: A Freudian Impression*. Eric Prenowitz, trans. Chicago: University of Chicago Press.
Domenici, D., and V. Domenici. 2003. *I nodi segreti degli incas*. Milan: Sperling and Kupfer.
Downing, Pamela, Susan D. Lima, and Michael Noonan, eds. 1992. *The Linguistics of Literacy*. Amsterdam: John Benjamins.
DRAE. 2001. *Diccionario de la Real Academia Española*. 22nd ed. Vol. 2. Madrid: Espasa Calpe.
Dresner, Manuel. 1997. "La ortografía." *El Espectador*, Bogotá, May 10, p. 4a.
Dubin, F., and N. Kuhlman, eds. 1992. *Cross-Cultural Literacy: Global Perspectives on Reading and Writing*. Englewood Cliffs, N.J.: Prentice-Hall.
Ducrot, Oswald, and Tzvetan Todorov. 1977. *Encyclopedic Dictionary of the Sciences of Language*. Catherine Porter, trans. Baltimore: Johns Hopkins University Press.
Dueñas, Alcira. 2010. *Indians and Mestizos in the "Lettered City."* Boulder: University Press of Colorado.
Dumézil, Georges, and Pierre Duviols. 1974–75. "Sumaq T'ika: La princesse du village sans eau." *Journal de la Société des Américanistes* (Paris) 63 (1974–75): 15–198.
Durston, Alan. 2003. "La escritura del quechua por indígenas en el siglo XVII – nuevas evidencias en el Archivo Arzobispal de Lima (estudio preliminar y edición de textos)." *Revista Andina* 37: 218–228.
——. 2007a. *Pastoral Quechua: The History of Christian Translation in Colonial Peru, 1550–1650*. Notre Dame, Ind.: University of Notre Dame Press.
——. 2007b. "Notes on the Authorship of the Huarochirí Manuscript." *Colonial Latin American Review* 16(2): 227–241.
——. 2008. "Native-Language Literacy in Colonial Peru. The Question of Mun-

dane Quechua Writing Revisited." *Hispanic American Historical Review* 88(1): 41–70.

Duviols, Pierre. 1971. *La lutte contre les religions autochthones dans le Pérou colonial.* Lima: Instituto Francés de Estudios Andinos.

——. 1979. "La dinastía de los incas: ¿Monarquía o diarquía?" *Journal de la Société des Américanistes* 66: 67–83.

——, ed. 1986. *Cultura andina y represión: Procesos y visitas de idolatrías y hechicerías. Cajatambo, siglo XVII.* Archivos de Historia Andina 5. Cuzco: Centro de Estudios Rurales Andinos Bartolomé de Las Casas.

——. 2003. *Procesos y visitas de idolatrías: Cajatambo, siglo XVII.* Lima: Fondo Editorial Pontificia Universidad Católica del Perú and Instituto Francés de Estudios Andinos (IFEA).

Economist, The. 2007. "When Teacher Is a Dunce; Education in Peru," March 31.

Egido, Aurora. 1995. "Los manuales de escribientes desde el siglo de Oro: Apuntes para una teoría de la escritura." *Bulletin Hispanique* 97(1): 67–94.

El Comercio [Peru]. 1945. "Inaugurόse un centro escolar en Matucana." P. 15, col. 7.

Encinas, José Antonio. 1986 [1932]. *Un ensayo de escuela nueva en el Perú.* Lima: Imprenta Minerva.

Escobar, Ana María. 1990. *Los bilingües y el castellano en el Perú.* Lima: Instituto de Estudios Peruanos.

——. 2007. "On the Development of Contact Varieties: The Case of Andean Spanish." In *Spanish in Contact: Policy, Social and Linguistic Inquiries,* K. Potowski and R. Cameron, eds., 235–50. Amsterdam: John Benjamins.

Espinoza Soriano, Waldemar. 1960. "El alcalde mayor indígena en el virreinato del Perú." *Anuario de Estudios Americanos* 17: 183–300.

——. 1971. "Agua y riego en tres ayllus de Huarochirí, Perú, Siglos XV y XVI." PEMN/R (*Revista del Museo Nacional,* Museo Nacional de Historia. Lima) 37: 147–66, map.

——. 1992. "Huarochirí y el estado Inca." In *Huarochirí: Ocho mil años de historia,* V. Thatar Alvarez, ed., 119–94. Huarochirí, Peru: Municipalidad de Santa Eulalia de Acopaya.

Estenssoro Fuchs, Juan Carlos. 2003. *Del paganismo a la santidad: La incorporación de los indios del Perú al catolicismo, 1532–1750.* Gabriela Ramos, trans. Lima: Instituto Francés de Estudios Andinos (IFEA).

Ethnologue Nambikuára, Southern. 2008. Web pages of Ethnologue: Languages of the World, www.ethnologue.com, printouts on files with author.

Faber, Alice. 1992. "Phonemic Segmentation as Epiphenomenon: Evidence from the History of Alphabetic Writing." In *The Linguistics of Literacy,* Pamela Downing, Susan Lima, and Michael Noonan, eds., 111–34. Amsterdam: John Benjamins.

Fasold, Ralph. 1984. *The Sociolinguistics of Society.* Oxford: Basil Blackwell.

Fell, E-M. 1990. "La construcción de la sociedad peruana: Estado y educación en el siglo XIX." In *La escuela rural: Variaciones sobre un tema*, C. Montero, ed., 65–71. Lima: FAO.
Ferguson, C. A. 1959. "Diglossia." *Word* 15: 325–40.
——. 1994. "C.A. Dialect, Register, and Genre: Working Assumptions about Conventionalization." In *Sociolinguistic Perspectives on Register*, D. Biber and E. Finegan, eds., 15–30. New York: Oxford University Press.
Finnegan, Ruth. 1988. *Literacy and Orality: Studies in the Technology of Communication*. Oxford: Basil Blackwell.
Fisher, John H. 1996. *The Emergence of Standard English*. Lexington: The University Press of Kentucky.
Fishman, Andrea. 1988. *Amish Literacy: What and How It Means*. Portsmouth, N.H.: Heinemann.
——. 1991. "Because This Is Who We Are. Writing in the Amish Community." In *Writing in the Community*, D. Barton and R. Ivanič, eds., 14–37. London: Sage.
Fogelson, Raymond. 1974. "On the Varieties of Indian History: Sequoyah and Traveller Bird." *Journal of Ethnic Studies* 2: 105–12.
Fonseca, Juan. 2001. " 'Sin educación no hay sociedad': Las escuelas lancasterianas y la educación primaria en los inicios de la república (1822–1826)." In *La independencia del Perú: De los Borbones a Bolívar*, Scarlett O'Phelan Godoy, ed., 265–317. Lima: Pontificia Universidad Católica del Perú.
Foucault, Michel. 1989. *The Archeology of Knowledge*. London: Routledge.
Frake, Charles. 1983. "Did Literacy Cause the Great Cognitive Divide?" *American Ethnologist* 10(2): 368–71.
Friedman, Jonathan. 1985. "Our Time, Their Time, World Time." *Ethnos* 50 (3–4): 167–83.
Frost, Ram, and Katz, Leonard, eds. 1992. *Orthography, Phonology, Morphology and Meaning*. Amsterdam: North-Holland.
Fundación Flora Tristán. 2002. *Hijas de Kavillaca: Tradición oral de mujeres de Huarochirí*. Lima: CENDOC-MUJER, Centro de la Mujer Peruana.
Galinier, Jacques, and Antoinette Molinié. 2006. *Les néo-Indiens: Une religion du IIIe millénaire*. Paris: Odile Jacob.
Gallegos, Luis. 1902. *La escuela de Utawilaya: Manuel Z. Camacho*. Puno, Peru: Ministerio de Agricultura.
García, María Elena. 2005. *Making Indigenous Citizens: Identities, Education, and Multicultural Development in Peru*. Stanford: Stanford University Press.
García Calderón, J. 1934. "Monografías provinciales: Huancané y Asángaro [*sic*]." *Boletín de la Sociedad Geográfica de Lima* 51(3): 297–99.
García Márquez, Gabriel. 1997. *El nuevo siglo* [Bogotá], April 12, p. 9.
Garcilaso de la Vega, Inca. 1966 [1609]. *The Royal Commentaries of the Incas*. H. Livermore, trans. 2 vols. Austin: University of Texas Press.
Gareis, Inés. 1993. "República de indios—República de españoles. Reinterpreta-

ción actual de conceptos andinos coloniales." *Jahrbuch für Geschichte Lateinamerikas* 30: 259–77.

Gee, James Paul. 1986. "Orality and Literacy: From the Savage Mind to Ways with Words." *Tesol Quarterly* 20: 719–46.

——. 1992. *The Social Mind: Language, Ideology, and Social Practice.* New York: Bergin and Garvey.

——. 1996. *Social Linguistics and Literacies: Ideology in Discourses.* 2nd ed. London: Taylor and Francis.

——. 1999. *An Introduction to Discourse Analysis: Theory and Method.* London: Routledge.

——. 2000. "The New Literacy Studies: From 'Socially Situated' to the Work of the Social." In *Situated Literacies: Reading and Writing in Context,* D. Barton, M. Hamilton, and R. Ivanič, eds., 180–96. London: Routledge.

Gelb, Ignace. 1952. *A Study of Writing.* Chicago: University of Chicago Press.

Gelles, Paul H. 1984. "Agua, faenas, y organización comunal en los Andes: El caso de San Pedro de Casta." M.A. thesis, Facultad de Antropología, Pontificia Universidad Católica del Perú.

Gewertz, Deborah, and Frederic K. Errington. 1991. *Twisted Histories, Altered Contexts: Representing the Chambri in a World System.* New York: Cambridge University Press.

Gimeno Blay, Francisco M. 1999. " 'Misivas, mensajeras, familiares . . .' Instrumentos de comunicación y de gobierno en la España del quinientos." In *Escribir y leer en el siglo de Cervantes,* Antonio Castillo Gómez, ed., 193–209. Barcelona: Gedisa.

Gisbert, Teresa, and José de Mesa. 1966. "Los chipayas." *Anuario de Estudios Americanos* 23: 479–506.

Glave, Luis Miguel. 1991. "Los campesinos leen su historia: Un caso de identidad recreada y creación colectiva de imágenes (Los comuneros canas en Cusco, Perú)." In *Los Andes en la encrucijada: Indios, comunidades, y estado en el siglo XIX,* Heraclio Bonilla, ed., 221–75. Quito: Ediciones Libri Mundi.

Godenzzi, Juan Carlos. 1991. "Discordancias de ayer y hoy: El castellano de escribientes quechuas y aimaras." *Boletín de Lima* 75: 91–95.

——. 1992. *El quechua en debate: Ideología, normalización y enseñanza.* Cuzco: Centro de Estudios Regionales Andinos Bartolomé de Las Casas, 1992.

Golte, Jürgen, and Norma Adams. 1987. *Los caballos de Troya de los invasores: Estrategias campesinas en la conquista de la Gran Lima.* Lima: Instituto de Estudios Peruanos.

González Holguín, Diego. 1952 [1608]. *Vocabulario de la lengua general de todo el Perú llamada lengua quichua o del inca,* Raúl Porras Barrenechea, ed. New edn. Lima: Impr. Santa María.

Goodman, Dena. 1996. *The Republic of Letters: A Cultural History of the French Enlightenment.* Ithaca: Cornell University Press.

Goodman, Nelson. 1976. *Languages of Art: An Approach to a Theory of Symbols.* 2nd ed. Indianapolis: Hackett Publishing.
Goody, Jack. 1986. *The Logic of Writing and the Organization of Society.* Cambridge: Cambridge University Press.
Goody, Jack, and Ian Watt. 1996 [1962]. "Las consecuencias de la cultura escrita." In *Cultura escrita en sociedades tradicionales,* J. Goody, ed., 39–82. Barcelona: Gedisa.
Gow, Peter. 1990. "Could Sangama Read? The Origin of Writing among the Piro of Eastern Peru." *History and Anthropology* 5(1): 87–103.
——. 1991. *Of Mixed Blood: Kinship and History in Peruvian Amazonia.* Oxford: Clarendon Press.
Grace, George. 1981. "Indirect Inheritance and the Aberrant Melanesian Languages." In *Studies in Pacific Languages and Cultures,* 255–68. Auckland: Linguistic Society of New Zealand.
Graham, Laura R. 1995. *Performing Dreams: Discourses of Immortality among the Xavante of Central Brazil.* Austin: University of Texas Press.
——. 2011. "Quoting Mario Juruna: Linguistic Imagery and the Transformation of Indigenous Voice in the Brazilian Print Press." *American Ethnologist* 38(1): 163–82.
Granda, Germán de, ed. 1999. *Español y lenguas indoamericanas en Hispanoamérica.*Valladolid: Universidad de Valladolid.
Gruzinski, Serge. 1993. *The Conquest of Mexico: The Incorporation of Indian Societies into the Western World, 16th–18th Centuries.* Cambridge: Polity Press.
Guaman Poma de Ayala, Felipe. 1980 [1615]. *Nueva corónica y buen gobierno del Perú.* John Murra and Rolena Adorno, eds.; Jorge L. Urioste trans. 3 vols. Mexico City: Siglo XXI.
Gudeman, Stephen, and Alberto Rivera. 1990. *Conversations in Colombia: The Domestic Economy in Life and Text.* New York: Cambridge University Press.
Guerra Martinière, Margarita, and Lourdes Leiva Viacava. 2001. *Historia de la educación peruana en la República (1821–1876).* Lima: Fondo Editorial de la Biblioteca Nacional del Perú.
Gumperz, John J. ed. 1982. *Language and Social Identity.* Cambridge: Cambridge University Press.
Guzmán y Valle, E. 1923. *El libro de la escuela elemental peruana: Primera Enseñanza.* 13th ed. Lima: Ministerio de Instrucción.
Hall, Kira. 2001. "Performativity." In *Key Terms in Language and Culture,* Alessandro Duranti, ed., 180–83. Oxford: Blackwell.
Hamilton, Mary, David Barton, and Roz Ivanič. 2000. *Worlds of Literacy,* London: Routledge.
Hampe Martínez, Teodoro. 1985. "Visita de los indios originarios y forasteros de Paucarcolla en 1728." *Revista Española de Antropología Americana* 15: 209–40.

——. "Los libros del cacique." 1989. *El Comercio* [Lima], March 21 1989, p. A2.
Harris, Roy. 1995. *Signs of Writing.* London: Routledge.
Harris, Z. 1952. "Discourse Analysis." *Language* 28: 1–30.
Harrison, Regina. 2002. "Pérez Bocanegra's Ritual Formulario: Khipu Knots and Confession." In *Narrative Threads: Accounting and Recounting in Andean Khipu,* J. Quilter and G. Urton, eds., 266–90. Austin: University of Texas Press.
Havelock, Eric A. 1996 [1986]. *La musa aprende a escribir: Reflexiones sobre oralidad y escritura desde la antigüedad hasta el presente.* Luis Bredlow Wenda, trans. Barcelona: Paidós.
Hazen, Daniel C. 1974. *The Awakening of Puno: Government Policy and the Indian Problem in Southern Peru.* Ph.D. diss., Yale University.
Heath, Shirley Brice. 1982. " 'What No Bedtime Story Means': Narrative Skills at Home and School." *Language in Society* 11: 49–76.
——. 1983. *Ways with Words: Language, Life, and Work in Communities and Classrooms.* Cambridge: Cambridge University Press.
Heller, Monica. 1999. *Linguistic Minorities and Modernity.* London, New York: Longman.
Herzog, Tamar. 1996. *Mediación, archivos y ejercicio: Los escribanos de Quito, siglo XVII.* Frankfurt am Main: Vittorio Klostermann.
Higgins, James, ed. 2003. *Heterogeneidad y literatura en el Perú.* Lima: Centro de Estudios Literarios Antonio Cornejo Polar.
Hildebrandt, Martha. 1969. *Peruanismos.* Lima: Moncloa Editores.
Hill, Jane, and K. C. Hill. 1986. *Speaking Mexicano: Dynamics of Syncretic Language in Central Mexico.* Tucson: University of Arizona Press.
Hill, Jonathan D., ed. 1988. *Rethinking History and Myth: Indigenous South American Perspectives on the Past.* Urbana: University of Illinois Press.
Hornberger, Nancy. 2000. "Bilingual Education Policy and Practice in the Andes: Ideological Paradox and Intercultural Possibility." *Anthropology and Education Quarterly* 31(2): 173–201.
Hostnig, Rainer, Ciro Palomino Dongo, and Jean-Jacques Decoster, eds. 2007. *Proceso de composición y titulación de tierras en Apurímac-Perú, siglos XVI–XX.* Vol. 1: *Abancay, Antabamba, Aymaraes, Chincheros.* Cuzco: Asociación Kuraka.
Howard, Rosaleen. 2007. *Por los linderos de la lengua: Ideologías lingüísticas en los Andes.* Lima: Instituto Francés de Estudios Andinos (IFEA).
Hrdlička, Aleš. 1914. *Anthropological Work in Peru in 1913, with Notes on the Pathology of the Ancient Peruvians.* (Copy at Museo Nacional de Archaeología has date rubbed out and handwritten "1913.") Smithsonian Miscellaneous Collections, vol. 61, 18, Publication no. 2246. Washington D.C.: Smithsonian Institution.
HRUC *(Huarochirí, Revista de Unidad Cultural).* 1991. Lima.
Huertas Vallejos, Lorenzo. 1992. "Aspectos de la Historia de Huarochirí en los

Siglos XVI y XVII." In *Huarochirí: Ocho mil años de historia*, V. Thatar Alvarez, ed., 241–70. Huarochirí, Peru: Municipalidad de Santa Eulalia de Acopaya.

Hughes, Diane Owen, and Thomas R. Trautmann. 1995. *Time: Histories and Ethnologies*. Ann Arbor: University of Michigan Press.

Hugh-Jones, Stephen. 1989. "Wnribi and the White Men: History and Myth in Northwest Amazonia." In *History and Ethnicity*, Elizabeth Tonkin, Maryon McDonald, and Malcolm Chapman, eds., 53–70. ASA Monographs, No. 27. London: Routledge.

Hyland, Sabine. 2003. *The Jesuit and the Incas: The Extraordinary Life of Padre Blas Valera*, S.J. Ann Arbor: University of Michigan Press.

Hymes, Dell. 1974. *Foundations in Sociolinguistics: An Ethnographic Approach*. Philadelphia: University of Pennsylvania Press.

Iciar, Juan de. 1960 [1550]. *A Facsimile of the 1550 Edition of Arte Subtilissima*. London: Oxford University Press.

INEI (Instituto Nacional de Estadística e Información, Perú). 2004. *Censo Nacional del Perú, 2000*. Web pages of INEI, www.inei.gob.pe, printouts on file with author.

Irolo Calar, Nicolás de. 1996 [1605]. *La política de escrituras*. M. del P. Martínez López-Cano, ed. Mexico City: Universidad Autónoma de México.

Itier, César. 1991. "Lengua general y comunicación escrita: Cinco cartas en quechua de Cotahuasi." *Revista Andina* 9(1): 65–107.

——, ed. 1995. *Del Siglo de Oro al Siglo de las Luces: Lenguaje y sociedad en los Andes del siglo XVII*, Cuzco: Centro de Estudios Regionales Andinos Bartolomé de Las Casas.

——. 2002. "Quechua, Aymara and other Andean Languages: Historical, Linguistic and Socio-linguistic Aspects." Paul Gouldner, trans. Paper presented at Maison de l'Amérique Latine, Paris, January 16, 2002. Web pages of Brunel University, people.brunel.ac.uk, printouts on file with author.

Ivanič, Roz, and Wendy Moss. 1991. "Bringing Community Writing Practices into Education." *Writing in the Community*, ed. D. Barton and R. Ivanič, 193–223. London: Sage.

Jacobsen, Nils. 1993. *Mirages of Transition: The Peruvian Altiplano, 1780–1930*. Berkeley: University of California Press.

Jakobson, Roman. 1960. "Concluding Statement: Linguistics and Poetics." In *Style in Language*, Thomas A. Sebeok, ed., 350–77. Cambridge: MIT Press.

Janzen, J. 1985. "The Consequences of Literacy in African Religion: The Kongo Case." In *Theoretical Explorations in African Religion*, W. van Binsbergen and M. Schoffeleers, eds., 225–52. London: KPI.

Johnstone, Barbara. 2000. *Qualitative Methods in Sociolinguistics*. New York: Oxford University Press.

——. 2002. *Discourse Analysis*. Malden, Mass.: Blackwell.

Jouve Martín, José Ramón. 2005. *Esclavos de la ciudad letrada: Esclavitud, escritura y colonialismo en Lima (1650–1700)*. Lima: Instituto de Estudios Peruanos.
Julien, Catherine J. 1988. "How Inka Decimal Administration Worked." *Ethnohistory* 35(3): 257–79.
Jung, Ingrid, and Luís Enrique López. 1988. *Las lenguas en la educación bilingüe: El caso de Puno*. Lima: GTZ editorial.
Kalbermatter, Pedro. n.d. *20 Años como misionero entre los indios del Perú*. Puno, Peru: n.p.
Kalman, Judy. 1999. *Writing on the Plaza: Mediated Literacy Practice among Scribes and Clients in Mexico City*. Cresskill, N.J.: Hampton Press.
——. 2005. *Discovering Literacy: Access Routes to Written Culture for a Group of Women in Mexico*. Hamburg, Germany: UNESCO.
——. 2009. "San Antonio: ¡Me urge! Preguntas sin respuestas acerca de la especificidad de dominio de los géneros textuales y las prácticas letradas." In *Lectura, escritura y matemáticas como prácticas sociales: Diálogos con América Latina*, J. Kalman and B. Street, eds., 130–55. Mexico D.F.: Siglo XXI Editores.
Kalmar, T. M. 2001. *Illegal Alphabets and Adult Biliteracy: Latino Migrants Crossing the Linguistic Divide*. Mahwah, N.J.: L. Erlbaum Associates.
Kapsoli, Wilfredo. 1980. *El pensamiento de la Asociación Pro Indígena*. Cuzco: Centro Las Casas.
Kessler, J. B. A. 1993. *Historia de la evangelización en el Perú*. Lima: Puma.
King, Linda. 1994. *Roots of Identity: Language and Literacy in Mexico*. Stanford: Stanford University Press.
Klaiber, Jeffrey. 1988. *Religión y revolución en el Perú: 1824–1988*. Lima: Centro de Investigación de la Universidad del Pacífico.
Klaren, Peter. 2000. *Peru: Society and Nationhood in the Andes*. Oxford (UK) and New York: Oxford University Press.
Klee, Carol, and Caravedo, Rocio. 2006. "Andean Spanish and the Spanish of Lima: Linguistic Variation and Change in a Contact Situation." In *Globalization and Language in the Spanish-Speaking world: Macro and Micro Perspectives*, C. Mar-Molinero and M. Stewart, eds., 94–113. Hampshire: Palgrave Macmillan.
Korreas, Gonzalo. 1971 [1630]. *Ortografía Kastellana nueva i perfeta, Salamanca, 1630*. Facsimile. Madrid: Espasa-Calpe.
Kowalewski, Stephen A. and J. J. Saindon. 1992. "The Spread of Literacy in a Latin American Peasant Society: Oaxaca, Mexico, 1890–1980." *Comparative Studies in Society and History* 34(1): 110–40.
Krech, Shepard. 2006. "Bringing Linear Time Back." *Ethnohistory* 53(3): 567–93.
Kristal, Efraín. 1987. *The Andes Viewed from the City*. New York: Peter Lang.
Kugelmass, Jack. 1988. *From a Ruined Garden: The Memorial Books of Polish*

Jewry. Jack and Jonathan Boyarin, eds.; Zachary M. Baker, author of geographical index and bibliography. 2nd ed. Bloomington: Indiana University Press.

Labov, William. 1972. *Sociolinguistic Patterns*. Philadelphia: University of Pennsylvania Press.

Lafont, Robert, et al. 1984. *Anthropologie de l'écriture*. Paris: Centre Georges Pompidou Centre de Création Industrielle.

Landaburu, Jon. 1998. "Oralidad y escritura en las sociedades indígenas." In *Sobre las huellas de la voz*, L. E. López and I. Jung, eds., 94–113. Cochabamba, Bolivia: S.L., PROEIB, Ediciones Morata.

La República. 2008. "Con bailes y tradición: También se realizó una misa en quechua en la Catedral de Lima." (Lima, Peru), January 14.

Larson, Brooke. 2003. "Capturing Indian Bodies, Hearths, and Minds: The Gendered Politics of Rural School Reform in Bolivia, 1910–1952." In *Proclaiming Revolution: Bolivia in Comparative Perspective*, M. Gindle and P. Domingo, eds., 183–209. Cambridge: David Rockefeller Center for Latin American Studies, Harvard University: Distributed by Harvard University Press.

———. 2004. *Trials of Nation Making: Liberalism, Race, and Ethnicity in the Andes, 1810–1910*. Cambridge: Cambridge University Press.

Laurencich Minelli, Laura. 1996. *La scrittura dell'antico Perù: Un mondo da scoprire*. Bologna: CLUEB.

———. 2005. *Exsul inmeritus Blas Valera populo suo e historia et rudimenta linguae peruanorum: Indios, gesuiti e spagnoi in due documenti segreti sul Perù del XVII secolo*. Bologna: Cooperativa Libraria Universitaria Editrice Bologna.

Lavigne-Delville, Philippe. 2002. "When Farmers Use 'Pieces of Paper' to Record Their Land Transactions in Francophone Rural Africa: Insights into the Dynamics of Institutional Innovation." *The European Journal of Development Research* 14(2): 89–108.

La Voz de San Damián. 1957. Lima: n.p.

Levaggi, Abelardo. 2001. *Revista de estudios histórico-jurídicos* (Valparaíso) 23: 419–28. Web pages of Scientific Electronic Library Online, www.scielo.cl, printouts on file with author.

Levillier, Richard, ed. 1925. *Gobernantes del Perú, cartas y papeles, siglo XVI*. Madrid: Imprenta de Juan Pueyo, 8: 337–38.

Lévi-Strauss, Claude. 1992 [1955]. *Tristes Tropiques*. John and Doreen Weightman, trans. New York: Penguin.

Lienhard, Martin, ed. 1992. *Testimonios, cartas, y manifiestos indígenas (desde la conquista hasta comienzos del siglo XX)*. Caracas: Biblioteca Ayacucho.

———. 1997. "Writing from Within: Indigenous Epistolary Practices in the Colonial Period. Literates." In *Creating Context in Andean Cultures*, R. Howard-Malverde, ed., 171–84. New York: Oxford University Press.

Lira, Jorge. 1982 [1941]. *Diccionario kkechuwa-español*. 2nd ed. Cuadernos Cul-

turales Andinos, No. 5. Bogotá: Secretaría General del Convenio "Andrés Bello."
Lobo, Susan. 1982. *A House of My Own: Social Organization in the Squatter Settlements of Lima, Peru*. Tucson: University of Arizona Press.
Locke, Leland L. 1923. *The Ancient Quipu, Or Peruvian Knot Record*. New York: American Museum of Natural History.
——. 1928. *Supplementary Notes on the Quipus in the American Museum of Natural History*. Anthropological Papers of the American Museum of Natural History 30: 30–73. New York: American Museum of Natural History.
Lockhart, James. 1982. "Views of Corporate Self and History in Some Valley of Mexico Towns: Late Seventeenth and Eighteenth Centuries." In *The Inca and Aztec States, 1400–1800: Anthropology and History*, G. Collier, R. Rosaldo, and J. Wirth, eds., 367–93. New York: Academic Press.
López, Luís Enrique. 1989. "Educación bilingüe en Puno: Lo hecho y lo por hacer." *Amazonía Peruana* 9: 127–44.
López Beltrán, Clara. 2005. "Lo que se escribe y lo que se entiende: El lenguaje escrito en la sociedad colonial de Charcas (hoy Bolivia)." In *Usos del documento y cambios sociales en la historia de Bolivia*, Clara López Beltrán and Akira Saito, eds., 9–26. Osaka: Senri Ethnological Studies, No. 68.
López Beltrán, Clara, and Akira Saito. 2005. *Usos del documento y cambios sociales en la historia de Bolivia*. Senri Ethnological Studies, No. 68. Osaka, Japan: National Museum of Ethnology.
Loza, Carmen Beatriz. 1998. "Du bon usage des *quipus* à l'administration coloniale espagnole (1500–1600)." *Population* 1–2: 139–60.
Lund, Sarah. 1997. "On the Margin: Letter Exchange among Andean Non-Literates. " In *Creating Context in Andean Cultures*, R. Howard-Malverde, ed., 185–95. New York: Oxford University Press.
——. 2001. "Bequeathing and Quest: Processing Personal Identification Papers in Bureaucratic Spaces (Cuzco, Peru)." *Social Anthropology* 9(1): 3–24.
Macera, Pablo. 1990. "La educación elemental y la enseñanza de los indios." In *La escuela rural: Variaciones sobre un tema*, C. Montero, ed., 45–49. Lima: FAO.
MacGaffey, Wyatt. 1986. "Ethnography and the Closing of the Frontier in Lower Congo." *Africa* 56(3): 263–79.
Mackey, Carol. 1970. *Knot Records in Ancient and Modern Peru*. Ph.D. Department of Anthropology, University of California, Berkeley.
——. 1990. Hugo Pereyra et al., eds. *Quipu y yupana: Colección de escritos*. Lima: Consejo Nacional de Ciencia y Tecnología.
Mac-Lean y Estenós, R. 1944. *Sociología educacional del Perú*. Lima: Editorial Gil.
Mallon, Florencia E. 2005. *Courage Tastes of Blood: The Mapuche Community of Nicolás Ailío and the Chilean State, 1906–2001*. Durham: Duke University Press.
Mannheim, Bruce. 1984. " 'Una Nación Acorralada': Southern Peruvian Quechua

Language Planning and Politics in Historical Perspective." *Language and Society* 13: 291–309.
———. 1991. *The Language of the Inca since the European Invasion*. Austin: University of Texas Press.
———. 1992. "The Inka Language in the Colonial World." *Colonial Latin American Review* 1 (1–2): 77–108.
Mannheim, Bruce, and Dennis Tedlock. 1995. "Introduction." In *The Dialogic Emergence of Culture*, D. Tedlock and B. Mannheim, eds., 1–32. Urbana: University of Illinois Press.
Marden, Orion [*sic*] Sweat [*sic*]. 1913. *Abrirse paso; principios generales sobre educación colectiva, escritos en inglés por y adaptados a la evolución educativa del pueblo mexicano por Rafael Téllez Girón*. México DF: Imprenta de la Secretaría de Fomento.
Mariátegui, Aldo. 2009. "¡Qué nivel! Urge coquito para congresista Supa." *Correo*, Lima, April 23, 2007 (headline on front page, article, pp. 12–13).
Marquilhas, Rita. 1997. "Orientación mágica del texto escrito." In *Escribir y leer en el siglo de Cervantes*, Antonio Castillo Gómez, ed., 111–28. Barcelona: Gedisa.
Martí, Miguel. 2007. "Kuniraya Pariakaka y Kawillaka." Video footage on YouTube, www.youtube.com.
Martínez Chuquizana, T. Alejandro. 1996. *Historia y geografía del Distrito de San Andrés de Tupicocha*. 3rd ed. Mimeo. Ricardo Palma, Huarochirí: Ediciones Villa la Paz.
Martínez Compañón y Bujanda, Baltasar Jaime. 1985 [c. 1779–89]. *Trujillo del Perú*. Vol. 2. Madrid: Instituto de Cooperación Iberoamericana.
Mateos, Fernando. 1944. *Historia general de la Compañía de Jesús en Perú*. Madrid: Consejo Superior de Investigaciones Científicas.
Matienzo, Juan de. 1967 [1567]. *Gobierno del Perú*. G. Lohmann Villena, ed. Paris and Lima: Travaux de L'Institut Français d'Études Andines.
Matos Mar, José, et al. 1958. *Las actuales comunidades indígenas: Huarochirí en 1955*. Lima: Departamento de Antropología, Facultad de Letras, Universidad Nacional Mayor de San Marcos.
Matute, Esmeralda. 1998. "Transparencia de los sistemas ortográficos y la idea de estrategias diferenciales de procesamiento de la lengua escrita." Paper presented at the conference V Encuentro Internacional de Lingüística en el Noroeste, Sonora, Mexico.
Maxwell, K. 1983. *Bemba Myth and Ritual: The Impact of Literacy on an Oral Culture*. New York: Peter Lang.
Mayer, Enrique. Repensando. 1980. "Más allá de la familia nuclear." In *Parentesco y matrimonio en los Andes*, Enrique Mayer and Ralph Bolton, eds., 427–62. Lima: Pontificia Universidad Católica del Perú.

——. 2002 [1980]. "The Rules of the Game in Andean Reciprocity." In *The Articulated Peasant*, 105–42. Boulder: Westview.

Mckay, Sandra. 1996. "Literacy and Literacies." In *Sociolinguistics and Language Teaching*. Sandra McKay and Nancy Hornberger, eds., 421–45. Cambridge: Cambridge University Press.

Medelius, Mónica, and José Carlos de la Puente. 2004. "Curacas, bienes y quipus en un documento toledano (Jauja, 1570)." *Historica* (Lima) 28(2): 35–82.

Meisch, Lynn A. 1998. "Qumpi and Khipucamayuks: New Perspectives on Textiles on Colonial Ecuador." Paper presented at the 38th Meeting of the Institute of Andean Studies, Berkeley, California, January 10.

——. 2002. *Andean Entrepreneurs: Otavalo Merchants and Musicians in the Global Arena*. Austin: University of Texas Press.

Mejía Xesspe, Toribio. 1947. *Historia de la Antigua Provincia de Anan Yauyo*. Lima: n.p.

Meli, Bartomeu. 1998. "Palabra vista, dicho que no se oye." In *Sobre las huellas de la voz*, L. E. López and I. Jung, eds., 23–38. Cochabamba, Bolivia: S.L., PROEIB Ediciones Morata.

Messick, Brinkley. 1993. *The Calligraphic State: Textual Domination and History in a Muslim Society*. Berkeley: University of California Press.

Metcalf, Eric. 1997. "(Review of) Angel Rama: *The Lettered City*, John Charles Chasteen, ed. and trans. Durham: Duke University Press, 1996." Web pages of Zona Latina, www.zonalatina.com, printouts on file with author.

Mignolo, Walter. 1995. *The Darker Side of the Renaissance: Literacy, Territoriality, and Colonization*. Ann Arbor: University of Michigan Press.

Mills, Kenneth. 1997. *Idolatry and Its Enemies: Colonial Andean Religion and Extirpation, 1640–1750*. Princeton: Princeton University Press.

Milroy, James. 2001. "Language Ideologies and the Consequences of Standardization." *Journal of Sociolinguistics* 5(4): 530–55.

Montero, Carmen. 1990. *La escuela rural: Variaciones sobre un tema*. Lima: Proyecto Escuela, Ecología y Comunidad Campesina.

Mosterín, Jesús. 1993. *Teoría de la escritura*. Barcelona: Icaria Editorial.

Munn, Nancy D. 1992. "The Cultural Anthropology of Time: A Critical Essay." *Annual Review of Anthropology* 21: 93–123.

Murra, John V. 1975. "Las Etno-Categorías de un *Khipu* Estatal." In *Formaciones económicas y políticas en el mundo andino*, 243–54. Lima: Instituto de Estudios Peruanos.

Nebrija, Antonio de. 1977 [1517]. *Reglas de orthographía en la lengua castellana*. A. Quilis, ed. Bogotá: Instituto Caro y Cuervo.

——. 1980 [1492]. *Gramática de la lengua castellana*. A. Quilis, ed. Madrid: Editora Nacional.

Niederehe, E. F. K. 2001. "Introduction." In *History of Linguistics in Spain II*, E. F. K. Koerner and H-J. Niederehe, eds. ix–xxii. Amsterdam: John Benjamins.

Niño-Murcia, Mercedes. 1997. "Ideología lingüística hispanoamericana en el siglo XIX: Chile (1840–1880)." *Hispanic Linguistics* 9 (1): 100–142.
——. 2004. " 'Papelito manda' literacidad vernacular en una comunidad andina de Huarochirí." In *Escritura y sociedad: Nuevas perspectivas teóricas y etnográficas*, Virginia Zavala, Mercedes Niño-Murcia, and Patricia Ames, eds., 347–65. Lima: Red para el Desarrollo de las Ciencias Sociales en Perú.
——. 2009. "The Roots and the Growth of Women's Writing in a Peruvian Village." In *Interdisciplinary Approaches to Literacy and Development*, Kaushik Basu, Bryan Maddox, and Anna Robinson-Pant, eds., 145–64. London: Routledge.
Niño-Murcia, Mercedes, Juan Carlos Godenzzi, and Jason Rothman. 2008. "Spanish as a World Language: The Interplay of Globalized Localization and Localized Globalization." *International Multilingual Research Journal* 2(1): 1–19.
Nissen, Hans J., Peter Damerow, and Robert K. England. 1993 [1990]. *Archaic Bookkeeping: Early Writing and Techniques of Economic Administration in the Ancient Near East*, Paul Larsen, trans. Chicago: University of Chicago Press.
No, Song. 1999. "La oralidad y la violencia de la escritura en los 'Comentarios Reales' del Inca Garcilaso." *Revista de Crítica Literaria Latinoamericana* 25(49): 27–39.
Ochs, Elinor. 1979. "Planned and Unplanned Discourse." In *Syntax and Semantics*, T. Givon, ed., 12:51–80. New York: Academic Press.
Oesterreicher, Wulf. 1994. "El español en textos escritos por semicultos: Competencia escrita de impronta oral en la historiografía indiana." In *El español de América en el siglo XVI*, Jens Lüdtke, ed., 155–90. Madrid: Iberoamericana.
Olachea Labayen, Juan B. 1958. "Opinión de los teólogos españoles sobre dar estudios mayores a los Indios." *Anuario de Estudios Americanos* 15: 113–200.
Oliart, Patricia. 1999. "Leer y escribir en un mundo sin letras." In *Cultura y Globalización*, C. I. Degregori and G. Portocarrero, eds., 203–23. Lima: Red para el Desarrollo de las Ciencias Sociales en el Perú.
Olson, David R. 1994. *The World on Paper: The Conceptual and Cognitive Implications of Writing and Reading*. Cambridge: Cambridge University Press.
Olson, David, and Nancy Torrance. 1991. "Introduction." In *Literacy and Orality*, D. Olson and N. Torrance, eds., 1–7. Cambridge: Cambridge University Press.
Ong, Walter. 1982. *Orality and Literacy: The Technologizing of the Word*. London: Methuen.
Oré, Luis Jerónimo de. 1992 [1598]. *Symbolo cathólico indiano, en el qual se declaran los mysterios dela fe*. Lima: Australis.
Orlove, Benjamin. 2002. *Lines in the Water: Nature and Culture at Lake Titicaca*, Berkeley: University of California Press.
Ortiz Rescaniere, Alejandro. 1973. *De Adaneva a Inkarrí: Una visión indígena del Perú*. Lima: Retablo de Papel.

——. 1980. *Huarochirí, 400 años después*. Lima: Pontificia Universidad Católica del Perú, Fondo Editorial.

Pando Pacheco, Edgardo, and Edgardo Pando Merino. 2004. *Talento: Lenguaje-comunicación. Educación secundaria*. Lima: Distribución Gráfica S.A.

Paniagua Loza, Félix. 1991. *El Jaq'e Arjatiri Maestro Telésforo Catacora Defensor del Indio*. Juli, Peru: Ministerio de Educación, Región "José Carlos Mariátegui."

Paredes, A. M. 1970. "Apuntes monográficos de la provincia de Azángaro, Heróico Pueblo de Vilca Apaza." In *Album de oro: Monografía del Departamento de Puno*. Vol. 1, S. Frisancho Pineda, ed., 61–74. Puno, Peru: n.p.

Paredes Ochoa, Pedro Antonio. 1998. *Ensayo monográfico del distrito de Chupa provincia de Azángaro*. Puno, Peru: Editorial Samuel Frisancho Pineda.

Pärssinen, Martti. 1992. *Tawantinsuyu: The Inca State and Its Political Organization*. Helsinki: Societas Historica Finlandiae.

Pärssinen, Martti, and Jukka Kiviharju, eds. 2004. *Textos andinos*. Vol. 1: *Corpus de textos khipu incaicos y coloniales*. Serie Hispano-Americano, 6. Madrid: Instituto Iberoamericano de Finlandia.

Pavez, Jorge. 2008. *Cartas mapuche: Siglo XIX*. Santiago, Chile: CoLibris.

Pease, Franklin. 1990. "Utilización de Quipus en los Primeros Tiempos Coloniales." In *Quipu y yupana: Colección de escritos*, C. Mackey et al., eds., 67–72. Lima: Consejo Nacional de Ciencia y Tecnología.

Penny, Ralph. 1991. *A History of the Spanish Language*. Cambridge: Cambridge University Press.

——. 1993. *Gramática histórica del español*. Barcelona: Editorial Ariel.

Percival, W. K. 2001. "Nebrija's Syntactic Theory in Its Historical Setting." In *History of Linguistics in Spain II*, E. F. K. Koerner and H-J. Niederehe, eds., 3–1. Amsterdam: John Benjamins.

Pérez Bocanegra, Juan. 1631. *Ritual Formulario, e Institucion De Curas, Para Administrar a Los Naturales De Este Reyno, Los Sanctos Sacramentos Del Baptismo, Confirmacion, Eucaristia, y Viatico, Penitencia, Extremauncion, y Matrimonio: Con Aduertencias Muy Necessarias*. Impresso en Lima: Por Geronymo de Contreras.

Pérez Silva, Jorge Iván. 2004. *Los castellanos del Perú*. Lima: PROEDUCA.

——. 2007. "La investigación científica del castellano andino: Contra la discriminación lingüística." *Summa Humanitatis*. Revista Electrónica Interdisciplinaria del Departamento de Humanidades, Pontificia Universidad Católica del Perú 1: 1–32. http://revistas.pucp.edu.pe/ojs/index.php/summa, viewed November 28, 2010.

Perrin, Michel. 1986. "'Savage' Points of View on Writing." In *Myth and the Imaginary in the New World*, E. Magaña and P. Mason, eds., 211–32. Dordrecht, Holland: FORIS Publications.

Peru. 1878. *Censo General de la República del Perú formado en 1876*. Vol. 6: Departments of Lima, Loreto, y Moquegua, Lima: Imprenta del Teatro.

Peru, Dirección Nacional de Estadística y Censos (DNEC). 1994. *Censo Nacional, 11 julio 1993. Resultados Definitivos. Departamento de Lima.* Vol. 1, no. 2: *Aspectos generales*. Lima: Dirección Nacional de Estadística y Censos.

Peru, Ministerio de Hacienda y Comercio, Dirección Nacional de Estadística. 1941. *Censo nacional de población de 1940*. Vol. 8: Departments of Cuzco and Puno. Lima: Ministerio de Hacienda y Comercio.

Peru, República del Perú, Ministerio de Hacienda y Comercio, Dirección Nacional de Estadística. 1944. *Censo Nacional de Población de 1940*. Lima: Dirección Nacional de Estadística.

Piedra, Maria Teresa de la. 2004. "Oralidad y escritura: El rol de los intermediarios de literacidad en una comunidad quechua-hablante de los Andes peruanos." In *Escritura y sociedad: Nuevas perspectivas teóricas y etnográficas*, Virginia Zavala, M. Niño-Murcia, and Patricia Ames, eds., 367–88. Lima: Red para el Desarrollo de las Ciencias Sociales en el Perú.

Pimentel H., Nelson D. 2005. *Amarrando colores: La producción del sentido en khipus aymaras*. La Paz: CEPA, Latinas Editores.

Pinaud, Alberto B. 1957. "Trozos históricos de San Damián." In *La voz de San Damián*, 153–56. Lima[?]: n.p.

Platt, Tristan. 1987. "The Andean Solders of Christ: Confraternity Organization, the Mass of the Sun and Regenerative Warfare in Rural Potosi (18th–20th Centuries)." *Journal de la Société des Américanistes* 73: 139–91.

——. 1992. "Writing, Shamanism, and Identity, or, Voices from Abya-Yala." *History Workshop* 34: 132–47.

——. 2002. " 'Without Deceit or Lies': Variable *Chinu* Readings during a Sixteenth-Century Tribute-Restitution Trial." In *Narrative Threads: Accounting and Recounting in Andean Khipu*, J. Quilter and G. Urton, eds., 225–65. Austin: University of Texas Press.

Polia Meconi, Mario, ed. 1999. *La cosmovisión religiosa andina en los documentos inéditos del Archivo Romano de la Compañía de Jesús, 1581–1752*. Lima: Pontificia Universidad Católica del Perú.

Polo, José. 1974. *Ortografía y ciencia del lenguaje*. Madrid: Paraninfo.

Ponce Sánchez, Hernán. 1957. *50 anécdotas del Sabio Tello*. Lima: Editorial La Universidad.

Poole, Deborah. 2004. "Between Threat and Guarantee." In *Anthropology in the Margins of the State*, Veena Das and Deborah Poole, eds., 35–65. Santa Fe: School of American Research.

Poole, Deborah, and Gerardo Rénique. 1992. *Peru: Time of fear*. London: Latin American Bureau.

Portocarrero, Gonzalo, and Patricia Oliart. 1989. *El Perú desde la escuela*. Lima: Instituto de Apoyo Agrario.

Pozzi-Escot, Inés. 1975. "Norma culta y normas regionales del castellano en relación con la enseñanza." In *Lingüística e indigenismo moderno de América*, 321–30. Lima: IEP.

Prinsloo, Mastin, and Mignonne Breier. 1996. *The Social Uses of Literacy: Theory and Practice in Contemporary South Africa*. Amsterdam: John Benjamins.

Pulgram, Ernst. 1978. *Italic, Latin, Italian: 600 BC to AD 1260: Texts and Commentaries*. Heidelberg: Carl Winter.

Quilis, Antonio, ed. 1977. *Introducción a las reglas de orthographía en la lengua castellana*. Bogotá: Caro y Cuervo.

Quilter, Jeffrey, and Gary Urton, eds. 2002. *Narrative Threads: Accounting and Recounting in Andean Khipu*. Austin: University of Texas Press.

Ráez Retamozo, Manuel. 2005. *Dioses de las quebradas: Fiestas y rituales en la sierra alta de Lima*. Avances de investigación, 5; Publicación del Instituto Riva-Agüero, 226. Lima: Pontificia universidad católica del Perú; Instituto Riva-Agüero.

Rafael, Vicente. 1988. *Contracting Colonialism: Translation and Christian Conversion in Tagalog Society under Early Spanish Rule*. Ithaca: Cornell University Press.

Rafoth, Bennett A. 1988. "Discourse Community: Where Writers, Readers, and Texts Come Together." In *The Social Construction of Written Communication*, B. A. Rafoth and D. L. Rubin, eds., 132–46. Norwood, N.J.: Ablex Publishing.

Raimondi, Antonio. 1945. *Notas de viajes para su obra "El Peru."* Vol. 3 [1862]. Lima, Peru: Imprenta Torres Aguirre.

Rama, Angel. 1984. *La ciudad letrada*. Hanover, N.H.: Ediciones del Norte.

——. *The Lettered City*. 1996. J. C. Chasteen, ed. and trans. Durham: Duke University Press.

Ramajo Caño, Antonio. 1987. *Las gramáticas de la lengua castellana desde Nebrija a Correas*. Salamanca: Ediciones de la Universidad de Salamanca.

Ramírez, Susan. 2008. "To Serve God and King: The Origins of Public Schools for Native Children in Eighteenth-century Northern Peru." *Colonial Latin American Review* 17(1): 73–100.

Ramos Núñez, Roberto. 1967. *Monografía de la provincia de Lampa*. Puno, Peru: Editorial Los Andes.

Rappaport, Joanne. 1990. *The Politics of Memory: Native Historical Interpretation in the Colombian Andes*. Vol. 70. New York: Cambridge University Press.

——. 1994. *Cumbe Reborn: An Andean Ethnography of History*. Chicago: University of Chicago Press.

Rappaport, Joanne, and Abelardo Ramos Pacho. 2005. "Una historia colaborativa:

Retos para el diálogo indígena-académico." *Historia Crítica* (Bogotá, Universidad de los Andes) 29: 39–62.

Read, Adam. 2006. "Documents Unfolding." In *Documents: Artifacts of Modern Knowledge*, Annelise Riles, ed., 158–77. Ann Arbor: University of Michigan Press.

Real Academia Española. 1726–39. *Diccionario de la lengua castellana, en que se explica el verdadero sentido de las voces, su naturaleza y calidad, con las phrases o modos de hablar, los proverbios o refranes, y otras cosas convenientes al uso de la lengua*. Madrid: Impr. de F. del Hierro.

——. 1984 [1771]. *Gramática de la lengua castellana.* Madrid: Editora Nacional.

Real Academia Española y Asociación de Academias de la lengua española. 2009. *Nueva gramática de la lengua española.* Madrid: Espasa Libros.

Reinoso, Susana. 2009. "Luego de 89 años, renovó su gramática la lengua española." *La Nación*, Buenos Aires, December 17 2009. http://www.lanacion.com.ar/nota.asp?nota_id=1212491.

Restall, Matthew. 1997. "Heirs to the Hieroglyphs: Indigenous Writing in Colonial Mesoamerica. Americas." *A Quarterly Review of Inter-American Cultural History* 54(2): 239–67.

——. 1999. *The Maya World: Yucatec Culture and Society, 1550–1850*. Boulder: NetLibrary.

Riles, Annalise. 2006. "Introduction." In *Documents: Artifacts of Modern Knowledge*, Annelise Riles, ed., 1–38. Ann Arbor: University of Michigan Press.

Rivarola, José Luis. 1995. "Aproximación histórica a los contactos de lenguas en el Perú." In *Lenguas en contacto en Hispanoamérica*, K. Zimmermann, ed., 135–60. Madrid: Iberoamericana.

——. 2000. *Español andino: Textos de bilingües de los siglos XVI y XVII.* Madrid: Iberoamericana.

Rivas Sacconi, José Manuel. 1949. *El latín en Colombia: Bosquejo histórico del humanismo colombiano.* Bogotá: Instituto Caro y Cuervo.

Rivera Cusicanqui, Silvia, Ramón Conde, Felipe Santos, and Universidad Mayor de San Andrés. 1992. *Taller de historia oral andina: Ayllus y proyectos de desarrollo en el norte de Potosí.* La Paz: Ediciones Aruwiyiri.

Roberts, Celia, and Brian Street. 1997. "Spoken and Written Language." In *The Handbook of Sociolinguistics*, Florian Coulmas, ed., 168–86. Oxford: Blackwell.

Roberts, Peter A. 1997. *From Oral to Literate Culture.* Kingston, Jamaica: University of the West Indies Press.

Robles Mendoza, Román. 1990 [1982]. "El kipu alfabético de Mangas." In *Quipu y yupana: Colección de escritos*, C. Mackey et al., eds., 195–202. Lima: CONCYTEC.

Romaine, Suzanne. 2000. *Language in Society*. 2nd ed. New York: Oxford University Press.

Romero, E. 1928. *Monografía del departamento de Puno*. Lima: Torres Aguirre.

Roseberry, William. 1994. "Hegemony and the Language of Contention." In *Everyday Forms of State Formation*, Gilbert Joseph y Daniel Nugent, eds., 356–66. Durham: Duke University Press.

Rostworowski, María. 1977. *Etnía y sociedad: Costa peruana prehistórica*. Lima: Instituto de Estudios Peruanos.

——. 1978a. "El avance de los Yauyos hacia la costa en tiempos míticos." In *Señoríos indígenas de Lima y Canta*, M. Rostworowski de Diez Canseco, ed. Historia Andina, No. 7, 31–44. Lima: Instituto de Estudios Peruanos.

——. 1978b. "Los Yauyos coloniales y el nexo con el mito." In *Señoríos indígenas de Lima y Canta*, M. Rostworowski de Diez Canseco, ed. Historia Andina, No. 7, 109–22. Lima: Instituto de Estudios Peruanos.

——. 1990. "La Visita de Urcos de 1652: Un kipu pueblerino." In *Historia y cultura* 20: 295–317.

Rowe, William. 2003. "Sobre la heterogeneidad de la letra en *Los ríos profundos*: Una crítica a la oposición polar escritura/oralidad." In *Heterogeneidad y literatura en el Perú*, Higgins, James, ed., 223–51. Lima: Centro de Estudios Literarios Antonio Cornejo Polar.

Rubinger, Richard. 2007. *Popular Literacy in Early Modern Japan*. Honolulu: University of Hawai'i Press.

Saito, Akira. 2005. "Las misiones y la administración del documento: El caso de Mojos, siglos XVIII–XX." In *Usos del documento y cambios sociales en la historia de Bolivia*, Clara López Beltrán and Akira Saito, eds., 27–72. Senri Ethnological Studies no. 68. Osaka, Japan: National Museum of Ethnology.

Salas, G. 1966. *Monografía sintética de Azángaro*. Puno, Peru: Los Andes.

Salomon, Frank. 1997. "Los quipus y libros de la Tupicocha de hoy: Un informe preliminar." In *Arqueología, antropología e historia en los Andes: Homenaje a María Rostworowski*, R. Varón Gabai and J. Flores Espinoza, eds., 241–58. 1st ed. Lima: Instituto de Estudios Peruanos.

——. 1998. "Collquiri's Dam: The Colonial Re-voicing of an Appeal to the Archaic." In *Native Traditions in the Postconquest World*, Elizabeth Hill Boone and Tom Cummings, eds., 265–93. Washington: Dumbarton Oaks.

——. 2001a. "How an Andean 'Writing without Words' Works." *Current Anthropology* 42(1) (2001a): 1–27.

——. 2001b. "Para repensar el grafismo andino." In *Perú: El legado de la historia*, L. Millones, ed., 107–27. Seville: Promperú.

——. 2002a. "Un-Ethnic Ethnohistory: On Peruvian Peasant Historiography and Ideas of Autochthony." *Ethnohistory* 49(3) (2002a), 475–506.

——. 2002b. "Patrimonial *Khipus* in a Modern Peruvian Village: An Introduction to the '*Quipocamayo*' of Tupicocha, Huarochirí." In *Narrative Threads: Explorations of Narrativity in Andean Khipus*, J. Quilter and G. Urton, eds., 293–319. Austin: University of Texas Press.

——. 2004a. *The Cord Keepers: Khipus and Cultural Life in a Peruvian Village.* Durham: Duke University Press.

——. 2004b. "Literacidades vernáculas en la provincia altiplánica de Azángaro." In *Escritura y sociedad: Nuevas perspectivas teóricas y etnográficas*, Virginia Zavala, Mercedes Niño-Murcia, and Patricia Ames, eds., 317–45. Lima: Red para el Desarrollo de las Ciencias Sociales en el Perú.

——. 2007. "Late Khipu Use." In *Script Obsolescence*, J. Baines, S. Houston, and J. Cooper, eds. Oxford: Oxford University Press.

Salomon, Frank, and Emilio Chambi Apaza. 2006. "Vernacular Literacy on the Lake Titicaca High Plains, Peru." *Reading Research Quarterly* 41(3): 304–26.

Salomon, Frank, and Armando Guevara Gil. 1994. "A 'Personal Visit': Colonial Political Ritual and the Making of Indians in the Andes." *Colonial Latin American Review* 3 (1–2): 3–36.

Salomon, Frank, and Karen Spalding. 2002. "Cartas atadas con khipus: Sebastián Franco de Melo, María Micaela Chinchano, y la represión de la rebelión huarochirana de 1750." In *El hombre y los Andes: Homenaje a Franklin Pease G.Y.*, J. Flores Espinoza and R. Varón Gabai, eds., 857–70. Lima: Fondo Editorial de la Pontificia Universidad Católica del Perú.

Salomon, Frank, and George L. Urioste, eds. and trans. 1991. *The Huarochirí Manuscript: A Testament of Ancient and Colonial Andean Religion.* Austin: University of Texas Press.

Sampson, Geoffrey. 1985. *Writing Systems: A Linguistic Introduction.* Stanford: Stanford University Press.

Sanabria, H., et al. 1989. *Apurimac.* Vol. 1. Lima: Editorial Atlántida.

Sansevero di Sangro, Raimundo. 1750. *Lettera Apologetica dell'Esercitato Accademico della Crusca contenente la difesa del libro intitolato "Lettere d'una Peruana per rispetto alla supposizione de 'Quipu' scritta alla duchessa d'S**" e dalla medessima fata pubblicare.* Naples: n.p.

Santo Tomás, Domingo de. 1951 [1560]. *Lexicon o vocabulario de la lengua general del Peru.* Facsimile edition. R. Porras Barrenechea, author of prologue. Lima: Instituto de Historia [de la] Universidad Nacional Mayor de San Marcos.

——. 1995 [1560]. *Grammatica o arte de la lengua general de los indios de los reynos del Perú.* Introductory study and notes, R. Cerrón-Palomino. Cuzco: Centro de Estudios Regionales Andinos Bartolomé de Las Casas.

Sapir, Edward. 1949. *Selected Writings of Edward Sapir in Language, Culture and Personality.* D. G. Mandelbaum, ed. London: Cambridge University Press.

Sarmiento de Gamboa, Pedro. 1942 [1572]. *Historia de los Incas.* Buenos Aires: Emecé.

Saussure, Ferdinand de. 1960 [1916]. *Course in General Linguistics.* Charles Bally and Albert Sechehaye, eds.; Wade Baskin, trans. London: Peter Owen.

Schieffelin, Bambi B., and Rachel Doucet. 1994. "The 'Real' Haitian Creole: Ideology, Metalinguistics, and Orthographic Choice." *American Ethnologist* 21(1): 176–200.

Schieffelin, Bambi B., and Elinor Ochs, eds. 1986. *Language Socialization across Cultures*. New York: Cambridge University Press.

Schiffman, Harold F. 1997. "Diglossia as a sociolinguistic situation." In *The Handbook of Sociolinguistics*, F. Coulmas, ed., 205–16. Malden, Mass.: Blackwell.

Scholes, Robert J., ed. 1993. *Literacy and Language Analysis*. Hillsdale, N.J.: Lawrence Erlbaum Associates.

Scollon, Ron, and Suzie Scollon. 1981. "The Literate Two-Year Old: The Fictionalization of Self." In *Narrative, Literacy and Face in Interethnic Communication*, 57–98. Norwood, N.J.: Ablex.

Scribner, Sylvia. 1984. "Literacy in Three Metaphors." *American Journal of Education* 93: 6–21.

Scribner, Sylvia, and Michael Cole. 1981. *The Psychology of Literacy*. Cambridge: Harvard University Press.

Seed, Patricia. 1991. "'Failing to Marvel': Atahualpa's Encounter with the Word." *Latin American Research Review* 26(1): 7–32.

Sempat Assadourian, Carlos. 2002. "String Registries: Native Accounting and Memory According to the Colonial Sources." In *Narrative Threads: Accounting and Recounting in Andean Khipu*, Jeffrey Quilter and Gary Urton, eds., 119–50. Austin: University of Texas Press.

Serruto Loayza, Andrés Avelino. 1953. *Monografía del distrito de Pichacani (Album gráfico, histórico y descriptivo)*. Puno, Peru: n.p.

Silverstein, Michael. 2000. "Whorfianism and the Linguistic Imagination of Nationality." In *Regimes of Language: Ideologies, Polities, and Identities*, P. Kroskrity, ed., 85–138. Santa Fe: School of American Research Press.

Sotelo, Hildegardo R. 1942. *Las insurrecciones y levantamientos en Huarochirí y sus factores determinantes*. Ph.D. diss., Writing Faculty, Universidad Nacional Mayor de San Marcos. Lima: Empresa Periodística S.A. "La Prensa," 1942.

Sousa, Lisa, and Kevin Terraciano. 2003. "The 'Original Conquest' of Oaxaca: Nahua and Mixtec Accounts of the Spanish Conquest." *Ethnohistory* 50(2): 349–400.

Spalding, Karen. 1974. *De Indio a Campesino*. Lima: Instituto de Estudios Peruanos.

——. 1984. *Huarochirí: An Andean Society under Inca and Spanish Rule*. Stanford: Stanford University Press.

Stahl, Ferdinand. 1920. *In the Land of the Incas*. Mountain View, Calif.: Pacific Press Publishing Association.

Stevens, Wallace. 1965 [1947]. "Adult Epigram." In *The Collected Poems of Wallace Stevens*, 353. New York: Alfred A. Knopf.

Stiglich, Germán. 1922. *Diccionario geográfico del Perú*. Lima: Imprenta Torres Aguirre.

Street, Brian V. 1984. *Literacy in Theory and Practice.* New York: Cambridge University Press.

———, ed. 1993. *Cross-cultural Approaches to Literacy.* New York: Cambridge University Press.

———. 2001. *Literacy and Development: Ethnographic Perspectives.* London: Routledge.

Street, Joanna C., and Brian V. Street. 1991. "The Schooling of Literacy." In *Writing in the Community,* David Barton and Roz Ivanič, eds., 143–66. London: Sage.

Stubbs, M. W. 1983. *Discourse Analysis.* Oxford: Blackwell.

———. 1996. *Text and Corpus Analysis.* Oxford: Blackwell.

Talavera Cervantes, Juan Manuel. 1985? *Monografía de Azángaro: Pasado y presente.* Puno, Peru: n.p.

Tamayo Herrera, José. 1980. *Historia del indigenismo cuzqueño, siglos XIV–XX.* Lima: Instituto Nacional de Cultura.

Tannen, Deborah. 1982. "The Oral/Literate Continuum Discourse." In *Spoken and Written Language: Exploring Orality and Literacy,* Deborah Tannen, ed., 1–16. Norwood, N.J.: Ablex Publishing Corporation.

Taylor, Gerald. 1974–76. "*Camay, camac, et camasca* dans le manuscrit quechua de Huarochirí." *Journal de la Société des Américanistes* 63: 231–43. Paris.

———. 1987. *Ritos y tradiciones de Huarochirí del siglo XVII.* [With biographical material by] Antonio Acosta. Historia Andina, No. 12. Lima: Instituto de Estudios Peruanos.

———. 1999. *Ritos y tradiciones de Huarochirí.* 2nd ed. Lima: Instituto Francés de Estudios Andinos (IFEA).

———. 2001a. *Waruchiri ñiŝqap ñawpa machunkunap kawsaŝkan Tomáspa makinwan plumanwanpaŝ qillqaŝqa.* Lima: Instituto Francés de Estudios Andinos.

———. 2001b. *Introducción a la lengua general (quechua).* Alasitas/Biblioteca andina de bolsillo, 14: Ritos y tradiciones, 3. Lima: Instituto Francés de Estudios Andinos.

Tedlock, Dennis, and Mannheim, Bruce, eds. 1995. *The Dialogic Emergence of Culture.* Urbana: University of Illinois Press.

Teel, Charles, Jr. 1989. "Las raíces radicales del adventismo en el altiplano peruano." *Allpanchis* 33: 209–48.

Tello, Julio C., and Próspero Miranda. 1923. "Wallallo: Ceremonias gentílicas realizadas en la región cisandina del Perú central." *Inca: Revista Trimestral de Estudios Antropológicos* 1(2): 475–549. Lima.

Terraciano, Kevin, and Matthew Restall. 1992. "Indigenous Writing and Literacy in Colonial Mexico." UCLA *Historical Journal* 12: 8–28.

Thurner, Mark. 1995. "'Republicanos' and 'la Comunidad de Peruanos': Unimagined Political Communities in Postcolonial Andean Peru." *Journal of Latin American Studies* 27 (2): 291–318.

Topic, John R. 2004. "From Audiencias to Archives. The Changing Social Contexts of Andean Recordkeeping Technologies." Paper given at conference "Archive and Empire," Notre Dame University, April 3–4.

Torquemada, Antonio de. 1970 [1552]. *Manual de escribientes*. Ma. Josefa C. de Zamora and A. Zamora Vicente, eds. Madrid: Real Academia Española, Anejos del Boletín de la Real Academia Española XXI.

Tufte, Edward R. 1983. *The Visual Display of Quantitative Information*. Cheshire, Conn: Graphics Press.

Turner, Terence. 1988. "Ethno-Ethnohistory: Myth and History in Native South American Representations of Contact with Western Society." In *Rethinking History and Myth: Indigenous South American Perspectives on the Past*, Jonathan D. Hill, ed., 235–281. Urbana: University of Illinois Press.

Twaddle, Michael. 1974. "On Ganda Historiography." *History in Africa* 1: 84–100.

Ugarte Chamorro, Miguel Angel. 1997. *Vocabulario de peruanismos*. Lima: Universidad Nacional Mayor de San Marcos.

Urquiaga Vásquez, Alberto. 1981? "Huella histórica de Putina. Sicuani, Peru?: Talleres Offset de la Prelatura de Sicuani.

Urton, Gary. 1990. *The History of a Myth: Pacariqtambo and the Origin of the Inkas*. Austin: University of Texas Press.

——. 2002. "Spanish Colonial Commentary." In *Narrative Threads: Accounting and Recounting in Andean Khipu*, J. Quilter and G. Urton, eds., 3–25. Austin: University of Texas Press.

——. 2003. *Signs of the Inka Khipu: Binary Coding in the Andean Knotted-String Records*. Austin: University of Texas Press.

Valderrama Fernández, Ricardo, and Carmen Escalante Gutiérrez, eds. 1996. *Gregorio Condori Mamani and Asunta Quispe Huaman*. Paul Gelles and G. Martínez Escobar, trans. Austin: University of Texas Press.

Valdivia Rodríguez, M. 1999. "La educación en Puno." *Allpanchis* 31: 163–75.

Van Acker, Geertrud. 1995. "Dos alfabetos amerindios nacidos del diálogo entre dos mundos." *Amerindia* 19–20: 403–20.

Vaughan, Mary Kay. 1990. "Primary Education and Literacy in Nineteenth Century Mexico. Research Trends, 1958–1988." *Latin American Research Review* 25(1): 31–66.

Vidal, Lux, ed. 1992. *Grafismo indígena: Estudos de antropologia estética*. São Paulo: Livros Studio Nobel.

Vilcayauri Medina, Eugenio. 1983–91. *Tupicochanos a tupicochanizarse*. Chosica, Peru: n.p.

——. 2009. *Tupicochanos a tupicochanizarse.* 2nd ed. Lima: Ediciones Paradigma.

Villavicencio Ubillus, M., et al. 1983. *Numeración, algoritmos, y aplicación de relaciones numéricas y geométricas en las comunidades rurales de Puno*. Lima: Dirección de investigaciones educativas, Ministerio de Educación.

Viñao Frago, Antonio. 1992. "Alfabetización, lectura y escritura en el Antiguo Régimen (siglos XVI–XVIII)." In *Leer y escribir en España: Doscientos años de alfabetización*, Agustín Escolano, ed., 45–68. Madrid: Fundación Germán Sánchez Ruipérez.

——. 1999. "Alfabetización y primeras letras (siglos XVI–XVII)." In *Escribir y leer en el siglo de Cervantes*, Antonio Castillo, ed., 39–84. Barcelona: Gedisa.

Viza Yucra, Antonio. 1977. *Monografía sintética del distrito de Achaya*. Puno, Peru: Editorial los Andes.

Vološinov, V. N. 1973. *Marxism and the Philosophy of Language*. Ladislav Matejka and I. R. Titunik, trans. Cambridge: Harvard University Press.

Wachtel, Nathan. 1994. *Gods and Vampires: Return to Chipaya*. Carol Volk, trans. Chicago: University of Chicago Press.

Warkentin, Germaine. 1999. "In Search of 'The Word of the Other': Aboriginal Sign Systems and the History of the Book in Canada." *Book History* 2: 1–27.

Weismantel, Mary J. 1988. *Food, Gender, and Poverty in the Ecuadorian Andes*. Philadelphia: University of Pennsylvania Press.

Widdowson, H. G. 2004. *Text, Context, Pretext: Critical Issues in Discourse Analysis*. Oxford: Blackwell.

Wierzbicka, Anna. 1997. *Understanding Cultures through Their Key Words: English, Russian, Polish, German, and Japanese*. New York: Oxford University Press.

Wijk, Axel. 1959. *Regularized English: An Investigation into the English Spelling Reform Problem with a New, Detailed Plan for a Possible Solution*. Stockholm: Almqvist and Wiksell.

Wogan, Peter. 2004. *Magical Writing in Salasaca: Literacy and Power in Highland Ecuador*. Boulder: Westview Press.

Wood, Robert D. 1986. *Teach Them Good Customs: Colonial Indian Education and Acculturation in the Andes*. Culver City, Calif.: Labyrinthos.

Wuthnow, Robert, ed. 1992. *Vocabularies of Public Life: Empirical Essays in Symbolic Structures*. London: Routledge.

Zavala, Pedro José. 1892. *Memoria del prefecto del departamento de Lima, Sr. D. Pedro José Zavala*. Lima: Imprenta del Estado.

Zavala, Virginia. 2002a. *(Des)encuentros con la escritura: Escuela y comunidad en los Andes Peruanos*. Lima: Red para el Desarrollo de las Ciencias Sociales en el Perú.

——. 2002b. " 'Vamos a letrar nuestra comunidad': Reflexiones sobre el discurso letrado en los Andes peruanos." In *Estudios culturales: Discursos, poderes, pulsiones*, Santiago López Maguiña et al., eds., 233–52. Lima: Red para el Desarrollo de las Ciencias Sociales en el Perú.

——. 2004. "Literacidad y desarrollo: Los discursos del Programa Nacional de Alfabetización en el Perú." In *Escritura y sociedad: Nuevas perspectivas teóricas y etnográficas*, Virginia Zavala, Mercedes Niño-Murcia, and Patricia Ames, eds., 437–59. Lima: Red para el Desarrollo de las Ciencias Sociales en el Perú.

———. 2008. "Mail That Feeds the Family: Popular Correspondence and Oficial Literacy Campaigns." *Journal of Development Studies* (UK) 44(6): 880–91.

———. 2009. "¿Quién está diciendo eso? Literacidad académica, identidad y poder en la educación superior." In *Nuevas direcciones en estudios de cultura escrita en América Latina*, Judith Kalman and Brian Street, eds., 348–63. Mexico, D.F.: Siglo XXI Editores.

Zavala, Virgina, Mercedes Niño-Murcia, and Patricia Ames, eds. 2004. *Escritura y sociedad: Nuevas perspectivas teóricas y etnográficas*. Lima: Red para el Desarrollo de las Ciencias Sociales en el Perú.

Zúñiga, Madeleine. 1990. "Educational Policies and Experiments among the Indigenous Population in Peru." Prospects (Paris), 20 (3): 365–75.

INDEX

Page numbers in italics refer to illustrations; those followed by "n" and "t" indicate endnotes and tables, respectively.

Frank Salomon is the John V. Murra Professor Emeritus of Anthropology at the University of Wisconsin, Madison, and adjunct professor at the University of Iowa. He is the author of numerous books on Andean ethnohistory and ethnology, including *The Cord Keepers: Khipus and Cultural Life in a Peruvian Village* (Duke, 2004), to which the present study is a companion piece.

Mercedes Niño-Murcia is professor and chair of the Department of Spanish and Portuguese at the University of Iowa. She is the editor (with Jason Rothman) of *Bilingualism and Identity: Spanish at the Crossroads with Other Languages* (2008) and (with Virginia Zavala and Patricia Ames) of *Escritura y sociedad: Nuevas perspectivas teóricas y etnográficas* (2004).

Library of Congress Cataloging-in-Publication Data
Salomon, Frank.
The lettered mountain : a Peruvian village's way with writing / Frank Salomon and Mercedes Niño-Murcia.
p. cm.
Includes bibliographical references and index.
ISBN 978-0-8223-5027-9 (cloth : alk. paper)
ISBN 978-0-8223-5044-6 (pbk. : alk. paper)
1. Writing—Peru—Tupicocha. 2. Literacy—Peru—Tupicocha. 3. Sociolinguistics—Peru—Tupicocha. 4. Indians of South America—Peru—Tupicocha—Language. I. Niño-Murcia, Mercedes. II. Title.
P211.3.P4S25 2011
809′.898525—dc23   2011021964